CRITICAL ACCLAIM FOR PR[illegible]
PUSHING LIMITS: MEMOIR OF A MAVERI[illegible]

"I loved the book. Extraordinary job of mal[illegible] come alive . . . with great energy and dialog."

—David Ignatius, *Washington Post* columnist and associate editor, author of *Body of Lies*

"Much more than a chronological replay of the exciting, wacky adventures and events of his life . . . *Pushing Limits* gave me a glimpse of a world of adventure and challenge, risk and reward, math and military, and right and wrong."

—The Cyber Defense Review

"Ted Hill is an original. Mathematician. Adventurer. Activist. His life has seen both his mind and body tested to extremes. . . . Insightful, entertaining and—in a very good way—unlike any other book you will ever read by a mathematician."

—Alex Bellos, author of *Here's Looking at Euclid* and *The Grapes of Math*

"Straddling the military and the mathematical worlds, Ted Hill's life is full of contradictions, daring exploits and accomplishments, and outright fun and adventure. A fascinating read."

—John Allen Paulos, author of *Innumeracy* and *A Mathematician Reads the Newspaper*

"Thirty years [after *Surely You're Joking, Mr. Feynman*], Ted Hill's *Pushing Limits* conveys the exact same sense of exaltation. Ted is a world-class mathematician—and, like Feynman's, his tales are almost unbelievable . . . adventures of an academic set loose in the world."

—Bernoulli News

"Ted Hill is unique in having both a very exciting internal mathematical life . . . and an action-filled, adventurous, external life. . . . His natural gift, very rare for mathematicians, of storytelling [makes this] a page-turner."

—Doron Zeilberger, winner of MAA Ford Prize, AMS Steele Prize, and ICA Euler Medal

"Ted Hill's incredible life story shows that a mathematical life can be heroic."

—Reuben Hersh, coauthor of *The Mathematical Experience*, winner of National Book Award in Science

"This [memoir] will thrill and perplex the reader, by the seamless mixture of mind adventure and body adventure, and for the unconventional academic path traveled by its author. Hill perpetually runs into trouble with authorities. . . . A life that touches on the highly exceptional, rich in friendship, thought, and humane warmth."

—Mircea Pitici, Cornell University, editor of *Best Writing on Mathematics*

"This book is a celebration of an unusual odyssey towards a mathematical career . . . [recounting] his days as a West Point cadet, a trainee Ranger, army captain in the Vietnam War, a PhD candidate at Berkeley, a twenty-year itinerant professor at Georgia Tech, and an ambassador of mathematics. . . . Hill is a master storyteller."

—Mathematical Reviews

"This insightful and entertaining book's first half covers Hill's military career. . . . The second half tells just about everything you would want to know about the study of mathematics at the highest levels. . . . His determination to pursue problems to their conclusion won my admiration."

—The VVA Veteran

"He has always had a maverick side . . . [with] little need for possessions. . . . Like Feynman, [Hill] insists on the need for a real understanding of the fundamental ideas of a problem."

—The Mathematical Gazette

"The author's goal is to dispel the notion that mathematicians are stodgy and lead boring, reclusive lives—he succeeds admirably!"

—Choice Reviews

"This reviewer has no doubt that in a hundred years or so this autobiography will be read as an attractive, vivid, and generally reliable description of political and academic, in particular, mathematical life in the United States of America in the second half of the twentieth century."

—Zentralblatt MATH

PUSHING LIMITS

MEMOIR OF A MAVERICK FROM SOLDIER TO SCHOLAR

TED HILL

WISE INK

Print ISBN 13: 978-1-63489-351-0

Library of Congress Catalog Number: 2020910379

Printed in the United States of America
First Printing: 2020
24 23 22 21 20 5 4 3 2 1

Cover and interior design by James Monroe Design, LLC

WISE INK

Wise Ink, Inc.
807 Broadway St. NE, Suite 46
Minneapolis, Minnesota 55413
wiseink.com

To order, visit itascabooks.com or call 1-800-901-3480.
Reseller discounts available.

CONTENTS

PREFACE

The path to a career as a mathematician is normally as straight and narrow as one of Euclid's lines: high school math club, college math major, math graduate school, tenure-track university math professor. No dangerous assignments, no daring adventures, no detours. My path was just the opposite—a mathematical carpet ride.

This book fulfills a promise I've made to several generations of students and colleagues, Army buddies, friends around the globe, and sons and daughters of my widespread family of friends who call me "Uncle." For years they've badgered me to record these events. The civilian friends want details about daily life as a West Point cadet in the 1960s and surviving Army Ranger School. The Army guys want to know what it's like to write a PhD thesis in theoretical mathematics, and *how in hell* I can claim exploring math ideas can be every bit as spine-tingling as a solo night dive off a remote Bahamian reef. All of them want to know more about those condemned houses in St. Louis, Berkeley, and Atlanta that were my homes for decades, and how it felt to be invited to return to Saigon, thirty years after my tour of duty in the Iron Triangle, to lecture on my mathematical discoveries.

The last time a group of them cornered me in my living room, my good-natured inquisitors had the gall to *vote* on which episode they wanted to hear and then to correct me if I missed the odd detail. Each time, after the story smoke cleared, they again made me promise to get these happenings down on paper. When groups at San Jose and Cal Poly State Universities invited me to talk about my road trip behind the Iron Curtain and hitchhiking in Uganda during Idi Amin's reign of terror, their appeal for a written version finally clinched it. This book is for them and my extended family of friends; for Baby Boomers who missed or want to relive Haight-Ashbury and the Vietnam War; for armchair travelers who want to experience shoestring Third World travel vicariously; for prospective math majors who fear a career in mathematics would necessarily be too dull; and for anyone else curious about how at least one unorthodox research mathematician thinks and works.

This manuscript has been four decades in the making. I typed the first draft in 1970, and as unexpected new adventures unfolded, I topped off my burgeoning box of notes every few years with what the Army calls "after-action reports." In the process of knitting these incidents together, I suddenly realized for the first time how mathematics was the ambitious dream that got me through my military years, and how Army Ranger training in turn helped me survive both the PhD gauntlet in Berkeley and cutthroat academic politics much later. I now understand what might draw a country boy to shed his shyness, spend years at foreign universities, and devise an unusual classroom style. I finally appreciate the huge edge in life it gave me growing up with a dad who was half the Great Santini and half the father of "A Boy Named Sue." Wish I had seen that before he passed. These events span my experiences from Beast Barracks at West Point more than fifty years ago to present-day escapades, but not to worry. As Salinger so succinctly put it, "I'm not going to tell you my whole goddam autobiography."

My heartfelt thanks to the many people who helped me in this endeavor: Beth Rashbaum, Hillel Black of Author One Stop, Charlotte Raymond, and Paul and Terry Lichtman all provided invaluable editorial suggestions. My siblings George, Russ, and Margaret helped with insights and details, and the Oliver family made me a full part of their *ohana* during extended writing retreats on Kauai. Stephen Kennedy and Carol Baxter of the Mathematical Association of America were the first to commit to this project, and Lauren Foster, John Brady, and Christine Thivierge of the American Mathematical Society steered it smoothly through the production phases. I am also indebted for suggestions and corrections from compadres who shared some of these adventures: Leonid Bunimovich, Yuri Bunimovich, Wes Clark, Brett Eberhardt, Vince Ervin, Ron Fox, Jeff Geronimo, Ryan Hynd, Martin Jones, Al Lindseth, Noreen Lippits, Jack Miller, John Oneal, Marra Peché, Annette Rohrs, Cynthia Rostankowski, and Jon Steel.

PREFACE

Three people deserve special recognition for support above and beyond the call of duty: longtime friend and author Marylee MacDonald encouraged me from the very start and helped me begin to learn how to write non-mathematically; AMS Publisher Sergei Gelfand, with his personal commitment and leadership, was instrumental in forging the joint publication; and above all, my long-term companion Erika Rogers, whose unwavering optimism and years of outstanding editorial, technical, and research assistance helped make this a reality at last.

You asked for it, amigos!

—Ted Hill

ACKNOWLEDGMENTS

I'd like to thank the following people who were instrumental in publishing this new paperback version. First and foremost, Erika Rogers was the main architect and executive in this project, and it was her endless optimism, energy, and organizational skills that brought it to life. Marylee MacDonald's continued outstanding advice and encouragement were essential, and I am also grateful to Randy Peyser of Author One Stop for recommending the professional, friendly, and efficient team at Wise Ink, Inc.: chief publishing officer Amy Quale, Patrick Maloney, James Monroe, Graham Warnken, and especially project manager Alyssa Bluhm.

1

DAY OF THE HANDSHAKES

For a few short decades during the middle of the nineteenth century, the United States Military Academy at West Point was America's preeminent institution of higher education for mathematics. The country's leaders knew that the key to success on the battlefield was clean analytical reasoning, not Greek or poetry or philosophy. A good officer must study mathematics. When I entered the Academy on July 2, 1962, however, the last thing on my mind was mathematics. The first thing was survival.

"*Slam* those spines into that wall!" a deep voice bellowed. "*Yank* those necks in!"

Eight of us New Cadets stood flattened up against the wall in the cellar of the Seventh Division. It was the second night of Beast Barracks, the two-month indoctrination phase that precedes the freshman plebe year at West Point, and according to the official training schedule, we should have been fast asleep. Across from the dimly lit corridor where we stood, a passageway led to banks of porcelain sinks and urinals, and across from them on the left, the toilets and shower stalls. At the end of the prison-like passageway, a half-open window looked out onto Central Area, the football-field-sized cement quadrangle enclosed by Central Barracks. Black leather shoes and squeaky boots clicked across the cement, and I could hear the occasional orders barked in a raspy voice that caused those anonymous feet to pause or turn.

Gray lockers lined the sides of the corridor across from me, and the water pipes overhead dripped onto the cold cement floor. Recessed in the walls, painted a dingy lime green, mammoth vertical drainpipes gurgled with the flushing waste from the barracks above, while down here, in the cellar, odors of ammonia and chlorine mixed with those of body sweat and urine. "Thank God for that open window," I thought, not realizing that it was about to be my downfall, my first of many run-ins with the authorities.

Even waiting for a shower, we wore identical shower uniforms—white open-toed rubber shower slippers and a light cotton cadet-gray shower robe with matching cloth belt tied in a single overhand knot. Our right arms were bent perpendicular to the wall, elbows pressed against our right sides, with white towels folded lengthwise in thirds draped across our forearms. Displayed for inspection in our upturned right palms, green plastic soap dishes held the Army-issue white bars of soap. Spines pressed to the wall, we pulled in our stomachs and chins in the grotesquely exaggerated position of attention called "bracing." With newly inflicted Army skinhead haircuts and this robotic posture, we looked like the rows of condemned slaves on the glyphs of a pharaoh's tomb.

Pacing back and forth along our line, four upperclassmen in starched white shirts and gray trousers with a single 1-inch black stripe running from the hip down to mirror-polished shoes taunted, bellowed, and ranted. In my thin robe, I felt naked. Of course, that was the point: to break us. My squad leader, Mr. Williams, a short man with a permanent scowl blazing out from behind his thick gray military glasses, was distinguished from the other squad leaders only by the tiny ears jutting out from beneath his cap—and by his addiction to his new power to reign over us plebes, the lowest of the low. He scrutinized us for a loose thread or a tiny bit of lint or a stray whisker hair.

"You wackheads look *sloppy*!" Mr. Williams screamed, veins bulging in his neck. "Regulations say that you smacks are each entitled to a shower at the end of the day, whether you deserve it or not. But it isn't the end of the day yet, and I am here to see that you *earn* that shower! Showers are for sweaty bodies, and I want to see *sweat*! Then you can shower."

We had already stood motionless for twenty minutes, every voluntary muscle tightening until it ached, desperate to break into a sweat. My neck cramped and my arm twitched.

"McKnight—into the showers!" And exactly sixty seconds later, "McKnight, hot water off, cold water on!"

"Kirk, you're next! Move, mister!" Then Hammond, and Madison. One by one, my classmates went to the showers.

The small bones in my neck cracked as I tightened my muscles even more. Still no sweat. I was stationed at the end of the row, 2 feet from the passageway to the sinks and urinals. From the massive gray granite moats surrounding the barracks, through the half-open window, past the gleaming porcelain receptacles, a tiny breeze wafted its way, picking up a hint of disinfectant and urine but retaining its devastating coolness—strong enough to keep my brow ever so slightly refreshed but too light to be noticed by the pacing squad leader.

"Well, Mr. Hill, you are not trying as hard as your classmates. Are you some kinda prima donna or something? Why aren't you sweating, mister?"

"Sir, there is a . . ."

"Halt, mister! What are a plebe's three answers? *Irp*!"

This curious imperative, rhyming with *burp*, meant "immediate response please." I was just beginning to realize the complete unacceptability of all excuses.

"Sir, the three answers are 'Yes, sir,' 'No, sir,' and 'No excuse, sir.'"

"Why aren't you sweating?"

"No excuse, sir!"

Mr. Williams leaned closer, eyes glaring with hatred, and screamed his disapproval.

"Well I think you have a *bad attitude*, mister, and I will not have a plebe with a bad attitude in my squad, do you understand?"

"Yes, sir!" I replied sharply.

The other plebes finished their showers, and I stood alone, bracing against the metal locker, surrounded now by all four of the squad leaders in our company. From the minimum required distance of 3 inches, they took turns screaming and bellowing insults at me, when they weren't demanding answers to questions about military trivia. The more questions they asked, the fewer I was able to answer correctly. They turned purple with rage. My legs and arms cramped, my ears burned, and my throat was hoarse. At long last the merciful sweat appeared, thanks mainly to the phalanx of upperclassmen blocking the breeze. But by then I was a marked man.

Ten minutes later, showered and exhausted, I staggered back to my barracks room, which served as cramped quarters for four New Cadets. Across from the door of the 20x12-foot chamber, a small painted-brick fireplace housed a wooden shoebox instead of an andiron. On the wooden mantel above stood cans of Kiwi shoe polish and Brasso, rags, gloves, and caps—all in disarray. To the left, four gray metal wall lockers framed a small bookcase whose one book was the 2-inch-thick blue loose-leaf binder *Cadet Regulations*. Two government-issue metal desks and chairs filled the center of the room, and the window on the left wall looked down onto Central Area. Beneath the window was a cast-iron radiator, a slightly darker gray than the linoleum tile floor. To the right of the door, an 8-foot-long interior wall, lined with clothing hooks, partitioned the remaining space into two sleeping alcoves, each with dark-green metal double bunk beds.

I joined my three equally dazed and shell-shocked roommates polishing shoes and brass and feverishly memorizing pages from *Bugle Notes* and "The Army Fight Song"—*On, dear old Army team, on to the fray, fight on to victory*; the number of lights in Cullem Hall; the Military Code of Conduct; and the names of Secretaries of Defense, and of the Army, Navy, and Air Force; and on and on and on until lights out.

Alarms rang at 0530 hours. We sprinted outdoors to reveille formation in Central Area at 0550 hours and joined the other 853 New Cadets, bracing in ranks until the final head count at 0600. During the next twenty minutes we raced back to shave, polish brass belt buckles, shine shoes, and make beds military style, 45-degree hospital corners with drum-tight, black-gray-and-gold Academy wool blankets taut enough to bounce a dropped quarter. Then came breakfast formation in the Central Area at 0620, bracing and screaming answers in ranks until marching off to breakfast at 0630.

Washington Hall, the formal dining hall, had three wings and seated all 4,000 cadets simultaneously. As I marched through the 10-foot oak doors, I glanced quickly up at the 40-foot ceiling, the flags of each of the fifty states, and stern portraits of past Academy superintendents. A towering stained glass window on the west wall portrayed the life of General Washington, while a 70x30-foot mural on the south wall depicted twenty great battles and twenty great generals in world history, from Cyrus at Babylon to Joffre at the Marne. We sat at tables of ten, with three upper-class cadets at the head facing the elevated poop deck where the first captain and distinguished visitors were seated with Superintendent Major General William C. Westmoreland. We seven New Cadets took our assigned places at the foot of our table.

Breakfast was twenty minutes of bracing and reciting trivia, all while sitting rigidly, eyes down. If lucky, we managed to swallow a few bites of cereal or toast, or half a glass of juice or milk, but when we left the dining hall at meal's end, our plates still held the coveted scrambled eggs, home fries, and sausage. After breakfast we had twenty minutes more to brush teeth, polish shoes and brass, and prepare the room for morning inspection—dusting, folding socks, straightening hangers, aligning underwear, emptying ashtrays, cleaning rifles—and then change into the uniform for the first formation of the day. We had been issued more than two dozen uniforms, and for each activity only one was correct: Sierra Charlie short-sleeved khakis for squad drill; gym alpha for mass athletics; and for trainfire, full combat under arms with steel helmet and full field pack, combat boots, olive-drab fatigues, and web belt with first aid pouch and canteen. In between, we had shower uniforms for the five-minute showers between calisthenics and the next formation.

We struggled minute after hectic minute, on through uneaten "air lunch" and into the afternoon first aid lectures and forced marches up and down the ski slope, hazed and harassed at each formation, each meal, each drill exercise. My cap visor was dusty, trousers slightly wrinkled, execution of right oblique march sloppy, recitation of Scott's Definition of Discipline not perfect.

At dinner that night I watched my evening plate of food get dumped in the garbage and endured the screams of squad leaders, platoon leaders, and company commanders. Delivering mail, waking upperclassmen for reveille, shouting division orders and uniform changes on into the night, I strove to create five extra minutes sometime between 0500 hours and midnight to memorize the West Point definition of leather and synopses of the upper-class movie schedule. Otherwise it meant more bracing, Chinese push-ups, and "pinging"—slamming back and forth between the walls of a narrow hallway, smash after spinal smash.

All New Cadets suffered, but a marked man drew special attention. Word of my "bad attitude" had spread overnight among the upperclassmen. That tiny breeze had robbed me of the precious gift of anonymity. Upper-class platoon sergeants zeroed in on me at every formation, bellowing oaths at me, ordering me to brace harder and drop for push-ups, pressing me to crack. Each day brought only five hours of sleep, ten bites of food, fifteen minutes of solitude in the doorless toilets or curtainless showers.

Finally, the weekend arrived, and the official schedule showed three hours of free time in the late afternoons. This was time to polish shoes, find a new belt buckle, get to know roommates, and gorge on ice cream and candy at the snack bar of the government-run, on-post Thayer Hotel.

"Not for you, Mr. Hill." Mr. Williams, my squad leader, glowered down the table at the Saturday noon meal. "Report to my room during released time today and tomorrow. And do not eat any food obtained outside this mess hall. That is a direct order. I will run you out of the Academy by second detail. Hazing, demerits, starvation—whatever it takes. I won't pass such a sorry excuse for a New Cadet on to my successor. You can't make it here, Hill, and I guarantee I'll see you quit within a month. The sooner the better. Now pass your plate out and eat ice cubes."

My chest collapsed, my stomach drawing itself into a knot. I felt dizzy. Body and soul had counted on that precious bit of snack bar food and the brief glimpse of freedom. At released time my roommates and all the other plebes scurried off in the summer sun to buy Reese's peanut butter cups, potato chips, and pints of walnut ice cream. I quickly polished my belt buckle, shoes, and brass insignia, put on a new starched white Sierra uniform shirt, and marched briskly through the deserted barracks to my squad leader's room. Sitting with his bare feet propped up on his desk and the *New York Times* spread across his lap, Mr. Williams was relaxing in a T-shirt, his black suspenders dangling from his waist. He looked me up and down and shook his head.

"Your shirt is wrinkled, and your belt buckle is out of line. You need practice dressing properly. Report back here in three minutes in full dress gray under arms. And don't be late, mister. Post!"

I doubled-timed down three flights of black metal stairs, across the area to the Seventh Division, and up three flights of stairs to my room. Tearing off the Sierra uniform, I jumped into the gray wool trousers and snapped the starched white cuffs and collar into the formal wool dress coat, throwing the white cross belts and cartridge case over my shoulder. I buckled on the starched white waist belt and wiped a Blitz cloth over all my brass—breastplate, belt buckle, "frogs" on the leather rifle sling, and the fried-egg-sized Academy insignia on my tar-bucket full-dress cap. Then I dusted off my shoes and M1 rifle as I streaked out the door. Down three flights, up three flights. My squad leader lay on his bed and looked at his watch.

"You are late, Mr. Hill! And what's this? Did you forget to shine the brass on your hat? Are you *trying* to piss me off? You have two minutes to be back here in gym bravo. Post!"

Two minutes is a surprisingly long time, as the Beatles demonstrated with their clock animation in *Yellow Submarine*. There was a slim chance I could meet his new deadline. I sprinted desperately to my room, threw off the formal dress uniform, and sprang into white cotton athletic socks, black high-top sneakers, jockstrap, gray cotton athletic shorts, official Academy tee shirt, and the heavy official sweat suit. But my squad leader had calculated carefully, and his two minutes' allotment was short by thirty seconds. He walked up to me and screamed.

"Late again! You and I will go round and round. Drill India. Three minutes. Post!"

Ponchos, cross belts, combat fatigues, high-collared dress whites, and class uniforms hung in a tangled mess from every hook, chair, and alcove rail. Combat boots, high-top sneakers, shower sandals, dress shoes, and slippers lay strewn across the cold linoleum as if by a giant footwear salt shaker. T-shirts, boxer shorts, cartridge belts, dress hats, and white gloves were heaped on the desk and bed, spilling onto the floor. I flew around the room in despair, rummaging through the jumble to relocate a full dress uniform. Down the metal stairs again, then up the stairs in the next division.

"Later than last time! Wrinkled uniform, smudged brass, crooked cross belts! Your performance is getting worse! We'll just have to practice this exercise until you get it right—sharp uniform, on time. Or you resign." He ordered me to report again the next afternoon, a Sunday.

Luckily for me, Sunday noon meal table assignments were by religious denomination, and my squad leader was Catholic, not Protestant like me. After compulsory chapel attendance, my Sunday table commandant turned out to be a good-natured upperclassman with a thick Southern accent who had not heard about my attitude problem. For the first time in a week, I was allowed to eat most of the food on my plate. That modest meal gave me the strength and courage of a lion. I would not let simple hunger force me to resign, even though a new round of "clothing formations" awaited me that afternoon. My spirits rose.

After the afternoon hazing, I sorted through the piles of uniforms. Hopelessly wrinkled shirts, pant cuffs stained with shoe polish, belt buckles scratched. I pieced together the least incriminating combination for dinner formation and timed my arrival in formation so as not to be one of the first or last. I stepped into my empty slot in the ranks of rigidly bracing classmates, and the upper-class wolf pack descended on us, each cursing the regulations that tore him from his girlfriend or afternoon sailing. A diminutive upperclassman took one look at our line and stormed up to me. Not another "little man complex," I prayed.

"Let's hear the Flanker Poop, Mr. Hill," he ordered. "Sound off, smack!"

"Sir, intelligence is inversely proportional to the square of height," I bellowed.

He screamed at me for a smudge on my belt buckle and told me to report to his room directly after the formation. There, when he finally tired of hazing me, his roommate took over. Tag-team hazing.

"Get that neck in, Hill! I want to see more wrinkles under your chin. More sweat!"

The roommate also finally grew weary of this sport, slipped into his black parka, told his short friend he was going to play handball, and walked out the door.

"I'm going to take a nap, Mr. Hill," said my tormentor. "I want you standing there, sprouting wrinkles in your neck, until I relieve you. If I wake up and don't see you bracing, then you will read about it. Now get your neck in!"

He stretched out on his bunk, pulled the heavy brown comforter up to his chin, and fell asleep immediately, soft rock music flowing from the black plastic radio on his desk, which was tuned to the cadet radio station WKDT.

Although my back was literally up against the wall and my chin tucked in, in the relative quiet I had time to think, to reevaluate my decision to attend West Point, to regroup. "How the hell did I get here?" Every waking minute was dictated by regulations and penny-ante tyrants madly screaming at me and inflicting torture for no apparent reason. Somehow I had metamorphosed from a popular high school scholar-athlete into a military misfit in this Kafkaesque nightmare. "How the hell *did* I get here?" I started thinking back.

Perhaps my relationship with the military was doomed from the start. My mother told me she was driving my father to work at the Brooklyn Navy Yard three days after Christmas in 1943 when she went into labor, and they rushed her into the emergency room of the base hospital.

"You were not supposed to be born there," she told me. "I don't think those doctors ever delivered a baby before. They were experts in boiler-room injuries and war wounds, but as far as I know you were their first childbirth experience. Mine too," she said with a smile.

She was one of eight siblings in a literally dirt-poor Wisconsin potato farming family, the one child they could afford to send to college. For her, the unexpected Navy hospital episode was just another of life's little adjustments. But for me, in retrospect, it seemed to be my first challenge to "the system," and I guess she and I both won that round. My father, a twenty-two-year-old Navy ensign, was soon shipped out to fight in the Battle of Iwo Jima, while my mother and I moved from state to state, living with relatives, all the way to California, scraping by on a lieutenant junior grade's salary and the generosity of our cousins. As soon as the war was over, my dad left the military for a career in food production, and two years later, with his bachelor's degree in biochemistry, he landed a job at Comstock Foods in Upstate New York, well known for its apple, pumpkin, cherry, and mincemeat canned pie fillings.

As a little boy, I once asked him what he did at work, and he thought for a moment.

"I work in quality control at the canning factory," he said. Then he saw my puzzled look and added, "I taste pies every day." For a skinny kid with a high metabolism who ate everything put in front of him, that was a dream job if ever I could imagine one.

My brother Russ had been born in Wisconsin when my father was still overseas, and the four of us were living in Billsboro, a small hamlet at a rural crossroads a mile and a half west of Seneca Lake in western New York's Finger Lakes region.

"It's good for boys to grow up in the country," my father said. He knew his job in the canning industry would keep him away from home most of the time during the summer, and even though Comstock's factories were in villages and towns, he commuted so that we could live close to nature and learn to entertain ourselves. He loved us but was, by anybody's standards, a very strict disciplinarian.

"This house must be shipshape," he would bellow at the first sign of any infraction, standing beside photographs of himself as a young Navy lieutenant on duty in the South Pacific. Next to the photos was a small clear glass medicine bottle marked "Iwo Jima," filled with coarse black sand he had scraped from the bilge pump of an LST marine amphibious landing craft. Square-jawed, with premature baldness concealed by a khaki uniform cap and wide, muscular hands and wrists, he had been handsome in uniform. He had survived the Great Depression as well as the Okinawa invasion and was determined to pass on to his offspring the lessons learned in both.

My formal schooling began with first grade in Geneva Public School No. 5, Billsboro's one-room schoolhouse. Six rows of wrought iron and oak desks were bolted to the floor, facing the one teacher and a potbellied stove. Unlike me, all the other kids were from farm families, and since I was a December baby, my parents started me in school when I was five. I was quiet and shy, the youngest kid in school, and the smallest boy. The following summer we moved into the town of Geneva, where my brother George was born, and a year later we moved again, this time to the truck-farming region of southern New Jersey, where my father got a job with the frozen foods company Seabrook Farms. Once again, he settled us in the countryside, which we had already come to love, and for four years Russ and I rode the Blue Bird school bus to the small elementary school that served the company's factory workers, most of whom were from refugee families displaced during the war.

After my sister Margaret was born, we moved back to the Finger Lakes region into an 1890s five-bedroom country home a quarter mile from the hamlet of Alloway, New York, not far from the nearby village of Lyons, where I went to high school. As a growing teenager, I was still relatively small, but—fueled by plenty of adrenaline—I made it onto our high school football team, where I played starting guard on both offense and defense. By this time my shyness was long gone, and in our senior year my schoolmates elected me president of the Honor Society, of the Varsity Club, and of my high school class.

At home, however, there were more and more clashes with my strict disciplinarian father, and I longed for freedom and independence. Most evening meals in our home were formal affairs, dining on gold-rimmed china with heavy silverware, drinking from crystal water goblets. We had to be washed and at the table at 6 o'clock sharp, wearing a shirt with a collar. My mother sat at the foot of the table, and at the head, surrounded by a semicircle of serving dishes, sat my father. One by one he filled each of our plates in turn and passed them to us. If we wanted seconds, we had to pass him our plate with a request: "Dad, may I please have some more potatoes, and spinach?" and, more softly, "and some more meat?" This ritual of his clearly symbolized his role as sole provider, which was certainly fair enough, but we had to formally *ask* for literally every extra bite of food and everything else that cost money. Day after day, week after week, year after year, it ate away at me, and I began to crave the day when I'd never have to petition him for anything.

When it finally came time for college, I saw my chance to get away from his iron grip, and I applied to the far-off University of Wisconsin at Madison, ironically where my parents had met at college. Determined to be somehow financially independent, I left for college, taking with me only the $1,500 I had saved from summer jobs. Arriving on campus in the fall of 1961, I joined 7,000 other incoming freshmen, and $5 a week bought me half a bedroom in a private home on Chadbourne Avenue, the tree-lined residential neighborhood above Breeze Terrace. I shared my room with

Sam Steelman, a junior transfer student from American University. The first week I bought textbooks, joined the freshman crew rowing team, and strolled through the student union, pleasantly shocked by the beer on tap and racially mixed couples in the Rathskeller.

Though at first overwhelmed by the sheer size of the university—Alloway had only about eighty inhabitants—I quickly felt completely at home. Soon I was studying mathematics, busing tables for meals at the Green Lantern Socialist Eating Cooperative, and feeling like I had found the ultimate in freedom and independence. I loved the honors calculus course, botany classes, and even the grueling crew workouts on forest-lined Lake Mendota.

But once I'd settled in, except for classmates and teammates, I was completely alone most of the time. While growing up, I had learned to love the solitude of heading out into nature for hours at a time, taking only a .22 rifle and our family's black Labrador retriever, Cinder. Most of the rest of the time, however, I had spent immersed in our family of six and attending tiny schools in a village where every turn saw familiar faces. Almost everybody in town knew my family and me. This new isolation at Madison was a different world from my years of popularity in high school, and my loneliness built up, especially at night, often to the point of tears. It was difficult to stay in touch with family and friends with no email, no cell phones, and only one telephone in the whole house, which our landlady kept to herself.

I coped by concentrating on classes and crew but began to realize that what I really missed were those boyhood walks through the forests, alone. I needed a substitute for those, right here in the city. The University of Wisconsin's Camp Randall football stadium, two blocks from my room, was just as dark and deserted at night as those forests, so I began scaling its 10-foot cyclone security fence after midnight, to bathe in the moonlight and savor the eerie quiet of 60,000 dark, empty seats. Stopping at the center of the 50-yard line, I would imagine being in a Roman coliseum, the last gladiator standing.

Over the months, I slowly adjusted and eventually reached a plateau where I was at home with the solitude and anonymity. People I talked to who had been in this situation told me they had leveled off permanently at that stage. But as time went on, I reached another state of mind that no one had told me about. I came to *love* being alone for long periods of time and even came to enjoy taking meals alone. I still liked the company of friends as well, but this solitude was a special kind of bliss. It was a whole new world for me, and I felt myself growing free from family ties, especially my father's discipline, both mentally and physically.

I was still determined to somehow pay for my college education myself, but my father's executive salary ruled out any chance for a scholarship, and out-of-state tuition at Madison was triple what Wisconsinites paid. Though I had saved enough money to get me through most of my freshman year, after that it looked like I was going to have to either quit college temporarily to work full time or ask my father for money, which I was dead-set against. If I wanted my freedom from his early curfews and razor-strop discipline, then I felt I should also break free from his financial yoke. Going to college near home, even though it offered the huge benefit of in-state tuition, would also not be breaking free. One autumn afternoon after crew workouts, I was sitting at my desk when Sam walked in.

"What's up?" he asked.

"Answering a letter from my Congresswoman," I said. "Last year I thought about going to West Point but didn't research it very well and applied way too late. Her office wrote me to ask if I want to try again. I know it's a free education, but I like Madison and love mathematics, and I don't know how I'd handle all that discipline. I had enough at home, so I'm telling them I don't want to apply again."

Sam trembled, his eyes filling with tears. "Listen," he said, "it's fate, pure and simple. You have to go—for me. I wanted to go to West Point ever since I was six. I studied, lifted weights, joined the debate team, made Eagle Scout. Then on my admissions eye examination they said I have astigmatism. You have to go, for me!"

The tears did it—that and the dream of complete independence from my father. Without giving it a second thought, I changed the letter, and US Representative Jessica Weis added my name to the list of prospects she sent to the Army. Sam flunked out of school three weeks later. I would never see him again, but that letter changed my life.

Every Congressman was allotted one appointment to the Academy each year, and a few, Weis included, used a competitive selection system, hers administered by the Army. In the dead of a Great Lakes blizzard, I hopped a Greyhound bus from Madison to Ft. Sheridan, Illinois, for a three-day battery of physical, mental, and psychological exams by Army doctors and psychiatrists—Scholastic Aptitude Test (SAT), Combat Proficiency Test, MMPI personality test, and IQ test. I did a 1-mile run, pull-ups, kneeling basketball throw, and hour after hour of physicals—stool specimens, urine specimens, blood specimens, eye dilations, rectal exams, and fifteen-minute sessions with the Army shrink.

Two months later, I found out I had won an appointment to the United States Military Academy's class of 1966, with training to begin July 2, 1962. Neither my family nor I had any idea of what that really entailed, and now here I was, my grand plan for freedom and independence tied to surviving the most regimented life on Earth. It would be the first of many adventures in which I didn't do all my homework and stumbled headlong into a situation with unforeseen consequences. "What was I thinking? What the hell am I doing here?"

"Mr. Hill, squeeze that neck in! Are you bracing?" Red eyes blinked from the warm folds of the comforter. "Don't ever let me catch you with shoes like that in ranks again. Now, post!"

I couldn't be further from mathematics at ultra-liberal Madison. I was now in another galaxy, Beast Barracks at West Point. The next week, my right arm tingled with numbness. "Probably from slamming against the walls, or shining shoes for hours on end," I thought. Each day it worsened, and I became a left-handed shoe shiner. A week later, standing at attention during a formal parade, I heard the baritone command, "Right shoulder, arms!" My right arm froze, and in a split second I lifted the rifle to my right shoulder with my *left* hand and quickly jammed my right hand on the rifle's butt. But a split-second delay in precision drill, especially wearing white gloves, is an absolute disaster. After formation, my squad leader Mr. Williams extracted the reason and packed me off to the West Point Hospital on emergency sick call, where the neurology section diagnosed "brace-pack palsy." I marched back to the barracks with doctor's orders—"Excused from bracing" for a week.

"What?" The upper-class cadre fumed with rage. "Let me see that medical report! I've never heard of a plebe excused from bracing! Those damn Ivy League doctors. Go to your room, Mr. Hill."

That evening my squad leader and platoon leader banged on my door, and I called the room to attention.

"Mr. Hill, you may be excused from bracing, but you are not excused from plebe duties. Here is a list of items you are to memorize verbatim and be able to recite at dinner tomorrow. Your neck may be out at dinner, but you won't get much to eat."

I looked at the long list and cringed inside.

"One more thing, Mr. Hill. As long as you are excused from bracing, you will be division minute caller."

Minute caller duty meant standing at attention on the second floor, ten minutes before every formation, and calling the minutes that remained until the official roll call. That robbed a plebe of precious time between formations. Minute callers bellowed out announcements of uniform changes, parade cancellations, and results of athletic contests, as well as all the standard formations. This extra duty began immediately, and scores of times every day, my deep voice resonated through the stairwells.

Late in the week, in the middle of a parade announcement, my voice suddenly cracked and went dead. Again I was hustled off to the hospital, this time returning with a diagnosis of "canker sore on right tonsilar pillar," and a formal "Excused from talking!" Undaunted, my platoon leader had me write out, on three-by-five cards, all the answers to my required repertoire (including the three official answers), and the upperclassmen amused themselves watching me flash the answers to their barrage of questions.

I was more in shock than fear. Even the "poop schoolers" who had attended military prep academies were unprepared for the severity of Beast. Most of us had no bowel movements for days, literally shocked shitless. The authorities fully expected these reactions and, knowing they could lead to serious medical conditions, required us to report to our squad leader every evening, who dutifully recorded in his ledger the date of each New Cadet's last bowel movement. The officially sanctioned hazing and the food, water, and sleep deprivation were tough on everyone, especially for those few of us they had singled out as "troublemakers." Some New Cadets cracked and some didn't. Would I be the next to break? There was no good predictor of who would survive.

If my squad leader had only reasoned with me in a normal tone of voice, explaining sympathetically that I was just not cut out for the Army, more likely than not I would have agreed with him, immediately resigned, and returned to Madison. But these bullying threats, these predictions of failure, brought out something stubborn in me that would not give in. Teenaged MacArthur and Eisenhower had survived First Detail of Beast Barracks, and so had even Edgar Allan Poe and Timothy Leary. I decided I could too.

After a month of the Beast, our uniform coats hung loosely on bony shoulders, and trouser waists showed pleat upon pleat. The authorities made feeble attempts to see that we got enough to eat, but the hazing tradition was strong, especially among young men who were wielding power over other human beings for the first time. I continued to lose weight from an already lean frame. The less I got to eat, the weaker I became and the more mistakes I made, and those new mistakes were punished by additional food discipline. To help stave off the hunger pangs, I took bites of toothpaste or orange peels. We New Cadets talked food, daydreamed food, hallucinated food. Not lack of sex, or freedom, or sleep—just food.

Mr. Williams intensified the hazing at meals, requiring me to chew every bite a hundred times. The next weekend he forgot to order me not to eat sweets from the Thayer snack bar, and my roommate returned with a large sack for me just as I ended my latest gauntlet of clothing calls. That night at supper, my squad leader asked his standard Sunday evening question. A sadistic grin swept across his face.

"What did you eat this afternoon, Mr. Hill?"

"Sir, I ate a box of chocolate chip cookies, two Baby Ruth bars, three packets of peanuts, a pint of maple walnut ice cream, and four packages of M&Ms."

The three upperclassmen at the head of the table dropped their forks, staring at each other and then at my squad leader. His jaw muscles twitched, but when he spied my untouched plate of food, a new evil shone from his eyes.

"Pass Mr. Hill the zucchini. And the mashed potatoes. Eat *big* bites, Mr. Hill."

My squad leader's strategy was simple. If I started vomiting, or missed even one formation from stomach cramps or nausea, he could write me up for "Exercising extremely poor judgment." More demerits, clothing calls, unwanted attention. I downed the leftovers on our table, and then upperclassmen from nearby tables supplied new mounds of vegetables, cartons of milk, slices of bread. I choked down mouthful after mouthful, secretly as happy as Brer Rabbit in the briar patch. My belly swelled and gurgled but held tight, and at meal's end, much to Mr. Williams's dismay, I was able to march to the barracks unaided.

One month into Beast, I finally earned back one of my precious freedoms. After passing close inspection for spit-shined shoes and an immaculate Sierra short-sleeved, white-over-gray summer uniform, I signed out in the company departure book for Privileges Walking, beginning at 1500 hours on Sunday afternoon. This meant freedom to walk on the Academy sidewalks, to stroll along the parade ground overlooking the Hudson. Not free to meet or walk with non-cadets, but wonderfully free to amble along at my own pace, with my own uninterrupted thoughts.

As I stepped across the invisible line marking the end of the barracks sally port and the beginning of the public sidewalk, my neck relaxed. I rotated my head back and forth, feeling strangely guilty as I forced myself to vary the cadence of my pace and let my eyeballs wander from side to side at will. Suddenly the old familiar world came alive: women's and children's voices, the sticky-sweet smell of honeysuckle in the hedges, red and yellow and blue civilian cars and clothes. A young mother and her son stopped me, and I obliged the boy with my autograph. After a few minutes of small talk, I politely excused myself. A longer encounter would have required Privileges Escorting, and that incredible freedom was still weeks away.

I walked alone to Trophy Point, overlooking the sharp bend in the Hudson River far below, where it cut through the thickly forested old mountains. I lingered at Battle Monument, at Kosciuszko's Monument, and Patton's Monument, details of which I had memorized but never seen. I adjusted my hat ever so slightly back on my head and gazed up at the Cadet Chapel and at the turrets of the Academy library, whose familiar silhouette forms the insignia of the Army Corps of Engineers. Half expecting a sharp reprimand from behind, I sucked in the aroma of new-mown grass on a warm summer afternoon and closed my eyes, remembering long July afternoons of my boyhood baling hay on the Beal farm in Alloway. An hour later, my liberty ended. I re-crossed the invisible line, tucked my neck in, pulled my cap back into place, and resumed the strict military cadence as I marched to the company orderly room to sign back in from Privileges Walking.

Hazing increased halfway through Beast Barracks when a new upper-class cadre replaced those on First Detail. The Second Detail squad leaders were fresh, rested, and eager to assume power. Punishments increased. A dropped rifle now meant sleeping with it for a week, not in one manageable piece, but broken down into the three major components. We had more bracing, longer runs, and increased food and water discipline. More than a hundred New Cadets failed to survive the pressures of Beast—high school class presidents, honor students, state athletic champions. They returned their uniforms to the quartermaster and left on the next bus. Those of us who survived the shock of initiation were promoted from New Cadet status to that of full-fledged Cadet.

* * *

In September 1962, the two-month ordeal of Beast gave way to the beginning of nine months of coping with the academic freshman year. Suddenly there was an emphasis on scholastics, an intensely competitive sieve that added intellectual pressure. My first term consisted of twenty-one semester hours: Mathematics 103 (Analytic Geometry and Calculus); Mathematics 151 (Linear Algebra and Linear Programming); Advanced German; Advanced Freshman English; Engineering Fundamentals 101 (Measurements and Graphics); Environment 101 (Astronomy, Astronautics, and Physical and World Geography); and an hour and a half each of Tactics 101 (Basic Military Training) and Physical Education 101.

Even the civilian Advanced German professor, *Herr Doktor* Tiller, wore the green Army officer's dress uniform, with special insignia. Classes started as the wall clock's second hand hit vertical, with the whole class standing stiffly at attention as the ranking cadet saluted, reporting absences to the professor. Classes were small by civilian college standards, with no more than fourteen cadets seated in a semicircle facing the uniformed professor. In the mathematics classes, daily quizzes were worked at fourteen individual blackboard panels, solutions explained holding a pointer at a 45-degree angle and beginning with, "Sir, I am required to prove . . ." To my surprise, this new West Point method of instruction, imported in the early 1800s from France's École Polytechnique, suited me very well, and once again I started to shine in my classes.

In the stone tunnel sally port arches outdoors, professors posted weekly individual grades of each student, by name. Grades were calculated to *thousandths* of a point in each subject, showing the exact class standings, out of 800, for every cadet in every subject. At the end of each month, a mass re-sectioning took place in every subject based on the latest averages, allowing "men of nearly equal ability to be grouped within each section, the most apt students being in the top section," and so on down the list. The best students in each academic subject were soon identified and grouped together, where they constantly challenged each other. The authorities found that this hierarchal system also served the weaker students well, since they were more inclined to ask questions knowing that their classmates were also having difficulty with the same concepts.

A failing average on the daily quizzes in any single subject brought confinement to quarters, and failure of a single course at term's end brought separation from the Academy. But in spite of this rigidity, the basic course content was comparable to Ivy League curricula—vector spaces, Goethe and Kafka *auf Deutsch*, *Beowulf*, psychology, and solar wind. This went on week in, week out, Monday through Friday, with Saturday morning classes in mathematics and English. I quickly came to appreciate and love the academic part of this new life while trying to cope with the rest as best I could.

Tactics 101, or Military Science, was a single harmless weekly lecture, given by one of the non-academic tactical officers. The subject matter was essentially rote memorization—"the essentials of a reconnaissance are to identify METT—Mission, Enemy, Troops, Terrain" and "the essentials for firing a rifle are BRASS—Breathe, Relax, Aim, Squeeze Slowly." Phys Ed 101 was a specially designed additional Academy hurdle, its different components demanding in the extreme. Plebe Boxing class brought my first broken nose. Survival Swimming class was a lesson in panic control and willpower specially tailored to each cadet's swimming prowess. For me, this meant treading water with combat boots and a pack full of bricks, struggling to keep the heavy M1 rifle from touching the water. Wrestling class fostered aggressiveness, and Gymnastics demanded and honed the agility skills essential for a commando.

The academic year also brought new roommates, assigned at random by a staff officer. The two-man rooms had one bunk in each alcove and a separate desk for each cadet. Compared to the lack of privacy in Beast, it was pure luxury.

I first met my new "wife," as cadet jargon called them, as he returned from a swimming workout, eyes bloodshot and feet shuffling slowly. Of medium height, with a muscular chest and shoulders and the narrow hips of a swimmer, he had fine, almost delicate, handsome features—thin lips, small ears pinned close to his head, strong dark eyebrows, and thick black-brown closely cropped hair. His dark liquid eyes blazed determination and intelligence.

"Hi, Wes Clark, from Little Rock," he said as he stuck out his hand. The words were soft-spoken, with a heavy Arkansas drawl. At seventeen, Wes was a year younger than I, a Southern Baptist city boy who had attended exclusive Hall High School and maxed the SAT.

"I'm going to be number one in our class," he calmly told me that first week. This was not bragging, simply a statement of fact. That he would also become a Rhodes Scholar, command NATO and the allied forces in Kosovo, and seek the presidency, even he did not dare to predict. Who could have imagined that three decades later, this man in the next bunk would be collecting me at the tiny train station of Mons, Belgium, in the convoy of three armored black Mercedes assigned to the Supreme Allied Commander of Europe?

The required evening study periods of the academic year were free of hazing and left us alone in our rooms. Wes and I compared his Southern Baptist upbringing and my Yankee Presbyterianism. We debated the existence of God, the naturalness of monogamy. We questioned the importance of formal mathematical proofs and the morality of fondling girlfriends, or even fiancées.

We discussed just about everything *except* politics. Wes was deeply interested and informed, while I was just the opposite, a distinction between us that would never change. And, of course, the "insurrection" in Vietnam, which was to play such a significant role in both our lives, was not yet even on our radar. Over that fall semester, a friendship grew that would last into the next millennium, despite our radically divergent careers.

* * *

For us plebes, West Point was like living in a land where three-quarters of the inhabitants are ill-tempered, uniformed policemen, just looking for excuses to flaunt their authority and write tickets. Their harassments continued during the academic year, mainly at mealtimes in Washington Hall. All 4,400 cadets dined together at tables of ten, with white linen tablecloths, sterling silver coffeepots, and china embossed with the Academy insignia, black shields superimposed with the helmet and sword of Pallas Athene. Unlike in Beast Barracks, however, the plebes were now outnumbered at the tables seven to three.

During meals, we plebes had to perform a myriad of new duties, including memorizing and serving each upperclassman his choice of beverage at each meal. "For Mr. Wiley, at breakfast a plain glass of milk and black coffee with one lump of sugar, at lunch milk with two ice cubes, but no coffee, for dinner . . ." and so on down the line for each upperclassman. Each mistake cost us precious minutes of eating and the risk of seeing our dinner scraped into the garbage. Between bites, we recited synopses of the post movies for the week or the times and places of that week's athletic contests. Plebes still had no access to restaurants or snack bars Monday through Friday and, if in confinement, no access during the weekend. Plates of steak and potatoes and green beans continued to disappear into the trash can. More ice cube meals.

The enlisted and civilian kitchen staff at Washington Hall prepared excellent meals—roast beef, ham, corn, peas, fresh bread, coffee, and juices—sometimes even breakfast steak. Some of the homemade desserts, especially the chocolate layer cakes and brownies, were *so* good that cadets would rather have none at all than just whet their appetites with a standard portion. Thus evolved the tradition of "big dick," a casting of lots at a table of ten to distribute the coveted dessert.

The rules of big dick were that first each man picked up his dinner knife and rolled it out of his palm so that it landed on the table beside his dinner plate, pointing toward the center of the table. If the cutting edge pointed to the right, he gave a thumbs-up. If thumbs-up were in the minority, they alone rolled again—otherwise thumbs-down rolled. This continued until a single winner emerged.

The winner could take up to half the cake, and then he passed the remainder to the next man to his right, who could take up to half the remaining piece, and so on. When only a single-serving-size piece was left, the other cadets cast lots for it. The upperclassmen too craved this dessert, so a plebe had to be careful if he won. If he took too much, the senior at the head of the table might not get any, but if he took too little, he was accused of having "no balls." Plebe winners usually took only a quarter of the cake. The big dick rules also carried a penalty. If a cadet did not eat all that he had taken, he lost his dessert for a week.

I first won at big dick on a large, freshly baked chocolate layer cake with vanilla frosting. The sweetness filled my nose, and my emaciated body yearned for every single sugar molecule. The cake came to me, and four upperclassmen stopped eating long enough to glare down the table. I thought for a second, took a deep breath, and quickly sliced off the whole *top* half of the cake. The upperclassmen, momentarily dumbstruck, screamed in disbelief.

"What the *hell*?" one of them shrieked. "That was completely outrageous, Mr. Hill. Look at that cake. The rules say you can take half, but . . . *Jesus*! You had better eat every crumb, smack, or you will brace until you drop. And if you ever cut a cake like that again, I'll have you swimming to Newburgh."

I knew that torture well—lying lengthwise on my sternum on the 2x4 beam high above our alcoves, arms and legs flailing in pain. But my gamble worked. Their new ruling against taking the top half of a cake was not retroactive, and I shoveled down the whole thing, mouthful after mouthful. I even had room left for seconds on broccoli. The upperclassmen's faces burned as they cursed and sulked. This wacky solution of mine was manna from plebe heaven, inspiration born of desperation.

I won again on a layer cake several months later. This time I sliced off the annular outer half, leaving a naked pole of bare cake with a pancake of frosting on top. I reckoned my portion contained about 90 percent of the calories. My new ring-of-frosting cake cutting also was immediately banned by the livid table commandant and cost me an evening of hazing in his room.

Later that semester I received a Form 2-1 Delinquency Report for "taking food out of the mess hall in his mouth." Even my tactical officer, a West Point graduate himself, had never heard of such an offense, and when the report reached his desk, he had me standing tall in his office within the hour. Had the mess hall guard gone through my teeth with a dental pick? No, it was all because I had won big dick on the brownies at lunch. Instead of letting me eat the enormous piece I had sliced off, the furious table commandant ordered me to stop eating and recite Scott's Definition of Discipline and The Days. Ordinarily this was considered unfair, since not finishing the brownies I had won fairly would cost me dessert for a week, but the other upperclassmen had left the table, there were no witnesses, and the rules prevented me from offering excuses.

So, at the end of the meal, in the two seconds between the times when the first captain barked "Battalions attention!" and "Battalions rise!" I had jammed the remaining 4x8-inch slab of brownie so far into my mouth that I could neither talk nor chew. Screaming in disbelief, the table commandant ordered me to leave the dining hall at once, with my hands down to my sides, and the brownie protruding from my mouth. The mess hall guard at the door stopped me, grinned, and ordered me to bite off a piece and chew it. His smile turned to a scowl when he learned that this antic came not from some clever upperclassman but from me, and the guard wrote me up on the spot. My stunned tactical officer just shook his head and dismissed me.

Neither I nor my tormentors imagined then that this same quirky intuition of mine might one day be the foundation of a whole career in theoretical mathematics, and that three decades later, when I was a full professor of mathematics at Georgia Tech, the Academy would invite me back to lecture to its math professors on my research in fair division. The title of my lecture? "How to Cut a Cake Fairly."

My voracious appetite continued to attract more hazing. At dinner, our company first sergeant ordered me to stop eating and recite the Stuffgut Poop. Other plebes had no idea what he was talking about, but I did.

"Zowie, zowie, zowie! I am a stuffgut and a glutton," I bellowed, pounding the table three times with both fists.

"This is me left meat hook extended," I said, as I thrust my left arm in front of me, elbow locked, hand forming a likeness of Captain Hook's famous appendage.

"This is me right meat hook extended." My right arm now paralleled my left, separated by a few inches.

"These are me meat hooks extended and joined," I roared, and locked the two crescents.

"Zowie, zowie, zowie, I am a stuffgut and a glutton."

The first semester ended with "Christmas Buck-up" in Company E-2. As the three upper classes prepared for semester break, they forced us to serenade them after supper with "I'll Be Home for Christmas," rubbing it in that we plebes were not allowed to leave the Academy for the holiday. Many of my classmates were homesick, silently fighting back tears because they had always been home for Christmas. Spending those two holiday weeks inside the cold, gray granite walls would indeed be depressing but, as it turned out, blissful at the same time. While we couldn't go home to traditional family holiday meals and celebrations, at least our tormentors were gone, and we had the run of the Academy grounds. We enjoyed dining at ease in Washington Hall, twisting and waltzing at formal balls organized by the Cadet Hostess, watching movies, and enjoying civilian meals at the restaurant at the Thayer. My parents and sister dutifully drove down to visit for two days, but I was more intent on enjoying the freedom from hazing and on finding secret alcoves to sneak off to with my hop dates.

All too soon it was January. The three upper classes returned to the barracks, downhearted at their own renewed incarceration and the advent of Gloom Period in the long, dark months as winter winds howled up the frozen Hudson under perpetually gray skies. Six more months until the end of plebe year.

At the end of the fall term, Wes and I both ranked in the top 5 percent of the class academically, and for the next semester we were reassigned to different rooms, where we could help tutor plebe classmates who were in danger of failing out. The upperclassmen decided "to put the bad apples in one barrel" and paired me up with Gary Douglas Jackson, another marked man to whom several of them had taken an inexplicable dislike.

Gary was ruggedly handsome, with a solid jaw, high cheekbones, a broken nose, deep-blue eyes, and a light-blond crew cut—but when he smiled there appeared two embarrassingly cute dimples at the corners of his would-be tough-guy mouth. And under that crew cut hummed the brain of a scientific genius. While still a teenager, Gary had already invented and sold to the government designs for an electronic timing mechanism for satellites. At West Point, since he had already mastered the entire physics curriculum, the physics department would soon design a special course for him on the new device known as the laser. On the other hand, Gary crashed and burned in foreign languages, and the powers that be hoped I could help him pass German.

Gary's muscular 5-foot, 10-inch frame and lightning reflexes made him a natural in karate and squash. Trained from childhood in rural Ohio by his father, he delighted in the challenges of living off the land, and his eyes sparkled with the same excitement whether his quarry was moose or mushroom. He could track, stalk, and shoot with rifle or bow, and afterward would sell or trade the furs to the local tanner for cash or new traps or lures, and stew the meat for supper or jerk it for his next hunting expedition.

"Where are you from?" I asked him, as we both were emptying our barracks bags of cadet gear on our bunks in our new room.

"Near Dayton, Ohio," he said. "A town called Piqua." He had to spell it for me.

"Sounds Indian."

"Yep. They say it means 'man-from-out-of-the-ashes,'" he answered. "Say, have you heard the scoop on our new squad leader, McCaffrey? He's supposed to be one nasty disciplinarian, and they put him in the same room with Levin, the most indifferent, laid-back, plebe-friendly man in the class of '64. The Tac Department figures McCaffrey will soften and Levin will get tougher."

We were about to find out. Every morning at 0530, Gary and I reported to McCaffrey's room, where he demanded that we recite plebe knowledge as he lay still half-asleep. Then he stood beside us, with his pasty white face, bushy eyebrows, and acidic body odor. He wanted to strike like a cobra—we felt it—but he restrained himself. Thirty years later, when President Clinton appointed him national drug czar, McCaffrey could focus his malice on a whole nation of vicious marijuana addicts, but right now the two of us were his sole victims.

In between hazing formations, Gary and I soon discovered our common Huckleberry Finn boyhoods, love of athletics, and fascination with science and mathematics. But Gary and I were also in many ways very different. He was a gentleman in every sense of the word, even during the 1960s, when gentlemanly qualities were not always prized. His dates sometimes ridiculed him when he opened doors or held their chairs for them at dinner. One sadistic upperclassman learned that Gary abhorred profanity and forced him to recite crude ditties packed with every vulgar word he could think of. With a chip on my shoulder or a practical joke in mind, I often was asking for trouble, but even with his frontier-spirit brand of independence, Gary tried to avoid it, preferring to focus his energy on objectives more worthwhile than some of my pranks.

The Rite of Recognition was our ultimate plebe goal. Those who survived our eleven-month sentence would march in Graduation Parade on June 5, after which we would form up in Central Area, still in formal full dress gray under arms. The upperclassmen, starting with the graduating seniors, would then walk down the line, greeting each of us with a handshake. That handshake meant instant equality, a first-name relationship, and an end to hazing forever. *Recognition.*

An earlier handshake, even by accident, also meant automatic Recognition, and many upperclassmen taunted us with outstretched arms, jerking them back at the last moment. Purists never reached for anything from a plebe with their right hands. They used their left hands to grasp everything, from mail and coffee cups to maps and compasses.

The winter gloom oppressed everyone—short days, continually overcast skies, alternating snow and icy slush, daily exams. Upperclassmen's troubles with thermodynamics and nuclear physics classes brought foul moods and increased hazing. One of the yearlings in my squad, Mr. Ellenbogen, took out his frustration on me again and again. He was not a bad sort, just sagging under tremendous academic pressure and the dismal dark of a Northern winter. I overheard him tell his roommate that he was in academic confinement, unable to see his girlfriend that weekend. His harassments of me increased, and I sought to put a stop to them. I waited for the right moment.

The chance I was looking for came in the form of a fat, perfumed, pink envelope, addressed to Cadet Steve Ellenbogen in flowery turquoise script. A letter from his girlfriend. I was division mail carrier that night and practiced holding a notecard between my right thumb and forefinger, flicking it out again and again with a quick snap of the fingers. Then I waited until two minutes before taps to deliver the mail to his room, holding the bait envelope between right thumb and forefinger so the handwritten address was clearly visible, and marched briskly into his room. He stood poring over ordnance engineering books spread out all over his desk.

"A letter for you, sir," I said.

In a happy daze, Mr. Ellenbogen reached for the letter with his right hand. I flicked out the envelope and seized his palm with mine. He blanched, jerked back his hand, and gasped. By shaking my hand, he had instantaneously recognized me and could never haze me again.

"Thanks, *Steve*!" I said. I unbuttoned my stiff collar and stretched out my neck as his roommate dashed to the other side of a desk, ready to defend himself against a similar attack.

"Well, *Steve*, I've got to be going now. Sorry, but you have just been hazing me too much. See you later." I refastened my collar, tucked in my neck, and darted back to my room.

The next morning my squad leader seethed and called in other upperclassmen to decide my fate. After formation, a delegation pounded on our door. Gary and I stood at attention.

"We've never heard of such a thing, Mr. Hill. That was outrageous. Mr. Ellenbogen can't haze you any more, but *we* sure can, mister!"

They debated different punishments. None seemed severe enough for this new infraction.

"Let's send him on calls to *Moses*!" one finally suggested. George Leon Moses was a by-the-books, strict disciplinarian from Oklahoma whom even sophomores and juniors feared.

"That might be over the top," another said, but they voted for calls to Moses, a punishment of biblical proportions.

I was ordered to report to his room directly after breakfast, every day until graduation. It was a long night. Would this latest rebellious act be the end of my cadet career? I was so near to Recognition yet so incredibly far.

The next morning I braced against the wall in Mr. Moses's room, door closed.

His square jaw was 3 inches from mine. "I understand you tricked Mr. Ellenbogen into recognizing you," he said. "That was gross insubordination, Mr. Hill." He frowned, but then the hint of a smile and a wink caught me completely by surprise. "But it took *balls*!"

"Now who do you think is more anxious for spring to be here, plebes or first classmen?" he asked.

"Fourth classmen, sir!" I answered. Plebes were not permitted to use the word plebe.

"Wrong! When spring arrives, I get my new car and off-post privileges and am only a step away from getting out of here. *You* have three more years. Do you know the official West Point definition of spring?"

"No, sir."

"Find out."

The next morning he repeated the question. I was ready.

"Sir, the West Point definition of spring is when a tall Fourth Classman sees the sun above East Barracks while returning from breakfast through West Sallyport."

"Is it spring here yet?"

"No, sir."

"Why not? I want a *reason*," he said gruffly, in mock anger. He did not want the *No excuse, sir* answer.

"Sir, I did not see the sun as prescribed this morning."

That evening I went to the library. Several days later, Mr. Moses asked again why spring was not here.

"Sir, spring is not here since the sun's observed position on the celestial sphere has not yet reached that point where the ecliptic intersects the celestial equator from south to north."

His face lit up in delight. It became a game each day.

"Sir, spring is not here, since on 2 February of this year the North American marmot *Marmota moray*, in emerging from hibernation, failed to perceive its sun-cast umbra, thereby predicting six additional weeks of winter. The six weeks are not up yet, sir."

Then Apollo and his chariot, followed by the Egyptian Nilometer definition. Day after longer day, the sun crept higher, and it finally broke East Barracks as I returned from breakfast. With balled fist, I pounded on Mr. Moses's door so sharply the oak paneling cracked.

"*Enter!*" he bellowed.

Accompanied by an ear-shattering bugle fanfare by Gary, who had played trumpet in high school, I marched into his room and roared, "Sir, spring has sprung, the grass has riz, I wonder where dem boidies is!"

Mr. Moses leaned back in his chair and roared with laughter and after a few minutes got up to inspect the splintered door. It impressed him. Calls to him became a blessing. The other plebes endured the harassments of ordinary calls to their squad leaders, who smirked thinking of the hell I must be going through. They ignored me completely. I continued to win Mr. Moses's approval, writing his girlfriend letters praising his leadership and reminding him to send flowers on her birthday. In return, he shared hard-earned Academy insights and tips for survival but remained strictly formal and never, ever reached for a letter with his right hand.

Spring brought a new passion for me—introduction to the sport of rugby. I took to it immediately, relishing the broken-field running, the stiff-arming of opponents, and the bone-jarring tackles after long days of classes and hazing at meals. I was one of two plebes who made the first team on the intercollegiate squad and saw my first A-Team start in the Notre Dame game, where we decisively defeated a much larger scrum. Rugby also brought my first athletic Recognition Handshake, when upper-class teammates from other companies recognized us after the final cut lists. "Sir" was not an appropriate salutation inside the scrum.

Approaching June Week and Recognition, another *tiny* error of judgment at parade cost me dearly. By now I felt I could survive until the final week, no matter the hazing, but when two yearlings harassed me during the parade, calling for me to brace harder and recite trivia, I thought, "They must be joking, this close to Recognition." I gave them the finger.

After parade, all hell broke loose. Furious upperclassmen of all ranks, some from far-off companies, surrounded me at every formation, during every free minute.

"Mr. Hill," screamed a Rabble Rouser, one of the cadet cheerleaders, "I am a senior, and *I* don't give yearlings the bird! I've never heard of such insubordination here. Screw that neck in, mister! I promised myself never to yell at a plebe and made it almost three years. Now, one week from my graduation, you ruin my record. I am pissed. Hit the wall!"

I hurled my back into the wall with a smash and braced.

"One step forward, march! *Two* steps backward, march! One step forward . . ." he screamed until he was hoarse.

That last week saw a constant stream of angry upperclassmen coming to my room, to my spot in formation, to my table in the dining hall. I spent hours of Chinese push-ups and pinging and lying on my back with arms and legs held aloft in the "dying cockroach" position. Now, for the first time, their abuse was destructive, scratching my belt buckle with ballpoint pens, grinding cinders into my spit-shined shoes with their heels, tearing off correctly fastened buttons. Mr. Moses was too busy with graduation plans to give it a thought, and for the first time they left Gary alone. Gary was worried I might have gone too far, but it was done now, and there was no turning back. I dug in again, determined to endure even that final blaze of hazing. And I vowed that I would beat that Rabble Rouser's record and would get through my *entire* three years as an upperclassman without once yelling at a plebe.

At long last, June 5 arrived, bright and sunny. After Graduation Parade, we plebes lined up for the long-awaited Handshakes of Recognition. We stood at ease, as the upperclassmen came down the line one by one. A firm handshake and hearty congratulations from Mr. Moses, a mechanical clasp and reluctant uttering of "Ted" from my frowning squad leader, neutral words of well-wishing from lesser-known upperclassmen, and less-kind comments from those still angry about the bird incident. But grudges were officially forbidden now that plebe year was over. I had survived. But three more years?

2

THE STAR YEARS

What a difference a day makes. In the hours just before Recognition Day, I was treated like an outcast, a far cry from my popularity in high school. The upperclassmen, forbidden by regulations to fraternize with plebes, had continued to haze me, of course, but I was also shunned by many of my classmates, who could get in trouble just by knowing me. Gary returned to our barracks room one afternoon, glowered at me, and told me he'd run into a First Classman who'd questioned him briefly and then screamed, "What? You're Mr. Hill's roommate? Why aren't you straightening him out? Get that head in smack! Start bracing!" I couldn't deny there was often just cause for my run-ins with the authorities—sometimes it was not having a flawless gleam on my brass belt buckle or a mirror-like spit shine on my parade dress shoes. Other times, as in the big dick cake-cutting incidents and my lackluster performance in Tactics 101, I had woven my own noose.

After Recognition Day, however, I was no longer a marked man but just another upperclassman, and I made friends left and right. Classmates I'd previously seen in ranks who had hardly spoken to me before now warmed up, starting with summer training at Camp Buckner in the forested hills above the Academy proper. Every weekday morning at 0500 hours, paratroopers from the 101st Airborne Division rousted us yearlings from long rows of bunk beds in the wooden clapboard barracks to start the summer training day with a 3-mile reveille run. By sunrise we had showered, shaved, and wolfed down enough scrambled eggs, sausage, and toast from stainless-steel trays to energize us for the morning's obstacle courses, tank exercises, infantry squad drills, and mortar training. The Handshakes of Recognition had ended hazing, and Buckner now aimed to transform cadets into soldiers.

The physical challenges at Buckner brought back fond memories of rural boyhood adventures on the Canandaigua River, where my brothers and I had built tipsy rafts and armored tree houses and experimented with homemade pipe bombs and a zip line over the river. Although my father did not spend much time with us, especially during canning season in the summer, he made sure that we had plenty of freedom to develop basic country skills on our own. He carved our first slingshots for us, and when we mastered those, he replaced them with professional Wham-O slingshots. Next it was Daisy BB rifles, then Ruger .177-caliber pellet air pistols, Sears, Roebuck .22 rifles, and double-barreled 20-gauge shotguns. He never gave us a single lesson but carefully monitored our progress and then upgraded the arms when he saw we had mastered the last level. Hunting squirrels and woodchucks hones marksmanship, especially with a single-shot rifle, and I easily aced the Trainfire Course at Buckner to win an Expert Marksmanship Badge. From all the years of swinging on a rope into the river as a kid, I could climb like a monkey, and my classmates learned they could always count on me to scale the "enemy" wall or scoot up the rope attached to a grappling hook. The leadership I had honed in high school also began to shine through again, and the Regular Army sergeants began to select me for command positions. I practiced demolitions techniques with a classmate whose name I had often heard screamed in ranks during plebe year and mastered artillery tactics with a rugby mate. Bonding, plus building strength and confidence and new adventure skills, the Camp Buckner military training program was intoxicating, especially after the surreal experience of plebe year. Now *this* was more like it.

On weekends we were largely free from duty, and although we could not leave base, we could invite dates for the weekend, and the administration even converted an empty wooden barracks into a carefully chaperoned girls' dormitory. On weekends it was almost like summer camps everywhere. The third weekend, a mutual friend had arranged a blind date for me with a University of Bridgeport coed, and she and I spent that lazy summer afternoon strolling around the lake getting acquainted.

That night there was a dance in Barth Hall, and we jitterbugged and twisted to Chubby Checker and the Beach Boys on the rough, unpainted wood floor, brown-gray with age, that creaked and sagged as we moved. Our heavily starched, long-sleeved Drill India summer uniform, pure white from the top of its rounded clerical collar down to black spit-shined shoes, had a single row of thick, nickel-sized brass buttons from neck to navel, with new gold and gray class shields pinned to the epaulets. We called it the Snow Machine for its ability to transform the plainest of cadets into a handsome prince.

Our dates wore summer evening gowns with tight waists, strapless pink chiffons with full skirts, and low-cut lavender silk dresses that hugged the hips and thighs to below the knees. Some were stiff with lace and embroidered flowers, and others smooth and cool to the touch. All the girls wore the white gloves required by Academy regulations.

Creaking ceiling fans on the unfinished rafters above circulated the thick scents of Christian Dior, Old Spice, and the fine pine sawdust kicked up by our feet. Closer to the open screened windows that stretched the length of the makeshift ballroom, the fragrances of the surrounding Northern pine forest seeped onto the dance floor. Slicing vertically between the tall evergreens outside, reflections of the July moon shimmered off shallow Lake Popolopen 100 yards down the wooded slope.

Except for the formality of dress, it could have been a 4-H barn dance in Lyons or a sock hop in the student center on the shore of Lake Mendota at Madison. My partner's perfume, stunning figure, and quiet strong voice made me dizzy with desire as her soft satin dress pressed firmly against the Snow Machine during waltzes. Now, as we did the Mashed Potato and flirted, our eyes locked. My heart raced, and I felt my forehead flush red through my summer tan.

At a normal teenage dance or hop, I would have simply held her hand on the way to the punch bowl, or kissed her temple softly during a slow dance. But not here. Kissing, or even holding hands in public, was strictly taboo at West Point. As they tried to drum into us, "A career military man must be in control of his emotions at all times."

Too embarrassed to explain this to my date, I instead resolved to somehow share the kiss we both wanted. During the next band break, I suggested a walk outside in the moonlight, and she eagerly accepted. It was already pitch dark, a warm romantic summer evening, with small ripples in the water lapping the sand and rocks. The fragrant pine needles were slippery under my leather soles, and the crescent moon was just visible through the treetops. I walked ahead, her hand in mine, stopping every few steps and peering back through the pines to check that no officers followed. The Officer in Charge had earlier made his rounds at the hop, but I'd watched him leave in his command Jeep.

We now stood on the neck of a long wooded peninsula that jutted away from Barth Hall toward a small wooden boathouse on the other side of the lake, invisible in the shoreline shadows. No one had followed us, I was sure, and the path ahead dead-ended at a tiny pier at the tip of the peninsula. I glanced once more behind us toward the dance hall and then pulled her gently toward me.

Just as our lips met, a blinding beam of light suddenly slapped our faces. I threw up my hand as a visor and squinted, when a voice at the end of an Army flashlight gruffly demanded my name and company. As my eyes adjusted, I could make out the orange embroidered OC armband on the sleeve of the Officer in Charge. He ordered us to return to the dance, pointing to Barth Hall, and disappeared into the shadows. My date was stunned and could read the concern on my face. Back at the dance, I explained that any public display of affection (PDA) was against regulations and that our kiss might cost me a few hours walking punishment tours.

Two days later I was summoned to my first Regimental Board, the cadet equivalent of a summary court martial. I reported to the small wooden camp building that served as administrative headquarters, and the duty sergeant pointed me to a room where the Presiding Officer waited. There would be no witnesses, no jury, and, of course, no press. I hoped for a lenient judge, but my spirits sank as I opened the door. Behind the worn oak desk sat Major Turner, a tall, full-faced career officer with the stern features of a Baptist minister. Major Turner also happened to be Officer in Charge of the West Point Sunday School, and since I was charged with PDA, the prospects were not good—especially since the Form 2-1 Delinquency Report read "Prolonged kissing and embracing young lady." He came right to the point.

"Are you engaged to this young woman, Mr. Hill?"

"No, sir," I said, then hastily added, "not *yet*."

"Well, we really don't care what kinds of girls you associate with, but we don't want to expose other cadets' dates to such crass behavior. Do you have anything else to say?"

Even though my offense had occurred in the woods late at night, it was no use pleading that the incident was not "public." The fact that I had been *seen* was considered proof of that. I learned that the OC that evening had been shaved-headed Airborne Ranger Major Parmly of the Infantry, one of the most gung-ho of all our tactical officers. After he left the dance, he had secretly slipped back across the lake by *rowboat* to land on the tip of Picnic Point. I should not have been surprised. This latest ploy of his, a surprise amphibious landing, was downright admirable, and even though I was the victim, I offered him my silent congratulations.

The standard PDA punishment was "8&8," eight demerits and eight punishment hours, but this *prolonged* kissing and embracing upped the ante. I decided to contest that point, even though Major Turner's face betrayed no sympathy.

"Sir," I said, "a prolonged kiss is a matter of opinion. Why didn't the inspecting officer interrupt me *before* the kiss became prolonged, in his judgment?"

"Is that all, Mr. Hill?" he asked, and paused briefly. "If so, then I hereby award you fifteen demerits and twenty punishment hours. This is the first Regimental Board in your class this year and hopefully will serve as a reminder that regulations are not just for plebes. You will walk punishment hours as an example. Every weekend here at Buckner. You and your M-14 will march the asphalt back and forth in plain view of your friends and their dates, swimming and boating the summer away. Starting next Saturday. Dismissed."

I saluted, did a smart about-face, and walked out the door as he signed the punishment orders and dropped them in his wooden outbox, thereby putting an end to all the rest of my carefree summer weekends. The weekday military exercises sped by, as we learned to throw incendiary thermal grenades and drive 50-ton tanks, but those long weekend afternoons I was all alone, marching my hours on the Area. They seemed to last forever. I didn't regret the kiss but only my own lack of vigilance in getting caught.

Shortly after Summer Camp and the end of those punishment tours, I was marching again, but now it was on the grassy Plain back at the Academy, this time setting an example of another sort. The first fall semester Brigade Review formal parade every year honored the academically distinguished members of each class from the previous year. In July 1962, 850 cadet hopefuls had entered, and now 704 of us remained. The top 5 percent of those were now being pinned with gold brocaded five-pointed stars, worn on our stiff wool banded collars. Of the thirty-odd 66ers in Company E-2, three of us had won Stars, more than any other company. Wes, of course, just as he had predicted, finished number one in the General Order of Merit. The second E-2 Yearling was Jon Steel, who had been company clerk during our plebe year.

A 6-foot, 2-inch native of Virginia, Jon had clear blue eyes, curly thick brown hair, fine smooth features, and the lean and muscular physique of an accomplished athlete. Like me, he had spent a year at a civilian college before coming to West Point. At the University of South Carolina, Jon had earned straight As, reigned as campus Frisbee tournament champion, and excelled in intercollegiate gymnastics. When I first met him, I'd asked where he was from.

"Norfolk," he said. "You know our high school cheer?" He grinned and paused a second. "We don't smoke, and we don't drink. *Nor-folk, Nor-folk, Nor-folk*!"

As the rest of the Corps stood at attention, Academy Superintendent Major General Westmoreland, future commander of all American troops in Vietnam, moved slowly down the line of men. He stood at attention in front of each of us in turn, pinned the coveted stars on our uniforms, and glanced for a moment into our eyes as the Brigade Adjutant announced each of our names over the loudspeaker. The West Point Marching Band Hellcats blared John Philip Sousa as I marched back to my company a Star Man, even with glaring disciplinary problems and mediocre grades in

Tactics. None of that would change over the next three years.

As yearlings, we now no longer had to rush back to our barracks after class to memorize movie schedules and shine shoes. We were wonderfully free to just think and learn, but we still had to work hard to keep up. My class load that fall term was twenty-eight hours—Advanced German, Advanced Physics, Advanced Inorganic Chemistry, Advanced Calculus, History of Modern Europe, Human Relations, and an hour each of Military Heritage and Physical Education. After plebe year's monthly reshuffling of both instructors and students based on our grades, still calculated to three decimal points, the Honors Sections were now full of familiar faces. Wes and Jon from E-2 were there, as well as Star Men from other companies.

Some of our professors in the Honors Sections were the best instructors the Academy had to offer. Leading the discussions in those horseshoe-shaped classes of a dozen cadets were a Harvard PhD in Physics, several Rhodes Scholars, and a National Debate Champion. We even had a few future Army heroes, with their dynamic personalities evident even then. Norman Schwarzkopf, later commander of Operation Desert Storm and a well-known TV commentator on military affairs, taught Honors classes in Mechanics. Most instructors, however, were rank-and-file uniformed officers on a three-year assignment after completing their master's degrees on Army scholarships. Mathematics, at six credit hours a week, was the most highly regarded of the courses in the curriculum, since it was considered an indicator of future military success. Ironically, this contrasted with the lowbrow Tactics classes, which were allocated only one hour a week.

The relationship between mathematics and the military is curiously asymmetrical. On the one hand, a great many professional mathematicians look down their noses at the Army, a combination of academic snobbery and fashionable anti-military liberalism. But the military *worships* mathematics, since it has proved so terribly effective throughout history in designing instruments of war. From Dionysius the Elder's invention of the catapult at Syracuse and Napoleon's dependence on trigonometry for determining artillery settings to Turing's application of probability and automata theory in cracking Nazi Germany's Enigma code, mathematics has often turned the tide.

From its very inception, West Point had played a central role in nurturing American mathematics. Berkeley mathematician and Dean of Science Calvin Moore, in his book *Mathematics at Berkeley: A History*, points out that in the 1830s and 1840s, the best example of a polytechnic in the United States was West Point, which had been modeled after the École Polytechnique in Paris. He also quotes President Francis Wayland of Brown University, who wrote in 1850 that West Point did more to build up mathematics in the United States than all the other colleges in the US combined. Through 1850, the Academy was regarded as a paragon of scientific and technical training in the US, providing many faculty members for other American colleges and universities. Since that time, many of those civilian institutions had surpassed West Point in the rankings, but I found that my mathematics education at West Point was a perfect complement to the Honors Calculus sequence I'd taken two years earlier at the University of Wisconsin.

My math professor at Madison, Dr. John Nohel, was a true academic, about to be elected Fellow of the American Association for the Advancement of Science. As a teenager in a refugee family forced to flee from Czechoslovakia in 1939, he immigrated to America and volunteered to serve in the US Navy during World War II. After the war, he went back to school and finished his PhD at the Massachusetts Institute of Technology (MIT). Dr. Nohel and I both arrived on the Madison campus in the fall of 1961, I as a lowly freshman from rural New York, and he as a full professor of mathematics from Atlanta, where he had risen through the academic ranks from assistant professor to full professor at the Georgia Institute of Technology. What a coincidence that would turn out to be, when fifteen years later, after serving in a very different war, I too would go back to school, finish my PhD in mathematics, and then rise through the exact same academic ranks at Georgia Tech.

Dr. Nohel had close-cropped brown hair and wire-framed spectacles and came to class every day in a suit and tie. He knew each of us by surname and challenged us daily, his crisp Czech accent laced with good humor and warmth. His boundless enthusiasm for life and mathematics was evident in every class. But he was also very demanding, and our sloppy neophyte logic was slowly honed into a sharp cutting tool. Under his tutelage, we learned "epsilon-delta" proofs, a much higher level of rigor than that required in

Academy math classes, which I would not see again until graduate school at Stanford.

In contrast to Nohel, none of the instructors in our West Point mathematics classes were professional mathematicians, let alone members of national academies or parts of the elite group who regularly discovered and published new theorems. For most of them, teaching at West Point was simply one of their career-long series of two- or three-year assignments. On the other hand, none of them were absent-minded professors either—they were smart, dedicated, and exceptionally well prepared for every class. From them we learned a great deal of applied mathematics.

But it was in the other required classes—Advanced Physics, Advanced Electrical Circuits, Nuclear Engineering, Fluid Mechanics, Nuclear Physics, and Classical Thermodynamics—where the striking beauty and utility of mathematics in science and engineering came alive right before our eyes. It was concrete evidence of the famous essay by Hungarian-American physicist and Nobel laureate Eugene Wigner, entitled "The Unreasonable Effectiveness of Mathematics in the Natural Sciences." Differential equations could predict the bouncing trajectories in our laboratory double-mass-double-spring experiments, and imaginary numbers told us exactly what currents and voltages we would observe in our electrical circuits. As a math major at Madison, or any other civilian college, I'd never have seen those dramatic tabletop demonstrations of the power of mathematics.

There were distinct advantages to both systems. In Madison the homework problems might take us days to solve, and not all of us could crack them. In West Point math classes, however, there was no written homework at all, and the suggested problems were relatively routine exercises that every cadet was expected to be able to solve. But where at Madison we never had to stand and explain any mathematical argument, in the daily recitations at the blackboards at the Academy, we learned to do mathematics on our feet, under pressure. Both mathematical skills—the deeper epsilon-delta thinking instilled at Madison and the ability to reason logically on our feet at West Point—would stand me in very good stead in later years. I might not be hooked on a career in the Army, I was coming to realize, but I was certainly hooked on mathematics.

Even Physical Education was now enjoyable. In place of plebe survival swimming and boxing, we now all took formal classes in sports we could enjoy all our lives—squash, golf, handball, and tennis. The healthy doses of physical exercise and excellent food soon had me in top condition, my 6-foot, 2-inch frame now a solid 190 pounds, perfect for rugby. And unlike students at most civilian colleges, we played handball and proved theorems with exactly the same classmates, vastly increasing the level of bonding.

Despite these deceptively idyllic beginnings, however, surviving the upper three years was by no means a shoo-in. The pressures of academics—one single failed class still brought expulsion—and the all-or-nothing Academy Honor Code culled many classmates. As my first PDA conviction had confirmed, all upperclassmen were still subject to Cadet Regulations, and those were enthusiastically enforced by gung-ho cadet and commissioned officers alike.

Common offenses such as "Dirty rifle" or "Unshined shoes," or the more serious "Late to reveille formation," earned standard demerits and punishment tours. And, of course, there were catchall infractions such as "Exercising poor judgment," a one-size-fits-all statute that permitted the authorities to charge us with offenses not on the books and to impose a wide range of punishments. Less obvious common offenses included "Not sleeping between the sheets" and "Having clean laundry in laundry bag." A cadet caught not sleeping between the sheets was bunking under his cadet-issue heavy comforter on top of his perfectly made bed. This saved him the trouble of making his bed in the morning, gaining him perhaps five minutes of precious shut-eye. A cadet caught with clean laundry in his laundry bag was trying to avoid the frustrating and time-consuming task of folding his socks and underwear into perfect rectangular solids, to be displayed in his clothing locker. Instead, several sets of underwear, direct from the package and never used, were aligned on the proper shelves and periodically dusted off, while the rumpled clean underwear for daily use was stowed in the laundry bag.

Cadet Regulations governed our behavior with ever-changing rules, but the Honor Code, like the Ten Commandments, governed our character in one immutable short edict. The Honor Code, in principle, is extremely simple: "A cadet will not lie, cheat, or steal, nor tolerate any cadet who does." In contrast to the variable demerits and punishment tours awarded for breaking regulations, the punishment for an honor violation was immediate expulsion. Special cadet guards would instantly escort a convicted cadet to a holding tank called the Boarder's Ward, after stripping his room of everything bearing his name. Within twenty-four hours, he was evicted from the Academy, gone without a trace. It was possible to appeal an Honor conviction to a board of Army officers, but as far as the Corps of Cadets was concerned, the case was closed once the Cadet Honor Committee had voted.

At the end of plebe year, before we had a good chance to assess each other's values and characters, we had elected honor representatives who would oversee the whole honor process for the remaining three years. Some representatives had excellent, common-sense values, but many others were unrealistic goody-two-shoes types. To hear honor cases, a committee of twelve, selected from the senior company-level honor representatives, held a short hearing and arrived at a verdict in one sitting, usually during the midnight hours.

Even if an officer board overturned an honor committee guilty verdict, the entire corps was still required to silence the accused for the rest of his Academy life, reflecting the "nor tolerate any cadet who does" part of the Honor Code. He would then sit at a mess hall table by himself and room by himself, shunned by all other cadets. Gradations of punishment in questions of honor simply did not exist. A verdict of guilty or not guilty, with no gray areas, resulted either in permanent banishment or complete exoneration. The intent of the honor system was obvious—to codify the notion of gentleman's honor, or gentleman's word. The "nor tolerate" part of the Code, however, has also been interpreted as forcing a witness to report an honor violation by another cadet. Refusal to report an honor violation remained gray, even though Article 5 in the explanatory *Bugle Notes* stated, "Every man is honor bound to report any breach of honor which comes to his attention." Still, the witness himself had neither lied, cheated, nor stolen. Was tolerance of an honor violation itself dishonorable? The more I thought about it, the less clear and absolute it seemed.

Even the basic "will not lie" clause seemed murky to me. Honor committees tolerated social white lies such as "I really enjoyed your party, Mrs. Brown," and in fact they tolerated all lies to civilians. No cadet was ever convicted of lying to a car salesman, a girl's mother, or a hotel receptionist. On the other hand, "lying" officially included the crime of quibbling, defined as telling the truth in such a way that it leaves the wrong impression. Which lies are white, which truths are quibbling, and which deceptions are lies was quite arbitrary. Cadets viewed regulations as a necessary nuisance, like speed limits. The Honor Code, on the other hand, was feared and respected, with its potential for instant destruction of lives.

The Honor Code was useful to us cadets in that it forced us to trust one another. It demonstrated that honesty usually *is* the best policy, since little lies invariably require bigger lies. But the Code was often abused by the administration in its attempt to control several thousand energetic and adventurous young men. A complicated "All Right" and Absence Card inspection system incorporated into the Code made it much easier for the tactical officers and cadet guards to do bed checks and conduct secret inspections. If an inspecting officer asked for and obtained a verbal "All Right" from a room or saw an Absence Card marked "Hospital," he knew everything was in order without actually seeing the cadet. Every time a cadet returned from more than several hours off post, he signed a Leave Blank certifying that he was not, *and never had been*, married. Even a quickie marriage and divorce violated the Honor Code if the Leave Blank was signed. And the entire Academy system of daily examinations, which were identical from hour to hour, was possible only because of the strict Honor Code. In civilian universities, professors *expect* students to "cooperate" and compensate for that by writing multiple tests, spacing students out during exams, and close proctoring. But at West Point cooperation is grounds for immediate expulsion, and the only information cadets were permitted to pass between classes was whether or not there was a writ, or written quiz.

Surviving the Honor Code often depended on luck, since even trivial violations were grounds for dismissal. Just at the end of our plebe year ordeal, a good friend of mine from Los Angeles, an excellent scholar and champion rope climber, had been convicted of saying he had shined his shoes when he had not. Awakened from a nap to hand-deliver a message to another division, he stumbled out into the corridor with the message. In the hallway an upperclassman challenged him with "Did you shine your shoes before you left your room, mister?" In a daze he gave the standard answer

"Yes, sir!" when in fact he had not. In a state of shock, he soon admitted as much. It was never a question of whether his shoes were shiny—they *were*—but just what he had said. He was on a Greyhound bus back to the outside world within twenty-four hours.

I had one close call with the Honor Code myself. I was hiding contraband candy and a small black-and-white TV in my room, right in plain sight. I managed this by putting it in a false-bottom cardboard box addressed to my mother, and even affixed postage stamps. When an overly diligent classmate heard about my box, he questioned whether that might be *deception*. I immediately realized the danger and took the issue myself to the Honor Committee. Our Honor representative, Tom Hayes, was a Star Man I knew from many of my classes. Of medium height with a stiff flattop crew cut, Tom was the son of a two-star Army general. He was a bit strait-laced for my tastes, so we'd never socialized, but he was also brilliant and had won a National Science Foundation (NSF) scholarship in high school to study radiation-induced cancer in mice, long before any of the rest of us had even heard of the NSF. To my immense good fortune, his creative and clever mind bailed me out of this predicament. Tom neatly solved the problem by declaring that if the address on the bogus package was *not* showing, it was *not* deception.

I reversed the box for a few days and then removed it and its forbidden contents for good. No use tempting fate too far. A differently minded committee member might well have found me guilty of an Honor Code violation and sent me packing that same day, changing the whole course of my life.

A few of the first classmen in our company continued to pull rank on us yearlings. They were on a first-name basis with us, all right, but still wrote us up on Form 2-1 Delinquency Reports for various petty infractions. Our platoon sergeant was one of those over-the-top, gung-ho Army guys, and we decided something had to be done. Contractors had recently dismantled the West Point Library for restoration and would soon remount at the main entrance the cannon that fired the first shot at Vicksburg. In the meantime, the cannon, without its carriage, was temporarily stored just inside the construction site. The day before a formal Saturday morning inspection of cadet rooms, I organized a four-man team to slip out of the barracks after midnight and retrieve that cannon. We had not expected it to be so incredibly heavy—after all, it was only about 5 feet long. Who could have guessed that such a little cannon might weigh 1,000 pounds? But when we grabbed hold we could barely lift it and after a few awkward steps had to set it down again.

Freeing one of the construction safety ropes, I lashed it to the cannon and knotted loops as shoulder yokes. Trussed like the slaves building the pyramids at Luxor, by alternately lifting and pulling, we dragged the cannon across the sacred parade ground and into Central Area, leaving a nasty gouge in the immaculate manicured grass of the Plain. At the barracks, we slipped wool Army blankets under the cannon and used the rope to winch the cannon silently up the 6-foot stoop and into the barracks of the Seventh Division. Inside, we silently opened the platoon sergeant's door, where he was snoring away in his sleeping alcove. With one man standing watch at his side, we slowly and silently raised the cannon onto the platoon sergeant's steel-frame army desk. The desk creaked and groaned but held firm. Attaching a note reading "The Phantom Yearlings Strike Again," we ditched the rope in a dumpster and crept back to our bunks.

The next morning the Seventh Division was in chaos. The victim blundered into the cannon going to reveille but could not budge it, let alone remove it, by breakfast formation. The company commander, luckily for me one of the more liberal-minded cadet captains, came to my room. He needed to get that cannon out of his barracks immediately, before the officer in charge and the commandant got wind of it.

"Ted, do you know anything about that cannon?" he asked.

"Look, Frank, you can't ask that. It's using my honor against me. There's no reasonable cause to suspect me. Do you have any evidence, any witnesses?"

"No," he said. Then he smiled. "Look. I just need help getting it out of the barracks, and nobody can figure out how to get it down the steps. We figured you just *might* have an idea."

I told him it looked like an interesting challenge, and I would give it a try, if only he would speak to his platoon sergeant about his bad attitude toward us yearlings. He instantly agreed, and I enlisted a few plebes for the much-needed extra muscle power. We had the cannon back in its rightful place before the tactical officer's inspection, but the gouge in the Plain remained a mystery.

A full-sized cannon in a room was impossible to miss, of course, but the inspecting officers usually also found even the tiniest of contraband. Many of them were West Pointers themselves and were dead sure they knew every possible hiding place in the stark, identical rooms. They knew to check the dirty-laundry bag for clean laundry, the hollow gray metal bedposts for candy bars, and even up the chimney, using a mirror so as not to get a face full of soot. After close observation of many such inspections, I discovered a shoebox-sized space in the room, 4 or 5 inches beneath the center of the springs in the lower bunks, that even the most gung-ho inspectors missed. They checked the bed by patting it for telltale lumps, pulling back the covers, and feeling under the mattress. To check for contraband under the bed, they stepped back and bent their heads down slightly, avoiding the indignity of kneeling.

I experimented with boxes of various sizes, painting them dark colors and positioning them where they were hard to spot from different angles in the room. Soon I was convinced the inspecting officers would never see a small object suspended just *below* the bedsprings. There I hung a shallow wooden box by lengths of wire coat hangers, and inside the box lived a tan hamster I had bought in a Flatbush pet store. Mascot of the division, and named after my PDA accuser, little Yelmrap was *living* contraband.

Every afternoon before supper formation, I closed our door and released Yelmrap on the floor. He scampered happily around, not helter-skelter, but always clockwise along the baseboard, and for some curious reason circling one bedpost twice on each lap. During the thirty minutes prior to taps, inspections were forbidden, and during this release from quarters, all cadets, including even those in confinement, were free to go anywhere. Our room now saw a steady stream of visitors every night, some from far-off companies. They came to play with Yelmrap, to pet him, and spoil him with tidbits smuggled out of the mess hall. Animal lovers came, and curiosity seekers, but mostly just ordinary cadets bent on spending a few tender minutes with warm and cuddly Mr. Y.

The tactical officers never discovered Yelmrap, quiet in his hidden cage. But one night, during his own miniature release from quarters, my little furry friend darted into the narrow space in the doorjamb just as an unwitting mail carrier opened the door without knocking. My dive to reach the door came too late, and we heard a tiny, nauseating snap. When I picked him up, Yelmrap's legs twitched, and blood dripped from his nose. I ran to the room of a classmate who had worked as a veterinarian's assistant in high school, but he shook his head as he quietly massaged Yelmrap's chest with the tip of his little finger. Our mascot was dead. I mustered four plebes to assemble after midnight, in full dress tar bucket hats and black parkas. To the muffled drumbeat of wooden coat hanger on towel-covered wastebasket bottom, we marched to the basement. Removing a loose brick from the wall beside the sinks, I gently laid Yelmrap's kitchen matchbox coffin, draped in a square of cadet-gray wool cut from a discarded long overcoat, and replaced the brick. Little did we imagine that our midnight funeral march would soon be a dress rehearsal for a role in a national tragedy.

On a drizzly Friday afternoon in late November, as I dozed on my forearm at my desk, an uneasy stillness came over the division. I heard footsteps coming through the barracks halls, stopping briefly to knock softly at each door and utter a few low words. Still half asleep, I heard the steps stop at my door, and I opened it to see our company orderly. "The president is dead," he said, and turned to continue his mission. Thinking it was a dream, I staggered back into the room to turn on our small desk radio. As I slowly wakened, I pictured a rare form of superaggressive cancer or Air Force One crashing into a mountainside, but the WABC news soon erased that image. President John F. Kennedy had been assassinated.

The Academy went into controlled shock. Professors canceled classes, instructors postponed all drill and athletic practices, and an unearthly silence greeted the first captain at the poop deck as he announced a full-dress parade the next morning. There, in a cold mist, the new Superintendent, Major General James Lampert, read General Orders 117. This was our official notification of the passing of our commander-in-chief and the succession of Vice President Lyndon Johnson. The cannon at Trophy Point thundered every half hour until sunset, and the sacred Army-Navy football game was postponed for a week.

I somehow felt less affected than my friends, perhaps reflecting my growing doubts about a military career. But no one, even the most irreverent or indifferent man in the Corps, took the president's death lightly. Kennedy was young and vigorous, a World War II hero. He had just addressed the corps of cadets at the graduation of the class of 1962, stressing his support of the military and the Army's Special Forces, and predicting the new counterinsurgency warfare awaiting many of us in Vietnam. In many ways, especially through his death and anti-Communist strategies for Southeast Asia, JFK became a permanent part of our lives. The following Monday morning, as required by tradition, a contingent of West Point cadets led the state funeral procession in Washington, while the rest of us struggled to rebuild the fervor, expected by past generations of graduates, to support the football team's forthcoming battle against Navy.

Less than six months later, on April 5, 1964, the cadet chaplain again led us in prayer for another Academy idol—West Point's own General of the Army Douglas MacArthur. Three days later the entire corps boarded buses before dawn to march at the head of the four-block funeral procession in Manhattan. In a cold, drenching rain, I watched as the caisson and black riderless gelding, with empty boots reversed in the stirrups, slowly followed MacArthur's gunmetal gray government-issue casket through the city. The same caisson and riderless horse had followed JFK's coffin, and that funeral parade impressed even those schooled in pomp and ceremony. Our minds echoed with the closing words of MacArthur's famous last speech at the Academy: "My last thoughts will be of the Corps, and the Corps, and the Corps."

* * *

In the July–August break after yearling year, one of the compulsory summer duties was hazing plebes as a squad or platoon leader in Beast Barracks. I hated the idea of taking part in the Beast Barracks detail, where it would have been next to impossible for me to keep my promise to myself not to yell at plebes. Then something very fortunate happened. A new exchange program was to send four West Pointers from our class for summer duty at the German Military Academy in Munich. My academic Stars, rugby successes, and Honors German grades outweighed my blemished disciplinary record, and the administration selected me as one of the lucky four. In fact, due to the high grades in leadership my classmates had given me during the Camp Buckner military training, they designated me cadet-in-charge of the German exchange. Little could I imagine at the time that this would be the first of many academic exchanges and collaborations with foreign universities during the next five decades.

As the four of us met to get acquainted and prepare for the trip, I immediately hit it off with Al Lindseth, a representative from the First Regiment. Al was a North Dakota farm boy whose high school class size of fourteen was even smaller than mine. At over 6 feet, Norman Rockwell handsome with Nordic blond hair and blue eyes, Al was also in the top sections of mathematics. And he was physically tough, an intramural wrestler who would later be highly decorated as a paratrooper in Vietnam.

He and I didn't escape Beast Barracks duty completely, though, and the week before the exchange began, the administration assigned us administrative odd jobs. Al, wearing dress gray over white with a red sash, had to stand outside the cadet barber shop. Each of the thousand-odd New Cadets, upon exiting with his newly sheared skinhead, was required to give Al a perfect salute, and bellow, "Sir, New Cadet [so-and-so] reports to the Man in the Red Sash as ordered!"

At the end of the day, Al staggered to my room and gasped, "Only two in the whole damned lot got it exactly right the first time." He could hardly stand, leaned on my desk, and asked me how my job had gone. I was almost ashamed to tell him.

"I had to drive around in a Jeep all day," I said, trying to suppress a smile, "looking for runaway plebes. Some New Cadets arrived early, and a few smart ones quickly realized that by hiding out they could escape a few hours of hazing. Last year they found a handful of runaways cowering in the chapel. Today we got a couple down by the river."

The following week, the four of us flew an Air Force transport to Germany, where instead of being forced to haze and harass New Cadets at West Point, we joined our new German comrades-in-arms touring Bavarian castles, learning to throw anti-tank phosphorus grenades, and rappelling down Alpine cliffs on a "Sunday afternoon hike" with the *Hochgebirgsjaegertruppen*, Germany's elite High Mountain Pursuit Troops. As cadet-in-charge, I had made the decision that during the exchange, we would speak only German.

Broken German it was mainly, but our hosts were patient and very supportive. On our second evening in Munich, dressed in our finest uniforms, the four of us led dances as guests of honor at a formal German military ball. On weekdays, we and our new friends conducted joint exercises in a snaking line of six tiny, three-man French Alouette bubble helicopters, reconnoitering East German defensive fortifications and bouncing from peak to peak in the snow-covered Alps to explore the nearly inaccessible hunting castle of Mad King Ludwig of Bavaria. In the evenings we joined them in *Herrenabend* activities, drinking beer and playing ninepins on rough, hand-hewn bowling alleys in the *Bierhaus* cellars. My individual German counterpart, Peter Hupfer, was an engineer with a sharp sense of humor, and we hit it off immediately, especially with our common love of science.

The exchange ended far too quickly, but we would soon get a chance to reciprocate the hospitality our new friends had shown, since the four German *Kadetten* were coming to West Point in September. The other two in our own group immediately flew back to friends and family, but Al and I had already planned to explore Europe during our month's leave and agreed to link up two weeks later in Frankfurt to catch a flight to West Berlin. Al was flying to Norway to visit relatives, while I hitchhiked north through Denmark to visit Ricky Bodén, a business friend of my father's in Stockholm.

When I got to Sweden, Ricky welcomed me heartily at the family estate Örnäs and introduced me to his chef, who had once cooked for the royal family. She plied me with squab meatballs, dilled new potatoes, fresh-baked *knäckebrot*, and steamed crayfish. For me, even the snacks she put out were a feast. Ricky also immediately put me to work doing pick-and-shovel manual labor with his crew of German-speaking workers, and that visit initiated a lifetime friendship between our two families. Ricky's son Johann would later spend his senior year in high school living with my parents in the Finger Lakes Region, and my sister Margaret spent several idyllic summers at Örnäs.

Hitchhiking is always unpredictable, but I picked up a few tips on the road that summer. I learned to carry my wallet in my left front pocket—where it was difficult for a pickpocket to reach—and in my front right pocket, a switchblade knife. I built enough leeway into my hitching itinerary to meet Al in Frankfurt on schedule, and from there we caught an Army flight to West Berlin. One of his cousins was an airline stewardess based there, and she had given him the keys to her apartment while she was back in North Dakota on vacation. After visiting a few famous nightspots, including the Resi nightclub, Al and I were soon down to our last few Deutschmarks. We found a few basic staples in his cousin's cabinet and spent our last days in Berlin eating boiled rice washed down by cheap red wine before we caught an Air Force plane to the States and reported back to the Academy.

Although that trip to Germany was my first trip abroad, somehow I had felt right at home. For a country boy from the Midwest, this seemed unlikely, but when I reflected back on it later, I realized that my father had been exposing us to foreign cultures for as long as I could remember. At age seven, when we had moved to Seabrook Farms in New Jersey, my elementary school class had kids from Latvia, Estonia, Lithuania, Hungary, and Germany whose families had been displaced during World War II, as well as Japanese Americans on "parole relocation" from various internment camps. During the periods of severe labor shortage due to the war, Mr. Seabrook had had the brilliant insight to recruit these displaced families to work in his factories, which at one time produced 20 percent of the nation's frozen foods. After the warmest of welcomes by the Seabrook Farms factory community, which provided housing, good schools, and even free naturalization classes for all the immigrants, many had decided to stay.

The Farm at one time boasted twenty different languages, and my classmates had many unusual accents and age differences, up to six years depending on their English abilities. It was like an Ellis Island community, said to be one of the first "global bootstrap" villages. What that meant to me as a seven-year-old was that my playmates simply talked and looked a little different than members of my own family. Different accents and races were simply normal, and at that age almost completely unnoticed. What a wonderful four-year experience for a country boy! And were my new friends ever *smart*! While I later went on to win undergraduate academic honors in engineering and earn graduate degrees in operations research and mathematics at Stanford and Berkeley, here at Seabrook School I was just one of the class. That turned out to be the only time I ever got a C in science, and it was justified. Among these kids from refugee families, I was only average.

Not only did I see the world at school, but my father also often brought foreign visitors to our home for dinner. Once he told me that one of these visitors, a very black African man married to a very white Irish woman, had later told him it was the first time he had visited a family where the kids apparently did not even notice the anomaly but just showed them our toys and tree houses and pet lambs, as if there was nothing odd about racially mixed couples in the 1950s.

Most of our international visitors had been adults, of course, but in 1960 my father also arranged for an American Field Service foreign exchange student to be part of our family for my whole senior year. Vince Bruce, a tall, lanky eighteen-year-old from Australia, had already finished at the top of his high school class in Sydney and was a track-and-field athlete who held the state "schoolboy" (high school) mile record in track. For that whole year, he and I shared a bedroom in the old country home in Alloway, and physics and math classes at Lyons High. Vince liked politics and often debated them with our conservative mother. Although she had a bachelor's degree from Madison, it was hard for her to keep up her knowledge of politics and debating skills while raising four kids and managing the household. Had she known then that Vince would one day become a Supreme Court judge in New South Wales, she would have taken her political debate defeats with him more gracefully. These uncommon international experiences that our father had brought into our otherwise conventional country life made that first overseas trip to the German Military Academy seem very natural—just a trip back to my school days in Seabrook.

* * *

"Cow year" —from the warning to plebes, "You'll be sorry when the cows come home," i.e., when the second classmen or juniors return from summer leave—began with assignments to new companies in our regiment for our remaining two years. Al stayed in First Regiment, I went to Company D-2, and all my close friends in E-2—Gary Jackson, Wes Clark, Jon Steel—went to other companies in the Second Regiment. The academic year got off to a fine start for me, since the four German *Kadetten* arrived, and my counterpart Peter moved into the top bunk in my room. They dined with us in Washington Hall, where Peter marveled at the huge warm breakfasts, comparing them to the spartan coffee-and-bread fare in the German Army. The Academy rolled out the red carpet for our guests, including a trip on the Hudson in the Academy superintendent's official yacht, complete with beer, even though cadets were officially forbidden from consuming alcohol within 15 miles of West Point. Because of my high academic standing, the authorities assigned me to cut classes and take our four guests on an all-expenses-paid trip to New York City in an olive-drab Army stretch limousine. There, we billeted on Governors Island, caught the ferry to Staten Island, and took an evening boat trip around Manhattan. We saw *How to Succeed in Business Without Really Trying* on Broadway and visited the United Nations and Rockefeller Center. After the Big Apple junket, we returned to the Academy and bid *auf Wiedersehen* as our comrades returned to Germany and I went back to the new semester's classes.

That third year certainly saw no letup in academics—my fall classes were Thermodynamics, Law, German Seminar, Economics, Mechanics, Complex Variables, and Electricity 351—Advanced Circuits. West Point offered only four math courses beyond calculus, and I took all four. To help compensate for the fact that our instructors were not PhD professionals, the academic administrators chose outstanding textbooks. Our Complex Analysis text was Erwin Kreyszig's *Advanced Engineering Mathematics*, which became a classic and whose tenth edition is still a leading text fifty years later. From it we learned the sublime beauties and elegance of Cauchy's Integral Theorem and conformal mapping. Even as my disillusionment with the thought of a life under military regimentation grew, so did my enchantment with mathematics. I just had no idea how that would play out.

While the lectures challenged all of us, the Circuits Laboratory, infamously known as "Juice Lab," terrified many cadets. Some of the toughest men, from boxers and wrestlers to football linebackers, wore rubber overshoes to lab even on sunny days, preferring humiliation to repeated shocks of 110 volts AC. However, when Jon Steel was assigned to be my lab partner in the Honors Section of Juice Lab, I knew it would be an interesting semester, since he shared my need to question authority just a little now and then. He and I organized a clandestine "zap-the-prof" contest, where the goal was to tweak the electrical circuit design just enough to trick the instructor into getting a good stiff jolt while he was trying to analyze the "problem" we reported having with our circuit board. The instructors soon figured out our little game and welcomed the challenge, even after we had scored a few resounding points.

That year the Pentagon unexpectedly announced a new policy guaranteeing graduating Star Men a first assignment of attending the graduate school of their choice. This meant two years studying for a master's at any university in the US the Star Man wanted, with all expenses paid, instead of facing the new guerrilla warfare developing in French Indochina. A survey had revealed that West Point was losing many of its prospective applicants to the Air Force Academy, which had a liberal postgraduate education program, and West Point countered with its own new "5 percent program." The 5 percent Star status was, of course, calculated based on the General Order of Merit. Wes, still on track to graduate first in our class, dutifully kept up his grades in all subjects, including Tactics. And he refrained from flouting the regulations, to maintain his relatively high cadet rank. He and I still stayed close friends, often double-dating on post, and of course I saw him almost daily in classes. After yet another of my run-ins with the authorities, he came to see me.

"Ted," he said, "you've got to think about getting a better military aptitude rating. Don't forget that Tactics grades and military aptitude are included in the calculation for class standings. If you don't keep Star status, you won't get that scholarship!"

"Look," I told him. "I know that, but I just can't get motivated to memorize Army trivia when there's so much to learn about science and math. I'm going to take my chances. Thanks for the heads up, though. See you next weekend? Abe's band is playing."

My new roommate that year was Abe Dean, a hulking blue-eyed blond with a thick Southern drawl from central Florida who had been recruited to play football. His anti-authoritarian spirit put us in good company, and I learned he had even been kicked off the plebe football team after he threw a punch at one of the coaches. Abe started a small rock-and-roll band to entertain us on weekend leaves, playing a spirited lead guitar while polishing off Jack Daniel's. As third-year cadets, Abe and I served as squad leaders, responsible for seven or eight other cadets, including several plebes of the class of 1968. One afternoon, one of them, John Oneal from Oklahoma, knocked on my door. Nearly 6 feet, 2 inches tall and lean, with sharp, dark features, he reminded me of a thinner version of Clark Kent.

"Sir," he said, "Cadet Oneal requests permission to take a nap."

Plebes were not allowed to sleep during duty hours without direct permission from their squad leaders.

"Of course," I answered.

When he repeated this same request several more times during the next weeks, I checked his academic grades to make sure he could afford the break from studies. Not only was Mr. Oneal doing well, I could see from his General Order of Merit that he was well on his way to getting Stars. The next time he asked to take a nap, I was ready to save us both some trouble.

"Yes, Mr. Oneal," I said. "You hereby have *permanent* permission to sleep whenever you want."

Not only did he manage to get Stars every year at West Point, but he also later went on to write a PhD thesis in political science at Stanford. All, of course, due to the extra doses of rest I had bequeathed him as a plebe.

Two of Mr. Oneal's plebe classmates in my squad, however, did not fare as well. Mike C. had the body of a light heavyweight wrestler, with a square jaw and dark eyes. To come to West Point, he had turned down a combined athletic/academic scholarship to play football and wrestle at the University of Wyoming. He and his roommate George C., who the previous year had been captain of a 300-man Oregon crack firefighting team that parachuted into hot spots, became inseparable. They were quiet, powerful, and worldly young men. Neither had much use for the plebe system or Academy rules in general. Even upperclassmen sensed the inherent danger of provoking these two bears and concentrated their attention on less formidable plebes. Even the tactical officers avoided them, and for one full week Mike even sported ear-lobe-length sideburns.

As a yearling, George came to breakfast one morning with a black eye. He had gone over the wall, drinking beer in a local bar the night before, and had been worked over by some local toughs who hated cadets. The next night he and Mike went AWOL together, walked into the bar, and cleaned it out, standing back to back. When I was coaching our company intramural wrestling team, Mike attended practice to show us which illegal holds and arm bars could be used, depending on where the referee stood. He had years of experience in every conceivable form of fighting—wrestling, judo, karate, hand-to-hand combat, and even formal courses in dirty street fighting.

As their impatience with the class system grew, so did their liberties with Academy rules, including the Honor Code. While the Honor Committee never did establish clear honor violations for either of them, we were told that it finally found them both guilty of "disrespect for the Honor Code," as evidenced by their great number of borderline cases. Both were instantly expelled, and I expected never to see either of them again.

Meanwhile, my own skirmishes with the authorities continued. I was somehow drawn to questioning authority and almost random acts of insubordination—still subconsciously rebelling against a strict disciplinarian father, I suppose. Many of those skirmishes I lost. I was written up and punished for another PDA charge when I exited a dance hall with my arm around the waist of my date, and for riding a wheeled laundry cart while returning from our noon meal to serve punishment confinements. That little breath of freedom cost me yet more confinements. The worst delinquency report I got was "Bringing discredit on the Corps of Cadets," when I unbuttoned my stiff dress gray collar during a required evening lecture, "Unsafe at Any Speed" by Ralph Nader. After having been kicked in the face during an afternoon rugby scrimmage, I had let my guard down at the lecture and not noticed that several civilians were also present. That particular offense could have cost me dearly, but to my great relief, someone in the higher administration must have recognized it as an overreaction by an overzealous officer in charge, and the paperwork disappeared.

Our brief escapes back to the civilian world were sometimes all we lived for. During plebe year we had no leaves at all and could not even go away at Christmas. Even semester breaks all four years lasted only from the last math class Saturday morning until the following Monday math class at 0745. yearling year, regulations allotted us one weekend leave each semester, a whopping thirty hours from Saturday noon, after our last class, to Sunday evening meal formation. With the authorized paperwork in hand, we could leave the Academy, which usually meant a jaunt down Highway

9W along the Hudson to the Big Apple. We had almost no money and would pool our resources to rent several cheap rooms at the Times Square Motor Hotel or to buy bottles of bourbon to bring with us when we crashed at the seedy pads of friends of friends in Greenwich Village or, more often, in stewardesses' apartments when they were on reserve. They were sitting out their own form of confinement during those on-call duty days and were happy to see us.

Getting to and from the city, unfortunately, ate up many of those precious hours of freedom. Jon and I had eased that a bit when we borrowed an unregistered jalopy from a college friend of his. After the battered heap kept breaking down just when we needed it most, and a few close calls with the New York State Police, Jon and I decided to get a *legal* car. Legal, that is, in terms of New York State law but still in violation of Academy regulations. If we were caught, it would mean an automatic four months' confinement. We were, as usual, very short on cash, so we enlisted Jon's roommate, Chan McKearn. A short, red-haired, freckle-faced dynamo from Big Piney, Wyoming, Chan had often helped keep cadet morale up with pranks of his own. He once cut a huge Sasquatch footprint stencil, complete with sharp toenails, out of a large piece of cardboard box. Then, in the dark hours long after taps, he crept out into the Area with his stencil and a can of spray paint. The next morning, when we all stumbled out to reveille formation at 0550, we saw huge, gnarly, neon-green footprints leading directly to the tactical officer's headquarters from the sewer manhole cover. We were grateful for every little diversion.

Chan, Jon, and I pooled our resources, caught a lift to a used car lot in Newburgh, and for $120 cash we bought and legally registered a battered 1955 green and yellow Mercury station wagon. As far as we knew, we were the only cadets who owned a car, and it continued to amaze me how many very good minds worshipped and feared the regulations. New York law required insurance, but standard civilian auto policies were way beyond our budget, so I took a chance and applied for United Services Automobile Association Army insurance, even though it was officially available only to graduating cadets. I timed my paperwork to coincide with legitimate applications from members of the class of 1965. Luckily it slipped through the bureaucratic cracks, and soon we were on the road in a registered, insured car, albeit one that burned so much oil we had to stop every 40 miles for a top off.

A sympathetic Highland Falls mechanic offered to help, and before driving the 45 miles to New York City, we would swing by his shop and exchange our empty 5-gallon oil can for a full one, drained out of someone else's crankcase during an oil change. We stored our getaway car in an old wooden garage at the top of a hill in nearby Highland Falls, and the steep grade came in handy, since the car always needed a jump-start. To reach its hideaway, my usual strategy was to first get an authorized leave and then phone a civilian taxi to meet me at the Cadet Chapel. There I would meet the cab wearing civilian clothes under a long uniform overcoat or raincoat, which I removed in the cab. The MPs slowed them but routinely waved civilian taxis with civilian passengers straight through the gates.

That old station wagon was the perfect car to haul a load of friends and us away on weekends, and also the perfect car to learn to drive in Manhattan. It was already a battered heap, but it was heavy and solid and powered by a V8, so whenever aggressive cabbies tried to cut us off or squeeze us out of a lane, we just nudged them a little, stared them down, and indicated we were ready for more. It was playing "Broadway bumper cars" with full-sized vehicles. When we finally got a good feel for the city's unique traffic spacing and rhythm, it was easy to drive any car there, even a good one. We remembered to always park the Mercury on a hill, and that wonderful heap sped us to many rendezvous with airline hostesses and cadet parties in cheap motels where Abe's rock band often raised the rafters.

I never did get caught for owning the Mercury, but I did for other infractions. Near the end of first semester cow year, I had three regimental boards in two weeks—an Academy record, I was told—and they sentenced me to four months' confinement. The last board was for "argumentative and belligerent conduct" in the second board, i.e., offering a defense. "Confinement" meant restriction to quarters, akin to the civilian punishment of house arrest, but worse in the sense that no entertainments such as movies or even a TV were allowed, nor any outside visitors. No girls or family or civilian friends or even pizza delivery. Four months' confinement seemed impossibly long to me. Four straight months living day and night under all those rules and regulations, without the briefest beer run or rendezvous with a girlfriend?

Then I had an insight, one that is certainly second nature to jailhouse lawyers in cellblocks from coast to coast but was a major *aha!* for me. Yes, I was bound 24/7 by Academy rules and regulations, but so were the authorities! I hauled out my trusty loose-leaf blue binder of Cadet Regulations to see if I could find some loophole or obscure statute that might help me.

I learned that if a cadet was part of an intercollegiate team, official team trips trumped confinements, which would then be postponed. The fall season for varsity sports had already started, but I kept checking and found that the intercollegiate debate team qualified. I talked Gary into joining me, and after several tryouts he and I joined Wes, Gary's friend Rich Hood, and a handful of others as official members of the intercollegiate Academy Debate Team. Gary and I welcomed this new intellectual challenge, were selected as the best novice team at the Academy, and were soon off on debate trips from Ohio and South Carolina and all the way west to Los Angeles. On a debate tournament trip to Bowling Green, Gary and I rented a car for the following weekend to visit his parents in Piqua, where Gary took me canoeing in his own boyhood haunts. We usually didn't fly to tournaments commercially but rather in small planes piloted by West Point instructors working on keeping their pilot ratings.

Since these debate trips were official, we even got paid *per diem* when we were away, and the time away did not count against our weekend or annual leave quota. Many of the debate trips extended into the regular school week, so not only was I often away on trips more than "good" cadets were, but I was also getting paid for it and preserving my own leave time to boot. I was much better off than I had been before my punishment! My company tactical officer, Major Fuller, was livid but was bound by the regulations and bit his tongue.

During second semester of our cow year, the Pentagon announced an end to the traditional cadet summer Army Orientation Training (AOT) in Europe, as part of an austerity program to help reduce "unfavorable gold outflow." New AOT rules instead gave us stateside assignments, to hellholes such as Ft. Polk, Louisiana, and Ft. Hood, Texas, the armpits of the Army. I went to see Jon.

"Well, J," I said, "it looks like we don't get a second trip to Europe." Jon had been sent to the Britain's Royal Military Academy at Sandhurst while I was on the German exchange. "But I found out there are a few positions in *Hawaii*!"

He was one jump ahead of me. "I already checked it out, T," Jon said. "There are four hundred AOT slots nationwide, and ten of those are on Oahu. Seven Infantry, two Engineer, and one Signal. I'm going to apply for one of the Engineer jobs. I figure with my Stars and good military grades—unlike you, my friend—I'll have a good shot at it."

"Well," I said, "I figure most people will go with the odds and try for Infantry. And those will go to the straight arrows. I'm going to gamble on the Signal job. Most of our gung-ho classmates wouldn't touch Signal with a 10-foot pole."

Jon's solid application and my gamble both paid off, and within weeks we were in Hawaii for the first time. During the week we were third lieutenants on duty in the real Army, and on weekends, we were novice body surfers, driving another prohibited two-tone black-and-white 1955 Buick that we bought for $95. We used that car to explore jungle mountain valleys and hidden beaches and to pick up girls at Waikiki. It was also the getaway car when we crashed an Annapolis Midshipman's Ball at Pearl Harbor Officer Club, disguised in Middie uniforms, to smuggle out one of the young ladies I was dating whose parents had signed her up for the dance.

All too soon, our third lieutenant assignments in Hawaii were *pau*, and our annual leave was ahead of us. Instead of going home, as most cadets did with their month-long summer leave, I had another idea and talked to Jon.

"Hey, we're already halfway across the Pacific. Why don't we check out Okinawa and Japan? We can fly MAC. Never been to the Far East before."

"Sounds great to me, T," Jon said. "We can leave from Hickam."

Jon already knew about the Military Airlift Command. MAC offered one-way standby flights, often in cargo planes where the "seats" were canvas-and-aluminum benches bolted to the fuselage in a cold, vibrating hold full of pallets and heavy equipment strapped to the floor. On the positive side, the MAC flights were completely free—every active-duty serviceman could just show up at any Air Force or Army Air Base, in uniform with valid military ID and leave orders, and he could hop on any US military plane with space available, wherever it was going. And on the other end of every MAC ride, no matter what country or remote air base he wound up in, there was always a welcoming American military ground crew and hot coffee. I had heard of servicemen who took advantage of MAC travel, but only to visit friends and family, not to see the world.

"You know MAC doesn't guarantee any return transportation, right?" I said. "If we make it to Tokyo, we'll have to take our chances getting back here to Hawaii and then to the mainland and eventually New York. We could get stuck AWOL in Japan for a while, but when Al and I hopped a MAC flight to West Berlin and back last summer, it worked out fine. I'm optimistic."

So was Jon, but since neither of us had enough money for a commercial return flight from Tokyo to New York, we built in an extra week at the end, packed our duffel bags, and caught a bus to Hickam Air Force Base in Honolulu. Many flights were headed for Okinawa en route to Japan, and in two days we landed in Okinawa just in time to witness our first Typhoon Condition 3. After a week visiting the main city Naha and exploring the mountain caves where the last Japanese Army holdouts had hidden and died, we caught a flight to Yokota Air Force Base in Tokyo and checked in at the Bachelors Officers Quarters, where we got a room for $5 a night. Our shoestring budget didn't have any room for the usual tourist attractions, but we explored Tokyo on foot in ever widening rings, starting at the Imperial Palace and going as far as the Tokyo Tower to the south and the world-famous bookstore neighborhood at Jinbocho, stopping there to browse the English shelves and to sample exotic offerings from street vendors with whom we could not communicate. That short recon trip convinced me that some day I needed to learn a little Japanese and return for several months. Almost broke, Jon and I returned to Yokota early, and after a tense three days of no available return flights, we finally caught a MAC plane back to Hawaii, and from there to the mainland.

Jon and I made it back to West Point just in time for the start of our final fall semester. Both of us were awarded Stars again, but that did not carry much weight with Major Fuller. At mid-semester he summoned me to his office for my required semiannual consultation. Once a year tactical officers were required to review each cadet's record with him, inform him of his shortcomings, and suggest improvements to help make him a better officer: be stricter with subordinates, dress more smartly, develop better Army social skills, and so on. As he returned my salute, Major Fuller ordered me to sit in the wooden chair in front of his desk.

"Sir, before we start, may I make a statement?" I said, still standing.

He sighed, then nodded.

"Sir, I am not going to change my personality, personal habits, or values. The decision is up to you. If you think I will make a good officer as is, fine. Then there's no need to waste your time. On the other hand, if you feel I am lacking in certain qualities required of a good officer, then all you need do is say so, and I will quit the Academy. In either case, you won't have to counsel me."

This was no bluff on my part. By now it was clear to me that I would never succeed at a career in the Army. How in the world could I hope to toe the line for twenty or thirty years, when I couldn't even keep off the generals' toes for a few years as a cadet? I wasn't bitter. In fact, I respected much of what I saw in the Army, especially the selflessness, courage, and dedication. But I could not possibly behave like "an officer and a gentleman" for twenty straight years. Mathematics, on the other hand, seemed to welcome rebels and freethinkers, and mathematics had become my new long-range goal. I had a slight preference for finishing my time in the Army first, to share more honors science classes and adventures with my friends, but I was ready to quit the Academy and return to mathematics at a normal university if Major Fuller determined I was not officer material.

This completely disrupted his canned little speech, and Major Fuller groped for a new topic of conversation to fill the required half-hour interview. Clearly he was under pressure from above to keep a Star Man in the Army. He fidgeted, glanced at his watch, and looked around the room, his eyes coming to rest on a file cabinet.

"Well, as long as you are here, let's look at your aptitude ratings," he suggested, and opened the file.

Aptitude ratings measured the Academy's prediction for a cadet's success as an officer—for aptitude in the service. The aptitude ratings were notoriously unreliable. The numerical scores were largely based on semi-annual cadet peer ratings, where everyone rank-ordered each cadet in his own company, by year, who was in his and lower classes. For the two people he placed last on his list, he had to write a special subjective report we called a "poop sheet," stating why he had rated these two men at the bottom and what they could do to improve. By cow year, the truly inept had already been weeded out, and just from differences in personalities, the average cadet could expect two or three poop sheets. Six or eight were extreme. Major Fuller began leafing through my file, slowly at first and then much faster. His eyes widened and his mouth fell open.

"Mr. Hill, you got . . . sixteen, no . . . seventeen poop sheets, twelve from the first classmen! Listen to this. 'Mr. Hill is belligerent and insubordinate' . . . 'argumentative' . . . 'shows little respect for authority' . . . 'rebellious in nature . . .'"

He finally stopped and just stared at me.

"What do you think about these reports?" he stammered.

"I think they are probably right," I said, suppressing a smile.

Major Fuller was clearly tired of dealing with me. "Mr. Hill," he said, "I think I'll throw a party when you finally graduate and get out of my hair. Dismissed!"

As I walked back to my room, I felt a little sorry for the man. That night, after taps, I donned my black cadet parka, olive drab fatigue pants, and black combat boots and resurrected my Madison stadium walkabouts by going AWOL and sneaking up the hill to the Academy football field. The security fence at Michie Stadium was much smaller than that at Wisconsin's Camp Randall, since it was already inside a military base, but it still felt wonderful to be utterly free once again, if even for such a short time, especially since it was against regulations. Once again I gave serious thought to quitting, especially after my latest meeting with Major Fuller, but once again I decided to stay the course. Abe woke from a deep sleep when I crept back into our room and shook his head in disbelief at this latest of my escapades.

Fall semester passed, and I retained my position as the Star Man with the lowest cadet military rank in the class of 1966. In the spring semester of First Class Year, three classmates I had tutored in mathematics and nuclear engineering burst into my room.

"Ted—look. *You're one of us! You made the D-list.*" This was the deficiency list, for cadets failing in a subject.

"But you also made the *Dean's* List," they continued proudly. "That one-credit-hour failing Tactics grade couldn't pull down your math and nuke grades. Nobody ever made both lists at the same time!"

Tactics simply couldn't compete with my honors classes. Instead of attending standard lectures that semester, we pursued individual research projects. My self-designed project in advanced ordnance engineering involved evaporation of aluminum, at extremely high temperature and low pressure, to determine whether that method could be effective for depositing thin protective aluminum films on irregular surfaces. The experiment required equipment not available in standard cadet laboratories, so the professor gave me a key to the Ordnance Lab on Trophy Point. Each night, walking to and from the lab, I wasted a precious half hour. I researched my dog-eared Cadet Regulations once again and confirmed that it was forbidden for cadets to have automobiles, motorcycles, horses, and even roller skates. But, wonder of wonders, there was no mention of bicycles.

The teenage brother of a lady friend of mine from Newburgh cannibalized several old clunkers and supplied me, for the bargain price of $5, a solid, multicolored, one-speed bicycle. Part Schwinn, part Sears, part Raleigh, it worked as perfectly as Johnny Cash's "One Piece at a Time" Cadillac. The next day, while 4,000 cadets marched briskly to class in Thayer Hall, I soared merrily along on my bicycle. Peddling back for lunch, I passed the officer in charge. Saluting smartly, I kept cycling, and by the time he could react, I was long gone. A classmate from C-2 later filled me in on what had happened next. The OC had immediately stopped the next cadet he met, a plebe who lived across from my friend.

"Halt, mister!" the OC ordered. "Are you cadets allowed to have bicycles?"

"Sir, I do not know," he answered. Plebes were not allowed to use contractions—that much he did know.

The OC hurried to the central guard room to ask the duty officers and check the regulations. At the formal noon meal, the first captain's voice from the poop deck boomed down to the entire Corps of Cadets. "The officer in charge extends his congratulations to the ingenious cadet who has solved his transportation problems with a bicycle." My friends told me to stand and take a bow, but I knew better. Generals are not paid to have a sense of humor.

Sure enough, the brigadier general commandant had also seen the phantom bicyclist through his office window overlooking Central Area and notified all tactical officers to find the culprit. I was at the top of Major Fuller's personal list of usual suspects, and he phoned me immediately. Although he had no probable cause, and thus was using my honor against me, it was clear its days were numbered, so I admitted to having the bicycle of many colors.

"Mr. Hill, get rid of that bicycle by 1800 hours tonight!" he barked. The call from the general had disturbed him.

"But, sir, I've checked regulations, and nothing prohibits bicycles."

"This is a *direct order.* That's all the regulation you need."

The next afternoon Major Fuller paid me an unexpected visit. Abe was stretched out on the bed for a nap, and I sat at my desk. Major Fuller looked ruffled.

"Mr. Hill, have you gotten rid of that bicycle yet?"

It was his turn to sweat a little. The commandant would soon be writing Major Fuller's annual officer efficiency report.

"No, sir," I said. "Since I cannot sell it to one of the other cadets, and it's against regulations to throw it in the Hudson, I'll have to sell it off post. May I request a three day leave so I can take it to New York City and . . ."

"Leave denied," he interrupted and shuffled his feet uncomfortably. I waited out the awkward silence. "How much are you selling it for?" he then asked quietly.

"Five dollars. That's what I paid for it."

"Okay, Mr. Hill. Bring it to my house this afternoon and put it in my garage." He opened his wallet, handed me a $5 bill, and left our room.

Then I realized Major Fuller said *bring* the bike to his house. He didn't say *walk* it. I mapped out a long route passing as many barracks and officers' houses as I could, put on my informal cadet parka, and, tilting my uniform cap on the back of my head, soared through the Academy grounds. Down by Trophy Point and past the superintendent's quarters I rode, taking an extra lap around the parade ground. How beautiful and strange and free it felt, to be seeing these familiar sights in this period of twilight quiet and at this incredible speed. It was a wonderful last trip on that historic bike. Within a day, the authorities had printed and distributed a new page for all the cadet regulations books. Bicycles were now officially forbidden.

Of course I wasn't the only rebel in our class, and my friend Art Mosley had managed to pull off a much more impressive coup. Art was a tall, lanky fellow from the Florida Panhandle, and his thick Southern drawl concealed a sharp, analytical mind with a delightfully mischievous bent. He too was a Star Man, and I'd come to know him quite well between classes. Many considered him something of a cadet scofflaw, and Art had once managed to moon the entire Corps of Cadets from a barricaded barracks balcony room as they returned from lunch. This new caper of his, though, was much more serious. Late one night, during release from quarters, Art came to see me and pulled me aside.

"TP," he said, when we were out of earshot from the others, "I need a favor from you. I need to borrow that illegal car you have for a few days. I know you're still in confinement, so unfortunately you can't join us."

I figured it was some road trip to Wellesley or Greenwich Village, but he quickly set me straight.

"We're going to steal the Navy goat," he said quietly, his eyes blazing. "Armed Marines guard it round the clock, but we did a recon trip to Annapolis and figure it might be possible. We'll use bolt cutters to get through the chain-link security fence and a couple of sexy coeds to distract the guards. Wish you could join us!"

I pictured the official Naval Academy mascot, the billy goat with the long beard and Navy blue-and-gold painted horns.

"Here's the address where the car's hidden," I told him as I handed him the keys. "It's on a hill, needs to be jump-started. Car uses a ton of oil, there's a 5-gallon can of it in the back. Damned fine idea, Art! Good luck, my friend. And if you get caught, try not to tell them who owns the car!"

And damned if they didn't pull it off, causing an uproar at the highest levels of the two Academies. When Art returned the Mercury, it reeked of goat urine, but that old station wagon was now more beloved than ever, and we christened our Army-insured wreck the *Goatmobile.*

As we neared the end of that last year, Gary's outstanding talent in physics and mathematics led him to try to become the first West Pointer in history to win a National Science Foundation Graduate Scholarship in Physics. Every night he lugged back to the barracks old issues of *Scientific American* and *Physics Today* and typed out notecards on everything from electromagnetism to optics. Then he made tape recordings of formulas and physical laws to play in his sleep.

"Does it work?" I asked.

"Don't know. But what the heck, I'm sleeping anyway," he said, grinning. "But two days ago this special form of the Schrödinger equation just popped into my head at parade. When I got back to my room, I checked, and sure enough it was on the tape."

The qualifying examination for the NSF scholarship required approval from a candidate's college or university. Unfortunately for Gary, his great scientific talents did not make up for his struggles with German, which he had almost failed, thus lowering his overall grade point average. When he went to the academic office to request approval to compete, the dean denied him permission because of his undistinguished standing in the General Order of Merit. The Academy did not want to risk a poor showing in the competition by such a "mediocre" student. When Gary returned to our room still flushed with anger, he told me he had slammed his fist on the dean's desk and cried, "Damn, sir!" It was the only time I had ever known him to curse voluntarily, and that was to an officer.

That last spring we Firsties were finally allowed to have cars legally, so Jon, Chan, and I sold the Mercury and joined the rest of the class buying cars. Al was buying a cherry red 1966 Corvette, and everyone else I knew was also getting a brand-new car, taking advantage of the rock-bottom prices local dealers were offering for bulk sales. I too liked the idea of a sports car but opted instead for a ten-year-old black hardtop convertible 1956 Thunderbird, with its already classic lines—and at one-third the price of a new Corvette. When Jon saw it, he too went for a T-bird, a silver 1957 model with a continental kit.

Graduation Day came with its celebratory marches and fanfare. I was proud that I had been able to keep my promise to myself never to haze or even yell at a plebe. Many families, including mine, came to watch their sons, handsome in parade uniforms, receive their diplomas. "Fame will mix with '66" was our class motto, and we were ready to conquer the world.

In spite of my comparatively low grades in Military Science, I still finished nineteenth in our class, now reduced to 579, and thus was one of the lucky twenty-eight who qualified for the 5 percent immediate graduate school program.

In fact, the brass actually did not want us to take them up on the graduate school offer immediately, but rather to defer it for a few years. They herded us graduating Star Men into a lecture room, where a medal-bedecked and ruggedly handsome Green Beret captain assured us, "There is no substitute for grassroots experience as a platoon leader and lieutenant on a company staff," and one of our professors reminded us that after four years of books and exams, we were "ready for a well-deserved break from books." I'm sure that if they could have found a chaplain who would tell us it was better for our souls to go into the Army immediately, they would have had him speak too. Even without the theological angle, however, the brass managed to talk *more than half* of my Star classmates out of taking the offer. Both Art's close friend Jack Wheeler and my Honor Code savior Tom Hayes—number nine in our class in the final General Order of Merit—elected to go immediately into the *real* Army, along with all the rest of our class, including my friends Abe and Al and Chan and Gary.

Of my Star friends who jumped at the graduate school offer, Wes was off to Oxford as a Rhodes Scholar, Art to Harvard Business School, and Jon and I and our classmate Dave Linder were headed to Stanford in sunny, free-love California. My official program of study was for a master's in operations research, since the only graduate degree in mathematics that Stanford offered was a PhD, but I would be free to take as many electives in pure mathematics as I wanted. I was ecstatic, more than ready to leave the confines of military regimentation far behind me for a glorious two years to study mathematics as a civilian. Just enough time, I reckoned, to savor the wild freedoms of the Bay Area and let this new Vietnam War thing wind down to an end. Well, I got the first part right, anyway.

3

OUT OF THE GATES

Cooped up at West Point for four years, we had missed the simple pleasures other college students take for granted—sleeping late now and then, making our own sandwiches, having a beer or glass of wine with supper, holding a girl's hand in public in broad daylight. Times hadn't changed. President Ulysses S. Grant, the Civil War hero, had said that leaving West Point "was the happiest day of my life." When my class's ceremony ended at noon on June 6, 1966, with the ritual tossing of our white uniform hats high into the sky, we graduating cadets were like thoroughbreds exploding through racetrack gates. Except that we had no lanes, and the trajectories pointed in all directions.

The Army rewards each Academy graduate with a once-in-a-lifetime, two-month paid graduation leave, and most classmates sped home to be with their families and drink beer with high school friends. Many also rushed home to get married, happily filling the vacuum from leaving one institutional life by entering another. Some couldn't even wait to leave the Academy grounds, and in a four-day matrimonial marathon, wedding bells rang for nearly fifty 1966ers' nuptials right there in the Cadet Chapel. As different as our directions were, each of us was determined to cram as much living as humanly possible into those sixty days. The Vietnam War was now in full swing, and every one of us knew we would be ordered to Southeast Asia for combat duty. Nearly a hundred had already volunteered.

"I did," Gary told me cheerfully. "I figure we'll be ordered to Vietnam anyway, and this way I can get it over with and at least have a little say in the matter. Rich Hood and I set it up so we can serve in the same unit at the same time, and we'll watch each other's backs for the year. That'll maximize the probability we both come back alive."

I pictured our bookish debate teammate Rich and hoped he would be up to the task. As for me, I was off to study higher mathematics in free-speech and free-love California, while they'd be off "defending freedom" in an unknown land. Knowing that we'd soon be in different worlds, Gary and I had already hatched our own little graduation getaway, one suitable for two country boys to decompress after the Academy ordeal. While our classmates were planning parties and weddings, we decided to go prospecting for gold in the high Andes.

Gary and I had spent two months researching transportation and geology and had pinpointed two promising, remote regions of the Peruvian Andes. Our plan was to take MAC flights, as Jon and I had done from Hawaii to Japan and back. First, we'd try to catch a MAC lift from Ohio to South Carolina and hopscotch from there to Panama and then to our final destination of Lima. Between the two of us, we had enough money for one-way, half-fare military standby commercial tickets on Pan Am, so if we could make it to Peru for free, then in a worst-case scenario we figured we could return by half-fare civilian flights from Lima. Air traffic reports showed frequent military flights on each leg of our planned route. Delays of up to two or three days could be expected, but for the critical leg from Panama to Peru, the US military's scheduled Andes Run departed the Canal Zone once every week, visiting each capital city in South America to deliver diplomatic pouches and supplies to consulates and military attachés. In Peru we would use local transportation—trains, trucks, mules, and foot. The equipment we took would be limited to what two hardy hikers could carry in backpacks.

"If we use traditional gold panning techniques," Gary had explained, "competition from local *campesinos* will make it impossible to strike it rich. Those guys are willing to pan streams for 50 cents a day. So I invested in a portable gasoline-powered gold dredge that can sift thousands of times as much riverbed silt as a human. And we can work deeper streams. Its lawnmower-sized engine floats in an inflated inner tube on the surface and powers both the vacuum dredge and a compressor that pumps air down to a diver. One of us carries the whole contraption, and the other carries camping gear and supplies. And just in case," Gary insisted, "we'll bring my .357 Smith & Wesson."

We agreed to meet ten days after graduation at his parents' home in Piqua, conveniently close to the major military air hub at Wright-Patterson Air Force Base. I went home to Alloway to assemble my gear: backpack, boots, khakis, machete, and malaria pills. My parents and younger siblings George and Margaret were also packing. My father had decided to take a six-month leave of absence from Comstock Foods to go to rural Iran on a project sponsored by the International Executive Corps, a sort of Peace Corps for businessmen, to advise the region's first canning factory. Russ was staying behind to work during the summer and then to return to Cornell in the fall. The huge house would be vacant for half a year, and when Dad had first told Russ and me about the Iran trip, we'd joked that as soon as he left, we were going to set up a "whorehouse."

Several days before they were to leave, he called the two of us into the den for a formal talk.

"Boys," he said, "While we're in Iran, I'm renting out a room in the house to a New York State Trooper. You're both welcome to stay here, of course, but he's in charge. I'm sure you'll get along with him just fine. His name is Cy."

The expression on his face told us he wasn't joking. Forget the whorehouse—we probably wouldn't even be able to throw nighttime skinny-dipping parties. You had to admire my father's creativity, even if you didn't agree with his social politics. I finished packing and went out to continue celebrating graduation by drinking and partying with old high school friends at Sodus Point on Lake Ontario and at Mike's Bar and Grill along the New York Central Railroad tracks in Lyons. Then I flew to Ohio to meet Gary.

Mrs. Jackson fed us one of her typical two-meat, four-vegetable, and three-dessert Ohio country light snacks and then drove us to Wright-Pat.

An Air Force C-130, the military workhorse four-engine prop cargo plane, took us to the air base at Charleston, South Carolina, and another the same day from Charleston to Howard Air Force Base in the Canal Zone. The next morning, the Howard operations desk told us that although the next Andes Run would not depart for two more days, there was space to Lima that very afternoon in the hold of an unscheduled embassy supply cargo plane. We jumped at the chance, and once on board, we stuffed waxed cotton balls into our ears to dampen the deafening engine noise. We lashed towels to the cargo net on the fuselage walls to jury-rig semi-upright hammocks and covered each other with cargo blankets to ward off the chill of the frigid hold.

After eight long hours of cold vibrations, the Peruvian Andes finally came into view through the small, half-frosted porthole windows. The gray-brown barren western slopes of the mountains contrasted sharply with the lush green jungles on the eastern slopes, and Lima lay below in the thin north-south ribbon of land between the Andes and the Pacific, shrouded in the dense daily fog thrown up by the cold Humboldt Current. Now and then flashes of sunlight reflected off city buildings, and the long, gleaming seashore broke through the haze. Nearer Lima, irregular green checkerboard patterns revealed irrigated fields on the fertile desert coast. Gary and I were excited about exploring the high Andes and optimistic about finding gold. So far our luck had held, with three days of free air travel courtesy of Uncle Sam.

Someone had alerted the US embassy in Lima about our arrival, and a Peruvian sergeant met Gary and me at the airport and drove us to the US military attaché's office. Diplomatic and military flights used the same Lima airport as commercial planes but had minimal customs and immigration red tape, and all our equipment had been ushered right through, including the .357 with live ammo. The driver showed us to a small briefing room with long flat olive-green tables and wooden folding chairs facing a blackboard and a half-dozen wall maps. An American major from the attaché's office soon appeared, introduced himself coldly, and told us to sit down. He pulled down a large window shade topographic map of Peru and picked up a wooden pointer. A fidgety man, he kept tapping the map with the rubber tip of the pointer, making little dents. It seemed like long minutes before he spoke.

"I assume you gentlemen have maps," he said. "Now please pay close attention. There are certain areas of Peru you will *not* be permitted to visit." He swept the pointer across large areas shaded in red and pink. "Most of these areas are still run by bandito gangs and are particularly unsafe for gringos. All these pink, and especially the red areas. There's practically no law and order there—no government control at all."

He didn't say a word about us carrying loaded weapons in the mountains—he was more worried about *us* being shot than someone being shot by us. American deaths required much more paperwork. We thanked him, and his driver took us to a cheap hotel on the outskirts of Lima. Our research had not included interior political boundaries, and the objectives we had pinpointed were all in the forbidden red territories. But since we had come this far with all this special gear, Gary and I decided to at least slip into one of the gold-bearing valleys in a pink zone.

We repacked our gear from flight bags to backpacks, and at daybreak we caught a cab to Desamparados, the Lima train station. Between hotel and station, we caught our first glimpse of the inequities of Peruvian society, from the splendor of Spanish colonial haciendas and modern office buildings to the squalor of vast cardboard-and-corrugated-iron slums. But our immediate goal, far away from this urban nightmare, was high in the Andes to the east and above Lima, the old mining town of La Oroya.

To get there, we hopped aboard the nineteenth-century Lima–La Oroya Railroad Line, the world's highest railroad. The rickety, three-car wooden train zigzagged up and up through seventy-odd tunnels, the grade so steep the tracks could not wind directly up the mountain but instead were laid out in a herringbone pattern. Every few minutes, the brakes squealed—steel against rusty steel—the conductor stepped out to throw the switch, and we backed up to the next switchback. Forward, switch, back, switch, forward, switch, back, switch, higher and higher. For six hours the old train creaked and shuddered and groaned, and I closed the window against the cold. The view out one side of our old wooden car was a barren rocky mountainside covering the whole window, with not even a sliver of sky framing the top. The panorama in the other direction was *all* sky. The drop-off from the tracks was a steep embankment where a derailed car would plummet and crash, end over end, for several long vertical miles down the mountain, before disappearing below in the clouds covering Lima.

The only other passengers were small groups of Indians, mostly women and children. La Oroya was above 12,000 feet, and when we finally reached there, Gary and I both had severe frontal headaches. We wrote these off to sinus problems, not realizing they were symptoms of altitude sickness, of oxygen deprivation in the brain. (In the 1990s, that train began providing oxygen tanks.) Under heavy packs, our heads throbbing with shooting pains, we staggered to an adobe inn and collapsed in a heap in our sleeping bags on the dirt floor. Our first aid kit contained aspirin and Darvon, but no painkiller strong enough to ward off these piercing pulses.

We slept through the whole next day, and at dusk our headaches began to subside, but we were still dizzy. Part of our weakness, we realized, was now also due to hunger. In our nausea, we had eaten nothing since two oranges on the mountain train. We stepped outside and walked through the streets of La Oroya, a desolate, windswept, has-been mining town. A blanket of gray dust choked the treeless streets, and frigid gusts of mountain wind pierced the seams of our jackets. No restaurants were open, but an innkeeper pointed us to a small café a mile down the dirt road.

In its small dining room with cracked, yellow-brown plaster walls lit by kerosene lamps, we sat at one of the half-dozen rough wooden tables. I pointed to a line on the short handwritten menu that contained a word I recognized—*arroz*—and ordered, "*Dos, por favor*," holding up two fingers.

Gary and I propped our weak frames up on our elbows, still wearing our windbreakers, until the girl returned from the kitchen with two steaming plates. The neon green concoction had the texture of oatmeal but smelled like swamp scum. Slowly I forced myself to swallow bite after bite of my serving, blocking out the current sensory signals and substituting memories of Thanksgivings past. But Gary stared silently at his plate and bent to sniff it several times, the way a starving junkyard dog returns to a rotting cabbage.

"Look," I said, pointing to his plate. "In Beast Barracks you'd have wolfed that down in a heartbeat and hoped for seconds. Are you telling me you'd rather be spending graduation leave at home eating wedding cake?"

He then poured two full bowls of sugar over the mixture, stirred it all together, and slowly and mechanically swallowed mouthful after mouthful. He never looked down at his plate once, until the entire mound disappeared. Luckily, the food stayed down, and when we awoke the next morning, we felt much stronger. We packed our prospecting gear, paid the innkeeper for two more nights, and struck out into the hills with maps.

The next two days we trudged all over the surrounding slopes with our heavy backpacks, sampling streambeds and investigating rock outcroppings in the barren high Andean landscape. Nada.

"Hey," Gary said. "Whoever named La Oroya is probably the same joker who named Greenland."

We rechecked our maps and notes and decided to move to a different area, the fringes of a pink zone near Cuzco, the ancient Inca capital 350 miles southeast of Lima. There were no trains from the village of La Oroya to Cuzco, and the bus station in the village was a small adobe hut.

"The bus," said the clerk, as he pointed to a dilapidated heap parked next to the shack, "leaves tomorrow. We guarantee a 75 percent chance of reaching Cuzco in three days."

Gary and I looked at each other. The clerk recognized our puzzled look.

"The only north-south route is a narrow one-lane mountain road through the high Andes. It's one way northbound on even days, and southbound on odd. The bus goes as far as it can in one day and then stops for twenty-four hours. There are very few places to turn around."

The odds of getting to Cuzco that way looked too slim to us, so we took the herringbone train back down the mountain and the next day caught a sputtering, twelve-passenger Aero Peru plane to the high-altitude Cuzco airstrip. Stepping down the aluminum passenger ladder to sunny clear skies and thin, 50-degree mountain air, we collected our packs on the tarmac beside the plane. A fellow passenger eyed our US Army duffel bags and asked, in English, about our plans. Friendly, in his thirties, he was tall and lean, with a short-cropped crew cut and American accent. "Perhaps Army Intelligence," I thought—"from the looks of his light-gray suit and tie—or CIA." Gary and I briefly described our little celebratory graduation outing, the Lima attaché's warning, and our disappointing La Oroya probes.

"You two are *West Pointers*?" he said, shaking his head. "I thought they had more sense than that! Don't you realize the extent of anti-American and anti-capitalist activities going on here? President Belaunde just nationalized the American-owned International Petroleum Company, and Shining Path guerrillas, *Communists*, are trying to overrun Peru. Killed nine rural policemen. And even if the bad guys don't get you, the mountains will. This is no picnic in the Catskills. Is that all the gear you brought for this trip? *Jesus*." He pointed to our packs and walked away, still shaking his head.

Of course he was right. That coat-and-tie fellow, CIA or whatever he was, knew ten times as much as we did about our own expedition. We should have prepared as though it were an Everest climb and certainly should have researched the political scene. But this close to the gold of the Incas, we decided to give it one last shot. The next morning, loaded down with our heavy gear, we made more exploratory excursions, testing arroyo faces and streambeds. Still unaccustomed to the altitude, we made excruciatingly slow progress. Our panning and dredging "showed color," which is exactly what is promised at the $5 tourist panning stalls in the California goldfields near Sutter's Mill. Enough gold to *see*, but not enough to pick up, at least without tweezers. Still it thrilled us, testing our strength and ingenuity amid the spectacular background of Andean peaks. And the more deeply we probed into the forbidden pink zone, the more samples showed color.

On our deepest penetration behind the invisible border of safety, we began working a small stream that cut through the pebble-lined bed of an old river. A sharp bend in the stream sliced deeply into the 8-foot bank of the riverbed. After dropping our packs next to the stream, I climbed the bank and scanned the surrounding gray rocky hills for signs of civilization but saw nothing—no adobe huts, no simple shelters, not even a burro or llama. Somehow we had not pictured the headwaters of the Amazon as runoff from Andean snowfields in a cold, rocky, and barren mountain valley. Since the icy stream was only 2 feet deep, Gary and I panned by hand, standing on the rocks, our fingers red and swollen. Our packs and the .357 lay on a gravel bank 10 feet away, on the inside curve of the streambed.

A shout broke the stillness, and we turned to see a lone figure standing on the embankment, his rifle steadily sweeping back and forth from Gary's chest to mine. Tucked between the dirt-stained brown pants and faded flannel shirt of the short, stocky bandito, a bone-handled knife caught the edge of his homespun *serape*. Black eyes flashed from a weather-beaten brown face, half concealed by a thick bushy mustache and the leather chin strap of his crumpled, wide-brimmed brown felt hat.

"*Manos arriba!*"

I glanced at Gary as we raised our hands slowly. The man stared at our packs and machete. Compared to him, we were millionaires. But it wouldn't be easy for him to rob us. To clamber down the bank, he would have to sling his rifle momentarily, and maybe then we could turn the tables on him. And it would be hard for him to shoot us both before one of us reached the .357 and the cover of nearby boulders. He had to decide if our gear looked worth the risk or not. At least he couldn't see our gun. Finally he motioned with his rifle toward our packs.

"*Váyanse de aqui, gringos!*" Get out of here!

We moved slowly toward our packs, realizing now that our assailant had decided not to rob us, or he would have motioned us *away* from our gear. We were lucky. Since the man didn't make a move toward us, pulling our gun would be a stupid mistake. In ten minutes Gary and I were out of sight over the next ridgeline, moving as fast as we could under the heavy packs. By the time we got back to Cuzco, we had decided to stay out of the pink zones—and perhaps hire burros to carry our packs.

Back at our inn, the owner told us he knew of no place where a gringo could buy or rent a burro, but since we were *soldados*, he told us, perhaps we could get some from the small Peruvian Army garrison a few miles down the dirt road. The next day we walked there, but the guards refused us admission until I showed them our Army IDs. They finally led us to the office of the captain of the garrison, a wiry pockmarked man in an immaculate, starched, and tailored fatigue uniform. I introduced Gary and me in slow, broken Spanish, but the captain immediately broke into a huge smile. He welcomed the chance to speak English, he told us, and led us to a small officer's canteen where he opened three bottles of *cerveza*.

"I was in the US Army for three years. Fort Benning, Georgia, Airborne School—yes, those were good years. The American officers treated me well. But I returned here where I am needed, and now I am a *capitán*.

In my opinion, the best way to eliminate poverty and illiteracy in Peru is to *force* education upon the people. Bring them into the army and start with basic sanitation. Force them to brush their teeth every day. Force them to wash with soap, to boil their water. Soon they will learn." He paused to finish his beer. "So, what brings you to Cuzco?"

We explained our plans and spread out our annotated map. When we finished, he pointed on the map to a mountainous region several hundred miles southeast of Cuzco.

"Here is the good gold region," he said, "but you need a moderate-sized expedition to reach it. First you must cross backcountry for six days by truck to the end of the dirt track, then two days by horseback, and finally on foot another five or six days, crossing this pass. The goldfields there are *muy rico.* With your equipment, you should be able to make about $200 a day."

I followed the movements of his finger, my heart sinking at the remoteness of the site.

He was reconfirming the assessment that the CIA guy had made of our expedition. We thanked him, and when we left his stockade, decided to give up on gold panning and close the trip by hopping a mountain train up the Urubamba River Valley to Machu Picchu. From the train stop, a sputtering, recycled Blue Bird school bus took us and a few other passengers up the steep mountainside, leaning into the dozen hairpin curves cut into the cliffs, until we finally reached the mostly deserted ruins. There Gary and I explored the main structures and then picked our way up the steep path to the Huayna Picchu lookout, amazed that this narrow trail with loose rocks and 1,000-foot drop-offs was open to anyone who dared.

Gary and I returned to Lima to try to hustle a MAC flight back to Panama. The US operations shack at the Lima airport showed no scheduled flight north for the next twelve days, and later flights were booked solid. We called the commercial Pan Am agent in Lima to reconfirm their half-fare military standby rates.

"You have been misinformed," said the agent. "Pan Am has no half-fare military rates from Lima."

"But your agent in the Canal Zone told us we could get a half-fare return ticket," I said.

"We don't have any military fare rates outside US territories. The Canal Zone is a US territory. This is Peru."

Gary and I did not have the $600 to return by commercial airliner, and if it took two weeks for a free flight to materialize, we would be AWOL. Gary broke the silence with his usual positive attitude.

"Well, at least we aren't pressed for time yet. Let's check out the city, visit the museums and palace, and see if we can take in one of the anti-US rallies at the Plaza de Armas. Maybe see a local movie and see if there are any social functions at the American embassy."

His optimism was contagious. After two days of sightseeing, I decided to explore a few unofficial sources of information on military flights and went to the Gran Hotel Bolivar, the 350-room colonial landmark on Plaza San Martin that serves as a rendezvous for Lima high society, well-heeled tourists, and businessmen. As I walked up the steps and into the imposing lobby, I scanned the room for airline pilot uniforms but saw only civilians. Then I noticed a clean-cut *Yanqui* exchanging money at the cashier's desk. I recognized the Balboan coins—Panamanian currency.

"Excuse me. Are you coming from or going to Panama?" I asked. He looked like an American student or serviceman, and I figured he spoke English.

"Both. We flew in here on an unscheduled military flight and are leaving to go back to Panama right now. American?" he asked.

I nodded. "Do you have room for two more passengers?" I asked, trying not to sound desperate.

"Well, it's an Air Force plane, and I'm just one of the crew members. Why don't you talk to the pilot—that's him over there in the sport coat."

I walked over to the pilot, a guy of about forty with graying temples. "Do you have room on your flight to Panama for two officers?"

He stared at my unshaven shaggy head, dirty parka, and mountaineering boots.

"If you can be at the airport *in uniform* in fifty minutes, we do," he said. It sounded like a dare.

All that clothing formation hazing from plebe year was now about to pay off. I sprinted out the door to find Gary as fast as I could and caught up with him at Pizarro's Government House as he was adjusting his camera to capture the changing of the red-coated guards. We raced to our hotel, called a cab, dry shaved, threw our packs together, and jumped into our uniforms in the cab, still toweling off blood from the shaving nicks. We ordered the driver to bypass the main commercial airport building and pointed him to the one-room, battleship gray wooden building next to the civilian runway that served as operations center for military planes. We dashed inside to have our orders, shot records, and passports checked and hurried to the operations desk. The sergeant on duty remembered our phone call.

"You guys are really in luck," he said. "Three days ago there were no flights in sight for weeks, and today we have *two* unscheduled flights leaving for Panama. Both have space. I'll manifest you on the C-141. It's leaving later but arrives in the Canal Zone hours before the C-130. Much faster plane. That okay with you?"

We said yes, thanked him, completed the rest of our customs and exit visa forms, and sat down on the cracked vinyl chairs to relax and congratulate each other on our luck. Minutes later the tower air controller radioed the sergeant on duty that the C-141 would not be able to depart because of mechanical failure. Our hearts jumped to our throats as we rushed to the desk.

"Sorry, gentlemen! There's nothing I can do now. The other flight is already taxiing." He pointed out the window.

Just then a middle-aged man wearing a US Air Force colonel's flight jacket over civilian clothes burst into the operations shack with two bewildered Peruvian Army officers in tow.

"Sergeant," he said, "these two officers must get to the Canal Zone today." He pointed to his two companions. "I just heard the plane they're manifested on is disabled. *Stop that other plane*!"

"Sir, there's nothing I can do," said the dispatcher. "The pilot's on civilian tower frequency now, and I can't raise him on mine. By the time I go through channels to reach Lima Tower, he'll already be in the air."

"Look, I'm going to stop that plane," the colonel said. "Now, do you have anyone here who's going to Panama, who can see to it that these two officers get to the School of the Americas?"

Gary and I had been following this exchange and immediately jumped up and volunteered.

"Good!" he nodded. "Now grab that checkered flag and get in my car. On the double, gentlemen!"

I snatched up the red-and-white signal flag from its stand beside the operations desk, and the five of us dashed to his civilian station wagon. The two Peruvian officers plopped in the backseat in a rumpled daze.

"Just lean out the window," the colonel ordered, "and keep waving that flag until the pilot sees you."

He shifted from second gear to third, and we sped down the runway, chasing the plane. Head and shoulders out the front passenger window, I frantically waved the checkered flag. The huge four-engine cargo plane finished taxiing and began its lift-off leg. With the two driver's-side wheels off the edge of the narrow runway, we caught up with the plane, and the pilot spotted me frantically waving the checkered flag below.

The C-130 screeched to a halt, blue smoke hissing from the tires. All five of us jumped out of the car and sprinted toward the plane with our gear, and by the time the colonel apologized to the fuming pilot, the rest of us had climbed up the wobbly collapsible aluminum ladder one of the crew had lowered from the cargo door.

The colonel ran back to the bay door and yelled up at us, "Now you two lieutenants make damn sure those officers get to the School of the Americas!"

We nodded a smiling, "Yes, *sir*!" as the pilot motioned him back, and the engines revved up again. The cargo door slammed, and the next minute we were airborne. "I'll never complain about almost missing a plane again," I yelled over the din of the engines. Gary grinned and gave me a thumbs up.

After a two-day wait in Panama, Gary and I caught a MAC Air Force cargo plane to Florida and arrived on July 7, just as news broke of a nationwide commercial airline strike. We caught one of the last planes going north, a commercial jet to Cleveland, and arrived there just after midnight. The striking airline ground crew had stopped handling baggage, including our duffel bags, and the airlines canceled all US flights for what turned out to be more than a month. We made it back to Ohio but only with our carry-on. Gary rented a car to drive the several hours to Piqua, where he had one more week to relax before reporting to US Army Ranger School and then his tour in Vietnam with Rich and our other classmates.

"You damn well better stop on the way over to see me in California," I told him.

I set out to hitchhike the remaining 300 miles to Alloway. My uniform helped. An 18-wheeler Peterbilt stopped, and I climbed up into the cab. The driver was very friendly, and our conversation drifted between my Army and his trucking adventures. He and his partner, asleep in the berth behind our seat, had been on the road driving trucks together for eight years and loved every minute. At about 3 a.m. we stopped to gas up and change drivers at a crowded truck stop near one of the interstate junctions. After a hot shower for 25 cents, we sat down at the truckers-only counter and ordered. The waitress recognized my two companions by name.

The big rig was soon underway again, heading east on Interstate 90. After the hot meal, I slumped over against the passenger door and fell asleep. I woke up as dawn broke, and at Exit 42 on the New York State Thruway, we pulled over and I scrambled down the shoulder and over the fence, shouting back my thanks. The truckers were taking a chance, making an illegal stop like that on an interstate highway. I started hitching north on Route 14 and soon got a lift the remaining 4 miles to Alloway. Still groggy from the long hitch and the hot hike up the hill to our home, I had completely forgotten about my dad's threat to rent out a room to a state trooper when I barged in the side door and came face to face with a snarling watchdog. Almost immediately, a hulking brute in jeans and cowboy boots appeared through the kitchen door to calm the dog. Cy introduced himself with a big grin and told me that my brother Russ would be back that evening. I crashed. The hours seemed like only minutes when I awoke to Russ shaking me.

"Welcome back! Find any gold? Meet Cy yet? Great guy! Hell, a lot of times he gets in even later than I do. And he's our inside man. With him around we're practically immune from any police raids." Russ grinned. "He's very conscientious about keeping the house neat and grass cut and spends most of the rest of his off-duty daylight hours breaking and riding horses. Next week he's going to drive a stagecoach in one of the parades at Clyde or Palmyra. And he's got a really cool head—you'll see!"

I did see. Sunday morning about 7 o'clock he was just getting home and came up the back stairs, where he ran into a young woman in a nightie just outside the bathroom door. She was as calm as could be. "Oh, I'm sorry—were you next?"

"Nope, it's all yours," Cy said, and ambled back down the hall to his room, not giving it a second thought.

Those few days in the familiar surroundings of our family home, partying with girls and beer but absent the strict puritanical parental supervision we'd always associated with those rooms, reminded me of Plebe Christmas at West Point. I almost felt guilty.

After loading my few belongings in the T-bird, I took the northern route across country, stopping on the way in North Dakota to see Al on the Lindseth family wheat farm. When I finally entered California at Lake Tahoe, state officials at the huge agricultural Donner Pass inspection station did a more thorough check for forbidden fruit and vegetables than the customs officials in Lima had done for handguns and ammo. I followed Highway 50 down from Echo Summit through Forty-niner Gold Country, across the Central Valley, and into a land of contrasts. Past the "Psychedelphia" utopia of San Francisco's Haight-Ashbury district, I steered the T-bird down El Camino Real to ultra-conservative Palo Alto, whose citizens would soon help Ronald Reagan win a large victory in the Republican gubernatorial primary. West Point dropout Dr. Timothy Leary still reigned as the high priest of the drug culture, even though a month earlier, the California Legislature had passed the Grunsky bill that criminalized, for the first time in California, the sale and use of LSD. All that did was raise the street price from $3 to $10 a pop.

Even the Hit Parade reflected the growing rift in American society. Number one on the charts that week was Special Forces Staff Sergeant Barry Sadler's "Ballad of the Green Berets," perhaps the most pro-war ever of all number-one hits, followed closely by the upstart Doors' antiwar "Unknown Soldier." George Harrison meditated with Maharishi Mahesh Yogi, while the Black Panther Party held shootouts with the Oakland Police. The San Francisco Bay Area was a state-within-a-state that most conservative Californians wished would, someday soon, just break off at the San Andreas Fault line and sink into the Humboldt Current to become the Atlantis of the Pacific.

I steered west onto University Avenue and approached the classic Spanish architecture sandstone and red-tiled Stanford Quad through the campus arboretum, acre after acre of towering palms and eucalyptus. By sundown I was ready to stay forever.

A condemned man is traditionally granted his favorite last meal. But our immense good fortune to be assigned (in fact *ordered*, a crucial legal point later) to attend graduate school at Stanford for two years before reporting for Vietnam duty meant that we had some 2,000 last meals, with a paid furlough to boot. Most Saigon-bound soldiers had only several weeks' notice, but I looked forward to an all-expenses-paid, two-year sabbatical in the world epicenter for an emerging counterculture—flower power, free speech, free love—and center of intellectual activity of several great universities. I was determined to continue the optimistic and adventurous spirit of our gold-panning escapade, and California was exactly the place for that.

Jon and I both arrived a month before classes began and dove headfirst into this new world. We joined the throngs in San Francisco, where stoned hordes swayed to the music of Sopwith Camel, Strawberry Alarm Clock, and the 13th Floor Elevators. We saw the Grateful Dead and a young Janis Joplin belting it out at the Avalon Ballroom and discovered the Losers, a favorite dancing hangout in San Jose, whose house band was soon to become Sly and the Family Stone. Would-be rock stars practiced in suburban garages, and $150 rented us a party band with $15,000 worth of speakers and electric guitars.

Jon and I had signed in at the Stanford Reserve Officer Training Corps (ROTC) unit, as our orders directed. Since we were now on duty—no longer on leave—they wanted to get some work out of us for the several weeks remaining before our own classes began at Stanford and sent us off in uniform to counsel prospective ROTC students at nearby Foothill Junior College. The only inquiries we fielded there were from two worried mothers and one student asking about draft deferments. Most of our time at Foothill we spent reading or in the zoology lab helping feed the boa constrictor. One afternoon a campus cop stopped by our booth, a sturdy fellow who looked like a lumberjack in a crisp police uniform.

"Hey," he said, sticking out his hand. "Jim Eberhardt. Welcome to Foothill. Not too popular wearing a uniform on campus these days, so I thought I'd stop by and say hello."

When he learned we were new to California, Jim took us out to eat at an International Smorgasbord, got me a date with his girlfriend's sister, and invited us to his apartment, where he made the first tacos we'd ever eaten. He was a down-to-earth go-getter who'd spent four years as an enlisted man in the Navy and was now working part time as a student on the San Jose police force, selling candlesticks and burglar alarms out of his trunk. It was the beginning of a lifelong friendship.

The Foothill job ended with the start of the fall quarter at Stanford. I met with my academic advisor, Professor Frederick Hillier, and explained that my scholarship ended, and Vietnam began, the day I received my master's degree. Although the Pentagon felt this degree could be accomplished in four academic quarters, if necessary they would allow up to seven academic terms.

"I see," Professor Hillier said, looking at the course catalog. He flipped back and forth through the pages, as I waited in silence.

"Here we go," he said. "As your advisor, I officially recommend that you schedule *required* course OR 251 in your *seventh* quarter. I'll sign the paperwork today. Will that do it?" he said, smiling.

Yes, indeed it did. Now I had a guaranteed two full academic years to explore the wonders of higher mathematics and begin balancing the rational side of the scales. Unlike at West Point, classes at Stanford were not mandatory, weekly homework often contained problems that took days to solve, and the professors were career mathematicians. They were not always as well prepared or energetic as Academy instructors, but some of the theorems they presented carried their own names and were known from Madison to Moscow. Stanford professors dedicated their entire lives to mathematics, not just the two or three years of Academy teaching assignment tours of Regular Army officers.

The beauties of Euclid and scientific applications of mathematics were still fresh in my mind but receded into history as I now witnessed the thrill of new *theoretical* discoveries. For the first time, I began to see how alive mathematics is. Professors wandered the corridors, eyes locked on the ceiling, hands waving to help them visualize complex functions and surfaces. They often forgot students' names and office hours in their quests to push back the frontiers of knowledge. One Tuesday afternoon class, when Professor Hillier wrote one of his new theorems on the blackboard, would remain fixed in my mind forever. A slight, bespectacled, middle-aged man with short graying hair, he looked like a tax lawyer or accountant in his business suit and dark bow tie. But when he stepped to the board and modestly wrote down a new elegant equation-law in queuing theory, one no other human had proved or even dreamt of, the class was dumbstruck.

"Here is the theorem, but I won't write down the proof," he said apologetically, "since it hasn't been published yet."

In our minds he had just won a gold medal in a mathematical Olympics. The legendary feats of some of the other faculty also inspired animated lunch-hour conversations.

"Did you hear how Dantzig got his PhD?" asked one of my fellow graduate students.

I told him I didn't. I was only aware of Dantzig's world fame for discovering the simplex method for solving systems of linear inequalities, a cornerstone of applied mathematics. As one of my Stanford instructors, he struck me as brilliant but completely aloof.

"In graduate school," my friend said, "Dantzig came to class late one day, just as the professor finished writing two problems on the blackboard. Ten days later he showed up at the prof's office hours, looking terrible. Told him he was sorry the homework was late, and handed him a sheaf of coffee-stained notes. Then he said he found this assignment *much* more difficult than the previous week's homework. Guess what? Turns out these were not homework problems. They were two famous unsolved problems in mathematical statistics. When the prof had verified the solutions, he called Dantzig in, told him his PhD thesis was finished, and all he had to do now was complete the seminar requirement, and his doctorate was a done deal."

For the first time in my life I began to dream in mathematics and started going to bed with a pencil and paper at hand to scribble down dream-world insights. Usually the scrawls I found in the morning led nowhere, but several times they contained keys to problems I was working on, including my independent discovery of the powerful and elegant principle called Cantor's diagonal argument. I dove into this new world, taking classes in number theory, abstract algebra, and real analysis even though they were not required for my master's degree. The competition in classes was much keener than it had been at West Point, even in the Honors Sections, and was wonderfully invigorating. My analysis classmate Mike Harrison went on to become full professor at Stanford and to discover the first rigorous mathematical proof of the famous Black-Scholes formula. My love for mathematics took a huge leap in those years at Stanford and gave me a long-term goal that at the time was pure pipe dreaming. I wanted to make mathematical discoveries of my own, if and when I survived the next few years.

After a couple of months living with Jon and Dave in a rental house in East Palo Alto, I slowly came to realize that even though I liked them both and had my own bedroom, somehow I was missing the solitude of that simple rented room back in Madison. Yearning to listen to my own music or study math in dead silence with no interruptions, I was drawn to live on my own again. I found a studio flat in the top of a barn in Mountain View and furnished it with Salvation Army furniture, an electric hot plate, and psychedelic posters.

The Bay Area was teeming with young women from all points of the compass, drawn to the sun and music and new world order. Nurses, hippies, teachers, stewardesses, surfers, and blue-blooded Stanford coeds from the East Coast fluttered like moths around the new Fire. All wanted to motorcycle in the sun, smoke pot, and experiment with sex. AIDS, and even herpes, was unknown, and girls gobbled the Pill like vitamins. After four years of monastic living under constant threat of confinement and walking punishment tours for public displays of affection, I now dated three or four nights a week, on occasion twice the same night, experimenting with a sexual revolution of my own.

I didn't want to waste a single day in my efforts to cram in as much living as possible, and I joined the Stanford rugby team. Unlike West Point rugby, Stanford rugby was a full-fledged varsity sport, with its own locker room, team doctor and trainers, paid airline tickets to away games, and full-time coach, Pete Kmetovic, formerly of the Philadelphia Eagles. Teammates from Australia and New Zealand scrummed with future National Football League starters like Blaine Nye and walk-ons like me. At the Academy I had played prop, or front row, and the interior of the scrum had stifled my talent for rapid ball pursuit and hard tackling. When Kmetovic switched me from prop to wing forward, the new linebacker-like position was a perfect fit. He moved me up to the nationally ranked A-team, which would win the "national championship" Monterey rugby tournament the following year. I delighted once again in the incredible physical highs of a full-on contact sport.

I also added new extracurricular adventures to my list. The streets were full of motorcycles, from Hondas to Harley choppers. The Hells Angels, reeling from the aftereffects of a highly publicized gang rape in Monterey, were trying to win over the public by seeking out and aiding stranded motorists, leaving them with business cards that read, on one side, "You have been assisted by a Member of the Hells Angels, Frisco," and on the other, "When we do right, no one remembers. When we do wrong, no one forgets." For many of us, motorcycles, even standard Hondas and Triumphs, were vivid symbols of the anti-authoritarian freedoms of the Golden State. California law did not require helmets, shoes, safety inspections, training, or even a special motorcycle driver's license.

Jon already knew how to ride a motorcycle and bought a 250cc Honda. I wanted to join in, but not just as a passenger—I wanted to soar through the California landscape on my own. When I saw a used 350cc BSA one-stroke Goldstar advertised in the *Palo Alto Times*, I practiced for ten minutes on Jon's Honda and then went off to look at the BSA. On both sides of its blue mirrored bubble gas tank shone pointed gold enamel starbursts, blazing with the red letters BSA. I could see my face in the chrome fenders and, after a wobbly test drive, fell in love. As we finalized the deal, the owner handed me a large oily wooden box of spare parts and tools.

"That muffler I've got on the Beesa now is damned loud," he said, pointing to the short chrome megaphone on the right side. "Designed to be. I've got a standard one for you here in the box you might want to put on soon. If you see any cops on your way home, shift into high, lower the RPMs, and try to idle on by. When you come back later to pick up your car, you can take this whole box of spare parts with you. Hope you enjoy that bike as much as I have."

I straddled the bike and headed down his street, wobbling and crunching gears. By the time I reached Embarcadero Highway, I had already doubled my lifetime motorcycling experience and had pretty much smoothed out the ride. About 2 miles from home, in the middle lane ahead of me, a California Highway Patrol car signaled for a left turn. Shifting into fourth gear to keep the engine near idle, I coasted past him on his right and glanced at my side rear-view mirror. His blinker abruptly changed directions, the flashing blue light came on, and he closed down on me. I braked onto the gravel shoulder and hit the kill button before he got out of the squad car.

"Turn it back on," he said as he approached me on foot, removing his mirror aviator sunglasses.

I flipped on the ignition and kick-started it as gently as I could.

"Wind it out," he ordered.

I gave the accelerator grip a mild twist. *Brrt, brrt.* It already sounded loud to me.

"No," he said, and shook his head. "I said *wind it out*!"

This time I gave the throttle a good crank with my wrist, and the thunderous belch almost knocked him off his feet. He looked embarrassed to be caught off guard like that and readjusted his hat.

"Look, Officer," I said, reaching into my Levis jacket vest pocket for the bill of sale, dated that day. "You may not believe this, but I just bought this motorcycle this morning. I'm just driving it home for the first time. Also got a standard muffler in the deal." I sketched its size and form in the air with my hands.

"No, no," he said, after a pause. Then his eyes showed a mischievous twinkle.

"I *like* this one," he said. "It's just that you're going to get some trouble with it from other officers. What you need to do is to put in muffler waffles so you can adjust the noise when you have to. I *like* this one."

A New York State trooper would have skinned me alive. Man, did I love California!

Riding that Beesa plunged me into the soul of this new planet. Jaunts through Haight-Ashbury, teeming with hippies, and cruising Central Valley clad only in boots, Levis, and aviator sunglasses. Jon and I bungee-corded sleeping bags on the backs of our two cycles and leapfrogged down coastal Scenic Highway 1 to the Mexican border. Leaning into hairpin turns on moonlit nights, we drove with headlights out, the slaps and shimmering moonbeams from the Pacific waves far below.

A Spanish Montesa Scorpion motorcycle stalled at the curb by my mailbox one day, and there stood a beautiful Amazon hippie popping the kick-start again and again, her dark hair halfway down her back. I offered her a beer, and that was the beginning of a long romantic friendship, motorcycling side by side to Santa Cruz, camping in Big Sur, and going to outdoor rock festivals. Her half-brother was drummer for the Grateful Dead, and to some of her Palo Alto friends I was a motorcycling bohemian, but to others—like the Dead groupies she sometimes hung out with—I was about the Straightest Arrow they had ever met.

One Saturday I rode the BSA along the low, flat marshes of the West Bay, following the rough dirt access roads on the levees. Train tracks cut east-west through the salt-encrusted road at one point, leading to the Dumbarton railroad bridge. The miles-long structure stretched over bay marshland and then rose to span several miles of open water at a height that freighters and sailboats could pass beneath. On many motorcycling outings along this strip of land, I had never seen a train and often wondered if a motorcycle could make it across the old trestles. "What the hell," I thought. "I'm going to be sent to war anyway." Shielding my eyes against the glare, I traced the rusty rails across the Bay where they disappeared into the brown foothills of the coastal range. There was no smoke or sign of movement. I manhandled the BSA between the tracks and started across, bumping over the creosote-timber ties.

Unlike Amtrak trestles, freight-only bridges are not required to have either emergency pedestrian walkways or guardrails. Past the point of no return, where marshland ended and bay began, the jarring shocks of tire against timber numbed my forearms and fingers. I concentrated on maintaining balance, my eyes locked four or five timbers ahead. Between the ties, sunlight reflected off the water far below, lighting my face like a

Fillmore Auditorium strobe light. Constantly squeezing and relaxing the brake lever, my left hand began to cramp, and two-thirds of the way across, I paused to catch my breath and massage the hand. From this vantage point on the downhill slope, I could see the tracks miles ahead. As I stretched my neck to work out the kinks from the bone-jarring vibrations, a single yellow headlight suddenly appeared on the track in the distance, headed toward the bridge. "Oh, shit."

My mind raced. The narrow width of the tracks made turning around impossible, and the BSA weighed far too much for me to lift and spin her. I could either ditch the motorcycle into the bay far below and follow it with a lifesaver's jump off the bridge, or gun it like hell to the dry land, toward the oncoming train. I loved that motorcycle. I rubbed my left hand once more and gunned it. The intensity and frequency of the tie-against-tire shocks increased as the dreaded Cyclops headlight sped to meet me head-on. My teeth rattled and my inner thighs cramped, straining to control the vibrations and keep me in the saddle. I had just reached dry land when the engineer spotted me and the train emitted an ear-shattering warning whistle. Jerking the bike back out from between the rails onto the soft earth, I stood gently patting the mirror-blue tank of the BSA as the huge metal boxcars roared past. Riding home, I opted for the sedate overland route south of the bay. I took several deep breaths and promised myself *no more railroad bridges*. After all, cramming as much into life as possible, with a long-term goal of doing mathematics, does require actually staying alive.

Gary and I had been fortunate to return from our foolhardy gold-panning expedition unscathed, and since then I had been very lucky with my motorcycling escapades and several rugby injuries. Indulging in the new Sexual Revolution also had its risks, of course, but I somehow managed to avoid the usual venereal diseases such as crabs and syphilis. STDs, however, were not the only hazards in the free-love game. One day, one of my close women friends who worked in a local hospital came to see me.

"I'm pregnant," she said, and hesitated a few long seconds for that to sink in. "I don't know how it happened. You know I was on the Pill. My best guess is that medication I was taking for the yeast problem counteracted the oral contraceptive. No way I'm going to have a kid this young—I want to go back to college first. The bad news is the only way for me to get a legal abortion is to have some doctor certify that my mental health is in danger."

Even here, in the state that gave birth to free love, abortion was still a felony. Under threat of certain override of any veto, the new California governor, the staunchly anti-abortion Ronald Reagan, had just signed one of the nation's first laws permitting abortion if the mother's life or mental health were in jeopardy.

"But I don't want that mental health diagnosis on my record," she said. "I would automatically get fired from the hospital and would never be able to get a government job. I've done some research, and one of my friends recommended this clinic in Juarez." She handed me a business card stamped *ABClinic*, with an El Paso telephone number.

"Let me give them a call," I said. "No way I'm letting you go there alone."

I phoned the Texas number, and a strong, friendly man's voice with a heavy Spanish accent answered. I explained the situation.

"*Si, señor*," he said, "We can help you. Arrange a flight here to El Paso, call us to tell us the flight number, and we will pick you up at the airport. The cost is $500, and it must be cash."

I bought tickets for two from San Francisco to El Paso and phoned him back.

"Be very careful at the airport," he said. "Abortions are a felony in the US, and also here in Mexico. We have an arrangement with the Juarez police, but on your side of the border, FBI agents know about the illegal abortion traffic and are actively trying to intercept. *Do not speak to anyone!* A man in a green and yellow sweater, Mike is his name, will meet you at the gate. He will hand you business cards for a law firm in Juarez, and if anyone questions you, tell them you are going to Juarez to consult with divorce attorneys and show them the card. *Por favor*, be very careful!"

We flew to El Paso with the $500 in my shoe. Mike met us at the gate with the fake business cards, took us outside, and motioned us to sit in the backseat of a Ford station wagon with Juarez plates. He got behind the wheel, and in the shotgun seat, a Mexican man in a business suit turned around and introduced himself.

"Sit back and try to look relaxed when we cross the border," he then said. "Don't talk, and if anyone asks, you are coming to my law office. In fact, I am both an attorney *and* a doctor."

At the border, Mike slowed down, but the border guards glanced at him and his companion in the front seat, nodded, and waved us right through without saying a word or asking to see any documents.

"The border guards recognize our car," he explained. "And anyone with these border-town plates can pretty much come and go as he wants."

Across the border, we zigzagged through sunbaked *barrio* back alleys, kicking up clouds of red-yellow dust as the Ford bounced over the dirt potholes.

"We have to make sure no *federales* are following," he said.

"No telling how many felonies we're committing," I thought. "Crossing state and international borders to assist in a felony, in addition to the abortion itself, a felony in both countries. If I went to jail for this, would that keep me out of the war? Would I do my time in Texas or in a Mexican jail?" The men in the front seat knew we were carrying cash and that there was no record of us ever crossing the border. I kept making contingency plans as we drove—jump out of the car and both of us bolt for this *hacienda*, or roll down the window and start yelling for help near that *mercado*.

Just as I was convinced we were being set up, our driver pulled up in front of a modern two-story brick building with a sign reading "Law Offices." In the lobby inside, unseen faces screened us for what seemed an eternity from behind two-way mirrors. Then the inner doors buzzed open, and two young Mexican doctors led us into the clinic waiting room, where they explained the operation and follow-up care on a blackboard.

"Abortions will be legal in North America some day," one explained. "But in the meantime, there is a clear need for medicine to help society. People will get abortions one way or the other, and we provide an opportunity for that to happen in a safe manner."

They then escorted my friend to an operating room, and an assistant stayed behind with me. Nervous as I was, I could only imagine the terror my friend was going through as she exposed her most intimate parts to the scalpels of strangers in a foreign country. That same evening we flew back to the Bay Area in silence, as I held her to comfort her cramps. Would there be any serious complications or long-term effects? We hoped not, but there was no way to know, and we both returned to our separate lives, grateful that we had at least returned home safely. We never spoke of her ordeal again, but she followed her college dream, graduated from law school, and became a public defense attorney. Several years after that, one of the most joyous and welcome postcards I ever received announced the arrival of her healthy new baby boy.

* * *

While I was indulging myself in mathematics, motorcycling, rugby, and free love, news of combat deaths of West Point friends began to trickle in. Gary phoned me from Piqua.

"Rich Hood was KIA," he said, his voice shaking. "I should have been with him, watching his back! My departure date got delayed for medical reasons. You won't believe what happened to me, T. A hitchhiker I picked up over Christmas near Dayton pulled a gun on me. I karate-chopped the gun to the floor, and gave him another chop to his face. Smashed his nose—I could hear the bones crunching. I hit the brakes, we screeched to a halt, and both scrambled for the gun on the floor. He got it first, jumped out, and fired three shots back through the passenger window. Hit me in the stomach, calf, and foot, and then ran into the bushes. I drove myself to the hospital.

"Know what the investigating detective said to me?" Gary went on angrily. "He asked me if I had shot myself to get out of going to Vietnam. Damn. The bones in my foot took forever to heal, and I missed shipping out with Rich. I should have been there."

Then he told me that Tom Hayes, the president of the Academy Honor Committee in 1966 who had rescued me from the Honor Code, was also KIA and had been awarded a posthumous Silver Star. Tom had postponed his Star Man scholarship, afraid the war might be over before he finished his master's degree. Near the end of his tour, he left his rear-echelon support unit to volunteer for a long-range reconnaissance platoon and died in a firefight a month before he was to come home, shot down dragging a wounded soldier to safety. What came back from Vietnam for his family? Two Silver Stars, three Bronze Stars, a fistful of other medals, and an Army casket.

A week later Al phoned to say he would be passing through the Bay Area en route to Vietnam.

"Come a week early," I insisted. "North Dakota farm boys need extra preparation." I was thinking about the news of our classmates' deaths and hoped that someone had given them good send-offs.

Al made the overland trip from Munich, North Dakota, to Palo Alto in record time, thanks both to his overpowered Corvette and to his copies of his orders for Vietnam, which saved him several speeding tickets from sympathetic fellow officers in highway patrol uniforms. When he arrived at my barn apartment, I gave him his choice of dates with beautiful California sophisticates or with less fashionable but more sexually liberated ladies. Naturally, Al chose both. His red convertible whisked him to North Beach nightclubs with the green-eyed blonde cover girl heiress of Saks Fifth Avenue and to more basic rendezvous with free-spirited hippie women in the Fillmore District.

He was headed for command of an infantry platoon in the 173rd Airborne Division, and I put him on the troop transport at Sacramento's Travis Air Force Base so drunk he couldn't walk. I should have insisted he arrive in California even a month earlier than I had. Al was about to stumble into the bloody battle of Hill 875, which killed four more West Point 1966 classmates.

The only requirement the Army made on my Stanford active duty years was for me to earn a master's degree, and since Professor Hillier had arranged to spread this out over seven quarters, that left me forty credit hours of electives to choose for myself. During the academic year, I took courses in pure mathematics like number theory that were not required for my degree, but also classes in public speaking, astronomy, and diving. For the summer term, when no advanced math courses were offered, I decided on an eight-week intensive Russian course, from 8 a.m. to noon five days a week, designed to cover a full college year of beginning Russian. Our instructor had studied at the Defense Language Institute, the famous "spy school" in Monterey, and I had no idea at the time how handy those two months of Russian would come in later.

During the short academic break between the end of Stanford's summer term and the beginning of fall term, I tried to temporarily drown out all the bad news with a return to nature, one that I had always wanted to do. I packed a small rucksack and set out for a solitary hitchhiking trek through eastern Australia. I caught another free MAC flight from Travis (where I too would depart for Vietnam eighteen months later) to Honolulu, another cargo plane from there to Pago Pago, then New Zealand, and from there to the military airfield at Richmond, just northeast of Sydney.

I hitchhiked north to the Gold Coast, a surfing paradise south of Brisbane, where bikini-clad meter maids put pennies *into* expired parking meters. Past fisheries and banana plantations along the coast, then southwest into the outback I thumbed, using up three weeks of "last meals" on meat pies and kangaroo steaks and baked beans on toast. I watched young koalas frolicking in eucalyptus trees and sheepdogs culling out selected animals, guided only by the ranchers' whistles. Bumping along in the backs of pickups or beat-up Holden sedans, I covered about 100 miles a day, watching rural rugby and Australian Rules football matches, downing pints of Foster's, and playing euchre in Outback pubs, all the while managing to put the war out of my mind. After a brief visit to Sydney to take in a professional rugby game with Vince Bruce, I returned to the Richmond base to catch MAC flights back through Hawaii to California.

With only thirty weeks of classes remaining, I should have had trouble concentrating on academics. But with the classic soldier's illogical sense of immortality and my ever-increasing love of mathematics, studying stochastic processes seemed natural. But reality also kicked in, and I decided to add specialized physical training to my daily schedule. I did chin-ups to strengthen my shoulder after a rugby injury and 3-mile runs in the midday heat in heavy combat boots. Gary called from Piqua to tell me when he was arriving in San Francisco, en route to Vietnam. I picked him up at the airport.

"The next time you go to war, you bastard," I said, pausing to enjoy his wince at my intentional profanity, "you damn well better give me more than two days' notice. I told you to come *early*!"

As he and I drove back to Mountain View, I gave him the standard send-off activity choices of drinking and chasing skirts.

"No," he said. "Time is too short. I just want to walk on the beach and in the redwoods."

I asked about his foot, and he told me the tiny bones in his foot had finally, slowly healed.

"But way too late to go over with Rich. I should have been with him, T. The VC murdered him."

"It's war, not murder," I answered.

"They *murdered* Rich. Ambushed his company in the jungle at dawn, caught them half-asleep, opening C-rations for breakfast. Overran them, took Rich and others prisoner. Now that's all fine. It's war. But then they simply executed him, smallbore shot behind the ear. They could have shot him in the foot and put him out of the war, or taken him prisoner. Nope. Too much trouble. They just plain snuffed him out."

Rich, who had survived plebe year, Juice Labs, and Ranger School, had now been deemed an inconvenience by his enemies in the jungle and simply exterminated. Several in his company had survived, feigning death as North Vietnamese Army soldiers shot them repeatedly in the back and severed their fingers with trench knives for small rings of gold. Gary and I took one long last walk in the nearby eucalyptus grove the afternoon before his evening departure, and then I helped him pack.

"What's that?" I asked as he fumbled to conceal a small, shiny metal object.

"A derringer."

"*What?* This is the twentieth century. Why are you taking a damn *derringer* to Vietnam? That's for a riverboat gambler, not a soldier."

"They advised me to bring one. That and a high-powered riflescope. Don't ask any more questions, T. I volunteered for a special assignment, and it's classified." He paused, and smiled. "By the way, T, I graduated number one in my class at Vietnamese Language School. You know how bad I am in languages. If you hadn't tutored me in German, I wouldn't have graduated from West Point. Thought you'd be proud of me."

"I am," I said. "I am. Now I'm getting you drunk whether you like it or not."

At Travis that night, I passed his limp body to the processing sergeant and wept as I drove home. If I had been a seer, I would have kidnapped him and hidden out in the Sierras.

Three months later, my Mountain View mailman delivered a wrinkled letter with no return address, only an APO zip code, and the word "Free" written in longhand where the stamp normally goes. Combat duty offered many perks, including franking privileges. It was a letter from Vietnam, my first and last. I recognized Gary's flowing script, written in blue ballpoint, and realized he had carried the letter in his fatigues pocket for many days. Along with a paramedic and teacher, Gary had gone out as part of a three-man team in the Northern Highlands to aid a village of Montagnard tribesmen. He served as military advisor for the village, supervising defense works and strategies. One night the Viet Cong had broken through their perimeter defenses, kicked open hut door after hut door, and opened up with flamethrowers. Men, women, and children were incinerated, nearly a third of the village. I could make out tear stains on the dirty letter.

"I tracked them down," the letter said, "and did what I had to do. Eliminated them. No other choice—we have to keep the confidence and support of the villagers we're assigned to defend, to show them we're professionals and mean business. I wasn't surprised to find the VC assassins were on drugs, but T . . . they were *women*."

That must have ripped his heart apart. He had been lightly wounded once, he wrote, and then severely wounded by a rocket-propelled grenade. Two Purple Hearts, and he now had earned a free trip home.

In the meantime, I prepared to say goodbye, possibly forever, to my California life and friends. The intense experiences of those two fleeting years after West Point made deep impressions on me and reinforced the lessons I had begun to learn five years earlier in Madison. I knew the joys of living alone in simple surroundings, balancing intellectual highs with physical adventures, and an ever-increasing love of mathematics.

But now it was time for me to put normal civilian life and mathematics dream goals on indefinite hold. I skipped the master's graduation ceremony in Stanford Memorial Chapel, packed up my few belongings, and drove the T-bird to storage. After a long farewell ride along the levees, I shipped the Beesa to live with my brother Russ in St. Louis. Then Jon, Dave, and I drove an auto-transport car across country to Ft. Benning, Georgia. It was back to the Army now, to get ready for war. And it couldn't just be an "easy" transition like boot camp or Beast Barracks. It had to be *Ranger.*

4

PREPARING FOR WAR

It was not my idea to become an Army Ranger. Congress required certain West Point classes, including mine, to attend US Army Ranger School. Not to pass it, or even to *survive* it, just to attend. If I had a second chance to prepare, I'd wear sweats and combat boots on my conditioning runs, without socks or underwear, and I'd carry a heavy iron pipe. Socks and underwear are fine for absorbing perspiration and shock at first, but after several days on patrol, they're a smelly, wet nuisance. Better to have endured ahead of time the discomfort of bare feet against leather boots and the blisters that slowly develop into useful calluses. And better to have gotten used to the awkward weight of the pipe, strengthening the special muscles that can help a man lug a heavy machine gun through the mountains.

At Stanford there had been no sense trying to prepare for the upcoming sleep and food deprivation—I had to concentrate for final exams. During those two years in graduate school, I'd heard many tales about Ranger training. West Point classmates who had finished it told tales of stake-and-water tortures, and rumors of deaths and even suicides. But most of the stories simply focused on obsessions with sleep and food.

Late one cold, rainy California winter night in 1967, I sat in front of a blazing hearthside fire in East Palo Alto talking with Chan, who had just returned from Ranger School. After several hours drinking wine and catching up, we both yawned widely. Then Chan stood up.

"I just can't sleep anymore if I'm warm and dry. I'm going outside." He laughed and winked at me, shaking his head. *You'll see.*

A month later, my Academy rugby teammate Tom Kinane and I were driving up Highway 101 toward San Francisco in his Austin-Healey. Tom was fresh out of Ranger, and we were reminiscing about our rugby days. I was riding shotgun and navigating and asked if he had a map. Tom pointed to the glove compartment. When I opened it, a flood of candy bars and packets of raisins and peanuts sprang out all over my lap and the floor. My friend looked at me sheepishly and apologized.

"Sorry man, forgot about those. Ever since Ranger, I swore I'd never be more than an arm's length away from all the food I could eat. Map's in there too somewhere."

My Stanford physical regimen—rugby, running, motorcycling, and chasing women—had kept me physically trim and hard, but had those two years in paradise turned me soft in other ways? Mathematics had kept me sharp analytically, but I wasn't sure I had the mental toughness to function efficiently under the rigors of Ranger. Chan and Tom had both assured me it was much worse than Beast Barracks. We were about to find out for ourselves.

When Jon, Dave, and I reached Ft. Benning, our first stop was Ranger Joe's, an Army-Navy store in Columbus. There we purchased used combat fatigues, jungle boots, camouflage rain ponchos, and a few other special items that Ranger Joe recommended from his years of experience outfitting Rangers. After cramming down one last steak at the Black Angus Restaurant, we walked through Ft. Benning's main gate. The MP guard spotted the captain's insignia on our Class A uniforms and saluted smartly. Stenciled signs—RANGERS REPORT HERE—led us past wood-frame World War II barracks nestled among tall, thin, black-barked pine trees topped with sparse branches of long, dark-green needles. The barracks and the Ranger Headquarters Building rested on cement blocks 3 feet above the flat, hard-packed Georgia red clay, just high enough to allow ventilation but still discourage rats and scorpions.

Inside, a square-headed man with a massive neck, wearing camouflage jungle fatigues and a black beret, ordered each of us to immediately change into jungle fatigues displaying "no rank or insignia, *sir*" and announced that, as Ranger students, we were "lower than whale shit" and about to be chewed up by "the Bear Named Ranger." As captains we formally outranked him and most of the other instructors, but the Ranger platoon sergeant took one look at me and immediately ordered me to shave off my mustache or else "We will use the Ranger method to remove it," with hints at both fire and boulder abrasion techniques. I shaved.

We linked up with Art, who also had been ordered to Ranger after his two years at Harvard Business School, and the four of us changed into our fatigues in the barracks, storing our civilian and regular Army clothes in individual Army footlockers. We were curious to see who our new fellow trainees were going to be. Although designed by and for the Army, our Ranger Class 69-1 of 244 men was an unusual mix—Green Berets, Marines, Long Range Reconnaissance Patrol specialists, Navy SEALs, an assortment of other military hyper-testosterone types, and the four of us West Pointers. Some of our classmates were underwater demolition experts. Others were anti-terrorism specialists, combat paramedics, and paratroopers. They all had one thing in common—each one was hell-bent on learning commando skills and earning the right to wear the Ranger Tab. Two had just returned from a year in combat in Vietnam and had already volunteered for a second tour. It was as motley and motivated a band of professional soldiers as one could imagine.

Of the 244, all but two had formally volunteered for Ranger training. Art and I were the only holdouts, and even Jon and Dave, like us required by law to attend, had caved in under pressure and "volunteered" at the last minute. Immediately after the first formation, Art and I were summoned to Ranger Headquarters to report to the Ranger first sergeant.

"You two Rangers!" bellowed a voice from behind an olive-drab Army wooden folding desk. The Ranger sergeant's thick-fingered, scarred hands fumbled with our application forms, and his lips moved as he read our statements again. He flung the papers down on his ancient Remington typewriter, and his face broke into a scowl.

"You marked your questionnaire forms incorrectly! You marked that you do not wish to volunteer for this course," he said. "We *will* have an all-volunteer class, do you understand?"

"Yes, we do understand, Ranger Sergeant. But the forms are correct. We wish to report that we do *not* wish to volunteer," I said.

"I'll put you both through the Ranger meat grinder. I know Congress sent you here, but it's up to me to decide who makes the grade. If you try to quit or feign injury, I'll just recycle you for your entire Army career. Now get out of my office."

We had been warned about *recycling*. If a trainee failed to complete one of the three three-week phases, the instructor could recommend that he repeat that phase. Theoretically it could mean repeating, for years, the most torturous training in the US Army. But Art and I stood our ground and silently vowed to grunt and starve and claw our way through whatever was in store. From the antiwar West Coast spirit of flower power to the Spirit of the Bayonet—*which is to kill, Sergeant!*—would be a long haul, and here I was, a marked man once again.

At our first formation, the Ranger sergeant explained the Ranger Buddy system.

"It's very simple," he said. "If two Rangers go into a swamp, then either *both* come out alive or *neither* does." If one Ranger crossed a gorge on a rope bridge, then so did his buddy, if not under his own power, then lashed to the back of the first. Rappelling, slogging through swamps, jury-rigging plastic explosives—either both survived or neither did.

I had the unexpected good fortune to be teamed up with Jon as my Ranger Buddy. Between his athletic prowess and his strikingly calm, clear-headed thinking, I couldn't have asked for a better person to rely on in the upcoming survival training. Jon thrived under stress and, unlike me, had been one of the very few to somehow breeze through Beast Barracks. And unlike my abstract math skills, his master's degree in aeronautical engineering might well come in handy in the following weeks. I promised myself I would not let him down.

In the next formation, I caught a glimpse of another Academy acquaintance, one I had never expected to see again. Mike C., my squad member from the Class of 1968, who had been expelled from West Point three years earlier for alleged Honor Code violations, had now mysteriously appeared in my platoon in Ranger School. He was still built like a rock.

"Hey Mike, good to see you again!" I said. "I figured you were long out of the Army."

"I was. Went back to college, worked in a normal job, but missed soldiering. Decided on a military career, reenlisted, made sergeant, and then won an appointment to Officer Candidate School. Guess what—I was *president* of the OCS Honor Board! I'm a lieutenant now." He promised to tell me more between exercises.

Phase I at Benning began with the objective to train us to "find and kill guerrillas." The instructional technique was to batter us physically and mentally until either we cracked or we emerged as tough, resilient, small-unit, behind-enemy-lines combat leaders, worthy to be counted among the Army's legendary shock troops.

The training staff had scientifically calculated the average Ranger energy expenditure and intentionally gave us 500 calories a day less. For someone like me, at over 6 feet, 2 inches and 190 pounds, with a high metabolism, carrying the standard 65 pounds of gear, and often as not stuck with carrying the machine gun on a patrol, that was a near disaster. Two hours a day were allotted for sleep, as Ranger Sergeant Boyle told us, "whether you Rangers need it or not." A bad compass heading often robbed us of that. On reveille runs in combat boots, we carried our rifles overhead and finished nightmarish obstacle courses in dry heaves. At night we struggled through brambles and up rocky slopes, crossing swamps and icy rivers, and during the day we pummeled each other bloody in pugil stick bayonet drills and hand-to-hand combat training in the Pits.

"Hand-to-gland," we called it. Set into a 30-yard-wide clearing cut in the sparse pine forest, a 3-foot-high ring of sandbags enclosed a fighting arena of sawdust known as the Pits. Here, in the Ranger equivalent of a gladiator ring, we practiced the deadly arts and dirty tricks of unarmed single combat. First, combat veteran Ranger instructors drilled out of us all our boyhood notions of fair play. When an enemy was down or weakened, then *that* was the time to deliver the death blow. The sergeants taught us to aim kicks at the kidneys and groin and temples and throat, throw dirt in faces, and gouge and claw at eyes and balls. Our kicks and karate chops in training were not meant to seriously cripple or maim our fellow trainees, of course, but they were meant to cause pain. Instead of a potentially lethal toe kick to the kidneys, we used the flat instep of our boots to stun and discipline our buddies. But if a Ranger held back to keep from hurting his buddy—upon whom his life might depend in the river crossing that night—then a Ranger sergeant jumped between them.

"No, Rangers, no! That is not a proper kick. Now *I* will demonstrate a proper kick to the kidneys."

Smash! came a kick ten times as painful as it would have been had it been done properly in the first place by the kind-hearted buddy. Each day in the Pits brought a variety of injuries, but as a tribute to the Ranger sergeants' expertise, Class 69-1 suffered only a few broken ribs and noses, and one broken back. The instructors knew just how far to push.

The graduation ceremony for hand-to-gland training was an event called King of the Pits. Two hundred Rangers went into the pit, and at the end only one was left standing—the last gladiator, the King of the Pits. My solid frame and wrestling experience from West Point gave me an edge, and I slowly battled my way to the top, often using a wrestling takedown that the Ranger sergeants had not taught. I reached the finals and found myself squared off against Mike.

Mike was 20 pounds heavier than I was, and all of that must have been muscle. From our cadet years, I recalled his lightning-quick reflexes and his formal training in every conceivable form of fighting. I knew I was up against the perfect fighting machine, and the other Rangers, the fallen gladiators, sat silently on the sandbag ring and watched, too exhausted to cheer or wager.

I realized my only hope against Mike was an instant attack, nothing fancy. Just take him down with my momentum. I charged, and in one of the smoothest countermoves I've ever seen, he fell and rotated with me so fluidly that I was on my back in a split second. It was all over so fast that the Ranger sergeant referee thought we'd both fallen, and he signaled us to square off again. Mike and I looked at each other and shrugged. We both knew he'd beaten me, and this time I knew Mike's technique would be somewhat less subtle. There would be no doubt in the Ranger sergeant's mind this time around. I charged again, and Mike pulverized me with a forearm block and put two of my teeth clean through my lower lip. "Sorry, TP," he said as medics ushered me out of the pits to have four stitches close the hole in my lip. The Ranger doctors were under orders not to "mollycoddle" us, and they didn't even wash off the blood or sawdust. I didn't miss an hour of training—*or* get the cookie or lollipop that I really needed. All I got was a 25-point Good Spot Report, the Ranger equivalent of a silver medal. Mike won the gold and became King of the Pits. The following week, he was also winner of the equally bloody pugil stick event—the only instance I know when the same Ranger won both.

Between hand-to-gland bouts, we practiced other tools of guerrilla warfare, especially patrolling behind enemy lines in all terrain and weather conditions. We learned to navigate with only a compass and map, pacing off a marked 100 meters in forest and foothills, again and again, until we could do it in our sleep. We kept track of distance traveled by tying knots in a cord in our pocket, one for each 100 meters, so every ten knots was 1 kilometer. Some Rangers were uncannily accurate, and we remembered who they were so we could select them for navigators on our exercises. We learned to patrol at night without using lights or probing sticks and to avoid ambushes by tediously bushwhacking cross-country. Ranger sergeants just back from Vietnam taught us how to set patrol-sized and company-sized ambushes, L-shaped and U-shaped ambushes, and convoy and helicopter ambushes. And they taught us how to survive *being* ambushed, beginning with the dreadfully counterintuitive Rule Number One: if caught in the killing zone, *charge* the ambushers. Never mind if that means storming directly into a hail of fire from well-entrenched machine guns, grenade launchers, and Claymore mines. By counterattacking immediately, maybe 10 percent will make it through a well-planned ambush alive, as opposed to 0 percent if we instinctively dove for defensive cover. We learned how to navigate through dense undergrowth and around obstacles, to endure pain and hunger and fatigue. But not all of us learned—a third of our class failed to make it through Phase I and dropped out of Ranger School.

Phase II was at Dahlonega in the North Georgia mountains, home of the US Army Mountaineering School. During the troop transport convoy from Columbus to Dahlonega, I fell into a deep sleep sprawled out on my combat gear in the bed of the open deuce-and-a-half Army truck. The "food discipline" was taking its toll on me. We averaged two hours of sleep a day and one cold meal of combat C-rations. Ranger sergeants carefully controlled and inspected our food allotments and were well aware of tricks like replacing the olive-drab tin of fruit in a standard-issue C-ration package with an extra tin of meat.

But we were permitted to carry as many canteens as we wanted for our halazone-laced swamp water, and during the four-hour rest break we had between phases, I prepared three canteens—one for water, one secretly filled to within an inch of the brim with pure honey and then topped off with water at the last minute before the inspection, and the third with a jury-rigged, hinged false bottom. I cut the base off a standard-issue Army canteen with my bayonet and reattached it with thumbtacks and rubber bands, after fitting the neck from below with an open medicine bottle. I then filled the medicine bottle halfway with water and screwed on the canteen top. I jammed beef jerky and butterscotch candies into the cavity of the canteen, enough so it didn't rattle. When I shook the whole canteen, the water in the medicine bottle gurgled, and opening the cap revealed only brown water. I felt ready for Phase II.

At Dahlonega we mastered the basics of mountaineering and mountain combat patrol techniques—how to rappel, day or night, with little or no equipment but a rope, and how to take wounded comrades, bound in makeshift stretchers, up and down cliffs. We learned free climbing; construction of one-rope, two-rope, three-rope, and four-rope bridges; strategies to cross cold, raging streams; and night navigation in mountainous terrain.

Our single-file columns moved cross-country in order to surprise the enemy, and out in front walked the point man, our distant early-warning system. A human point dog, he led the way through dense undergrowth and across streams, serving as the eyes and ears of the entire patrol. Often only this one man's intuition, or sixth sense for danger, could save the whole patrol from blundering into an ambush or minefield or over a cliff. Just behind the point man, several meters back in heavy fog or thick foliage, but 20 or more meters back in open country, walked the compass man, followed by the patrol leader, his radioman, and the rest of the patrol strung out far behind. After checking his map with a flashlight under his poncho or receiving instructions from base camp via his radioman, the patrol leader whispered directions and distances to the compass man, who used hand signals to keep the point man on the correct heading. Every twenty minutes the patrol leader turned back to the radioman and ordered: "Pass up the count." Then each man in turn relayed this command to the man behind him, if he could see one. If not, he caught up with the next man in front of him, tapped him on the shoulder, and whispered "One." That man reached the next and reported "Two," and so on up the line. If the count was short, as often happened after crossing stream thickets or after firefights, the patrol leader called a halt and sent back scouts.

Patrol leaders were free to select any Ranger they wanted as their point or compass man, and back in the Benning patrols, Jon had quickly emerged as the point man of choice. His silent, quick pace, exceptional night vision, and calmness saved us from ambushes and natural obstacles on practically every patrol. Using stars and an uncanny sense of direction, Jon kept us on course with minimal guidance from the compass man. While other patrols weaved back and forth through the forests, constantly underestimating and then overcorrecting, our patrol traced a crow's-line path to the next checkpoint.

Here in the mountains, patrolling was much more difficult than in the forests near Benning. Now we found ourselves fighting up loose rocky slopes at night, without lights or walking sticks, poked and torn by dead branches, wait-a-minute vines, and thorn bushes. Struggling up and down those steep mountainsides, our machine guns, 30-pound radios, ammo, and full combat packs turned to lead. When starlight breaking through the trees in the slope ahead suggested we were near the summit, we found new energy for the final push up the slope, only to find another small, level plateau and the *real* mountain looming as a dark slope in the distance behind that. Plateau after hidden plateau sapped our strength and resolve.

Moving down the mountains, one small misstep threw us headlong into boulders or fallen tree trunks, or into hollows we then had to crawl back out of. At the bottom were cold streams with impenetrable rhododendrons and lilac bushes, moss-covered stones, and slippery, decaying logs. Each log, each bramble, each unexpected rock overhang added new lacerations on my hands, cheeks, and neck. My boot tops chafed against swollen, raw skin. At one halt I rested next to King of the Pits Mike, who carried the

M60 machine gun but who had been moving slower than usual, slightly favoring one foot. I looked down and saw the leather uppers of the toe of his right boot had been cut away. Through the hole I could see his big toe was swollen and black.

"Broke it two days ago," he said. "If I tell the sergeants, they'll pull me out and send me to the base hospital. I cut the boot open with my bayonet. Long as it doesn't go gangrene, I'm okay—I can handle the pain. Does it smell okay to you?" He sat down on the ground and elevated the foot on a stump until the patrol continued.

The cold of the North Georgia mountains cost even more calories. Had this been a survival course, we could have easily lived off the land by trapping small animals and gathering roots and berries. But the Ranger course emphasized patrolling techniques—we were not in training to become hunters and gatherers. Struggling single-file through the undergrowth, day after night, cursing our swollen feet and chigger-infested waists and bleeding fingertips, I thought of nothing but food. Forget sleep, forget warmth, forget resting tired muscles. For every bug and worm and wild onion I saw, I roughly estimated the foot-pounds of energy it would cost me to stoop over, pick it up, and chew it, and weighed that cost against the number of calories the tidbit would provide. Never mind the taste. *Was the sum positive or negative? Is auto-cannibalism energy efficient? In an emergency, could I save myself from starvation by severing and eating my own arm, or would the energy needed to recover from the injury outweigh that provided by the flesh?* Food. Food. Food.

At dawn halfway through a twenty-four-hour patrol, the Ranger in front of me stumbled across a nest of baby rabbits. One rabbit panicked and bolted head-on into the toe of his combat boot, knocked out cold. Without missing a step, he scooped up the prize and stuffed it into an empty ammo pouch on his waist web belt. All I could think of was how damn lucky that guy was, winning the Rabbit Lotto. I wondered, "Would I even bother to cook the little critter?"

On seeing that rabbit, my thoughts drifted back to one of our lessons on ambushes in Phase I. Our patrol sat on a 4-foot-high, crescent-shaped hummock in a small clearing deep in the woods. The Ranger instructor stood at the center of the natural mini-amphitheater, describing the basics of an L-ambush. In the midst of his lecture, he said he was thirsty, excused himself, and reached down behind a stump to produce a canteen cup and a live rabbit. He drew his bayonet, slit the rabbit's throat, drained the warm blood into the cup, and gulped it down.

"Thanks for your patience, gentlemen," he said as he wiped the blood from his chin with the sleeve of his jungle fatigue jacket. "I needed that. Now to continue . . ."

At the next halt, I asked the Rabbit Lotto winner which Ranger recipe had he decided upon—stewed in an ammo can or simply raw? The fellow looked at me incredulously. He had released it! I could not imagine that.

Rappelling and free climbing, we slowly gained confidence navigating the mountains. It isn't the Alps or the Andes, but the 900-foot sheer rock face of Yonah Mountain provides more than enough vertical cliff to practice combat mountaineering. We struggled to overcome our natural fear of heights.

At the first sign of a Ranger balking while traversing a 60-degree wall, a Ranger sergeant barked out the order "Give me ten, Ranger." The bewildered trainee started to count out the required ten push-ups, rendered almost effortless by the steep uphill slope, when he heard the second command. "Not that way, Ranger. Face *downhill*!" For an agonizing ten minutes, the trembling Ranger slowly rotated, like the hand of a giant human clock, inch by inch, until he faced down the feared slope. With white knuckles and ashen face, he counted out the ten push-ups and then slowly rotated back to the high noon position. By that time he was so grateful to be upright again that the slope had lost its terror. Ranger sergeants had mastered the psychology of fear and knew exactly how far to push a trainee. As far as I know, they have never lost a man on Yonah.

The patrols in the mountains now averaged three or four days each. For three or four days with little or no sleep, I stumbled through briars and into low-hanging dead branches in the dark. Wounds on my shins reopened just above the tops of the jungle boots. Chigger eggs hatched under my belt, and I doused the skin with diesel fuel to suffocate the little buggers and stop the incessant itching. I stopped wearing a fatigue shirt or T-shirt and instead stripped my upper body clothing down to a rubber camouflage parka. The cold rain ran off in sheets, and the parka trapped body heat—as long as I kept moving. When we stopped, I started to shiver.

Our spirits sagged. The food and sleep discipline had transformed us into a band of gaunt, hollow-eyed desperadoes, bent only on surviving the next hour or day. One of our fellow Rangers had already served a tour in Southeast Asia.

"I'd rather spend a month in 'Nam than a week in Ranger!" he told us. "No doubt about it."

Orders for the next patrol included an inspection of our gear, and I was summoned to a waist-high, 6x8-foot wooden stand on the grassy clearing, in front of my fellow Rangers. As they sat and watched, a Ranger Captain who wanted my non-volunteer head ordered me to empty my pack and fatigue pockets on the table. As I stood at parade rest, he patted down my parka and shook out the contents of the ammo pouch, first aid pouch, and field pack. Then he slowly picked his way through, confident at first, as if he had been tipped off about my contraband. All I could think about was the dreaded *recycling*. He even unrolled my socks, where many Rangers hid packets of instant Kool-Aid to mask the bitterness of disinfected swamp water. I had heard that trick from another Ranger, but minutes before the patrol, I removed the Kool-Aid. If other Rangers knew that trick, so did the Ranger instructors. Instead, I relied on my own secret inventions, the canteens.

The Ranger Captain hastily inspected each canteen, and yanked the one with the beef jerky and butterscotches out of its case, hoping to find packets of Kool-Aid or dried soup stashed flat underneath. The two Rangers sitting closest to the stand saw a flash of light from the thumbtack hinge, and both blanched. Neither said a word, and the inspector gave up in disgust. Even my C-rations checked out standard issue.

A half hour later, at sunset, we boarded the open deuce-and-a-half trucks in a cold rain, about to be dropped off at some godforsaken coordinates to begin another three days of agony. Spirits were *low*. Then I quietly opened my canteen and passed each man in my patrol a fat golden butterscotch. Since they had all watched me being searched from head to toe, they couldn't believe their eyes and nodded and smiled in silent gratitude as they sucked the candies slowly to absorb every calorie. My honey-filled canteen, however, I kept secret even from them, and shared its treasure only with Jon. Our own survival, after all, took precedence.

We Rangers took turns as patrol leader, and that was the only thing that counted toward the Ranger Tab. The only test was how well we could lead, motivate, and make battle plans under extreme stress. There were no intermediate grades—each patrol was either a pass or a fail for the leader. Some of the best barracks leaders crumbled quickly. Often it was something intangible that destroyed a man—a whiny voice or hesitation in making a decision or giving an order. Other times the leader showed poor judgment—trying to cross a stream at the wrong point or deviating from the correct compass heading to try an "easy" approach to the objective. And some of the mildest-mannered men blossomed. Unflappable and decisive, they suddenly became creative and self-confident in the midst of confusion.

A few patrol leaders fell victim to circumstance. When resupply helicopters dropped our rations on the wrong ridgeline once, we automatically blamed the patrol leader. The Ranger sergeant, we later learned, had intentionally given the wrong coordinates to the choppers. He radioed in a location close enough so we could see and hear the food drops being made, but just far enough away to be out of reach. That meant yet another Ranger Meal—tightening our belts one notch and announcing, "That was great—I feel full now." But with the missed airdrop, that unfortunate patrol leader lost our confidence and was unable to rebuild morale. The Ranger sergeant checked the box "fail."

Once in a while, though, the Bear of the Mountains smiled on us. On one night patrol, we lost the Ranger sergeant, who fell over an embankment and tore the ligaments in his knee. He had been harassing us all night, moving up and down the patrol line in the dark, calling us "pussies" and "wimps." Then he stepped over the edge of the ravine. We heard him crash below, and his low cries: "Rangers, where are you? Rangers, I'm down here." We stopped dead in our tracks and set out listening posts at the 12, 4, and 8 o'clock positions.

The rest of us fell into a deep sleep in the center, taking turns to relieve the lookouts. The instructor in the gully below hacked a crutch out of a tree branch with his bayonet and limped out to the nearest road to get help and report the coordinates of the lost patrol. We caught three hours of much-needed sleep before he returned with bandaged knee and had the good fortune to trip over one of the sleeping Rangers in the dark. To his credit, he limped his way through the rest of the patrol—but was much quieter.

Two days before the end of our longest exercise, they split our patrol into two night reconnaissance sections, and the instructor went with the other section. The section I led filed into the dark mountains to evaluate the defensive line we were supposed to penetrate the next day. A three-quarter moon lit the sky, and I stood under the cover of some trees at the top of a hill, looking down into the wooded valley and making notes on my map about the enemy's positions. I turned to my assistant patrol leader and explained my strategy for crossing the one bad stretch of open ground.

"What do you think, Skip?" I asked.

"I think," he answered numbly, craning his neck back to look skyward, "I think this is an *apple tree*."

My dazed nostrils suddenly awoke to the sweet smell. As I feasted my eyes on the fruit in the tree and on the ground around us, my thoughts flashed back to a day at Stanford when Al had mentioned finding an apple tree during one of his own Ranger patrols. If the Ranger sergeants caught us taking the apples, they would confiscate the fruit and fail the patrol for breakdown in discipline and "compromising the mission." I decided to put our Ranger training to immediate practical use. As patrol leader, I set up a ring of sentries around the tree and told each of my men to grab three or four of the apples nearest him. One by one, each of us emptied his pack of everything he could possibly jettison, filled his pack and pockets with apples, and then relieved one of the sentries. After we had stuffed our packs and pockets and stomachs, we completed the original reconnaissance mission and linked up with the other patrol, trading our apples for welcome scraps of C-rations. The whole next day was almost pleasant.

When the three weeks of Phase II mountaineering training ended, those of us still left in Ranger Class 69-1 were rewarded with another four-hour break before the final jungle warfare Phase III, in the swamps of the Florida Panhandle. I had heard stories about the ill-tempered big brother of the Bear of the Mountains. The Bear of the Swamp boasted fire ants, coral snakes—deadliest of all North American snakes—and chest-deep muck. Phase III exercises included torturous rubber boat amphibious assaults and a final, infamous 17-mile Death March. But I was two-thirds done, and although famished, exhausted, and covered with festering scratches and chigger bites and welts, I was mentally tougher and more determined than ever.

On our first Phase III patrol, we immediately learned that unlike the mountains, just finding our way was going to be an absolute nightmare. The North Georgia mountains had offered hundreds of clues to an experienced patrol leader with a decent topographic map, but here there were no distinctive silhouettes on the horizon to run back-azimuths, no ridgelines that led to the objective, no streambeds to follow. Difficulty in navigation increased tenfold.

Before setting out on patrols, I doused my grimy fatigues with heavy doses of DEET insect repellent and painted my hands and face with insecticide-laced green and black camouflage sticks. Every single step in the bogs was potentially perilous. *Was this simply another inch-deep puddle of algae-covered black water, or did it mask a waist-deep hole or quicksand? Is that a luminescent fungus on that branch or a coral snake?* In the mountains I had cursed the ventilation holes in the insteps of my jungle boots, when each step in the tiniest streamlet let icy water seep into my boot. Here in the swamps the ventilation holes were godsends, and the Rangers who had opted for standard combat boots soon regretted it. As soon as I stepped into a hole that was much more than a foot deep, swamp water filled my boots. But when I next stepped onto dry land or a log, the water squirted out through brass screens covering holes in the instep. Algae and decaying cypress leaves soaked our fatigues, and at each rest stop we smeared on more repellent and checked our legs and toes for black leeches.

The starvation continued. My fake canteens still helped, but on a six-day patrol, one quart of honey and a pound of pemmican does not go far for two Rangers. I learned it was easy for me to trade a C-ration canned beefsteak tin for two of the unpalatable chopped ham and eggs, or ham and lima beans. To hell with the taste—my food lesson with Gary in Peru had taught me to maximize the protein and calories.

Our C-rations also included a four-pack of cigarettes, which I wrapped in plastic and carefully protected during the first days of a long patrol. Up to my nose in swamp water, I'd keep this cigarette stash dry, even if it meant dragging my rifle or maps in the muck. On the last day or two of the patrol,

I was the only Ranger with an abundance of dry cigarettes, and I easily traded them with the smokers on the patrol for C-ration packets of dried cream, or the tiny sugar packets that came with the coffee substitute. Every morsel helped, and occasionally, even the enemy helped.

A company of seasoned paratroopers—the "aggressors"—played enemy Red Force in our war exercises. It was rumored that some of them had tortured one of our classmates, and we heard of beatings and fist-fights, but my experiences with Red Force were quite the opposite. They knew how starved we were, so some of them intentionally carried candy bars in their pockets in case they were captured and searched. After we had ambushed and "killed" a Red Force patrol, one would whisper, "Hey, Ranger! You forgot to look in my shirt pocket." To mimic real guerrilla warfare, the aggressors sometimes dressed as civilian hunters or fishermen. Rangers in another patrol jumped one and were rolling him in the dirt, going through his pockets when an instructor ran up, shouting, "He's not in the problem, Ranger!" Real hunters and fishermen also sometimes strayed into our war games.

Sent ahead as scouts, Jon and I once found our airdropped C-ration resupply three minutes before the rest of the patrol. We ripped open one unit and choked down as many mouthfuls as we could, quickly burying the empty container under some rocks, and disappeared as we heard the rest of our patrol approach. The instructor screamed in fury when his inspection of the cache showed one unit missing, but he did not discover us. He then distributed the remaining rations equitably, so Jon and I had literally taken the food out of the mouths of the rest of the patrol. Had they been in our shoes, we would have expected exactly the same treatment.

Ranger Mike, by now my hero of Ranger School, showed me a trick to trade food for sleep. During a tactical halt in a patrol to send out scouts or erect a rope bridge across a river, the rest of us could sometimes catch twenty minutes of sleep. Most of us were kept half-awake the whole time by the stinging attacks of fire ants, but Mike seemed surprisingly immune to their harassments. I asked him the secret.

"This is between you and me, TP," he whispered. "I just wait until the two Rangers on both sides of me doze off, and then I sprinkle a little sugar around each one. Then I have no problems with ants."

* * *

We began to think like bank robbers and terrorists. "Using the school solution will buy you a body bag," the instructors told us again and again. "Be creative. Be alert. Expect the unexpected."

Just after dusk, three days into a long patrol, we halted on a patch of high ground in a bog near a small creek. The patrol leader and compass man pored over a map to plan a village reconnaissance. Navigation in the swamps at night required intense concentration. The rest of the patrol was deployed in a hasty perimeter security, and the patrol leader sent me to get water for the patrol. I collected one canteen from each man, which I tied together with my 10-foot Swiss seat mountaineering rope, and slung it over my shoulder as I picked my way through the palmettos and mangroves toward the creek. Just as I submerged the first two canteens in the stagnant water and knelt to cap them, a deafening *CRACK* and blinding flash of light exploded behind me. The concussion knocked me to the ground. On hands and knees, I turned back toward the patrol and began to rise as I heard the cries "Medics! . . . Men down! . . . Casualties! . . . Radioman! . . . Ranger Steel . . ."

I jumped to my feet. "Jon, no, not Jon!" screamed my brain.

Two steps toward the patrol came the sharp command, "Hit the dirt, Rangers!" and I again flung myself to the ground as nearby thunder and lightning crashed to the earth.

"Pass up the count!" shouted the patrol leader. The count came up five short, and as my eyes readjusted to the darkness, I saw dim figures bending over a pile of bodies scattered around a charred pine tree and a smoking PRC-25 radio backpack. The wind shifted slightly, bringing the acrid smell of burning rubber and plastic, smoldering pine bark, and singed hair.

The cry *Ranger Steel* echoed again and again through my head, and after an eternity of waiting, choking back tears I could blame on the smoke, I low-crawled toward the prone figures. There knelt Jon, calmly counting cadence aloud as he administered CPR to one of the victims. Without warning the tropical lightning had struck vertically into the middle of the patrol, shooting down the radioman's antenna and blasting sideways into the four men nearest him. Jon raced to check vital signs and found two men with no pulse. He revived one but lost the assistant patrol leader. He didn't have to check the radioman, who died instantly, scorched from the inside out.

I wiped the smoke and tears from my eyes with the sleeve of my rain parka and at the Ranger sergeant's orders pulled back to the perimeter. Radios crackled nearby in the swamp as another patrol moved toward us. In twenty long minutes, the rhythmic chop of helicopter blades penetrated the silence. As our patrol regrouped, medics carried the two dead and two severely wounded out of the swamp, slung in Army ponchos. I mouthed a silent prayer to the Big Ranger in the Sky, with special thanks for Jon's safety. His heroism and quick thinking had just saved a man's life, but there was no time in the training schedule for awards and back patting—or grieving either, for that matter.

We simply returned to base camp for instructions on the next patrol, a quick review of CPR, an impromptu briefing on the peculiarities of tropical lightning, and a demonstration on the use of body bags. We knew that comrades in Vietnam were finding death every day and chalked up this experience as a preview of real combat. It was almost as if the lightning trauma were a planned part of the Ranger School curriculum. On the next night's patrol, hearing thunder, we all hit the ground again and flung aside rifles and radio. A vertical bolt of lightning again struck two men, but fortunately they survived.

Less than a week now remained before Ranger School graduation. Following my initial run-in with them, the Ranger staff had made me the lowest-ranking squad member, to try to weed out this disgusting non-volunteer. Although I was a captain in real life, in Ranger School I took orders from enlisted men, some as low as Specialist E-3. However, over the long weeks of hand-to-gland and patrolling in the mountains and swamps, those same Ranger sergeants gradually elevated me to platoon leader, second in command among all Ranger trainees. Even for them, getting the job done right took precedence over punishment or retaliation.

After the grand finale 17-mile march two days later, our putrid, raw-beef, swamp-water-softened feet bled and throbbed as I doubled-timed the exhausted remnants of my platoon across the rough tarmac runway of Auxiliary Field Seven for our graduation ceremony. Emaciated as concentration camp survivors, those of us who had also survived the Bear of the Swamps stood at attention as the Ranger sergeants pinned the coveted Ranger Tabs on the left shoulders of our filthy jungle fatigues. Of the 244 highly motivated, superbly fit soldiers who had started Ranger Class 69-1, only 127 received the Tabs.

The two-month training was now over, or so most of the Rangers believed. Back at Benning, the Ranger Instructors threw a huge chicken-and-steak barbecue for us newly graduated Rangers, just to prove that Ranger sergeants were human too. But visiting me during his send-off to Vietnam, Chan had warned of one last torture.

"Be careful," Chan said. "Your stomach will be the size of a walnut after all those weeks of starving. Just eat a few mouthfuls of barbecue and wait a couple of hours."

I tried to warn as many of my fellow Rangers as would listen, but an hour after the feast began, many were bent over at the edge of the woods, retching violently. *Expect the unexpected.* The Ranger sergeants smiled at one another.

While the weeding out and indoctrination period of Beast Barracks at West Point had been rough, I found it mere child's play compared to the agonies of Ranger School, where soldiers who are good spit-and-polish barracks leaders are either broken and discarded, or else are rebuilt into tougher physical and psychological versions of their former selves. Ranger School uses the calculated stresses of food and sleep deprivation, personal humiliation, pain, discomfort, and physical danger to strip soldiers to reveal their innermost potentials and trains the survivors in "kicking in doors" behind enemy lines, in jungles, swamps, or mountains.

I may joke about it a lot, but Ranger training affects me to this day. I still have "food moments" when I unconsciously start devouring everything in sight. Whenever I *think* I'm cold or wet or tired or hungry, I remind myself of those months in Ranger and feel instantly refreshed. There is no place I couldn't sleep, and nothing I would not eat to survive, including human flesh and excrement. Ranger School also taught me a kind of mental toughness that would later help me survive Berkeley's brutal mathematics PhD program.

* * *

The Pentagon wisely decided I should have a few months' experience in a real Army unit before leading troops in Vietnam, so after Ranger School they ordered me to Ft. Devens, Massachusetts, to become commanding officer of Company B of the 18th Combat Engineer Battalion. Most captains had been in the army at least four or five years, but with the high attrition rate in Vietnam, promotion from first lieutenant to captain was now down to a record low of two years. My two years as a lieutenant had been spent not in standard Army units but as a shaggy-haired, motorcycle-riding mathematics graduate student at Stanford. Ranger School had taught me survival, hand-to-hand combat, and patrolling, but nothing about managing a company. To make it worse, I had no instruction in the technical aspects of combat engineering—demolitions, laying and traversing minefields, or disarming booby traps. In an effort to get me to Vietnam as quickly as possible, the Army brass had waived the standard requirement that every company-level officer attend Officer Basic Course, where I would have learned those skills. Instead, they assigned me to Ft. Devens for on-the-job training as a Combat Engineer company commander.

As soon as Ranger School ended, I flew to California to pack a few mathematics books and to pick up an Army field manual on the Class A uniform. I took the Thunderbird out of storage and retraced my route, back up California Highway 50 into Nevada and east to Massachusetts. I rented an unfurnished one-bedroom apartment in Lowell, a short drive from the base, and unpacked my tropical-worsted, medium-weight Army green dress uniform. I had never worn one before, and using the diagrams shown in the manual, I pinned the official brass "US" on the lapel, exactly three quarters of an inch inside and parallel to the seam. My brand-new uniform, with its shiny new insignia and Ranger Tab, advertised the unlikely status of a Ranger captain with no other decorations or overseas service awards. A normal Army captain's uniform would have been faded and frayed from six years of service and bedecked with a small fruit salad of medals.

The next morning I reported to Ft. Devens. The military police sentry at the main gate spotted my captain's bars and snapped to attention as I drove the black convertible across the line from civilian world to military. Past the sentry box, the same wooden, World War II–era barracks as at Ft. Benning came into view, this time set on rocky slopes partly hidden by an early autumn, scarlet-and-green patchwork of oaks and maples. I drove past marching formations of young men in sloppy olive-drab fatigues, past motor pools filled with row after row of identical green deuce-and-a-half trucks and Jeeps, and past the run-down post exchange (PX) and base theater.

My thoughts flashed back to the Stanford campus, with its student cars of every make and hue, its flowering fragrant star jasmine bushes and palm trees, and its green expanses of lawns where Frisbee players, poets, mathematicians, and lovers relaxed in the sun. I longed for California, my friends, my freedom, my mathematics.

Inside the company headquarters building, I met my company first sergeant, a stocky Puerto Rican career soldier, perhaps fifteen years my senior, with several missing front teeth and his uniform almost bursting from his pot belly. After a short introduction, Sergeant Landau suggested a tour of the battalion area and barked an order to the headquarters driver to bring around the commanding officer's Jeep. Two minutes later, he put on his fatigue cap and led me down the front steps to the waiting vehicle. As I stepped to get in the backseat, the first sergeant gave me a strange look and blocked my entry politely with his arm.

"No, sir," he said in a deep voice, laced with a heavy accent. "You should sit up front."

I told him I thought it would be easier for him to give directions to the driver, and since the canvas top of the Jeep was down, I would have no trouble seeing his landmarks.

"No, sir," he said again. "This is your Jeep, and you know the CO always rides up front."

Perhaps he had already read my new uniform. I now vaguely recalled, from some West Point tactics class I had nearly failed two lifetimes before, that the Old Man always rides shotgun. There he has more protection from rain and snipers and is closer to the command radio and driver. From lieutenant to general, from platoon and company to battalion and brigade, the shotgun seat is always the mobile throne of the commanding officer, and that was now me. I nodded and quickly climbed in next to the driver.

It was almost noon when we returned from the first sergeant's Jeep tour, and I told him if he needed me during the lunch hour, I would be at the Company B mess hall. Again he looked at me strangely, and when I walked in the door of the mess hall, the shock on the mess sergeant's face told me it had been a long time since he had seen an officer in the chow line. This soon after Ranger School, I still treated every hot meal as a blessing, and the reconstituted powdered potatoes and meatloaf on stainless steel tasted just fine to me. But Army mess hall food sent most officers scurrying to the officers' club instead, and in Company B, I learned, even the enlisted men chose to buy most of their meals at snack bars. No wonder my company's mess hall was practically empty.

Two weeks later, shuffling through the never-ending mound of paperwork requiring the CO's signature, I came across the mess hall meal count report. The figures looked suspiciously high based on my observations, even though the food had improved slightly since my first visit. I called in Sergeant Landau.

"Sir," he said, "every company inflates those reports. It's the only way we can get decent rations. Our allotment is based on meal count signatures, and we just pad the books. Everybody does it—if we didn't, our mess hall supplies would be cut, and the meals even worse."

"I'm not signing this, Top," I told him. Although I was commanding officer, he was the top sergeant and had earned this respectful nickname. "You find a way to solve it. And I want good meals for the troops."

He again gave me that quizzical look. I now realized that my naive integrity, commendable as it might have been in the halls of the Academy, could now actually harm my own men. The West Point Honor Code had no place in the "real Army." Sergeant Landau did find some creative solution to circumvent another of his new CO's idiosyncrasies, and I never saw the meal count form again.

A dedicated professional soldier, my first sergeant set himself the task of completing my education. A few days later, he knocked and entered my office.

"Sir, Private Foster would like to speak with you. He wants to get married. He needs your permission, you know," he said. And of course he was dead sure I didn't know.

"Right, Top," I answered. "Uh, what do you suggest?"

Hands behind his hips, still stiffly at parade rest, his eyes swept the room, from the Company B Guide-On flag in its corner stand, past President

Johnson's commander-in-chief portrait on the bare wall behind me, and then down to me.

"Well, sir, I've seen this girl before. She's already been engaged twice to guys who had orders for 'Nam. She puts out a week or two, gets a diamond ring and new car on their credit, and dumps them soon as they ship out. And this guy Foster is right off the farm—never seen a city girl before. *And* he has orders for Saigon."

The first sergeant had covered me again. When the soldier came in, I softly denied him permission to marry until he returned from Vietnam. Crestfallen but clearly somewhat relieved as well, he saluted and marched out the door.

One afternoon, as I sat wading through still more paperwork in my office, I happened to glance at the official training schedule. Physical training was scheduled for 1500 hours for the entire company. My watch showed 1510, and I looked out the window, but the company area was completely deserted. I called the first sergeant in.

"Top, what about PT? Where's it held? I'd like to see it."

"Sir, we haven't had any PT in years," he said. "We just pencil it in, another of the required activities."

"Well, I think it's important. Let's get out the troops."

"Sir, we don't have anybody that can lead it. Don't worry about it, sir, nothing will happen. Nobody in the battalion does PT."

"Top, I'll lead it. I can use the exercise. Ring out the men. We start in ten minutes."

I took into account that my post-Ranger physical condition was far above that of most of the men and toned down the exercises to a few basic jumping jacks, squat thrusts, push-ups, and a slow mile at double-time. On the run, more than half the troops fell out to gasp and retch in the grass.

Two days later, a half hour before PT was scheduled again, the first sergeant came to see me.

"Sir, the four platoon sergeants are here. They'd like to talk to you."

Of course I agreed. After I put them at ease, their spokesman, a young man in immaculate sergeant's fatigues, snapped to attention and stepped forward.

"Captain," he said, "it's the job of us noncommissioned officers to keep the men fit. We know you are very busy and just want you to know you can leave PT to us."

I told him I appreciated the offer but needed the exercise myself, and it would be no trouble for me to lead PT again. As they left my office, I could hear the quiet groans as they slowly kneaded the soreness in thighs and calves. The grumbling and moaning continued during the exercise drills, but less each day. After a couple weeks of my PT, the men double-timed past our rival companies' barracks, bellowing out cadence chants and friendly insults. Morale improved dramatically.

In addition to PT, I ordered Top to make sure that first aid and drivers' education took place as scheduled and were not simply penciled in on the training charts. All these skills could save lives, I reminded him, in the Army or out. I gave some of the lectures myself and made unannounced inspections of the others. While I gained confidence in my ability to lead and relied on my own creativity more and more, there was still so much to learn, especially those tricks-of-the-trade solutions that are passed down by word of mouth and do not appear in any Army field manuals or Tactics 101 courses. After one Saturday morning inspection, I asked the first sergeant why the men didn't seem very enthusiastic about their upcoming free afternoon. At West Point, cadets lived for Release from Quarters and Privileges Walking, but these troops seemed completely indifferent.

"I know they don't have money to paint the town red, Top, but don't they look forward to cranking up the jukebox and playing Ping-Pong and poker?" I asked. "Isn't there a battalion recreation room?"

"No, sir," he answered. "We used to have one, with a pretty good stereo and pool table. But officers requisitioned them and took them home."

Exposing corruption under any circumstances is a nasty business, and in hierarchical organizations like the Army, it is usually professional suicide. That night I thought about the West Point Cadet Prayer that we had been forced to memorize in Beast Barracks: *Make us to choose the harder right instead of the easier wrong . . . Endow us with the courage . . . that scorns to compromise with vice and injustice and knows no fear when truth and right are in jeopardy . . .*

At the next weekly battalion commander's meeting, with the four other company commanders and the battalion staff present, I brought up the idea of building a rec room for the troops. The battalion executive officer interrupted me and said that he had looked into it before, but that there was no recreational equipment listed in our TOE, the Table of Organization and Equipment, which itemizes every single item an Army unit is authorized to have, down to the last pencil sharpener.

"I believe there is," I said. "My troops tell me the TOE has a stereo and pool table for the enlisted men but that officers took them home."

The battalion commander scowled at his executive officer, who asked to see me after the meeting adjourned.

"Never, ever make accusations like that unless you have proof," the major snarled at me after the CO left.

"Sir, I believe you will find a stereo and pool table for enlisted men listed in the property book," I answered.

The sacrosanct property book listed every piece of equipment that we actually did have, with dates acquired, location, signatures of receiving party, and serial numbers. I had already done my homework—the book showed that the stereo and pool table had been checked out and signed for by officers who had long since left the battalion.

"The property officer has been here since 0500," Top told me when I came in the next morning. "Some sort of investigation. Scuttlebutt is we'll have a rec room soon. The men want me to thank you, sir. That was a tremendous risk you took for us."

Top knew that speaking out often ruined an officer's chances for career advancement. He had mistakenly assumed that any West Point Ranger Captain was going to be Regular Army for thirty years. Of course he didn't know that this one was secretly planning instead to become a freewheeling mathematician.

Unlike most other officers, I rarely spent off-duty time at the officers' club, preferring instead to explore the New England countryside in my T-bird or to trade Ft. Devens social life for Boston nightlife and the company of a Wellesley senior from West Virginia, whom I'd met at Stanford. Just strolling through campus to meet her made me yearn for the tranquility and the intellectual challenges of university life. The New England countryside and villages surrounding Ft. Devens are a world apart from the military life inside the base, and the Wellesley campus is yet another world away from that. On one side of the invisible campus border are traffic, parking meters, window shoppers, ice cream stores, and advertisements for going-out-of-business sales and Rotary lunches. On the other side, students and professors stroll quietly along winding campus lanes and footpaths, some deep in thought, others in animated conversations about philosophy, evening poetry readings, weekend dates, and politics. Pink and orange notes on the campus's cylindrical outdoor bulletin boards announced reggae concerts, Spanish tutors, drama club tryouts, and "roommate needed." I went to Wellesley as often as I could.

The week before Halloween, I dropped by the bar at the officers' club after work one night to deliver a training message to one of my lieutenants.

"Hey, Cap'n Hill, how about a drink?" said a voice at the bar behind me.

Our battalion operations officer, Bob—a freckle-faced, sandy-haired, slightly pudgy lieutenant—and his tall, dark, athletic sidekick we called "the Geek" because of his peculiar aspirating laugh—sat at the rounded corner of the wooden bar with a pitcher of draft beer and two half-empty mugs. Off-duty Army officers were filling up the half-dozen tables and standing at the bar admiring the battalion award plaques and framed citations displayed on the faded veneer walls.

"We never see you around here," said Lieutenant Geek. "What the hell do you do on Friday nights anyway, sir?"

Most officers spent Friday happy hour at the officers' club. The Army supplied Jack Daniel's, Chivas Regal, Southern Comfort, and practically every other brand of quality liquor at rock-bottom government prices. Perhaps the happy hours fostered camaraderie, but they also spawned widespread alcoholism.

"Thanks, gentlemen," I said, and winked. "But I'm driving down to Wellesley to meet a girl, and somehow, don't ask me why, I prefer her company to sitting here at the bar with you guys."

"Hey, are those Wellesley girls snooty or friendly?" the Geek asked. "Think you could line us up a couple of dates too, sir?" The Boys from Battalion were finally beginning to show some signs of intelligence after all.

"If you guys are serious, I'll give it a try. Cost you change for the phone."

I called her at the dorm and passed on the request, leaving it up to her to decide. It was Friday night, Wellesley was an all-women's college campus, and not surprisingly, she didn't have far to check before she drummed up two more dates.

As we drove Bob's huge old Buick to campus, I heard something rumbling in the trunk.

"What's that noise?" I asked.

"Oh, just some pyrotechnics left over from the last field exercise—a few tear gas grenades and *artillery simulators*—stuff like that," he said with a gleam in his eye. We slapped him on the shoulders and immediately dubbed him the Mad Bomber.

Artillery simulators are about the size and shape of a shaving cream can, designed to imitate incoming artillery rounds in war games. Pull the pin on them, throw them in a pit dug for the purpose, and they first emit a piercing, high-pitched scream. The noise increases at a steadily lower pitch to simulate the Doppler frequency shift effect of an oncoming train, or in this case, an incoming round. Then comes a tremendous explosion, loud enough to be heard inside a tank during field exercises. The overall effect is exactly that of a high-explosive artillery round landing and detonating a few yards away. It adds realism to war games training. "Now those could be amusing," I thought.

We parked in a visitors' lot on campus and walked to the dorm. Cazenove Hall's huge reception hall, in the style of an English men's club, was filled with Oriental rugs and tapestries, oak desks and bookcases, Victorian davenports, coffee tables, and leather chairs. An elderly woman receptionist, dressed in a stiff, faded brown business suit, instantly challenged us when we crossed an invisible line just inside the threshold. I gave her my friend's name, and she relaxed slightly and motioned us to a nearby sofa.

Soon all six of us were stuffed into the Buick, making the rounds, drinking beer in a campus bar, dancing, and cruising. It was a run-of-the-mill typical college triple date. Then I casually worked the phrase "artillery simulator" into the conversation. The girls were curious and beer-brave enough to see one detonated. We hauled the simulators out of the trunk and drove around town, pulling the pins and dropping one here beneath an overpass, and there by a factory wall. Speeding away just far enough to enjoy the explosive sound-and-light show, we then picked out the next target. Porch lights went on, and cars screeched to a halt, but no one was hurt, and the girls told us it was bringing a spark of life to the sleepy college town. We almost missed their 1 a.m. curfew, and the frowning dorm mother quickly gathered her flock with a sweep of her shawl, turned out the porch light, and bolted the door. Just after kissing goodbye, my friend had reminded me that Halloween was approaching, and then she threw down the gauntlet.

"We already have a jack o'lantern," she teased, "but it's up in the window of the fifth floor where you can't get it."

Back at the car I repeated her dare to the Mad Bomber and the Geek.

"No way," the Mad Bomber said, shaking his head. "Did you see that place? The fire escape starts on the second floor, and the main entrance has security guards round the clock."

"I'm going for it," I said, by now full of courage from a few beers and the untapped energy from the boring life on base. "All I need is a boost up to the fire escape. You guys stand lookout below. C'mon."

They reminded me of the serious trouble we would be in if caught. But the crisp autumn air stirred fond memories of boyhood Halloween pranks, and now here I was, twenty-four years old and expecting orders for Vietnam any week. *Of course I was going for it!* The Mad Bomber and the Geek finally agreed to act as lookouts while I scaled the wall. Standing on their shoulders as they leaned against the brick building, I reached the lower rungs of the fire escape and pulled myself up. Rounding the corner up to the fourth floor, I heard the leaves rustle below me and looked down to see the shadows of my two lookouts disappear. A police car was rounding the corner of the dorm, heading directly toward my part of the wall. *Uh-oh.*

My mind raced. The fire escape above me ended below the roof, so my only chance was to break into the dorm or try to beat the squad car to the base of the building. I raced down the metal stairs as fast as I could, spinning around corners and clanging down the metal stairs to the bottom step, 10 feet above the asphalt. The squad car jerked to a halt a few feet from the brick wall, its high beams illuminating the whole side of the building. I was trapped—a brick wall behind and above me and a police car in front of me.

I hung from the bottom rung of the fire escape and dropped to the ground between the squad car and the brick wall. The two patrolmen in the front seat flung open their doors, drawing their service revolvers. I landed on all fours and instinctively broke into a dead sprint for the corner of the building, ten long strides to my right, picturing the Road Runner's windmilling legs hitting the canyon floor. This impossible escape attempt caught the cops by surprise and gave me a split-second advantage. I was at full tilt halfway to the edge of the dorm when I heard the command "Halt or I'll shoot!"

If I'd had more time to think about it, I would have halted. Just as I reached the corner of the building, two shots rang out. The sound of the bullets crashing into the branches around me triggered another surge of adrenaline. I rounded the corner and dashed for the small grove of trees next to the dorm. The cops chased me in hot pursuit. Having shot at me, they now desperately needed to make a collar.

Ranger training kicked in, and I charged headlong into the underbrush, ignoring the pain of the brambles and invisible branches snagging me in the dark. I struggled through the thicket at breakneck speed and then suddenly dropped to the ground and froze, listening for thrashing in the pitch-dark bushes. There was silence, followed by distant voices and slamming car doors. Hadn't I told my men PT could save lives? My pursuers, burdened with drawn revolvers, dangling nightsticks and handcuffs, and long police flashlights, could not match my pace, even had they been in top form.

Crawling on my belly, I could now see flashing blue lights crisscrossing the dark campus roads around me, a dragnet of squad cars from the Wellesley Campus Police, the Wellesley City Police, and the Massachusetts Highway Patrol. All I had to do was evade their noose and somehow cover 30 miles in five hours to make reveille at Devens. I finally made it out to Massachusetts Route 135. Crawling in a gully across from the visitors' parking lot, I heard voices and peeked up to see the Mad Bomber and the Geek casually pacing up and down the sidewalk near Bob's car as if nothing had happened. I whistled a poor imitation of a bird call.

"Get down! In the ditch!" I whispered loudly.

"Hey, Ted, c'mon up here. They've got nothing on us. Let's just get the hell out of here."

"Didn't you guys hear the shots? There are cops swarming all over campus. And besides, look at me." I was scratched, bleeding, muddy, and covered with bits of leaves and twigs.

"Don't be a pussy, man. They don't know jack shit. We'll just say you're drunk, fell into the culvert, and we're taking you home. Haven't seen a thing."

Like an idiot I gave in and acted drunk, and they propped me up under both arms and walked me toward the car. But the cops were on us in minutes, manhandled us into the back of a squad car without a word, and sped us to the Wellesley city jail, where they locked us up in separate cells, out of earshot from one another, and interrogated us one after the other.

"We've been getting bomb and explosion reports all night," the officer on duty said. "Do you know anything about that?"

"We heard some explosions in town earlier too," I said, careful not to lie. They apparently had no evidence linking us to the explosions. It appeared that the younger cops felt that stuffy Wellesley College could use a little excitement, but the older cop would now have to file a formal written report on his use of deadly force for firing the two shots at me. He wanted to throw the book at us.

"Look, if you're not going to formally arrest us, I'd sure appreciate getting back to Ft. Devens before reveille," I said.

"You guys are Army *officers*?" they said, looking at my ID again in disbelief.

"Yes," I said. "I'm a captain stationed at Devens, and my two buddies are lieutenants. I talked them into this stunt. It was my idea, and I'm the senior officer. I want to take full blame." My adrenaline-charged brain strove to find some way to minimize the damage.

"No can do," said the lead investigator. "You're all in it together. This is some serious shit, gentlemen!"

They knew that if we didn't make reveille the next morning, the Army would investigate and then court martial us for "Conduct unbecoming an officer" and AWOL, for starters. The deputy locked us back up while they made the decision.

I paced back and forth in my cell, kicking myself for using such poor judgment. While this glorified panty raid, or whatever I wanted to call it, could easily cost me my freedom and give me a permanent police record, that was a risk I accepted. But involving two casual friends now weighed heavily on my mind. I had not thought about the consequences to their careers and lives, and I felt guilty. From now on, I promised myself, I would not involve others in my own hazardous undertakings. I paced and brooded as the lesson slowly sank in, and it seemed like hours before the guard unlocked the door and led me to the police commander.

"Okay," he said. "We'd like to charge you with trespassing and throw you in jail for a few days, but we know what the Army will do if we do that. If we had any evidence connecting you to the bomb reports, we'd nail you good. Here's the deal. You're not under arrest, but we're entering this incident in the official police log. We're releasing you tonight, under one condition. You are hereby *banned from Wellesley College for life*."

Finally they returned our wallets and released us just before dawn, with barely enough time to make reveille. My first permanent relationship with a university was not exactly what I had hoped for.

* * *

A few short weeks later, on a cold Monday morning in mid-November, Sergeant Landau knocked softly on my office door. His eyes avoided mine and focused instead on the papers in his hand.

"Your orders came in, sir," he said. He handed me the documents and quietly closed the door as he left, a sad look on his face.

My head spun as I stared at the official letter—orders for Vietnam with a reporting date not later than 24 January 1969. Long expected, but a shock just the same. Should I have quit West Point long ago and forgone graduate school at Stanford in the hopes the war would end? Should I now consider desertion and exile in Canada or Sweden? I telephoned Jon in North Carolina, where he was undergoing his own eleventh-hour crash course in the "real Army."

"I got my orders too, T," he said. "Reporting date January 12. Thought about splitting." Then came a long pause. "Well, we talked it over, and

Laurie and I decided I should just go to 'Nam and get it over with." Another long pause. "And we're going to get married before I leave. Christmas Eve, T. West Point chapel. Can you make it?"

I promised him I'd be there and called my parents in Alloway to let them know there was good news and bad news. For once I would be home for a few days for Christmas and my birthday, I told them. The bad news was that on this trip, I would be en route to Vietnam.

After turning over Bravo Company at Ft. Devens to the next commanding officer, I drove the 300 miles to Alloway in a blizzard. Within five minutes of getting home, I buckled on knee-high pack boots and parka and walked out the back door with my old single-shot .22 rifle. Three inches of new snow obscured the trail and hidden pitfalls, but I still knew the woods and riverbank by heart and soon left all signs of civilization behind in the long winter shadows. The worn wooden stock of the .22 felt warm and familiar in my hands.

My thoughts raced forward to Vietnam. I tried to picture tropical vegetation in place of the snow-laden bare branches in front of me. In place of this puny .22 in my hand, I imagined a man-killing M16 assault rifle, with tumbling trajectory specially designed to circumvent the Geneva Convention's ban on soft-nosed bullets, which tear huge hunks out of human flesh. A tumbling, hard-nosed bullet does the same thing. In my mental picture, I would be the hunted as well as the hunter, and the ghostly faces of fallen West Point classmates flashed through my mind. "How absolutely beautiful these woods and hills and river are," I thought, "and how incredibly silent just before dark." A light snow drifted down through the mute winter air. I wondered if Vietnam would be this lovely.

When I returned, my father called me into the den for another private chat.

"There's something I want to discuss with you," he said. "You're twenty-five now and should start a savings program. You're not married yet, but some day you will be, so I bought you a life insurance policy. I'm the beneficiary, and I'll pay the premiums this year. When you get back you can start paying them yourself and change the beneficiary if you want."

I thanked him and suppressed a smile. My friends found it cold-hearted, but I admired his purely pragmatic point of view. He certainly didn't want to lose his oldest son, but if he did, why not ease the pain a little? It's called "hedging a bet" in gambling lingo. And maybe he realized that that insurance policy might just make me all the more determined to come back alive.

5

VIETNAM

After flying half-fare military standby on a commercial flight to San Francisco, I changed into civilian clothes in the terminal restroom and picked up a Hertz car. The next four days I drove around the Bay Area, visiting friends in both pro- and antiwar camps, smoking Maui Wowie one night around a lava lamp in Santa Cruz with *Sgt. Pepper's Lonely Hearts Club Band* in the background, and drinking beer with returning West Point classmates the next night in the Moffett Field officers' club. Some of my anti-establishment friends had burned their draft cards and withheld the 50 percent of their income tax going to the war effort. Other friends had volunteered for first and then second tours in Vietnam. I had agreed to serve in the Army in exchange for those six years of college at West Point and Stanford, so after weighing all the options again, it did not seem right for me to avoid the war. "Buy the ticket, take the ride," as Hunter S. Thompson said.

Coincidentally, the annual National Canners Convention was in San Francisco that week, and my father and mother were staying at the Fairmont Hotel. I drove to San Francisco to meet them, and the whole city below was bathed in golden sunshine, all the way to the Pacific. I met my parents in the lobby, and we walked outside to say our last goodbyes. My father, in his standard dark business suit and tie, stood tight against my mother, his hand holding hers in a white-knuckled clutch. They both looked tired and slightly stooped over, and my mother's eyes darted left and right. As my father shook my hand—we never hugged—a brisk breeze kicked up paper scraps and leaves in the gutter. My father's eyes watered.

"Dad, do you have something in your eye?" I asked.

He stood silently, and my mother answered quietly. "He's watching his son go off to war. He's been there himself."

How stupid I felt. I had never seen him cry before and had forgotten that at almost exactly my age he had left California for the Pacific War. I waved goodbye and left to return the rental car and catch a shuttle to Travis.

Given the decision to go, I had developed a simple strategy for the year: keep a low profile and concentrate on defensive actions. I could only hope to be half as brave as the unarmed battlefield medics and front-line ambulance helicopter pilots I later came to know personally and pray there would be no orders from war-crazed commanders to "kill gooks" or "massacre villages."

I went to war with a positive attitude, even optimistically packing a paperback copy of Konrad Knopp's famous *Theory of Functions* and a text on number theory from the class at Stanford. The tour in Vietnam, I told myself, would be an involuntary adventure, like being sentenced to spend a year in a police squad car or hospital emergency room in an inner city combat zone. I would see bloodshed and insanity, life-and-death decisions both good and bad. The junkets at West Point and Stanford were over. Now was payback time.

At Travis I joined the other faceless jungle fatigues boarding the transport plane. Heads shaved, we labored under the weight of our duffel bags, and the soles of our jungle boots clanged up the aluminum stairs. Sober or completely drunk, as I had delivered Gary and Al, every man boarded in complete silence. They all looked so young—probably I did too.

The government-chartered Flying Tiger flight that took us to Vietnam felt like a flying funeral parlor. Every seat in the Lockheed Constellation was filled. Three hundred young men, all wearing green camouflage combat fatigues and skinhead haircuts, sat quiet and somber all the way from Travis to Tan Son Nhut Air Base, with refueling stops in Anchorage and at Tokyo's Yokota Air Base. The flight was long, nearly twenty-four hours, and gave me plenty of time to think.

The math books stayed stowed in the overhead compartment the whole trip. As it turned out, I might just as well have left them at home. I had the time to read them that year, just as I did on this long flight, but I just didn't have the proper frame of mind. As the plane droned on through the night, I thought of my West Point classmates who had taken this trip before me, several of whom had already returned wounded or in government-issue gray metal caskets. I wondered how many on this plane would make it back alive.

We disembarked at Bien Hoa in the dead of night, and briefing officers directed us to wood-frame billets. "If you hear sirens, we're under attack. Just get down and stay down. Don't move. You won't even have weapons yet. The gunships and combat units will take care of everything. Stay calm."

The hot, damp air reeked with diesel fumes, the stench of decaying tropical vegetation, and whiffs of Army chow and high-explosive powder burns. We stumbled into the wooden barracks and dropped onto the bunks, bewildered and jet-lagged and terrified. Sirens pierced the night twice. Peering out the corner of the window, I could see distant flashes of light followed by dull explosions. Howitzers returned salvos, while helicopters darted back and forth overhead. Without a clue about what was happening, I felt weak and vulnerable, especially with no weapon, not even a bayonet.

After several days in the 90th Replacement Unit, I slowly grew accustomed to the heat and humidity and humdrum. Helicopters were darting left and right, cargo and transport planes were landing and taking off every few minutes from the airstrip, and lines of olive-drab trucks took GIs to their new units. MPs led the convoys in Jeeps and 3/4-ton trucks armed with .50-caliber machine guns on tripods. At every stop, security guards probed under the vehicles with shaving mirrors attached to telescoping handles, checking for severed brake lines and improvised car bombs.

One by one, the duty sergeant called our names and assignments. Officers in Vietnam were typically sent to a combat unit for six months and a support unit for six months. As a Ranger West Point Combat Engineer Captain, I could expect almost anything. Finally my in-country orders arrived: Captain Hill, T. P., OF107742. 25th Infantry Division, Cu Chi.

The 25th Tropic Lightning Division protected Saigon's northern flank at Cu Chi in III Corps. Dubbed the Iron Triangle by AP correspondent Peter Arnett for its fiercely nationalistic population, Cu Chi District would remain "unpacified" during the entire war against the Americans, just as it had against the French. (After the war, Hanoi formally awarded it the official title Iron Land of Cu Chi.)

Iron Triangle could just as well have referred to the district's rusty red-brown soil. Predominantly laterite, an iron and aluminum compound in clay binder, it reminded me of reddish pumice. Laterite was made to order for tunnels. When the 173rd Airborne had established Cu Chi base camp in 1966—on the site of an abandoned peanut plantation—they unwittingly plopped it down dead center over an old tunnel complex. The Viet Minh had burrowed underground in the 1940s to fight the French, and now, in 1969, it was known that there were "problems" in that region with Viet Cong tunnels, but no one had an inkling about the magnitude and complexity of the tunnels.

It wasn't until much later that the US Army realized that individual houses and villages were linked by 200 *kilometers* (125 miles) of subterranean passageways. There were not only escape tunnels and supply routes, but also sleeping areas, command posts, weapons caches, and hospitals complete with operating rooms. There were printing shops, flag-making workshops with sewing machines, and even stables for water buffalo—all underground and invisible.

My specific assignment in the 25th was to the 65th Combat Engineer Battalion, sister to the 18th I had served with at Ft. Devens. The 65th's motto, "First In—Last Out," boasted that combat engineers often cleared the path ahead of the infantry, sweeping minefields, destroying obstacles with plastic explosives, or erecting rope bridges across ravines. And they were last out—laying defensive minefields, blowing up bridges, and erecting obstacles. My battalion commander, Lieutenant Colonel Gibson, called me in to discuss my assignment. Of medium height with ruddy full cheeks and stocky frame, he glanced up from my personnel folder and rose to shake my hand.

"Well, Captain Hill, you look like a leader to me. Top twenty in your class in West Point, Stanford graduate degree, Ranger. I think I'll start you off with S-1 or S-3, and after you get your feet on the ground, will let you take over Charlie Company."

From Ranger School, I knew S-1 meant personnel and S-3 meant operations officer, officially "counterinsurgency." To be commanding officer of a combat unit in war is every career officer's dream and virtually a requirement for reaching the rank of general. But I saw it differently. I thanked him for the opportunity and his confidence in me but reminded him that I had spent nearly all my time in the Army as a civilian in graduate school and had not even attended Officers' Basic Course. I told him that I didn't feel I had the right to learn combat engineering at the expense of men's lives.

"And if possible, sir," I added, "I prefer to take part only in *defensive action*."

His shoulders jerked slightly as he put his palms on his desk, and furrows ran across his forehead. I hoped he wouldn't press me for my views on the war. I was sticking my neck out. Other commanders would have run me out on a rail or had me court-martialed. After staring at my folder in silence for a few minutes, he dismissed me, promising to give the matter more thought.

Much to his credit, Colonel Gibson granted my request but immediately saw to it that I got more than my share of *dangerous*—albeit defensive—missions. He appointed me as the .50-caliber machine gunner standing in the back of his command Jeep, an unheard-of, sitting-duck assignment for a captain. I preceded him through fields where booby traps had just wounded several of our men, and he often selected me as his "bodyguard" on his command and control helicopter, an open Huey with machine gun tripods affixed outside the bay doors. Like many combat leaders, Gibson always wanted to be where the action was, the scene of an ambush or active minefield, and neither the chopper pilot nor I had a vote.

On one of these chopper missions, we landed where one of our battalion teams had just discovered a manned Viet Cong tunnel complex. Bulldozers from our Delta Company at Tay Ninh were digging them out, ready to return fire. The VC refused to surrender, and one dozer unearthed an armed sniper several yards from our chopper's landing site. Seconds later there was a loud crack when a frustrated Army of the Republic of Vietnam (ARVN) scout, attached to us from South Vietnam's ARVN, shot him in the forehead at point-blank range. I was so close that a pencil-lead-sized piece of brain, gray with tiny red capillaries, spattered onto my rifle barrel. I left that dried speckle on my rifle, staring numbly at it several times a day. Although I never said a word about it, I knew my sergeant sensed my distress.

One morning the battalion executive officer, Major Frink, called me into his office.

"Captain Hill, you've been in-country almost two weeks, and I think it's time you had some reconnaissance experience. The assistant division commander, General B., wants us to build him a tennis court—in our battalion area, of course, so his staff won't see him playing all the time. Well, there's an old French tennis court here," he said, pointing to a spot on a 1:25,000 topo map of Tay Ninh Province, "and from the air it appears to be holding up pretty good. What we want you to do is make a recon, to see how it was built, especially the surface and substructure and drainage. A chopper will pick you up this afternoon at our LZ at 1400 hours, drop you off there, and pick you up an hour later. Any questions?"

I didn't have any—too dazed, I imagine—and hurried off to pack a small notebook, find a map case, and load my CAR-15, a sawed-off shotgun version of the M16, with a very short barrel and collapsible steel stock. I talked to one of the more experienced sergeants in S-3, who told me what soil conditions to expect and what construction features to look for. He told me to concentrate on the foundation and shook his head at my assignment. Cu Chi had too many serious problems with tunnels and sappers and mortar attacks to be wasting resources on a mission like this.

At exactly 1400, the Huey dropped in to pick me up at our landing zone. The pilot had not been informed of my mission and rolled his eyes when I told him. His charts showed recent enemy activity in that region, and he would be in and out of there as quickly as he could. As we approached the long-neglected tennis court from the air, I saw no sign of old French barracks or fortifications, just a solitary tennis court surrounded by a few palm trees in the midst of flat fields. Surrounding the two red clay courts, an old cyclone fence supported towering vines with yellow flowers. We planned my drop-off and agreed on a different pickup point to lessen the chance of ambush. He flashed me a thumbs-up for good luck and hovered 6 inches above the ground, to avoid setting off land mines. I bolted out the door and away from the whirling blades, clutching my carbine and notepad in one hand and clamping my steel helmet to my head with the other.

I low-crawled to the tennis court, probing the substrata with my bayonet and making notes, but mostly scared as hell. Straining to detect any sign of movement or booby traps, I kept my finger close to the trigger of the CAR-15. *Would it be considered a combat death on this mission if I bought the farm, or in this case, bought the tennis court?* It seemed like hours before I heard the welcome *wacka-wacka-wacka* of the approaching Huey.

Right on schedule, the chopper hovered at our designated rendezvous point, and I dashed for it, glad to still be alive. The pilot, also relieved to be finished with this insane mission, sped me back to the safety of Cu Chi, where I described the construction to our executive officer. I told him the foundation was apparently the key to its durability, and a laterite-based substratum provided support and drainage for the clay court surface.

Soon General B. was working on his tan and backhand on a new tennis court near our battalion mess hall. We heard that personnel sergeants in Bien Hoa had screened records of incoming enlisted men to turn up a tennis pro and found one. They assigned PFC Woods to our battalion as chaplain's assistant, and soon he was passing out hymnbooks at Protestant services and playing tennis with General B. on a tennis court partly designed by me.

Just after midnight on February 26, our base camp came under heavy mortar and rocket attack. Whining whistles preceded sharp, deafening *CRACKS* and flashes of bright light from incoming rounds. Then came a series of dull *WHUMPS* and flashes from *inside* our fortifications. These were not mortar rounds any more, but satchel charges tossed into bunkers by enemy commandos. The cry went out: "*VC are inside the wire!*" Men peering out from the gun ports of interior bunkers had no idea which direction to shoot. There were more blasts, followed by screams and shouts for "Medic!" Parachute flares illuminated the camp in white-yellow light from above, like the dancing arcs of giant welders. As the parachutes drifted jerkily to the ground, shadows flickered around every sandbag, Jeep, and tent. Our perimeter bunkers sprayed the tree line with machine gun bullets, and rocket-propelled grenades roared out into the night. But the dangerous VC darted from bunker to sandbagged barracks inside the perimeter, leaving chains of explosions in their wake.

Suddenly it was over as quickly as it had begun. Dac Cong sappers, the enemy special commando forces, had emerged from hidden tunnels, some even within our perimeter. Synchronized with the mortar and rocket attacks from outside the camp, they ran amok inside the wire, demolishing troop bunkers with plastic explosives and blowing to smithereens all fourteen of our big troop-carrying CH-47 Chinook helicopters with thermite grenades. Thirty-eight Americans died in the melee, and, in the confusion, all but thirteen of the attackers miraculously escaped, running out through the gaps in the concertina as our perimeter guards held fire, unable to distinguish counterattacking friend from fleeing foe. It was pure luck that I had been in one of the bunkers missed by the enemy's mortar fire and hand-delivered plastic explosives.

Major General Williamson, the Tropic Lightning commander, had always scorned the suggestion of a tunnel problem. He immediately placed the smoldering remains of the Chinooks off limits and ordered the evidence buried by bulldozers. Curious about how a single heat grenade could destroy a whole helicopter, I borrowed a Jeep and, pulling rank as a captain, drove past the MP guards before the dozers arrived. The lightweight magnesium alloy of the Chinooks had consumed itself in the heat of the thermite explosion. Each helicopter, dreaded by the VC for its fierce firepower and surprise attacks, had now been melted into a tub-sized puddle of still-warm silvery metal, congealed like gigantic drops of mercury on the red dirt. Black propeller blades rested flat, like crosses over a corpse. I walked around the remains and could still feel the heat of the metal from several yards away and smell the acidic burn of powder. Our casualties had already been taken to field hospitals or to the battlefield morgue.

So now I was at war. In the air, flying over the battlefield, one could think about fighting in the abstract, questioning its morality, and how it fit with his notions of right and wrong. But here on the ground, war was personal and confusing. I was in a strange land where people wanted to kill me, just because of the shape of my eyes or the color of my clothes. To them I represented a foreign power that had invaded their country to interfere in their own civil war. I didn't hate these people. In fact I'd never met one and meant them no harm, but if I took a stroll in the countryside here, I might get killed just because of the way I looked. The survival instinct kicks in quickly, however, and I reacted. The highbrow political debates of the war in the press and in Berkeley cafés were suddenly and effectively replaced by the low-level concreteness of coping and surviving.

On my first Jeep trip from Cu Chi to Saigon, two sergeants and I, armed to the teeth, were motoring down Route One when I noticed a tall stand of trees about 50 yards from the road. Their rows of smooth black trunks receded to vanishing points, like columns in a Greek temple, and the thick green canopy far above cast the bare forest floor in dark shadow. From each trunk hung a small wooden bucket beneath a bamboo spout.

"What's that?" I asked, pointing to the trees.

"Rubber plantation. They used to be all over here. Part of the Fil Hol Plantation. See the buckets?"

I nodded. I had never seen raw latex before, and Indian Country or not, I was determined to get a firsthand look.

"Stop the Jeep," I ordered.

The two enlisted men mumbled curses as I grabbed my M16 and hopped out of the Jeep.

"Keep an eye out, and cover me if there's any fire from the tree line," I ordered.

Stooping over to keep a low profile, I darted across the open land toward the rubber trees, conscious of the usual dangers of war but driven by this curiosity attack to smell and feel raw rubber, the same liquid latex in which the Incas had dip-coated their feet to provide skin-tight boots. Safely at the edge of the plantation, I crouched at the base of a rubber tree to examine the contents of its collecting bucket, affixed to the trunk just below a short bamboo spout leading from a diagonal gash in the bark. The sap was less viscous than I expected, milky white with a thick, dank smell. I tasted it, rubbed it between my fingers, tested its tackiness on my uniform and skin, and spread some on my nostrils. For two precious minutes I lingered in another world, a world away from the war, a world driven by scientific curiosity. Too soon I was back in the Jeep again, heading toward Saigon with my relieved companions.

I was assisting a minesweeping team clearing a dirt road one day when the platoon leader motioned me to where he stood on the muddy shoulder. At his feet lay a wooden ammunition crate, about a yard long and foot square.

"Hey, Lieutenant, be careful!" I yelled. "You remember what happened to that Spec 4 in Charlie Company two days ago."

The Specialist 4, a trained combat engineer, had spent almost a whole year at the fire-support base, sweeping the same stretch of track every morning, looking for mines and booby traps. He found and disarmed, or blew in place, three or four a week, and then was careless just once. His company commander had just written to his widow.

"It ain't no biggie, sir," the platoon leader said, drawing his bayonet and stepping up to the crate.

I jumped back instinctively as he probed gently under the lid with the tip of his bayonet, feeling for trip wires. Then he looked at me and grinned.

"It's a booby trap all right."

I took one more quick step back and pulled my steel helmet lower over my forehead. Those frontal lobotomies can be killers. He held the bayonet in place on the wire and flicked open the lid with his left hand.

"Yep, just as I thought," he said. "A Type Bravo trigger, and enough C-4 to blow one hell of a crater."

But what if it had been a Type Alpha? Or one they didn't teach yet in Combat Engineer's Officer Basic Course, rigged up with a tiny bamboo lever and human-hair tripwire? His way to cope with combat was to make it a game, and he enjoyed testing his wits. It was a quiz show: behind one door was a little satisfaction from seeing he guessed right, and behind the other grinning death. He could just as easily have backed off and detonated the bomb with a hand grenade, but instead he had to open a door. Luckily it was the right door, and I didn't have to send a letter to *his* widow.

Slowly I was becoming used to my part-time job as machine gunner on Colonel Gibson's command Jeep. Most of the time it just meant hanging on for dear life, standing in the back of the open Jeep and trying to keep hold of the stock and tripod of the .50 caliber, as the Jeep jumped potholes in trails and irrigation trenches in the rice paddies. I learned that if I flexed my knees, inertia would keep my center of gravity parallel to the ground, instead of parallel to the base of the bouncing Jeep. The Jeep would bang up and down below me while my torso remained moving on a smooth, straight line, much like the continuous level trajectory of a cheetah's head above pounding feet below.

Our battalion doctor periodically needed a bodyguard for our unit's Medical Civic Action Program. "Doc" and several medics, all volunteers, would pile supplies into an open three-quarter-ton truck, pick a local hamlet at random, and drive there unannounced to set up a temporary mobile medical clinic. It seemed like an excellent humanitarian project to me, and although I knew very little about emergency medical procedures, I did now know something about being a machine gunner, so I signed up. Word of mouth would spread quickly at the site of the makeshift clinic, and soon there was a small crowd of villagers. Our team dressed infections, set broken bones, pulled abscessed teeth, and gave penicillin shots for a quick hour before we scooted. The villagers were very grateful, and if there was danger, they'd quickly whisper, "VC, VC!" and we'd spin around and speed back down the dirt track.

One defensive assignment I did *not* volunteer for was leading a patrol at dusk outside the bunker line at Cu Chi. Just before dark, a sister unit on the east perimeter discovered a tunnel leading into the base camp from outside the barbed-wire defenses. Not knowing whether this was part of another coordinated attack plan, the division duty officer alerted all troops standing guard on the perimeter to probe for similar tunnels outside the wires. I happened to be the officer in charge of our sector that night, and I quickly organized an eight-man patrol equipped with ropes, lights, and plastic explosives, as well as the usual M16 rifles and M-79 grenade launchers.

Those months of patrolling in Ranger School, supervised by experts and performed under nerve-racking pressure, now paid off in spades. I soon had my patrol sweeping the no-man's-land outside our lines exactly where sappers had broken through in February. The point and flank men reported two dry earthen wells, often used to disguise tunnel entrances. I set out a three-man team around us as security and assembled the rest of the patrol near the first well. Even with our flashlights, we couldn't see far into the shadows of the well.

"I need a volunteer to go down to see if there is any tunnel offshoot," I told them. If we just blew the entrance in place, the VC could dig it out in an hour. We needed to know.

Silence. No volunteers. I could order them to do it, one by one, and if they refused could have them court-martialed, or, theoretically, could even shoot them on the spot. That didn't seem like a good idea. Even though the 25th Infantry's policy clearly stated that officers were not to enter tunnels, I saw no other option. I was not trained as a "tunnel rat" specialist and was far too big to even be considered, but it had to be me.

I fought to block out thoughts about the VC's penchant for dispatching tunnel trespassers by skewering them alive through the groin, pinning them screaming to the walls of the tunnel. They would then ambush the rescuers as they squirmed through the tunnel to aid their comrade. The Americans' obsession with retrieving their dead and wounded played right into Charlie's hand. VC in the tunnel were safe from hand grenades and gas attacks as long as a live American remained underground, even a mortally wounded one.

"Okay. *I'm* going," I whispered to my men. "If anything happens," I said to the ranking sergeant, "you're in charge. Give me that rope, and when I nod, lower me slowly."

I lashed a makeshift Swiss-seat rope harness around my waist, grabbed an Army flashlight in one hand and .45 in the other, and they lowered me inch by inch into the black hole. A strange calmness came over me. Whether it was the same emotional blinders that one experiences when diving into a raging river to save a drowning child or simply a protective mental shock, I have no idea. But my mind cleared, and I stared into the shadows, listening intently and drawing quiet breaths through my nostrils to smell for telltale hints of diesel or perspiration. The rope cut into my sides for thirty of the longest seconds of my life. But luckily the tunnel was "cold," as the professional tunnel rats say, and ten minutes later I stood at the bottom of the second well. We marked the exact locations of the holes on our map for demolition and continued the sweep. I still felt strangely calm during the remainder of the patrol, but when I returned to base camp and reported to Colonel Gibson, my knees buckled and my hands trembled. My reward, better than any medal, was delivered the next day by one of the sergeants.

"Sir, the men really appreciated the way you handled that patrol last night," he said. "They wanted you to know."

I felt strong, confident, and happy to be alive.

As I grew accustomed to the physical stresses of war and the adrenaline highs, my thoughts turned more frequently to female companionship. Not sex *per se*, as I had expected, having arrived in Vietnam directly from free-love San Francisco. But I missed a woman's touch, her voice, her smell and tenderness. In Cu Chi's base camp of some 25,000 soldiers, a few Vietnamese women worked as day laborers, but I had not seen an American woman in months. Then one day at a supply center, I literally bumped into one, a slim young woman in her twenties with huge brown eyes and a marvelous smile.

Back in the battalion I described her clothes, a light-blue seersucker summer dress, floppy dark-blue field hat, and tennis shoes. She was a civilian, head to toe, but still it looked like some sort of a uniform. The old-timers explained that she was one of the seven Donut Dollies, or Red Cross workers, stationed with the 25th. I asked if they had ever gone out with a Donut Dolly, and they roared with laughter. The thousand-to-one gender odds were impossible, and besides, what did "going out" mean, anyway, in the midst of sandbagged bunkers, mortar attacks, and Army chow? I had not yet seen the movie *M*A*S*H*.

"To hell with the odds," I thought. I called the Red Cross headquarters on our field phone, and to my great surprise, the girl remembered me and accepted my invitation to visit our battalion officers' hooch for a drink. Privacy was impossible, but I scrounged some candles and wine and a book of Rod McKuen poetry. She and I took turns reading aloud behind the sandbags, while every officer in the battalion found some excuse to stop by, including the chaplain, fresh from an outdoor barrel bath, dripping wet and buck naked except for an olive-drab towel. He heard that Captain Hill had conjured up a real live "round-eye" woman and wanted to see the apparition for himself.

Later the girl and I took a short evening stroll along the earthen berms, oblivious to the deafening howitzers around us, spewing out fire and high-explosive rounds, and the flares drifting slowly toward the barbed wire in their white silk parachutes. It could have been the Fourth of July in Kansas. I saw her once more, when a mortar attack interrupted our poetry readings. Division headquarters frantically radioed our command post to send her back to the Red Cross barracks at all clear. The higher-ups could afford to lose hundreds of soldiers in battle, but a single civilian death, and a woman at that, would have meant mountains of paperwork.

* * *

A helicopter mission late one afternoon brought home to me both the impotence of our mighty technological forces and the sublime beauty of the Vietnamese countryside. I hopped aboard a Huey to help resupply the handful of men we had atop Nui Ba Den (Black Virgin Mountain), which overlooked rice paddies and the Cambodian border. Flying at an altitude above 1,500 feet, where small-arms fire from the ground lost its punch, our helicopter crossed a vast network of silver mirrors and lush green carpets, the flooded fields of young rice shoots. Suddenly, on the horizon of this green-and-silver checkerboard, there appeared a perfect volcanic cone, like an immense jet-black pyramid. Nui Ba Den thrust up from the center of the fertile tableland.

Our tiny base camp on its peak, perhaps 100 feet in diameter, served as observation post and radio relay station, facilitating contact among ground units. As we set down on the makeshift heliport, the men there were happy to see us, especially the ammunition, food, and mail.

"Better get that chopper out of here pretty quick, sir," said the sergeant. "It's almost time for the evening attack."

"*What?*" I asked.

"We own the peak here," he said, "and our armor owns the rice paddies below. But the damn VC have held the sides of the mountain the whole war. Tunneled deep into the lava rock. We've blasted 'em with artillery barrages that would level Manhattan, but they're still there. And they usually attack after sunset every night, just to remind us. We're ready. It's almost a game.

Last week we made gigantic Molotov cocktails out of 50-gallon drums of aviation fuel tied with flares and rolled them down the mountain. Number one light show, but I don't think Charlie even got warm enough to toast weenies. They'd love to score a helicopter, sir."

We got the hint and didn't even shut down our engines.

To help keep our minds off the absurdities of the war and the obvious but unpublicized fact that we were not winning, the Army distributed medals like handbills, flew troops on R&R to Hawaii and Bangkok, and sometimes even brought entertainment into the middle of the combat zone. One morning, Division HQ ordered us to construct a small outdoor wooden stage, not too near the perimeter bunker line.

"It's for a rock-and-roll concert, sir," said one of the old-timers with a laugh. "*Really*. You weren't here for the last one. They bring in Korean rock bands from Saigon to entertain the troops. Ain't Bob Hope, but it's somethin'."

The first scheduled concert was rained out. Mortars, not monsoons. The next one came off. Choppers whisked in the performers just before dusk, with their amplifiers, spotlights, drums, and electric guitars. Off-duty GIs crammed the red dirt bleachers as the heavy green Army canvas curtain lifted to a loud but barely recognizable version of Creedence Clearwater Revival. Tiny Korean go-go dancers, in scanty red, white, and blue halter tops, short-shorts, and knee-high white cowboy boots, jerked mechanically to the wailings of the enthusiastic but pitiful band.

"Light My Fire" brought hundreds of army Zippo lighters flashing in the dark. The skinhead olive-drab audience cheered and screamed in the hot, humid night air, less than 200 yards from the trenches where their friends guarded the barbed wires, huddled over M60 machine guns and starlight scopes. The dancers tried desperately to be sexy, the vocalists to sing English. *Wok and woe*, we called it. It ended punctually at 11 p.m., unlike its famous sister Woodstock rock festival that same month, back in The World, that drew acid-dropping crowds matching nearly exactly one-for-one the half million head count of all US troops in Vietnam. Years later I often had to explain to non-Vietnam friends that the unlikely jungle rock concert scenes in *Apocalypse Now* were not just the figment of some Hollywood scriptwriter's imagination. They were real.

Army construction engineers in Vietnam built air-conditioned movie theaters and post exchanges, fancy swimming pools, and posh officers' clubs. Troops watched John Wayne on Armed Forces Network Television and listened to rock music on AFN Radio. Those in Saigon could dine at fine French restaurants, frequent fancy brothels, and take night college courses from the Far East Branch of the University of Maryland. Even in our combat engineer unit, Colonel Gibson slept in a generator-powered, air-conditioned hooch, drank Jack Daniel's, and played eight ball in our battalion officers' club.

This was the part of the war that angered me the most. The morality of every war is debatable, and the Vietnam War would have been just as popular as the later Persian Gulf Conflict, had it been over as quickly and had we won. But the deceitful extravagances in Vietnam, the sheer waste, revolted me. It was far worse than anything I had seen in my limited experience at Ft. Devens. I even naively risked going over the generals' heads once and wrote directly to Senators Stuart Symington and Edward Kennedy to volunteer to serve on a fact-finding committee to Vietnam, pointing out that my firsthand experience might help cut through the various bureaucratic smoke screens. Only Kennedy's office responded, and that with a short kiss-off note. His staff was apparently up to its eyeballs in the Chappaquiddick scandal. The swimming pools and movie theaters were in for the duration, because the Army needs combat-experienced troops, and combat troops need diversions.

To cope with the decadence, the futility, the absurdity, and the fear, I fell back on my two basic strategies. I gave myself new physical challenges, including teaching myself inverted commando rappelling on the nearby Special Forces practice tower, and I kept reviewing mathematics on scrap paper during off-duty hours, trying to reconstruct theorems and proofs in geometry and analysis. My lieutenants noticed this, and one day one of them brought me Department of the Army Pamphlet 70-5. Chapter 15 contained a complicated mathematical differential equation model based on the Lanchester Square Law, which says that military force is proportional to the square of the number of units it has. For example, doubling your own numerical superiority will result in reducing your losses by one fourth.

As an application of how accurate the mathematical model was, Figure 15-1 plotted the predicted curve versus actual real-life—in this case real-death—statistics on the invasion my father had fought in at Iwo Jima. The predicted versus actual casualty rates, *in thousands of Allied troops killed per day*, were sawtooth curves that were eerily close. That accuracy certainly bolstered the pride of some bean-counting bureaucrat sitting safely at his desk in Washington in 1945, and today his bean-counting successor in the Pentagon was undoubtedly applying the same mathematical model to Vietnam casualty rates, where my whole company and I were no more than an errant fly speck on his graph.

And when the Pentagon brass found it increasingly difficult to convince politicians and the public that we were winning the war, they simply dropped standard statistics altogether and resorted to the most basic of all mathematics—counting. Success, they now declared, was measured by the new criterion called "body count"—the number of enemy bodies that could be tallied. So now platoons were losing even more men on patrols digging up makeshift enemy graves to bolster the count.

* * *

In May I learned that Abe Dean, my junior-year West Point roommate, was stationed with a nearby Army Aviation unit. He and his fellow pilots flew small, fixed-wing planes to monitor paratrooper jumps, advise the Laotian Air Force, and conduct special reconnaissance missions not suitable for Air Force planes or helicopters. My operations officer located Abe's unit's call sign and patched me through. I gave Abe my company's location, and he promised to fly in for a short visit the next week.

"We don't really have a runway," I told him. "Only a short strip of dirt and potholes, so maybe it's better if you fly in at the air base."

"No problem," Abe said. "See you at 1400 Tuesday at your coordinates. Take you up for a ride."

I expected a reasonably sophisticated aircraft, something befitting the year 1969. Perhaps not exactly up to the advanced avionics of the new attack helicopters and F-15 jet fighters, but up to snuff. After all, we had just heard the news that Americans had walked on the moon.

Abe arrived in a single-engine, propeller-driven Cessna O-1 Bird Dog, wingspan of 36 feet. The windows had been removed, so the two-seater, observer behind the pilot, was an open-cockpit, olive-drab combat crop duster. To me it looked like the same plane you still saw buzzing barns in Kansas. Minutes later Abe, the same old hulking red-blonde Florida country boy, stood grinning broadly in his leather flight helmet, pointing to the only armament he carried, the .45 at his waist. The plane had no machine guns, no rockets, not even the firepower of a single M16 rifle. And, with a cruising speed of only 104 knots, it was slower than your average arrow. Its strength, Abe said, lay in its solid and simple design, and as I climbed into the seat behind him, he assured me that this plane could land safely with 90 percent of the wing surface shot away.

"What," I asked, as I squeezed into the rear seat harness, "you don't have a TV in this thing?" recalling the illegal television he and I had once managed to conceal briefly in our barracks room at West Point.

He laughed, and off we went, with the O-1 practically flapping its wings as we jolted over the potholes and into the air. Airborne, Abe was all business, craning his neck left and right over the fuselage, dipping the wings, constantly on the alert for movement or hostile fire from the jungle and rice paddies below. The air felt cooler than I expected, our tanks and perimeter defenses looked like fragile sandbox toys, and the rubber trees seemed sparse and far apart. With no armament at all, our survival depended solely on Abe's reflexes and expertise as a pilot, on evasive maneuvers and his knowledge of enemy habits and activity. It was a wonderful rush, this thrill of primitive flight through the Wild West.

"You look like this place is getting to you," Abe said when we landed. "You should get laid." Then he winked and waved goodbye.

"Just to talk to a woman again would be enough," I thought. Then I remembered that Al Lindseth's sister-in-law Marra worked as an Army nurse in the 24th Evacuation Hospital at Long Binh. I called there to confirm and two days later caught a chopper lift from Cu Chi.

"She's in Ward 16, the last ward, NICU," said a medical corpsman outside the main entrance to the hospital. He pointed to the Neurosurgical Intensive Care Unit in the long row of gray, semi-cylindrical Quonset huts, ringed by chest-high walls of sun-bleached dark-green sandbags. A central passageway connected the ward huts, like the fuse running down the center of a string of giant firecrackers, lying half embedded in the red clay. Nonfunctioning air conditioners protruded from the boarded-up windows of the wards.

Opening the door at the end of the hut stenciled "Ward 16," I stepped into a surprisingly dark room, temporarily blinded after the intense midday tropical sun outside. I could see nothing for a few long seconds and stopped in my tracks as an unfamiliar breath-hot stench struck me in the face. I recognized the earthy odor of blood and human waste, but not the other, more pungent foulness. I involuntarily clamped my hand over my mouth and nose to stifle rising nausea, waiting for my eyes to adjust. Groans and the creaks of metal beds pierced the darkness.

Finally I could make out an aisle ahead of me, leading between two long rows of beds set perpendicular to the walkway. At the foot of each tubular metal gatch bed, a medical chart hung next to the hand crank used to raise and lower the head of the bed, emitting its characteristic *gatch* sound. I walked slowly toward the central passageway, where a simple wooden table and several chairs served as a nurses' station. The half-cylindrical wall of dingy gray ended in an unpainted rough cement floor. As I moved hesitantly past the beds, I saw gaping open wounds, oozing filth onto clean dressings as delirious young men strained against metal side rails.

Halfway down the gauntlet, a trembling, thin pale hand and wrist pointed to the Army Colt .45 strapped to my side.

"Shoot me, Captain," he pleaded. "*Please* shoot me."

I passed him silently, hand still over my nose, and tried not to look into their faces. The man in the last bed, however, *had no face at all.* No eyes, nose, mouth, or cheeks—just an open raw cavity with chin and cheekbones wired shut. As I staggered to the nurses' station, one of them stood up and introduced herself with a cheerful smile. Marra was short, with her sister's good looks, dark eyes, and dark hair. My eyes involuntarily shot back to the faceless patient.

"That's Jimmie," she said. "He's a sweetheart. Twenty years old. Shrapnel ripped off his whole face while he shielded two wounded friends, but his brain is completely unharmed. His thinking is clear as a bell. Unlike him," she said as she motioned to a handsome young man with no obvious injuries but vacant, staring eyes. "Half his skull and brain are missing. It's just covered by a skin flap. We sucked out the dead part of his brain with a suction catheter. In past wars, none of these cases would have made it out of the battlefield alive. But now, thanks to helicopter ambulances . . ." Her voice trailed off.

"A man just asked me to shoot him," I said quietly, "like they shoot horses."

"Those are the spinal injuries. Permanently paralyzed, chronically depressed. The head cases are easy. They're not worried at all. Behind the curtain," she said as she pointed to a canvas sheet separating off the far half of the Quonset hut, "are the ones who are going to die. Our unit has a policy. No GI dies alone. One of us is there holding his hand." She paused. "You don't look so good. Let's take a walk. The smell in this ward takes getting used to. It's *septicemia*, the infection caused by bullets and shell casings smeared with human feces. That's why we don't sew up the wounds. We keep removing the infected flesh. Nothing we can do about it. We keep them here five days at most and ship the serious cases to Japan for surgery."

We started down the connecting passageway leading past the other wards.

"See how these wards are better lit? Ours is intentionally dim. It's standard in neurosurgery units. We painted this corridor red because it's the only color we could get." She smiled.

"How do you do it?" I asked, "Stay so upbeat, optimistic . . ."

"We mostly use young medical corpsmen," she replied, "with a gallows sense of humor like ours."

"Bull*shit* to that," I said. "You're all saints. And what are you, twenty-four, or maybe twenty-five? Same as me."

Over coffee in the tiny hospital canteen, Marra described her disgust with the new hospital commandant, an MD colonel who wore jackboots and carried a swagger stick.

"Every couple of weeks he goes down to the hospital at LBJ," she said, referring sarcastically to the POW compound Long Binh Jail nicknamed after the president. "And any Vietnamese prisoners who refuse to stand at attention as he walks through with his swagger stick are transferred out, never to be seen or heard of again."

"I'm on graveyard shift tonight," she said, grinning at the pun. "You can sleep in my bunk in the women's BOQ. Nobody checks."

The shock of Ward 16 had left me numb. I slept fitfully, rose before dawn, and caught a flight back to Cu Chi. This was not the *laid*-back relaxing experience I had hoped to find. I felt sobered by the incredible courage and professionalism shown by these men and women who were mopping up as best they could.

* * *

After my six-month stint in the 65th Combat Engineers, the Engineer Branch Office reassigned me as management analyst in the Review and Analysis Section of the US Army Construction Agency, Vietnam. USARCAV was headquartered in a flimsy, modern, one-story, air-conditioned building with olive-drab aluminum siding, safely inside the huge rear-echelon base at Long Binh. I knew that my fellow '66er and non-volunteer Ranger, Art, was already stationed there. He greeted me warmly in his thick Southern drawl.

"Our boss over there is Colonel Myron," he said motioning to a short, cigar-chomping, middle-aged man with thin, short gray hair, "and he is one strict by-the-books sonofabitch. But we're on the road a lot, checking construction sites and plant maintenance, so we avoid him most of the time. The work is challenging—thought you might like it, and maybe you can even use some of that Stanford Operations Research degree. Pulled a few strings to get you here, TP—welcome aboard!"

Our mission was to oversee construction projects, from water purification plants and power plants to mess halls and officers' clubs. The futility of devoting all these resources to projects like that in this crazy war bothered me.

"Why the hell are we building all this?!" I asked Art. "Everybody knows this war can't last that much longer, and then what? All this for nothing."

"Not so," said Art. "See those job sites?" He pointed to nearby cement and wood-frame construction projects. "They've told us that when this war is over, those buildings will be part of Saigon University. No matter who wins!"

"Now this is a job I can put my heart into," I thought, never imagining in my wildest dreams that decades later those same universities in Saigon would invite me back to lecture on my own mathematical discoveries!

My new immediate supervisor, Major Mumford, was a dark-haired handsome man, intelligent and articulate. Art liked him, and he was friendly to me from the start. Although Mumford was a career officer and sensed that neither Art nor I was likely to be a lifer, he openly valued our out-of-the-box ideas. Unlike his superiors, he was determined to make the best of a couple of characters like us.

My first assignment, direct from Colonel Myron's office, was to represent the Army at the normally routine renewal of its $120 million annual contract with the civilian construction firm Pacific Architects and Engineers. To support its combat mission, the Army needed electrical power supplies and office buildings and huge supplies of fresh water. Instead of using American military forces to provide everything, they contracted out much of the maintenance and construction to PA&E. I only had a day's notice but studied the pending contract the morning before the final conference. I remembered a little bit about contract law from my West Point law classes, but this one struck me as unusual. It spelled out the agreement clearly enough. PA&E would construct a certain number of power generating stations and water purification plants and deliver specified amounts of electricity and fresh water during the coming fiscal year. In return the Department of Defense would pay $120 million to PA&E, but also would provide *everything except labor*—every pencil and lug wrench, every generator and dump truck, and even housing for PA&E workers. If PA&E drivers accidentally destroyed a truck, say by letting it run out of oil, then the Army simply replaced the truck. No money changed hands. In this contract, as in previous ones, it was specified that the Army would judge performance just as it judged regular Army unit performance—with unannounced inspections to monitor paperwork and dipstick oil levels in the trucks and generators. That was it! No estimates of the cost of spare parts or lost tools or replacement vehicles.

The meeting took place in a formal boardroom, unlike anything I had seen before in Vietnam, and I was the most junior person at the long table. The president of PA&E, a tall, middle-aged Texan civilian, sat on one side of the table, with several high-ranking civilian engineers from his company. Across from them sat the ranking Army engineer colonels. After the usual niceties, both sides were ready to wrap up the pro forma signing, and asked if there were any questions. I waited a few polite seconds and raised my hand.

"I'm new here," I said, "and have not worked with these projects before. But I'm wondering this. There seem to be significant amounts of supplies and replacement parts and vehicles that are not figured into any formula. Does anyone here know how much the US Army is actually paying PA&E for a kilowatt of electricity, or a gallon of water? The bottom-line cost?"

The room fell silent, and both sides of the table squirmed. No one knew the answer, and I could almost feel the *maybe it's cheaper to buy water directly from Seoul* thoughts going through their minds. The PA&E president and the head Army engineer looked at each other, whispered something I couldn't hear, and announced that the meeting would be adjourned and the contract renegotiated. After days of stalling and balking by PA&E, and another heated round-table meeting with the CEO, his team finally allowed me to write a few basics of cost analysis into the new contract, and he signed off. Colonel Myron personally came to my office to thank me, and he praised my independent thinking.

"I bet you bottom dollar that's the first time that guy ever thanked a subordinate for questioning authority," Art said, smiling.

I was happy with the bottom line and felt that I had gotten off to an unexpectedly good start.

USARCAV was always critically short of vehicles, and that hampered our inspections of PA&E plant operations and construction sites. Instead of simply hopping in a Jeep to go check out a reported engineering problem, Art and I had to call sister units and try to catch a lift in their trucks or Jeeps going in the right direction, and then catch one or two more rides to the final destination. Including the initial waits to find a ride, and the in-transit layovers, a job that should have taken only half a day now sometimes took several days. Often a long delay proved critical, so I went to Transportation Headquarters to requisition a Jeep, explaining how much it would improve our mission capabilities. My words fell on deaf ears.

"Look, Captain, there are colonels around here who don't have Jeeps," said the transportation warrant officer. "Sorry, sir, no can do."

"Okay, I understand that," I said. "But we need to get the job done. I'll just buy a used car in Saigon with my own money."

"That's against regulations. No POVs in Vietnam." Army regulations expressly forbid privately owned vehicles in combat areas, I now learned.

"Fine, then I'll buy a motorcycle," I said.

"No, sir. That's a POV too."

"Then I'll rent one. I won't own it."

"Nope. It's still privately owned—by the rental company."

I thought for a minute. "Okay, then, I'll buy a car and *donate* it to the US Army."

That stymied them for a few minutes. But it was the old catch-22 again when the transportation officer resumed.

"Never heard of that before, sir," he said. "But I'm sure there is no provision for it. So it's against regulations since there is no regulation permitting it."

I recognized the circular logic from my West Point run-in with the bicycle and realized once again that the authorities would never bend. I gave up trying to get a Jeep legally, and Art and I decided to "scrounge" one. First we needed a cover story, since we couldn't suddenly show up with a Jeep, without an explanation. I went to see our immediate boss, Major Mumford, and told him I might be able to get a Jeep up at my old combat unit in Cu Chi but warned him that it might be a maverick.

A maverick was a vehicle that was not on the official property books—as far as the Army was concerned, it didn't exist, or at least didn't exist *anymore*. Perfectly good Jeeps, trucks, and even tanks sometimes became these "ghost" vehicles through combat loss reports. Suppose a battalion motor pool has an on-the-books official Jeep and an enemy mortar round destroys it. No one "buys" a replacement, since no money changes hands for resupplies within the Army. Instead, the unit commander fills out a combat loss report, and his motor sergeant turns in the paperwork, along with some proof of the loss, say a piece of mangled bumper. Since the battalion is authorized to have one such quarter-ton truck, the quartermaster then issues them a new Jeep.

But suppose the mortar round just *misses* the Jeep. Remove a bumper, run over it a few times with a tank, file the same combat loss report together with the mangled bumper, and get issued a new Jeep. The first Jeep is now deleted from the property books, since it was officially destroyed, but the unit now has it as an extra vehicle, a maverick. Other maverick Jeeps were simply out-and-out stolen from another unit, with their serial numbers repainted. Art and I didn't have the combat loss report option at our disposal, since we were not commanders, so instead we decided to swipe a Jeep from another Army unit and repaint its ID numbers. Punishment for either kind of "Misappropriation of a government vehicle" ranged up to four years in a military stockade.

Major Mumford realized how much having a Jeep would help our mission and weighed that against the penalty of getting caught with a stolen Jeep.

"What do you need from me?" he asked.

"Three days," I said, "for me to go back up to Cu Chi. Combat units have more flexibility with paperwork. And when I return, no questions asked."

"You got it," he said.

If we swiped a Jeep from a nearby unit, we were almost certain to be caught, since all but the very newest of Jeeps are easily distinguished by their dents and scrapes and imperfect paint jobs. We decided to steal one from nearby Bien Hoa Air Base, but first we had to get there. One night, armed with bolt cutters hidden in the pant leg of my jungle fatigues and an old Army green T-shirt to muffle the sound, Art and I crept into the shadows where our own base camp Jeeps were parked and temporarily "borrowed" one by snapping the lock on the heavy chain that linked the steering wheel to the steel clutch pedal. I jumped into the driver's seat, and Art pushed me silently 100 yards and jumped in on the shotgun side as I cranked it up and aimed for the main gate.

The few dark miles to Bien Hoa passed quickly but tensely, as we drove unarmed outside the perimeter wires. Once inside the air base, we quickly located several Jeeps parked in the shadows near a motor pool. Art picked out a fairly new one, snapped its padlocked chain, and started it up. Then he followed me back to Long Binh, where we returned my Jeep to its original parking spot in our neighboring unit and hid the other Jeep out of sight near our supply room. At first light, we drove the Air Base Jeep to a local Vietnamese paint shop in a nearby village, where they altered the identification numbers in exchange for two cartons of Salem cigarettes. Then I drove the Jeep to Cu Chi to sit out the three days called for by our cover story.

When we returned to Long Binh with a practically new Jeep, we were the heroes of our section and avoided answering questions on exactly where it came from. Art and I were "in charge" of the Jeep. If someone wanted to borrow it, he was told in no uncertain terms that it was a maverick and that he could use it only if he agreed that, if caught, he would remain silent and take the full rap himself. That was the deal, clear and simple. The false paperwork we had made up to go with the vehicle would not stand up to close scrutiny. The system worked well, and our new maverick logged hundreds of construction-inspection miles.

Three weeks into my USARCAV assignment, Colonel Myron came to my office.

"Come with me, Captain Hill," he said. "I have another project you might like."

"Do I have a choice?" I asked with a smile as I followed him down the corridor.

"Yes, you have a choice," he answered coldly, his face flushing red at my little joke, which he interpreted as pure insolence. That man had absolutely no sense of humor.

In his office, he described the job in detail, a feasibility study on a new water purification facility, and then sarcastically asked whether I would *like* to work on it. He needed the final report in three days. The project looked interesting and challenging, and I accepted. I told him I would need to be able to concentrate intensely on this project for the next seventy-two hours, free from all other duties. The Colonel cleared it with Major Mumford, and for the next three days, I was in research heaven. I spent eighteen hours a day on the assignment, thinking, calculating, covering every angle, cross-checking with other reports, talking to engineers and on-site coordinators, and poring over documents in our little library. I even took a draft of my final report to an enlisted man in our unit with a master's degree in English from Harvard, and together we polished the exposition. By the time we were through, I felt it was perfect. Satisfied with every argument and phrase, I had a final version typed up and was carrying it to Colonel Myron's office, late at the end of the third day, when I ran into him in the hallway.

"Here's that feasibility study you wanted, Colonel."

"Thanks, Captain Hill. I'll look it over tonight and let you know what general changes I want you to make."

"I don't think you understand, sir," I said, perhaps a little too confidently. "This report reads exactly the way I think it should, like a poem. If you see changes you want, then it is probably best if you sketch them in yourself. But this is a *finished product*, sir."

He spun on his heels and stormed down to his office. Moments later he summoned Major Mumford, who came back to my office thirty minutes later, a grave frown on his face. The colonel had ordered him to reassign me immediately to another unit, as punishment for insubordination.

Ordinarily, disciplinary reassignment meant going to the boonies—front-line combat. This had just happened to one of my lieutenant friends, who had reported to the infirmary late one night with hashish-induced hallucinations. Asian dope was very potent, and smoking alone was risky. Officially, the Army gave amnesty to anyone who turned himself in for drug treatment, so my friend was not court-martialed. Instead, they reassigned him to a combat unit in the boonies.

Art and I speculated about my impending reassignment, got stoned, and went to see the Beatles' *Yellow Submarine*, shown with a jerky 16mm projector on a white sheet in a jury-rigged outdoor cinema covered with canvas Army tarps. Two days later, Colonel Myron ordered me to his office. He complimented me on the extremely high quality of my report—he had only one tiny "correction." Then he put down the document and looked up at me from his desk.

"Stand at ease, Captain. I feel that there is a certain amount of loyalty one owes his superiors, regardless of what he thinks personally, and I think that this loyalty is lacking in you. My tour here is almost over—otherwise I would keep you here under my command and personally readjust your attitude. But I don't want to leave a rotten apple in the barrel and will not leave you here for my replacement to deal with. I chose not to say anything to you until I found somewhere to send you. You will be leaving USARCAV *ASAP*! Report to the executive officer for instructions."

Once again the authorities were labeling me a bad apple. But to my great surprise, and that of all my friends, my new assignment was as *company commander* of a 300-man support unit in Bien Hoa. Shipping me out for insubordination, they were sending me to command another unit? It didn't make sense, and I asked Art.

"Myron was so bent on getting rid of you," Art explained, "that he literally jumped at the first possible reassignment that personnel came up with."

I still had a chance to say goodbye to my friends at the Construction Agency's next hail and farewell party, where an evening reception in the officers' club—with open bar, loud music, brass plaques, and drunken speeches—pays tribute to the arriving and departing officers. My friends were proud and told me it was a first at USARCAV. My eviction from Colonel Myron's command came so soon after my arrival that I was both "hailed" and "farewelled" at the same party. But I was also now officially branded as "insubordinate" and I wondered how this might come back to haunt me in the future.

A week later I left the maverick Jeep to Art, since as company commander of my new unit I would now have access to four Jeeps, twenty-four hours a day. Because of our take-the-rap code, I washed my hands of the stolen Jeep and put it out of my mind. I settled into the new company commander position and made new friends.

Compared to life at Cu Chi, life at Bien Hoa was luxurious, but the luxury also bred corruption. For starters, Vietnam had its share of the civilian evils of drugs and bribery and smuggling and extortion. Marijuana was cheap, plentiful, and potent, and a quart of a French weight-reduction tonic cost only a dollar, along with the needles to inject it for a speed-like high.

One of my warrant officers asked me for a captured Chinese Communist rocket launcher I had confiscated from souvenir-hunting troops, along with Swedish rifles and other non-automatic weapons that could be registered and brought back to the States. He traded the launcher for an Air Medal. His contact simply added his name to the official roster. My immediate commander at Bien Hoa, a major, had intermittent use of a general's small plane in exchange for wrangling the general's son a safe noncombat assignment. The major returned from "R&R trips" to Taiwan with briefcases full of gold and jade jewelry that he sold to the troops "at cost." It was easy. There were no immigration or customs inspectors at small airstrips in a war zone. He also collected kickbacks from South Koreans peddling mail-order white leather Bibles that troops paid to have sent to the soldiers' families stateside, and dictated lonely-hearts cassette tapes to his wife between sack-time with his in-country girlfriend, a teenage Vietnamese hooker.

He was by no means the worst of the lot. Officers in payroll ran intricate financial scams by exchanging dollars and piasters in one direction at the official rate, and in the other direction on the black market. Men in Graves Registration units smuggled drugs back to the States inside the corpses. The stories went on and on, and so did the operations.

One afternoon I returned to the orderly room of my new company headquarters to find an urgent message from the first sergeant. At 1300 hours that afternoon, the note said, I was to report to the Criminal Investigation Division at Long Binh. I phoned the CID to confirm the "appointment" and reminded the investigator that a commander takes orders only from someone in the direct chain of command above him. He apologized and asked if it were "convenient" for me to make the appointment. I told him I would be there at 1300.

On the drive over to Long Binh, I wondered what offense they might have cooked up. Smoking pot, maybe, or painting that peace symbol on the headquarters of the First Logistical Command? But I had never been caught at either. The CID had been looking for a case against me because it considered me "soft" on marijuana violations. Officially, smoking hashish was punishable by seven years in the slammer, whereas being drunk on duty was considered only a minor infraction. As company commander, though, I was the judge, and I treated both offenses equally. It didn't matter to me whether the guard-duty infraction was one kind of chemical mind bender or another—in fact, given the choice, I would prefer my guards to be under the influence of marijuana rather than alcohol, since reaction time was still excellent, and, if anything, the guard was even more paranoid about signs of VC incursions. The CID was frustrated by my actions, since after I had slapped a soldier's wrist with my standard booze-dope Article 15, higher authorities were prevented from increasing the punishment by the military legal code's double-jeopardy clause.

At CID headquarters, a basic Quonset hut ringed by a low wall of green sandbags, a sloppy, heavy-set man in a green Army T-shirt and trousers and jungle boots read me Article 31 of the Uniform Code of Military Justice—the right to remain silent and to have counsel present upon questioning. I knew Article 31 by heart—I read it to my own troops eight or ten times a week. Although I was in complete uniform, with name and rank clearly visible, he asked to see my ID. Then I asked to see *his* ID, and he squirmed nervously, slipped on his jungle fatigue jacket, and started calling me "sir." After all, he was only a warrant officer.

"I'm investigating the alleged larceny of a one-quarter-ton vehicle during the time you were here at Long Binh," he said. "I have here a sworn testimony that you used this vehicle for several weeks when you were stationed here. Do you have anything to say, sir?"

I told him I wanted to talk to a lawyer first, and he led me to the back room to take fingerprints and mug shots. After they released me, I drove back to my headquarters and tried to call Art to find out what in the world had happened with our maverick code. He was still in Hawaii on R&R, his sergeant told me, so I asked to talk to Art's '66 classmate friend, Jack Wheeler, who was now based at Long Binh. When Art had left for Hawaii, he told me he was going to let Jack use the maverick. Although I knew Jack quite well from West Point, we had never become friends, and I wondered how he had gotten involved in all of this.

When I finally got through to him, Jack told me he had used the illegal Jeep while Art was away, and that a jealous enlisted man reported him for having a maverick. When the CID questioned Jack, he spilled everything he knew, including his hunch that "Captain Hill stole it." He did somehow manage to patch through a call to Art, all the way in Hawaii, to tell him that the heat was on and to be prepared for trouble when he landed at the Tan Son Nhut Air Base. Apparently he even went back to the CID office the next day, to tell them more details he had forgotten in his first statement, but not once did he try to call or warn me in nearby Bien Hoa. As I said, we never were friends . . .

Since now three West Point captains were implicated, the decision on what to do with us passed all the way up to the Pentagon. Initially, I entertained thoughts of pleading innocent, since technically speaking, Art had stolen *that* Jeep, whereas I was the one who "borrowed" the first Jeep, which we had returned with a broken chain. A sympathetic and sensible Army lawyer soon convinced me of the ridiculousness of that defense. The decision finally came down all the way from Washington. A general would administer Article 15s to each of us, with forfeiture of pay. If we appealed, the Army would press for a full court-martial and maximum sentence of up to four years in Leavenworth. Officially, I was the only one of the three to be sentenced for "Wrongful appropriation of a government vehicle." Jack got it for "Conduct totally unbecoming an officer," which I secretly thought quite fitting, and Art got something similar.

General Mabry later cited our case in speeches across the US, as a warning to wayward soldiers, to prove that the Army punishes even its elite West Pointers for stealing Jeeps. The incident became well known throughout the Army, and Jack later blamed it for leaving what had been a traditional family career. For me, it was just another black mark on my military report card to add to all the disciplinary actions from West Point.

Ironically, I had weathered the six-month tour in the combat engineers with no "questioning authority" issues, but here in the relatively safe rear-echelon support units, I had already chalked up Army career-threatening "insubordination" and "misappropriation" blots on my record. Oh well. At least the one-year sentence of my Vietnam tour of duty was speeding by, and the only injuries I had suffered so far were administrative wounds.

6

RETURN TO REASON

Every American soldier in Vietnam always knew exactly how many days were remaining until his DEROS, his Date of Estimated Return from Overseas. We were like convicts marking the days of our sentences on a jail cell wall. Most soldiers' DEROS was the same as their ETS, their Estimated Time of Separation from the Army, that magical day of return to civilian life. My DEROS was one year to the day after I arrived in Vietnam, like most of my troops, but I had agreed to four years of Army service after West Point, and that ended about six months after my scheduled return from Vietnam. It was not clear how much additional time, if any, I owed for my two years of graduate school at Stanford, and I fantasized about that nebulous date in the future when I would be able to return to mathematics.

Checking my inbox at Bien Hoa one afternoon, I found a handwritten letter from my brother Russ, who was working on his PhD in microbiology at St. Louis University. Coincidentally, both he and our younger brother George were in St. Louis at the same time, with George studying physics at Washington University. Young men all across the nation were being yanked out of their jobs or schools and sent to Vietnam, a fate both my brothers dreaded. George had a little time to strategize, since he was six years younger, but Russ was expecting a letter from his draft board any day. He desperately researched ways to avoid the draft. Would getting married and having kids do the trick? Or finding a critical job in the defense industry or agriculture? Or becoming a bona fide conscientious objector? Had either brother been a California surfer, that also would have worked. Hardcore West Coast surfers sprouted egg-sized hard calluses on the top of each foot from spending years kneeling on surfboards as they paddled out to first break to wait for swells. Jungle boots didn't fit over the foot knobs, and Army physicians classified the very healthiest of California's youth as 4F, medically unfit. Russ's current plan was to flee to Canada or Sweden and live there forever. I wrote him back and advised him not to go into permanent exile just yet. Then I told him about the Universal Life Church.

One evening over beers, I'd had a long talk with one of my lieutenants about Europe and graduate school and the Free Speech Movement, and the next day he stopped by to see me.

"Hey, Cap'n Hill," he said, "I have something that might interest you. Forgot to tell you last night. I'm from Modesto, California, and a guy there name of Hensley thinks that established religions shouldn't have a monopoly on government perks and certifications. You know, have the right to marry people or keep a tax-free place of worship. He feels everybody should be able to believe whatever he wants—one god, no god, fifteen green gods—and should not have to belong to a standard religion in order to have the benefits of one. So Hensley founded something called the Universal Life Church, and anyone who wants can become a legally ordained minister, for free. It's already formally recognized by the State of California. You can do it by mail—here's the address. Never know when you might want to marry somebody." I had thanked him, sent off a letter to Modesto, and by return mail soon received my own official Certificate of Ordination. And, yes, he was right. There would come a time much later when that certificate would come in handy. In the meantime, maybe becoming a legally ordained minister could help keep Russ out of the Army, via the draft deferment classification 4D, Minister of Religion.

In his next letter, Russ reported that the Lyons draft board had rejected his ministerial ruse with no explanation and, after reviewing his request for 4D status, had him immediately inducted. Because of his education, just shy of a PhD, the Army offered him a commission as a second lieutenant, but he refused that offer because it required three years of service rather than two. Then the Army told him they wanted to make use of his microbiology training and would assign him as a private E-1 to the Criminal Investigation Division Laboratory "analyzing marijuana samples." Russ immediately accepted. Duty in the CID first required basic Military Police training, but after his MP schooling, the Army reneged on its promise of a laboratory job and told him he would instead be sent to Vietnam guarding front-line convoys as an MP. I knew convoy security troops here in South Vietnam had a very high casualty rate.

If Russ had been inducted only a few months earlier, the Army could not have sent him to war. After all the boys in one family, the five Sullivan brothers, died when a Japanese torpedo sank their ship at Guadalcanal, the Defense Department decided against having brothers in combat simultaneously. Unfortunately for Russ, my own Vietnam tour of duty was scheduled to end just before his next duty assignment, so they were free to send him wherever they wanted. Highest on that list, it seemed, was chaperoning supply trucks in Vietnam. Russ wrote me that he planned to desert, to flee to Sweden.

Although I still needed to work out my own Army exit strategy in the hopes of returning to mathematics, keeping Russ out of the war now became my first priority. I learned that if I extended my own tour in Vietnam to cover the crucial period of Russ's reassignment, the Saving Private Ryan policy would require them to send him to a noncombat zone. A three-month extension would suffice for Saving Private Russ, and I started looking for possible assignments.

One of my warrant officers suggested I apply for a job as R&R liaison officer. Posting options were Honolulu, Sydney, Kuala Lumpur, Bangkok, Tokyo, Singapore, and Taiwan. Key for me was the fact that although these liaison officers were stationed far from the war, officially they were assigned to Vietnam and even got the extra $65-a-month combat pay! Theoretically, it appeared, I could volunteer to extend my time in Vietnam, thereby keeping Russ out of the war, but could actually serve those extra months in some safe and exotic tourist haven.

Landing one of those liaison jobs, however, was definitely a long shot. Out of the half million US troops assigned to Vietnam, only seven were R&R slots. Requirements that the liaison jobs be filled by unmarried junior commissioned officers reduced the odds to the ballpark of perhaps 1 in 10,000. In addition, I now had two serious blots on my record from the insubordination and stolen Jeep incidents in the Construction Agency. But my natural optimism won out, and I decided *what the hell, nothing ventured, nothing gained.* I sent in an application form, and much to my amazement, they scheduled me to be interviewed for the R&R liaison job on November 10, 1969, at the headquarters of the First Logistical Command.

"We're looking for officers who are articulate and educated," the interviewer said. "And also unmarried and *worldly*. The R&R officer is a prime target for bribery. Last year a travel agency successfully hired a gorgeous local girl to tempt our man in Tokyo. After the officer fell in love with her, he started pushing that agency's travel packets. I see you're single, a distinguished graduate of West Point, Army Ranger, master's degree from Stanford, and have done some lecturing. West Point Debate Team, public speaking class at Stanford. Now convince me I don't have to worry about you falling in love with some travel agency floozy."

He must have liked my answers, because five days later, the officer in charge of the liaison teams phoned.

"You've got the job," he said. "Which do you want—Hong Kong, Bangkok, or Tokyo? The other slots are taken. The Pentagon will automatically process your orders soon as you decide."

"Thank you," I said, and my thoughts flashed back to my first trip to Japan with Jon Steel several lifetimes before. "I'll take Tokyo!"

And this unique job would also keep Russ out of the war. I couldn't believe it. There was almost a glitch when the "automatic processing" was delayed because the fine imposed by my Jeep-stealing Article 15 had not yet cleared. Luckily for me, by the time they resubmitted the paperwork for the R&R assignment, my monthly deductions were finished, and everything went through smoothly. Whether the interviewing officer had learned of my Jeep-stealing conviction and took that as further evidence of my "worldliness" or had never learned about it at all, I have no idea. But here I was, with both a General Article 15 and one of the Army's most coveted assignments. Deficiency list and dean's list all over again.

Within days I held in my hand the orders approving my extension and appointing me as the new R&R liaison officer to Japan for one hundred days. I immediately mailed copies to Russ and filled in the Army request form for my forthcoming post-Vietnam assignment. Normally an officer who voluntarily extended his assignment in a war zone was given his choice of next duty stations. My order of preference was Germany, California, and the East Coast. In last place I listed the Midwest.

I began working through Kiyooka's classic *Japanese in Thirty Hours*, and in early January, just short of a year after my arrival in Vietnam in 1969, I hopped on a "Freedom Bird" Boeing 707 returning a planeload of GIs to the States, with refueling stops in Japan and Hawaii. As the wheels left the ground at Saigon, the passenger cabin erupted in a spontaneous and thunderous cheer. Combat-hardened men, who had not shed a tear in Vietnam, now wept openly as they left the death and insanity of Southeast Asia for *The World*. I sat silently with mixed feelings. Had I not volunteered to extend my Vietnam tour, I might now be returning to my own friends in California on that very same plane. On the other hand, keeping Russ out of Vietnam also turned into a cultural adventure for me.

At our refueling stop at Yokota Air Base, I was the only passenger who deplaned and walked out into the subfreezing night air. A small blue Air Force transport bus took me to the US Army base at nearby Camp Zama, and I stared out the frosty window at sights long not seen: flashing neon restaurant signs, red cars and yellow cars and blue cars, families of pedestrians carrying shopping bags as little children laughed and teased each other, a light dusting of snow on the rooftops, steam hissing from manhole covers in the streets. It all looked so *normal*. Larry, the handsome young lieutenant I was replacing, sat in the hard metal seat beside me and began my orientation. Compared to me in my rumpled combat fatigues, he looked like a glossy *GQ* ad, in tailored sport coat and turtleneck.

Larry explained that I was authorized to wear civilian clothes at all times, travel anywhere in the country by rental car or bullet train, and even carry a concealed weapon, which he advised against. My boss would be back in Saigon, and my only duty would be to meet incoming government planes every second day at 0200 hours and brief the passengers, usually soldiers, on crucial facts they needed to know to survive an unsupervised week on their own in Japan. I shuddered at the thought of those early morning hours, but it dawned on me that with this schedule I would have every day and every evening completely free to meet the people and explore this fascinating country.

"I've got the staff here believing the R&R liaison officer is a living legend," Larry said. "It won't be hard for you to maintain that, and it'll make your job a whole lot easier. The support group based here already thinks you're some kind of god to be spending part of your Vietnam tour wearing civilian clothes in Japan. The Japanese see you as the military diplomat representing all American GIs in Vietnam, so you must be one special honcho. I'll show you the ropes, and if you just keep cool, you can keep all the power I've built up for the job. The important thing is to look sharp and to give a good briefing."

The way Larry said *briefing* made it sound sacred. Everything else, he explained, was handled by the local R&R support staff: billeting, AWOL reports, ground transportation, currency exchange, and tour planning. The briefing was not as crucial at the other Southeast Asia R&R sites as it was here in Japan, he told me, since at those other locations the R&R troops stayed only in approved hotels and traveled only in preapproved tour groups. At the Honolulu R&R site, nearly all the soldiers met wives or sweethearts, and there were no language or culture barriers.

Japan was different. The soldiers who chose Tokyo for R&R were camera and stereo buffs, ski bums, and hell raisers. They could travel anywhere they wanted in Japan and stay in any hotel or brothel. Their only real requirement was to be back at the airfield seven days later. When they landed at Yokota Air Base, they knew nothing about Japanese law or customs or geography or language, so the orientation briefing was vital. If it was a good briefing, forty-five minutes after being herded into the lecture room in the middle of the night, these restless R&R troops would now know enough Japanese customs and basic law to survive for one week: where to find the best camera and stereo deals, how to exchange money, what to see at Expo '70, ski conditions at Nikko, VD rates and cost of prostitutes in Yokohama, current con artist scams, and where to get medical and legal aid. My job was to know this information like the back of my hand, keep it current, and pack it into a stimulating and informative briefing. What an assignment!

Larry helped me check in to my quarters and then took me to his favorite nightspot in Atami, the seaside city 60 miles southwest of Tokyo called the Japanese Riviera. He showed me around the resort city, jammed with topless clubs, sushi bars, noodle restaurants, and fancy cabarets, flashing his official bilingual business card to each bouncer and maître d'.

"First thing we do," he told me, "is get one of these cards made up for you. Soon as they find out you're the new liaison officer, you'll get anything you want. These people know that your signature alone can put any place in Japan off limits. Many of these bars and whorehouses would lose 90 percent of their business overnight if you blacklisted them, or would increase their business 500 percent if you gave them a good plug in the briefing. You can walk into any clip joint here in Atami or Yokohama and pick out any girl you want. Here in Japan, bribery is a respectable business practice. Just use your head. See this suit?"

Although he had been of great help, I was glad to see Larry finally leave. He and I did not see eye to eye on all the perks. With every day and evening free, and travel expenses paid by the US Army, I explored from Kyoto to Nikko, beachcombing at Atami, riding bullet trains past Mt. Fuji to Osaka, and exploring the spectacular Jinbocho bookstores that Jon Steel and I had briefly seen five years earlier in the university section of Tokyo. I survived the rush-hour hordes at Shinjuku station and attended the wedding of my West Point classmate George Cox to his Japanese bride Kiko at the Meiji Shrine. I feasted daily on *iku sashimi* and *take-maki* at sushi bars, sipped noodles in the Tsukij Fish Market at 4 a.m., and relaxed in *ryokans* and love hotels.

It helped that I had arrived with an active Japanese vocabulary of about 500 words and a rudimentary knowledge of the grammar. My ability to conjure up an appropriate phrase or question at an opportune time opened many doors and brought many smiles. Many additional doors were opened by the bilingual calling card describing my special status as Vietnam liaison officer and, later, by my rare civilian Japanese driver's license with address listed as "US embassy." I had managed to finagle that with help from a secretary in the US embassy in Tokyo, since, coincidentally, my father had known Ambassador Meyers when both were in Iran. I leased a red Toyopet sports car with right-hand drive and left-hand four-on-the-floor, and gathered background material for my briefings, using the liaison calling card and US embassy driver's license to obtain VIP treatment everywhere I went, from Expo '70 in Osaka to the cabarets of Yokohama.

The Japanese travel companies were showering me with perks, from lavish invitations to grand openings of hotels to special engagements of kabuki theater and $200-a-plate Kobe steak dinners. R&R visitors came prepared to blow six months' salary in one week in Japan, and the travel companies were determined to rake in as much of that as they could. If an agency could persuade me to mention their company's hotel packages or Expo excursions in my briefing, it would increase their profits tenfold. I did take them up on the dinners and cabarets, but unlike Larry, I drew the line at free ski trips and GQ suits and pearl necklaces, and I refused to include plugs in my briefing.

The gorgeous-woman bait, on the other hand, almost sprang the trap on me. I started dating a Japanese go-go dancer, only to find out much later that she was working for the owners of a big hotel chain, and her assignment was to get close to me in order to set up a genuine sting with the *next* R&R officer. I don't know if that strategy worked, but luckily I wasn't compromised.

* * *

One night I was polishing off a sashimi plate at the Camp Zama officers' club when a West Point classmate I knew from Ft. Devens stopped by my table to say hello. I asked if he saw any of the Devens crew often.

"Not much," he said. "Wellesley is still buzzing about your raid. Students even composed a ballad about it, something about a renegade soldier from Ft. Devens. Can you believe that? If they're that short on excitement, send a few to 'Nam. Reminds me, you know Wes Clark pretty well, don't you? He got shot up real bad last week in combat, and they medevac'd him here for surgery. Touch and go for a while. He's in the base hospital here at Zama, in intensive care."

The waiter caught my signal and immediately brought the check. I hadn't seen Wes since his Oxford years, when he and Gert got married. My thoughts drifted back to our days as plebe roommates, to solving problems in juice and physics labs in Thayer Hall, and our first debate trip to the West Coast, when, at my first glimpse of the Pacific Ocean, Wes roared with laughter as I ran screaming into the surf fully clothed. And now he had nearly lost his life in this damned war.

At the Camp Zama base hospital, the receptionist directed me to the convalescent ward for non-ambulatory patients. As I walked into the room, I saw long rows of heavily sedated young men, stretched out in beds perpendicular to the aisle, with feet and medical charts facing the walkway. Unlike the Long Binh hospital's Ward 16, disinfectant and bleach odors nearly washed out the smell of bedpans and infections, and fluorescent lights kept the room well lit. Occasional moans interrupted the solemn silence as I walked slowly past the charts, looking for Wes's name and peering at bandaged faces in the hopes of spotting those blazing dark eyes.

When I found Wes's chart, I glanced at the head of the bed and barely recognized the face staring sideways from the white pillow.

"Wes, it's me. It's Ted. I just found out you were here."

He turned his head slowly toward me, bandages on his arm, leg, head, and back, and a cast immobilizing his chest and right arm.

"Ted, is that really you?" he responded groggily. He asked what I was doing in Japan.

His eyes slowly cleared. I pulled up a chair, and we started talking, very slowly. An Army nurse stopped by and told me Wes was lucky to be alive. He had been hit by four rounds from an AK-47 machine gun while on point of his company's patrol, and if either of the two bullets that passed laterally through his back had been 2 inches forward, he would have returned to the States in an aluminum casket with a tag on his foot. Even an inch forward would have landed him behind the curtain in Ward 16. But Wes had survived the five days of heat and infection and trauma before they air freighted him here to Japan.

He grimaced in pain as he spoke.

"I was afraid I'd never see my newborn son, Wes Junior. You're the first familiar face I've seen since we got ambushed. Not many visitors here.

They've taken me off the critical list, but no guarantees on my ever being able to walk again without a limp. Will I be able to stay in the Army? Ever play catch with my son?"

Tears came to his eyes as he spoke of Gert and how he missed her.

"Look," I said. "This damned place is a downer. Tomorrow night I'm gonna smuggle you outta here for a few hours. Do you good."

"I can't leave this ward," he said. "See our robes? White. White robes mean non-ambulatory. No Privileges Walking, no Privileges Escorting, not even in a wheelchair. Confinement to quarters." He pointed to the hallway, where nurses assisted patients in wheelchairs and four-legged walkers. "Those guys in the blue robes can leave their ward. But not us."

"Just be ready for tomorrow night," I told him. "We are getting out of here. During the day, I'm sending up a couple girls during visiting hours, and at supper, I want you to skip the sedative. This place is the pits."

During normal visiting hours the next night, I made off with a collapsible metal wheelchair and two blue hospital robes and hid them in a broom closet. After lights out at 2300, I returned to the dark ward disguised as a patient, wearing one of the blue robes. I slowly helped Wes into the other blue robe and eased him into the wheelchair, down the elevator, and out into the cold January night. I pointed to our goal halfway down the street on the other side, the officers' club. Even the slight jarring from sidewalk cracks made him wince with pain, and two elderly passersby stopped to see how we would negotiate the high curb.

I set the brakes on the wheelchair, stooped to measure the base clearance and angle of the foot pedal with my hand, and then rolled the chair carefully to the edge of the drop-off. With a sudden jerk I then yanked the wheelchair over the curb with a big *bang*! The look on those people's faces made Wes roar with laughter, even as he screamed from the painful shock. Enough of that pampering in the hospital. This was the road to recovery, I told him, the Ranger version of tough love. After sloshing down cheap drinks in the officers' club bar for several hours and solving most of the problems of the universe, we returned to the hospital staggering drunk and found a note pinned to Wes's pillow. *Captain Clark, report to the Head Nurse immediately!* Nurse Ratched's Army counterpart had discovered our escape.

Rolling erratically down the dark corridor toward the nurses' station, we joked about Snoopy reporting to the head beagle. I wheeled him into her office, bumping over a tray of instruments. She stood stiffly, grim and impassive, waiting for an explanation. Reeking with whiskey, Wes managed to raise his heavily bandaged right arm into what was obviously a very painful salute.

"Captain Clark reporting to the Head Nurse as ordered, *sir*!" he said gruffly.

She stifled a smile and scolded us for misconduct. Mostly, she was just relieved he was back in her inventory. Two days later, Wes flew back to the States for a thirty-day convalescent leave, telling me the whole ward would miss the attractive visitors I had been sending to see him.

* * *

During those first four months of 1970, I absorbed and processed and distilled as much visitor information as I could, returning to Camp Zama every second night to deliver "the briefing" to a new horde of sightseers. I based my reports on firsthand experience, and I distributed handouts, with essentials of Japanese law, spelled out in Army and embassy pamphlets. The codified legal system used in Japan, I told them, is completely unlike our common law system. In Japan you are presumed guilty until proven innocent.

An acquaintance in Japan had been involved in a minor fender bender and appeared in court unprepared. The fine was thousands of dollars, much more than the damages. On the other hand, another friend was more knowledgeable of Japanese laws and arrived in court knowing she could not bring a lawyer. Under Japan's legal system, she was already considered guilty. At five miles an hour, the police report said, she had bumped a drunken bicyclist who was crossing the road illegally on a foggy night. The judge asked her how she had shown remorse for her crime. With teary eyes, my friend sobbed that she had taken flowers to the man twice in the hospital and groceries to his family three times. The judge let her off scot-free. She saved thousands of dollars with her familiarity with local law and the freshly chopped onions in her handkerchief. These legal tidbits, along with vivid descriptions of unheated Japanese prison cells and seven-year sentences for smoking pot, brought home my point. As I told each new influx of visitors, Japanese law is different and not something to fool with.

My briefing also covered recent confidence games. The grifters didn't even try to scam me, since within a week of my arrival, every bouncer and bartender in Yokohama and Tokyo recognized me on sight, thanks to the travel agencies' grapevine. But other visitors were constant prey, and each new creative fleecing made it into my next lecture. After two months, I thought my warnings covered about every conceivable sting.

"Gentlemen, you have to watch yourselves in these bars," I told them. "Under Japanese law, it is considered larceny for a person to leave a bar or restaurant without paying his whole bill, no matter how unreasonable the check may seem. When you walk into a bar, the first thing you should look for is a price list of drinks in English. If you don't see one, my advice to you is to get up and walk out immediately. If you do see an English price list and decide to stay, I advise you to pay for each drink as you order it, to preclude accumulation of any hidden expenses like $20 napkins or swizzle sticks. Now, suppose you had a couple of drinks and paid for them and found the rates reasonable, when this cute little B-girl sitting next to you asks you to buy her a drink. Well, if you let *her* order it, you may soon find that the stuff she is drinking did not happen to be on the English price list and may cost 50 bucks a shot. So make sure you order the drink yourself and that it is one whose price you are willing to pay."

I paused to let that sink in.

"Now let's say you've followed all my advice but missed some little detail and find that you're still faced with an outrageous bill. Don't get mad and walk out. The Japanese police will arrest you for robbing the owner of the bar for the bill you didn't pay. What should you do? Call the R&R headquarters here, the US Military Police, the US embassy, or the Japanese authorities. Those numbers are all listed, in both English and Japanese, on the small card we have just passed out for you to keep in your wallet. Just stay in the bar, and phone us for help."

That still didn't cover everything. One of the R&R soldiers came back early to sleep free in the barracks and eat in the mess hall the last three days of his precious week. He asked to talk to me.

"Sir," he told me, "I really got screwed at the Superman Bar in Yokohama. I thought I did everything you said, but somehow they hit me with a cover charge or something for about $80. I began to argue with the bartender, but he just threw my bill at me and screamed: 'Captain at Zama tell you if you leave bar in Japan and no pay, then you go to jail, hai? And captain say if bill not fair, call police, yes? Well, we have our phone taken out last week, so pay up and get out!"

For the most part, however, our operations ran very smoothly, and feedback was positive and congratulatory. I received the highest officer efficiency rating of my short military career, and that from a general. Time flew by, and soon my own replacement arrived, and the cycle continued. The Army kept these liaison assignments short to minimize corruption. A week later I caught one of these same R&R flights back to Vietnam, and the best temporary job of my life came to an end.

That R&R liaison assignment also turned out to be a preview of my future career as a globetrotting professor. I would be acquiring and disseminating knowledge my whole life, but rather than Japanese culture, it would be mathematics. No wonder I loved the job. My months in Japan had sped by all too quickly, and I once again found myself back in Bien Hoa, getting ready for my final days in Vietnam before returning home.

A handwritten letter was waiting for me with the word "Free" scrawled where the stamp usually goes. It now had a double meaning. The return address, an Army post office in Korea, immediately told me my plan to keep Russ out of the war had worked. His short letter described his job as tower guard at a remote nuclear missile base near the Demilitarized Zone and his enchantment with Korean culture. I thought, "Thank God this will be his memory of Asian society, and not the absurdities of Vietnam." Now I could concentrate on getting myself back to the States and eventually back to a normal life.

But I was not yet free of the military, and when I finally received my new orders, I was shocked. My next duty assignment was to the US Army Administration Center in St. Louis, to an absurd paper-pushing job. Yes, St. Louis! The Midwest! The very *last* choice on my post-Vietnam assignment preference list. I didn't know if this was some kind of retaliation against me or simply another bureaucratic blunder, but this was the final indignity, and a new plan began to take form.

The idea stemmed from many conversations with friends and classmates about whether I had a moral obligation to remain in the Army two more years. My long-haired California friends, of course, thought it immoral for me *not* to get out of the Army as soon as possible. But for balance, I also talked to Academy friends who were bent on lifetime Army careers and who, like everyone else in our West Point class of 1966, had committed to four years of service after graduation. I had spent two of those years at Stanford, half a year in Ranger and Ft. Devens, a year in Vietnam, and three months in Tokyo. With leave time and a few months in St. Louis, this added up to four years after graduation, and the crucial question was whether the two years in graduate school at Stanford had increased my service obligation. After all, even though at Stanford I had been a card-carrying, active-duty Army lieutenant, for all practical purposes I was a civilian university student. Normally, when the Army sends an officer to graduate school, that incurs an extra obligation at the rate of two years' service for each year at the university.

Now, four years later, I racked my brain for the exact promises we had made at graduation. I called Wes in Virginia, where he was slowly recovering from the AK-47 wounds. I told him of my frustrations with the Army, this absurd new assignment, and my yearning to return to mathematics. Did he remember our original agreements?

"You're right," Wes said. "You stood up, twice, and asked them, fair and square, what we would owe for graduate school. We all heard you. You were the only one who thought, or dared, to ask. Both times they told us, 'Don't worry about that now,' and other vague generalities. There certainly was no agreement to anything. You did Ranger, and a full stint in Vietnam. If they aren't smart enough to keep you and use your talents, then get out—go back to mathematics. There's no moral obligation for you to stay in the Army."

It occurred to me that the same line of reasoning might actually also be the basis for a legal argument. I reported to my new unit in St. Louis without taking the usual post-combat month's leave, catching my new superiors by surprise. They had not prepared duties for an early arrival, and that gave me time to study the old Army regulations in the archives, just as I had pored over cadet regulations to find a way to get out of confinements. Late one afternoon, I hit pay dirt. The regulation in effect when I went to Stanford in 1966 stated that if an officer is ordered to an assignment that will increase his military obligation, that must be explicitly stated in the orders, along with the length of the additional service requirement. I rushed to the personnel office and requested a copy of the orders sending me to Stanford. There was no mention of any extra obligation or any requirement for me to remain past my four-year commitment. I put together a letter of resignation with a copy of the old regulation and my orders and then prepared to wait. Cut-and-dried as such logic might seem to a civilian, I already had ample evidence that the Army brass easily and often ignored logical arguments.

Two weeks later, my GS-14 supervisor walked into my office and angrily threw a crumpled ball of white paper on my desk. A slight, frowning man, graying at the temples, he had retired as a major after twenty years in the Army and detested my attempt at early release. I carefully unfolded the crumpled paper. Special Orders Number 158, dated 14 August 1970 at Headquarters, Department of the Army, Washington, DC, accepting the resignation of my commission and release from the Army as of September 8. And at the bottom: "BY ORDER OF THE SECRETARY OF THE ARMY: W. C. WESTMORELAND, General, United States Army, Chief of Staff." The same general who had pinned on my first Stars at West Point! A new Freedom Bird, in the form of that rumpled paper, and constructed by me from logic alone, would now carry me back to a civilian life and mathematics, back to reason. My spirits soared, buoyed by the same tremendous relief and exhilaration I felt when the metal Army Freedom Bird carried me back from Vietnam.

That unprecedented early release from the Army came with a very short fuse. In two weeks I would have no boss, no duties, no job. Complete and utter freedom. For the past eight years, through West Point, Stanford, and Vietnam, army regulations had dictated every waking moment of my life, and now suddenly I had the great privilege and burden of mapping out my own future. Many of my West Point classmates had not returned from the war alive, and I vowed to make the most of this reincarnation.

My desire for mathematics and university life provided a clear focus, and I set myself the ambitious goal of obtaining a doctorate. I had never heard of any West Pointer with a PhD in theoretical mathematics, but I wanted to try my hand at creating new theorems, an experience I had only observed as a passive bystander in the master's program at Stanford. First I sat down to figure out my finances. My salary as an Army captain during my tour in Vietnam had been a little over $700 a month, including subsistence allowance and our $65-per-month combat pay. Since all our clothing, food, and housing was gratefully provided by Uncle Sam, I had easily managed to save nearly all my salary, which I earmarked for going back to graduate school, hoping to convert swords into mathematical plowshares. With the Combat Zone Tax Exclusion of $500 a month, after fifteen months my college nest egg was now around $10,000, which I figured would buy me at least a couple of years in grad school.

That early and completely unexpected September release from active duty came too late for applications for that academic year, but I went ahead and applied to Stanford and Berkeley to start graduate studies in September 1971. I really wanted to get back to the Bay Area, and these were both top-tier mathematics departments. Since my whole future was wide open at that point, I also thought about spending more time in Germany, after that great experience during my exchange at the German Military Academy. So I did some library research and mailed off an application to study at the Georg-August-Universität in Göttingen, renowned for its long tradition in mathematics dating back to Gauss. To complete my shotgun approach, I also applied for a Fulbright Scholarship to help fund the Göttingen plan.

Surprisingly, I got a very fast response from Germany, but their university bureaucracy rivaled that of the military. First, they needed an official report from my hometown police department, even though I had been away in the Army for eight years. I wrote to Lyons, and luckily one of my high school classmates was now on the police force, and he soon sent off the official good-conduct letter. Next, the admissions office in Göttingen demanded an original, or certified true copy, of my *high school diploma*, even though I already had a master's degree from Stanford, to which they made no reference and for which they required no proof. I dug up a Xerox copy of the high school diploma, made a Xerox of that, carefully wrote "Certified True Copy" in longhand across the face, signed it myself, affixed it with a homemade rubber stamp, and mailed it off.

Finished with the application process, I next turned my attention to finding a job for the intervening year. A one-year college teaching position seemed like the perfect ticket. It would provide a little income, force me to brush up on my current math skills, and let me see whether I liked college teaching. The job market for math teachers was almost nil, and it was already August, but I phoned a dozen colleges and junior colleges in St. Louis anyway. Every administrator I reached immediately told me there wasn't any chance of a position opening up. I left voicemails at others, with no success. Then one day the chairman of the Applied Mathematics and Computer Science Department (AMCS) at Washington University phoned me, asking if I was still looking for a lecturing position. "Did they really understand I wanted a teaching job starting that month?" I wondered. Yes, the chairman explained, but only for one year. His predecessor had resigned unexpectedly earlier that month, and over one long weekend had left for Rice University, taking with him several professors and even the department files. The AMCS department immediately needed temporary instructors while it began to rebuild after the shock, and the new acting head was scrambling. I interviewed with him, and the next morning Dr. Ball offered me a nine-month position as lecturer. I barely had time to out-process at the Army Administration Center before classes began.

My experiment to sample university life for a year from a professor's point of view was to exceed all my expectations. Except for the handful of hours actually spent in class each week, this new life was totally unstructured. I attended seminars in theoretical mathematics, psychology, and art history, played racquetball and tennis at the sports complex, and watched documentary films in the campus theater. I lectured a graduate course on random processes and volunteered to teach the upper division section of numerical analysis, a subject I had never even taken myself. That course was crucial for physicists and engineers, and after the recent exodus of my department's professors to Rice, there was no experienced instructor available. I figured teaching numerical analysis would be a real test for me, as well as a service to the students.

One day my brother George, who was still studying physics at Washington U, came to my office hours.

"Hey, T," he said. "My advisor said I need to take numerical analysis next semester. I see you're listed as the instructor. Any problem with that?"

I told him I had no idea and went to see the department chair about the possible conflict of interest.

"No, no," Dr. Ball said with a smile. "By all means, go ahead. The Bernoulli brothers started the same way." He laughed, referring to the famous eighteenth-century probabilists, Jakob and Johann. "In fact," he teased, "I think the *younger* one was the real superstar."

I loved teaching. An academic version of hand-to-gland in the Ranger Pits, it quickly honed my analytic skills, especially with the high caliber of students in the hard sciences at Wash U. And with my brother in class, I had instant and uninhibited feedback. Academic life was truly wonderful. My monthly lecturer salary, a little over $1,000, was not much more than what I had earned as an Army captain, but the quality of life could not possibly be matched. I felt more determined than ever to return to graduate school, to become qualified to make this my permanent career.

But as I did more research, I found out that writing a dissertation in theoretical mathematics could take anywhere from five to ten years, if I could make it at all after my long absence in the Army. Student loans were almost unheard of, and I once again sat down to figure out how to finance a doctoral degree. For income during graduate school, I could rely on $200 a month from the GI Bill, my Vietnam savings, and part-time tutoring jobs. But I knew that this was not enough, and I needed to save as much as possible during my one-year Wash U lectureship, since that would be my last full-salaried job for many years.

Ever since Ranger training, I had been quite content with very simple meals, so there was essentially no more wiggle room for economizing on food, but shelter was a different story. As an Army captain, I had used my Army housing allowance to rent a two-bedroom house in suburban Creve Coeur, close to the Army Administration Center job, a half hour's commute from my new job at Wash U. The house would have to go.

I placed a "situations wanted" ad in the *St. Louis Post-Dispatch*, saying that I was a teacher looking for a cottage or carriage house near the university and offering to make repairs in exchange for rent. A woman from an investment company telephoned and asked me to meet her the next morning to look at their house at 4000 Lindell Boulevard. "On Lindell?" I thought. "The broad, tree-lined 'Fifth Avenue of St. Louis,' near Forest Park and the universities?"

I arrived early and slowly circled the block of large Victorian homes, parking my yellow Beetle convertible in front of the three-story white brick house numbered 4000. I got out and walked around the house, and through its *30-car parking lot*, looking for a carriage house or servants' quarters. But there was no cottage, and the house itself was in excellent repair. How could she have misread my ad?

The woman arrived exactly on time, wearing a gray business suit and carrying a briefcase. She introduced herself politely and pointed out the new roof, and that the exterior paint was only a few years old. She then led me up the gray flagstone steps to the massive front door and unlocked it while explaining the new, two-tiered, high-tech burglar alarm system. The house was a fifteen-room labyrinth, with central air conditioning, oversized kitchen, immense back office on the first floor, wall-to-wall carpeting on the second floor, and a small set of rooms on the third floor.

"The rent is $15 a month," she said, and saw the look of disbelief on my face. "My company bought this property as an investment just for the land, and if it is unrented and vacant, then our insurance costs are huge. But if it's *rented out*, even at a pittance, that pays for itself. I just need a formal signed lease."

That was perfect for me, and within a week I had moved into the mansion. After several months there, locals called me the "Lindell Good Samaritan." Friends of friends of friends knew that if they needed a simple meal or a place to sleep, they should go to 4000 Lindell. I lived mainly on the second floor and could spread out a dozen transients in sleeping bags on the first floor, with overflow on the third. My freezer was stocked with hot dogs and bread, and if a hungry crowd arrived unexpectedly, I plugged in my Presto Hot Dogger and soon filled bellies with my own standard fare: Wonder Bread and electrocuted hot dogs. During one of those soup kitchen meals, I met a band boy from the local rock group Rush. When he saw the huge empty back room on the first floor, he asked if the band could practice there. They had a truckload of expensive equipment—amplifiers, speakers, drums—but no place to jam and no money to rent a practice hall.

My father as a junior US Navy officer, pictured here on leave with my mother and me in 1944. He was just about to ship out for the war in the Pacific and the invasion of Iwo Jima. My brother Russ was born nine months later.

My family moved often, and I started different schools in first, second, third, and seventh grades. This may have been the initial impetus for a life of globetrotting. [1]

My fifth-grade class at Seabrook Farms School in 1954. At one time, Mr. Seabrook had the largest irrigated truck farm in the world. He welcomed and hired displaced and refugee families from the Deep South and from World War II, including Japanese-Americans "on parole" from their internment camps and former German and Russian prisoners of war. My classmates and school friends had different accents and ethnic backgrounds, and some of them were much older, depending on their English skills. [2]

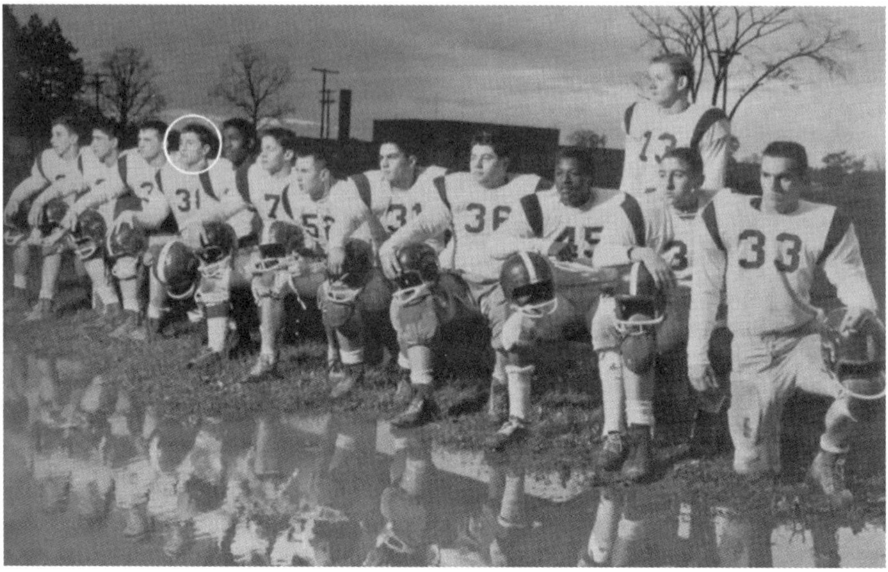

In the small village high school, 3 miles from our country home, I discovered for the first time the beauty of pure logic while proving Euclid's theorems; the thrill of contact sports playing first-string varsity football; and the allure of international academic exchanges through hosting Australian teenager Vince Bruce (right). [3]

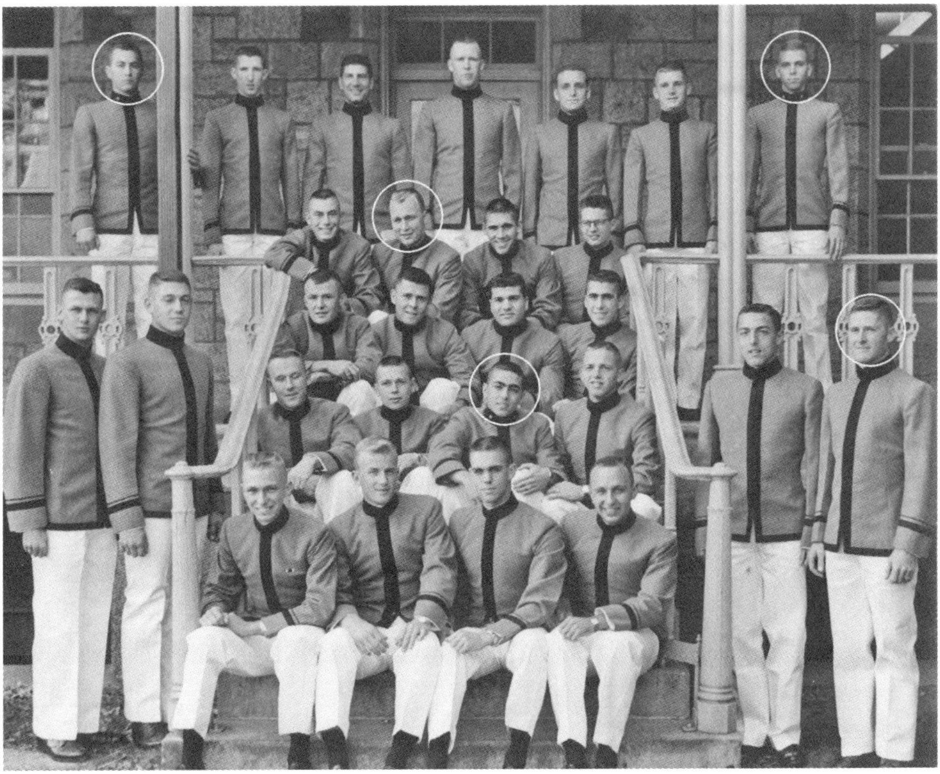

At the end of our West Point Plebe Year, the survivors of my Company E-2 gather outside our barracks in Central Area; (circled from left) me, my friend and future gold-panning comrade Gary Jackson, my roommate and future NATO Supreme Commander Wes Clark, my future Ranger Buddy and Stanford roommate Jon Steel, and my future scuba "instructor" and fellow Bahamas adventurer Chan McKearn. [4]

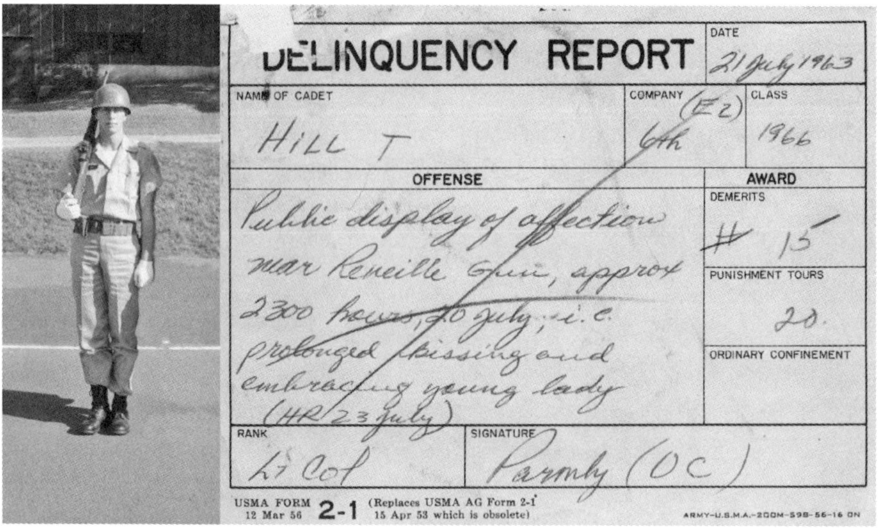

DELINQUENCY REPORT

DATE: 21 July 1963

NAME OF CADET: Hill T

COMPANY: 6th (E2)

CLASS: 1966

OFFENSE: Public display of affection near Reveille Gun, approx 2300 hours, 20 July; i.e. prolonged kissing and embracing young lady (HR 23 July)

AWARD

DEMERITS: 15

PUNISHMENT TOURS: 20.

ORDINARY CONFINEMENT

RANK: Lt Col

SIGNATURE: Parmly (OC)

USMA FORM 12 Mar 56 2-1 (Replaces USMA AG Form 2-1 15 Apr 53 which is obsolete)

ARMY-U.S.M.A.-200M-598-56-16 ON

Here I was walking a "punishment tour" at Camp Buckner during summer training in 1963. One single kiss cost me twenty such hours after I was caught with my date during a dance intermission by a zealous Officer in Charge. [5]

Practicing helicopter maneuvers in the Alps with West German High Mountain Pursuit Troops and German Military Academy *Kadetten*; (circled from left) me, my German counterpart Peter Hupfer, and my West Point classmate and new friend Al Lindseth. [6]

With the help of Chan McKearn, Jon Steel (right) and I bought this 1955 Mercury for $120, keeping it hidden in a shed in Highland Falls and using it for getaways from the Academy to New York City. The punishment for being caught with such an illegal car would have been four to six months of cadet confinement. [7]

The gold star on my collar was awarded for ranking in the top 5 percent of my West Point class academically, independent of demerits or other disciplinary problems, of which I had plenty. I used this graduation passport to go prospecting for real gold in Peru with Gary Jackson. [8]

Here Gary was using his camera auto-timer during our expedition to the Andes during Graduation Leave in the summer of 1966. Not shown is the .357 Magnum revolver that was in our pack, and not known to us at the time was the trouble we were about to have getting back to the United States. [9]

After the Peru trip, Gary went into the Army. I went to graduate school at Stanford, where I saw research-level mathematics for the first time, started motorcycling, and played A-Team varsity rugby. Here I was tackling Berkeley Rugger No. 28 in the 1968 Stanford-Berkeley big game. I would soon suffer a severe shoulder separation that cost me two operations to repair but did not keep me out of Army Ranger School or Vietnam. [10]

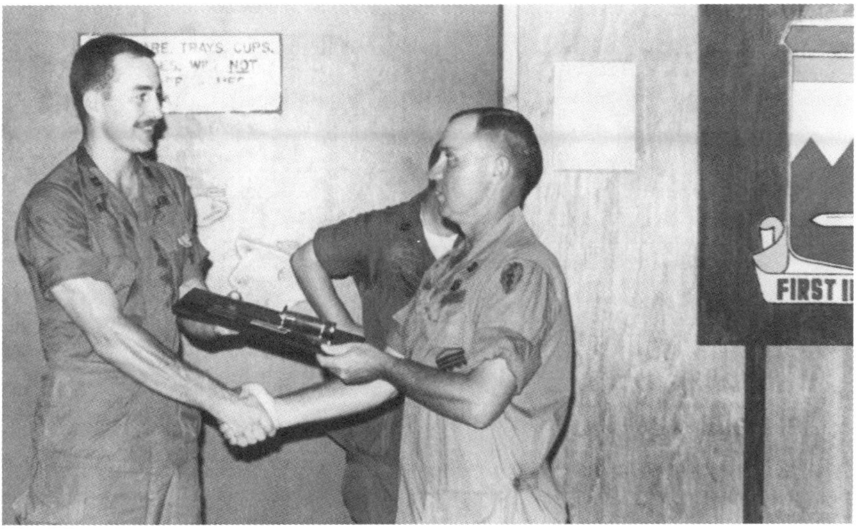

In June 1969, 65th Combat Engineer Battalion Commander Lieutenant Colonel Gibson presented me with an award in Cu Chi, Vietnam. The base camp for our 25th "Tropic Lightning" Infantry Division was later found to be infested with more than 200 kilometers (125 miles) of enemy tunnels. [11]

RECORD OF PROCEEDINGS UNDER ARTICLE 15, UCMJ
(AR 27-15)

This form will be used in ALL cases involving officers and warrant officers, and in those cases involving enlisted personnel when punishment OTHER THAN oral admonition or reprimand, restriction for 14 days or less, extra duties for 14 days or less, or a combination thereof is considered appropriate punishment.

NAME	SERVICE NUMBER/SSAN	BASIC PAY PER M	SEA OR FOREIGN DUTY PAY	TOTAL PAY
HILL, Theodore P.		$689.60	N/A	$689.60

ORGANIZATION	DATE OF BIRTH	GRADE	CONTRIBUTION TO QUARTERS ALLOWANCE (Class Q) (Para 131c (8) and (9) MCM, 1951)
520th Personnel Services Company, APO 96491	28 Dec 43	Captain	None

SECTION I - NOTIFICATION

1. It has been reported that, on or about 3 July 1969, at Bien Hoa Air Base, RVN while assigned to the USA Engineer Construction Agency, Vietnam, you did wrongfully appropriate a quarter-ton vehicle, USA Number 2R8972, the property of the 324th Aviation Support Detachment, Bien Hoa Air Base, RVN.

On September 24, 1969, I received a General Article 15 for "misappropriation" of a Jeep in Vietnam, a rare event for an Army captain, and one that could ruin his career. [12]

In February 1970, my hometown newspaper in the rural Finger Lakes region of New York announced my R&R Liason [sic] assignment to Tokyo. That 100-day duty to Camp Zama kept my brother Russ out of the Vietnam War. I was stationed near the Army hospital where I would soon see my friend Wes Clark after he was nearly killed in a Viet Cong ambush. [13]

Named Liason Officer

Capt. Ted Hill of Lyons, N.Y. has recently been named liason officer at the Rest and Recreation Center, Camp Zama, Japan. Ted, who graduated from Lyons Central School and is a 1966 West Point graduate, was awarded a Bronze Star during 1969, which he spent in Vietnam with the 25th Infantry Division

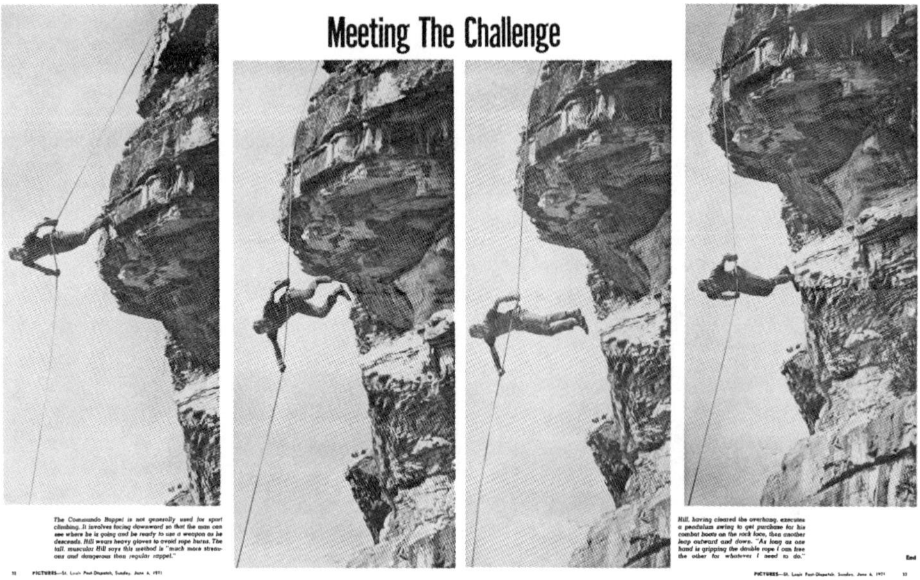

Meeting The Challenge

The Commando Rappel is not generally used for sport climbing. It involves facing downward so that the man can see where he is going and be ready to use a weapon as he descends. Hill wears heavy gloves to avoid rope burns. The tall, muscular Hill says this method is "much more strenuous and dangerous than regular rappel."

Hill, having cleared the overhang, executes a pendulum swing to get purchase for his combat boots on the rock face, then another leap outward and down. "As long as one hand is gripping the double rope I can free the other for whatever I need to do."

End

PICTURES—St. Louis Post-Dispatch, Sunday, June 6, 1971

Readjusting to civilian life after my early release from the Army, I let my hair grow. To help cope with the transition to academics, I continued some of my unusual Army physical activities, including facedown commando rappelling off the cliffs along the Mississippi. When editors from the *St. Louis Post-Dispatch* learned about it, they assigned a reporter and photographer, and on June 6, 1971, the paper published this article. [14]

The rock band Rush played at Forest Park Pavilion in St. Louis, a few blocks from the mansion I was renting on Lindell Boulevard. Rush regularly practiced and jammed in my backroom while I did math upstairs, amid a steady stream of transient visitors. [15]

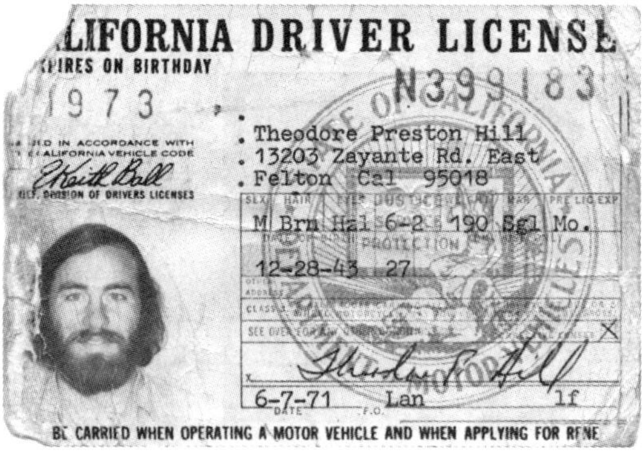

LIFORNIA DRIVER LICENSE
EXPIRES ON BIRTHDAY
1973
N399183
Theodore Preston Hill
13203 Zayante Rd. East
Felton Cal 95018
M Brn Hal 6-2 190 Sgl Mo.
12-28-43 27
6-7-71 Lan 1f
BE CARRIED WHEN OPERATING A MOTOR VEHICLE AND WHEN APPLYING FOR RENE

To help establish California residency for in-state tuition during my future PhD work at Berkeley, I made a quick road trip from St. Louis to Barstow, the closest city in California, to obtain this driver's license. I then returned to St. Louis to pack for a Fulbright year in Germany. [16]

Several days later I met the band—long-haired, tie-dyed, wild-eyed, acid rock musicians—and liked them immediately. Together we dragged in eight old mattresses and propped them up against the walls in the back room to absorb reverberations from Gene's huge trademark Marshall speakers. I gave them a key. The band's music was anti-authoritarian and loud. My favorite, "The Shit's Comin' Down," was well known in St. Louis, and some versions lasted over an hour. Rush and I had an excellent relationship. I worked on mathematics on the second floor while they jammed below. The real estate agent came by once after the electric bill increased tenfold, and I agreed to pay for it myself. As her unannounced inspection didn't happen to catch a whole crowd camping out, she left in peace.

I was sitting at my desk upstairs one afternoon, working on my math lectures, when the lead guitarist Ed Frillman came up after their practice session to thank me and to chat. The topic of conversation eventually drifted to the Army.

"I just can't believe you were a West Point captain!" he said, beaming with delight. "But I'll bet you had no idea the three of us have military backgrounds too!"

That seemed highly unlikely. Ed was tall and lean, with dirty shoulder-length blond hair, horn-rimmed glasses, and tattered Levis. Black-bearded, long-haired Gene Edlen, the lead vocalist, songwriter, and leader of the band, was the brains of the operation. And the drummer, in all the time I knew him, never uttered a complete sentence. He was a burnout in normal society, perhaps, but behind the drums he ruled. His rhythmic beat was wild, electric, spellbinding.

"He was even a paratrooper in Vietnam," Ed explained. "That's where he got into drugs. But Gene and I didn't make it that far. I was the only dude that ever went AWOL right from the induction center here in St. Louis. Man, I walked in the door, and before they had time to shake my hand, or take my fingerprints, or hand me a dog tag or anything, I just *knew* the Army wasn't for me. I shot right back out the door. When the MPs finally caught me several months later, they sent me where the paperwork said my first duty station was supposed to be, Fort Leonard Wood. I arrived at my first duty station strapped to a stretcher, with hair down to my chest on a bad acid trip. The captain there took one look at me and told me, 'Son, you don't want to be in the Army, do you?' and railroaded me out on an unsuitability rap. Cut my hair, and hassled me a lot, but let me out."

Ed continued, "Gene actually gave the Army a go, even made it through boot camp. But he couldn't hack the Army either, man, and kept going AWOL. They'd eventually catch him and put him in the stockade, but as soon as he got out, he'd go AWOL again. Then he came up with this crazy idea that there should be some easy, *legal* way to get out of the Army and started reading the regulations. He's a real smart guy and dug up this official Army regulation that says anyone with an *obscene tattoo* not covered by the uniform must be released from active duty."

That kind of spirit and jailhouse logic naturally appealed to me, and I pressed him for how it turned out.

"Well," Ed grinned, "we got real stoned one night, and he told me this idea of getting 'Fuck Off' tattooed on the knife edge of his hand so that when he saluted officers . . ." Ed demonstrated as I laughed out loud. "But I told him they'd just make him wear gloves. If he really was serious about getting out, I said, he'd have to get it tattooed on his *chin*. At first Gene didn't go for it, but then we got real fucked up and went down to South St. Louis. Had a helluva time convincing that old tattoo artist to do it, but he finally tattooed 'Fuck Off' on Gene's chin. Gene was AWOL three months that time, and when the MPs caught him at last and sent him to his unit, his new company commander almost choked when he saw Gene's long hair and beard. He ordered him to get a shave and a haircut and report to the bleachers, in uniform. A general was about to deliver a pep talk to the troops.

"Man, that old general was strutting up and down in front of the bleachers, like Patton, when he noticed Gene standing at extra-rigid attention up in the fifth row. He yelled up, 'Soldier, what is that on your chin?' So Gene answers, 'A tattoo, sir!' And the general says, 'A tattoo! . . . What does it say?' Then Gene bellows out as loud as he could, 'FUUUUCK OFF!' and the whole bleachers breaks out in cheers and catcalls. Man, that was it. The general called the MPs, and they ran his ass out of the Army in two weeks. That thing even made the papers."

Still laughing, we went downstairs to help Gene pack the speakers and extension cords. The saluting "Fuck Off" tattoo on his hand was still visible, but the chin tattoo was much fainter, thanks to a tattoo-eating, non-FDA-approved chemical he had smuggled in from Sweden.

I liked the trio and helped as a stagehand at their concerts in Forest Park and in Caveland, a huge limestone cavern in nearby rural Festus. Once I helped bail out their equipment, impounded by a truck rental company. Rush raised the last $100 by using my wall phone to make two hundred local calls in greater St. Louis to ask each acquaintance to bring one dollar to a mall clock tower at noon. It worked. I even acted as bodyguard on one of their drug deals, the only one at the rendezvous, I found out later, who was *not* carrying a gun. Basically good people, Rush often played concerts for free. Ed boasted that they even once had tidied up and played for the Annual St. Louis Policemen's Ball.

To balance the university intellectual life, I joined the St. Louis University rugby team and started motorcycling again, this time along the levees of the Mississippi on a brand-new Triumph 650 that an Air Force pilot friend stationed in England had shipped to me. Late into my first semester, I got a phone call from Chan, now stationed with an armor unit in Louisville. He was about to introduce me to another realm of physical adventure.

"Hey, TP," he said. "How's it hangin'? Wanna go scuba diving in the Keys and Bahamas during Christmas?"

"Sounds great, Chan. Never been diving before. Don't know how."

"Nothin' to it," he said. "I'll teach you. You made it through Mr. Sorge's Advanced Survival swimming class, and I figure since you didn't panic blindfolded in deep water wearing boots, a pack full of bricks, full combat gear, and a rifle, then a simple scuba outing'll be a breeze."

I borrowed my brother George's Ford 150 pickup, loaded my tent, sleeping bag, and Triumph 650 in the bed, and drove from St. Louis to Louisville the last Friday of final exams. In his garage, Chan and I added a Leer camper shell, his collapsible sailboat-canoe Folbot, and diving and camping gear. Also stationed in Louisville, Wes came by, took one look at our jumble of all-terrain gear, and laughed out loud in delight. Said he wished he could join us.

Our plan was to drive to Florida, then take the truck with all our gear to the Bahamas by ferry. We headed south on I-75, alternating driving and sleeping cramped but comfortable on the air mattress squeezed between the Triumph and the Folbot. We were in high spirits, but when we got to Ft. Pierce, we learned that shipping our loaded truck to Grand Bahama Island required approval of the British consulate. *And* a nonrefundable import duty cash payment of $1,500, about a month and a half of my salary. That was way beyond our budget, so we revised our plan. Instead of immediately taking the ferry to Freeport, we would drive to Key West and work our way back north to Miami, diving the various Keys. Then we would leave the truck, motorcycle, and canoe with Jon Steel's parents in Ft. Lauderdale and fly to the Bahamas, carrying only scuba and camping gear.

My first scuba experience was a textbook dive—from the "don't" page. I had no training, no air supply indicator on my tank, and no life vest, now called a buoyancy compensator, which hadn't been invented. To make things more interesting, an offshore storm brought moderately high seas and poor underwater visibility—only 6 to 8 feet of murky, liquid fog. I didn't realize it, but my regulator hose was leaking through a loose O-ring fitting, and halfway into the dive, I sucked desperately from an empty tank, flashing Chan the slash-throat, out-of-air signal he had taught me. My very first dive, and I was using emergency buddy breathing most divers never need in a lifetime of diving. Back on shore, Chan located the leak and tightened the hex nut. He then insisted on one more dive as soon as possible, realizing that the bad experience with equipment problems and poor visibility might otherwise sour me on diving forever.

At Key Largo, we rented a small outboard Boston Whaler to explore the reefs in John Pennekamp Coral Reef State Park. When we dropped into the water this time, a dream world suddenly appeared: black and white striped zebrafish; slender, long, gold-brown trumpetfish and royal purple wrasses darting between huge elkhorn coral heads; and sea fans waving in the gin-clear water. I had expected a world of silence, but the crunches of rainbow-banded parrotfish caught me by surprise as their beaks scraped algae tidbits from brain coral, and the raspy, baritone water rumbles of my air regulator marked my every breath. With a deep exhale, I sank noticeably toward the sand and coral beneath me, deep inhalations bringing me back up toward the surface. "This new world without gravity must be like a space walk," I thought, "but much more beautiful." There were octopi, crown-of-thorns seastars, queen conchs, and luminescent fish of every hue. It was magical.

Continuing north, Chan and I spent a day and a half canoeing and motorcycling in the Everglades, and on Christmas Eve we pulled the truck into the Miami YMCA for a shower. Only dim security lights shone in the cinder-block building, casting long shadows on the peeling paint, but the door to the main entrance was open, and two Goodwill-dressed men lounged on the steps. I walked up to one and asked if we could take a shower. From 4 feet away I could smell the MD 20/20 wine.

"Sorry," he said, "the YMCA Physical Department is closed for the next two days. It's a Christian holiday, you know." He explained that he was one of the live-in caretakers.

"Right," I answered. "Well, where can a *Christian* get a shower on *Christmas* Eve if it's not in the Young Men's *Christian* Association?"

He shrugged and said nothing. I asked if I could use the pay phone just inside the door, and he said I could if I made it quick. I found the number of Jon's parents on a crumpled bit of paper in my wallet and went inside to call them and ask about leaving the truck at their house. Back on the road five minutes later, I suddenly realized I had left the wallet in the phone booth. When we returned, the wallet was gone.

"I'm not leaving here until I get that wallet. Call the cops if you want," I growled to the caretakers.

"I'll help you look," volunteered one, and he immediately walked over to the vending machines near the phone booth, pausing only once to withdraw my wallet from the dispenser tray of a Marlboro machine.

At least it still contained my driver's license. Neither Chan nor I had any credit cards, which were uncommon luxuries in 1970 in our income bracket. Recovering my ID meant I could now still go to the Bahamas, but only Chan had cash.

We slept in the truck in a schoolyard that night and on Christmas morning caught a Mackey International flight the 68 miles to Grand Bahama Island, with only our camping and diving gear. Chan walked ahead of me in the immigration line at Freeport. A warning sign said *No Camping on Grand Bahama Island*. Yes, tourists were very welcome, but only tourists with money, it seemed—high-rolling gamblers and bonefish sport fishermen, not freeloaders or hippies.

"How much money do you have?" the immigration officer asked him, after checking Chan's return ticket and learning that we planned to spend ten days on the island.

"A hundred dollars," Chan said, looking in his wallet, realizing too late that amount would barely cover an ordinary tourist for about one day. "I'm with him," Chan said, and pointed to me.

The immigration officer looked relieved for a second, but when I told him that the hundred dollars was for *both* of us—that I had no money at all—he rang for his supervisor. That gave us a precious minute to think. Chan knew the name of an acquaintance in Freeport and gambled that his name was still in the phone book. Chan told the immigration supervisor we were invited to stay with a friend and gave his name and address. They checked the Grand Bahama Island White Pages, and luckily for us, it was listed. Both officers then cautioned us never again to come to their island broke. The only reason he allowed us to stay, the supervisor told us, was that the return flight had already departed—otherwise they would have shipped us back on the same plane. The airline agent in Ft. Lauderdale was supposed to have checked our finances before we left Florida, when they stamped our tickets "DOCS OK."

"Man, that was lucky," Chan whispered to me after we cleared customs. "That guy left the island last year. I was just hoping his name was still in the phone book."

Outside the tiny air terminal, where palm trees swayed in the Gulf Stream breeze and a line of beat-up taxis jostled for tourists, Chan and I regrouped. First on our priorities, far more important than lodging or food, was a vehicle to haul us and our heavy gear to dive sites at remote beaches and reefs. Across the street from the airport, two ramshackle rental booths advertised cars available. The cheapest deal, a Volkswagen beetle, required an $80 cash deposit for the week. Since banks were closed that whole week between Christmas and New Year's Day, there was no chance for us to get money wired. We had no other choice but to pay the cash deposit from our $100 stash and try to get creative about food. We would risk camping out in the bush and have to find some way to survive a week on our remaining $20, most of which we needed for air refills.

With the diving experience I now have, food is never a problem on Grand Bahama. We often give part of our catch to Mrs. Fountain at the Pepper Pot, who sometimes cooks it for us, or we trade it for steaming mounds of her delicious local staple, peas and rice. But on that first trip, neither of us knew where to find lobsters and triggerfish and conchs and octopi nor how to catch them and cook them if we did. Diving was our highest priority, not scrounging for food, so we bought two loaves of bread, stuffed our pockets with sugar packets from a fast food restaurant, and set up our tent in a clearing in the palmettos in the center of the island. We went to sleep hungry but reminded each other how much worse it had been in Beast Barracks and Ranger.

At first light we broke camp, ate a breakfast of sugar sandwiches, and went to a remote reef site for the morning dive. The coral and sea life were even more spectacular than at Pennecamp, and unlike the Keys, the reefs here were completely deserted. After a lunch of sugar sandwiches, we drove to a new site for the afternoon dive. The tremendous exercise and lack of protein left us exhausted, and after the second dive, we fell asleep on the beach for two hours under a cassowary pine.

When we woke, we felt lightheaded and knew we needed solid food. We drove the Beetle to one of the resorts, rinsed our gear at the outdoor freshwater beach showers, and then wandered from hotel bar to hotel bar to gulp down the free *hors d'oeuvres du jour.* A few bars boasted chicken wings and peanuts, but in most it was just popcorn and pretzels. If the bar was crowded, we simply mixed with the happy hour throng and ate the free snacks without ordering drinks. If the bar was quiet, we first found two hotel cocktail glasses where paying customers had left them in the restroom or the lobby telephone booth and added water from the men's room tap and ice cubes from the basement vending machines. Slowly nursing our "drinks," we would joke with the bartender and waiters and nibble our way through the small platters of bar tidbits. That got us over the low-blood-sugar dizziness, but we still needed something more substantial. I had an idea.

"Hey, Chan," I suggested. "When these rich tourists order meals up to their rooms, they usually put the dinner cart out in the hall when they're through. And they aren't all big eaters. Let's check it out."

For the whole holiday week, that became our meal routine. Sugar sandwiches for breakfast and lunch, bar hors d'oeuvres for late afternoon tea, and pilfered leftovers for the evening meal. The Princess Hotel, with two enormous turquoise cement-block wings, had eight floors with thirty rooms of gambling patrons on either side. Starting on the top floor, Chan and I would thread our way down, Chan checking one corridor and I the other. Wolfing down whatever we could on the spot, we then met at the end of the corridor to share any surplus. Forty years later, I can still smell and taste the delicious cold pork chop and half plate of spaghetti one of the Princess's guests left under a stainless-steel plate cover on a tray outside his room. So far, so good.

One night during one of our victual foraging rituals, I found two room-service trays in the hallway with leftover pasta. In my excitement to shovel a heaping spoonful of linguine into my mouth, I bumped one of the stainless-steel plate covers, sending it onto the cement floor with a loud clang. Noises came from inside the room, and I ran down the corridor to link up with Chan.

"There's a stack of trays down by 714," I reported. "There's some pasta in 'em, but I knocked over a lid and think someone in the room heard me."

Chan, who had not found much leftover food that night, said he was going back to take a look. Commando-style, he crept down the hall on bare feet, without making a sound. Just as he crouched in front of the door to examine the booty, the door opened and a woman screamed.

"Help! Peeping Tom! Call the police! Call the hotel detective! *Help*!"

The woman had probably heard my bumbling and put on a bathrobe to come to the door. By the time she opened it, there was the stealthy Chan, bent over exactly at keyhole height. Her shrieks echoed through the hallways as we sprinted for the fire escape, and we flew down the steps and out the door moments ahead of hotel security.

We sadly put the Princess off limits the second half of the week, continued our ration sorties at other hotels, and turned our attention to improving the main objective of our trip, namely, the diving. Up to now, without navigational charts or even decent land maps of the island, our dives had been hit or miss. We would swim out to sea on the surface, carrying our tanks but using just our snorkels, and then drop down to explore the reefs or sand bottom on scuba. When we surfaced, we faced a long kick back to shore, without life vests or other flotation devices. We hit upon the idea of bringing along a deflated air mattress, lashed to my weight belt, which we would reinflate when we surfaced and use to support us on the exhausting swim back to shore. The very first time we brought the air mattress, Chan suffered severe leg cramps during the dive, probably from our sugar-sandwich diet. Using the new jury-rigged lifebuoy, I managed to tow him to shore.

What we really needed was a boat. The day before our departure, combing the deserted stretch of shoreline east of Taino Beach, we came across a weather-beaten, heavy wooden boat about 12 feet long, partly filled with sand. It looked like it hadn't been used in years. The wood seemed solid though, and we figured it would probably float, at least for a while. Over the years, tropical storms had deposited bits and pieces of many wrecks on that beach, and we soon found a cement block for an anchor, a piece of fisherman's rope, and two boards we could use for paddling. Chan and I scraped the sand out of the boat, loaded our gear, and pushed out to sea. The craft leaked so badly that I had to bail full-time with my face mask while Chan paddled. Our plan was to reach the reef, drop anchor, bail the boat dry, and hope she was still afloat when we surfaced. If not, the swim for shore would be much farther than we had managed before.

We stayed down until we were out of air completely and surfaced to find the wood boat still there but filled with water. Chan and I leaned in, bailed with our face masks until it was half empty and we could slide over the gunwales, and then bailed feverishly to get set for the long haul back. The boat seemed to leak worse than before, and I spotted an open bail hole under one of the floorboards. Plugging it with a T-shirt cut the leak to a trickle, but a strong offshore wind and the outgoing tide were now taking us out to sea.

Our backs bent to the boards, we strained and pulled in silence. Half an hour later, the island looked even farther away. How long could we survive drifting in the Gulf Stream without food or water? Then the wind shifted slightly, and we began to make headway. An hour later, we finally dragged the boat ashore and dropped to our knees on the beach, completely shot.

At that moment, two Bahamians came running over the sand dunes toward us: an older man in tattered clothes and a giant, wearing a *tuxedo*.

"You're in big trouble, mon," the older man screamed. "Fucking big trouble. You think you just steal a boat here? Our laws are different here, *mon*! What you've done is you've committed *piracy*."

By sheer luck, our landfall was near where we had found the boat. The old man continued to rant, as we stood in shock and silence.

"I'm a fisherman and this boat is my only possession," he said. "You stole it. You'll have to pay big. *Piracy*! Don't let 'em move, Jake. I'll get the police."

The old man ran off, leaving the tuxedoed giant, a casino bouncer, to guard us. The boat rested at the water's edge 5 feet away and rocked back and forth from the surf's light waves. The bouncer told us we could pull the boat up farther onto the beach but could not go one step beyond. Tugging on the boat, Chan and I exchanged whispers. Should we make a dash for the sea, leaving our scuba gear behind? The authorities would certainly find our car and IDs. Should we sprint for the car? We were too exhausted and certainly too slow to outrun the giant. Then we heard voices and saw an angry gang of six or eight Bahamians storming toward us. I looked in vain for a police uniform, especially when I heard some of the angry words. It sounded like a lynch mob.

"Piracy . . . Stole the boat . . . I've been to the States, mon, and there a black man would be hanged for taking bread, mon, just because he was black!"

They approached us, then withdrew a short distance to discuss our fate. We cringed in fear, but then we heard arguing from within the huddle. Most of them wore ragged work clothes and dirty T-shirts, but one of them—a handsome middle-aged man in a clean, long-sleeved white shirt, pressed gray slacks, and polished black shoes—now stood a few paces apart from the throng, calmly facing them with his arms crossed. They shouted and shook their fists at him, stomping shabby shoes and bare feet in the sand and flailing their arms in the air. They yelled and waved toward the fishermen's shacks at the fringe of the dunes, and a few of their friends ran to join the heated debate. Then I heard one of the newcomers call the lone dissident *officer*. I raised my eyebrows silently to Chan and saw new hope on his face.

The shouting continued, but the off-duty policeman slowly quieted the mob. The boat had been returned cleaner than it left, he pointed out, with nothing damaged. These young men dared explore the underwater world most Bahamians never saw, ready to face sharks and barracudas local fishermen feared even in their boats. Gradually he won over everyone but the old man and finally forced him into shaking our hands. Then the officer pulled us aside.

"Technically speaking, you have committed piracy. If you ever need a boat here in the Bahamas, come to the police. If you need *anything*, come to the police. I have a boat you can use the whole weekend—all you have to do is supply petrol. But our sense of property rights is very strong here in the Bahamas. Much stronger than the States. Don't make that mistake again. Now I think this lot is cooled down, but I suggest you be on your way fast, mon, before they change their minds. Understand?"

The old man still fumed, and he smashed two air-hose fittings while the policeman turned to talk to the others. We scooped up our gear silently and dashed for the car. Our last day would be standard shore diving again, and when we returned the rental car just before our return flight, the refund from our cash deposit made us instantly rich. In Ft. Lauderdale, Chan and I downed plate after plate of Jon's mother's spaghetti but cut ourselves off when we still craved more, after reminding each other of the dangers of overeating on a shrunken stomach, as we had learned in Ranger School.

As we drove back to St. Louis, I again relished the thrill I feel after serious physical adventures—not only am I glad to be alive, but I also feel more drawn than ever to intellectual adventures and the dopamine rushes of mathematics. I couldn't wait to get my hands on some theorems, pencils, and paper. And, as I realized then, I didn't need to go to the Andes or Vietnam for these re-energizing Third World adventure trips—I could find them only 100 yards offshore on a deserted reef, on a sparsely populated sandbar 60 miles east of Florida. The trip made a deep impression on me, and Grand Bahama Island would lure me back dozens of times over the next four decades, to revel in its beauty and physical adventures, just when I needed it most. That first Bahamas trip with Chan was the perfect catalyst in my readjustment to civilian life.

* * *

Back in St. Louis, as I was preparing lectures for my Numerical Analysis class one night in the mansion on Lindell, my wall phone on the second floor rang. I recognized the voice of one of Russ's friends, who had recently finished his bachelor's degree in physics at nearby Webster College. Although I had met him many times, he had never phoned me before.

"Ted," he said. "I'm driving a cab in New York, waiting for a physics job to open up somewhere. Last night I picked up this fare, a woman, who was going to Bellevue Hospital, and we started talking. Something serious happened to your friend Gary Jackson. He was mugged in Central Park, beaten with a lead pipe, and left for dead."

I thanked him and hung up. "Jesus," I thought. "Would the trials of Job never end for that wonderful gentleman and scholar, my dear friend and fellow adventurer?" After Viet Cong rocket shrapnel had caused him brain damage in Vietnam, the Army evacuated him back to the States for medical examination and convalescent leave. When the blacking-out spells and partial paralysis continued, Walter Reed surgeons finally resorted to an exploratory brain operation and, after months of radiation treatments, released him from the Army and sent him home, telling his parents—but not him—that he had four months to live. He'd sensed something was not right and decided to live it up as much as he could. That's when he flew to New York to visit the girl in the cab, a girl I had introduced him to! He'd taken her to a concert in Central Park and, during an intermission, was on his way to get her coffee when he was attacked.

I waited until visiting hours the next morning and phoned the hospital. Gary was doing much better than could be expected. The doctors told me that if he had been hit once on the left side of the head, where the shrapnel injuries were, he'd have been killed instantly. After he regained consciousness, they transferred him to the military hospital at Wright-Patterson Air Force Base near Piqua, where he and I had started our Andes expedition.

The surgeons expected him to live, they said, but could not estimate the extent of permanent damage and were keeping him in the hospital. When they finally released him to his parents, I phoned Gary to tell him I was coming to Piqua, booked a flight, and, in a heavy snowfall, flew to Dayton and rented a car to drive to his parents' house.

When the door opened, I recognized only the voice and the clear blue eyes of the person who answered. An expensive wig sat slightly askew on a pale, stiff, homogeneous face that looked as lifeless as a car crash test dummy. The dimples were gone, as were the prominent strong jaw and high cheekbones. The Army plastic surgeons had done their best to rebuild his face after the beating and did remarkably well using old photographs. I couldn't see the scars, but I could hardly recognize him. His parents welcomed me with grief in their eyes.

Gary and I put on pac boots and heavy hunting jackets and walked along the river levee where we had canoed and speared snapping turtles in carefree summers long past. We crunched through the frozen snow banks in long silence before he stopped and spoke.

"I started back in graduate school at Purdue," he said. "Nuclear engineering. Just having a lot of trouble concentrating. But you know what the worst part has been for me, T? Not the pain, or the nausea and grogginess from medications. I can handle that. But it's *terrible* not being able to smile or cry. The injuries killed most of the nerves in my face. They're healing slowly now, but for months, I haven't been able to show any emotion at all. You cannot possibly imagine how awful that is."

We returned to his waiting parents, and I slept in his attic bedroom on a camping cot. The next day I flew back to St. Louis, blinking back tears. Gary phoned me a month later to tell me he had quit the nuclear engineering program and, motivated by his miraculous survival of all those near-death experiences, had begun seminary studies. He wanted to visit me in St. Louis, and we arranged a date.

On the way back from picking him up at the airport, Gary told me his dizzy spells had begun to recur, and when the doctors at Wright-Patterson looked at his thick medical file, they told him that the medicine he was taking would have killed a healthy man in six months. The surgeons who had performed the exploratory brain operation had been so convinced

Gary wouldn't live longer than four months that they had neglected to tell him to check back every few months.

Gary absolutely loved the Lindell mansion setup and called it "T's Good Samaritan Soup Kitchen." We talked for hours about graduate school and hunting and Vietnam, and the second night he broached the subject of my religious views. He knew I had been raised Presbyterian, but having met my father several times, he knew it was not by choice. What were my beliefs now, and could he convince me to accept Christ? After a long discussion, it became clear to him that it would not be easy to convince me of the superiority of any single religion. He cried and cried.

"How can I ever hope to be a minister, an evangelist," he said, "if I can't convince *you*—my dearest friend in the world?"

"You'll be a great minister," I told him. "You've seen the best and worst of life and beaten the odds again and again. Shot by a hitchhiker, shot by Viet Cong, mugged and left for dead by some New York slimeball. Even somehow survived that plate of green gruel in Peru! Who can doubt the power of your faith? You'll be an outstanding inspiration for people who are suffering or in trouble."

We finally changed the subject, and I breathed a sigh of relief. I knew he still had serious medical problems, but neither of us had any inkling that that would be the last time I would ever see him alive.

Late in the spring semester, I finally got responses about my graduate school applications. The first letter I opened was a flat letter of rejection from Stanford. That wasn't unexpected, since I didn't have any formal degrees in mathematics, but nevertheless it was disappointing. Then a week later, there was an envelope with German stamps on it, and to my delight, it was an unqualified acceptance from the University of Göttingen! And to top it off, Berkeley, then listed as the best mathematics department in the country, also accepted me in their math PhD program. It was admission as a walk-on—no tuition reduction, no financial aid, not even a chance to work for the meager wages of a teaching assistant, but at least they were giving me a chance to try! I was thrilled. Then came an official letter from the Fulbright Commission saying they were awarding me a full scholarship to study graduate mathematics for a year at the Technical University of Darmstadt. I phoned to thank them and asked them why my placement was Darmstadt instead of the more renowned math center at Göttingen.

"Because it would be too hard for us to get you into the graduate mathematics program at Göttingen," the Fulbright administrator said. "Maybe you're not aware of their reputation."

"I certainly am," I replied. "But I applied on my own and have already been accepted there."

The Fulbright office was amazed and delighted and immediately changed my appointment to Göttingen. Then I wrote the math graduate admissions office in Berkeley, explained that I had won a Fulbright to Göttingen, and asked for a year's delay in starting my walk-on status. They congratulated me and approved my request. *Hooah!*

The Applied Math PhD students at Wash U had just completed their grueling doctoral qualifying exams, and I decided to celebrate both their successes and my good news with a blowout party at the Lindell mansion. I told the grad students I needed help with the party lighting, and two math electronics whizzes and an electrical engineering student wired the whole first floor in hypnotic strobe lights, with two rooms in psychedelic ultraviolet. After dark we tested it. Just walking from room to room induced a respectable drug-like high, even without music and incense. "We set the strobes for brain wave frequencies," they explained with a grin. What did I know?

When Rush heard about the party, they insisted on being the house band. I distributed flyers and posters at Washington University, St. Louis University, Webster College, and Florissant Valley Community College. Then I called KSHE, the main St. Louis rock station, and arranged to have the party listed in their "Local Happenings" broadcasts. Next I phoned the St. Louis Police Department and told them there would be a loud party at my house at 4000 Lindell the next Saturday.

"*What?*" said the desk sergeant. "Let me make sure I got this straight. You're calling ahead of time to tell me about a loud party? Next week? Your *own party*?"

"It'll be noisy," I said. "The rock band Rush will be playing, and I expect several hundred people. I don't think it'll disturb anyone in the neighborhood, since this block is deserted after dark, but just letting you know.

Some people will be using marijuana and acid, I'm sure, but it shouldn't get out of hand, and I won't be supplying any drugs. You'll probably send some narcotics officers out anyway when you hear about it, so I'm just telling you in advance, so you can plan on it."

The desk sergeant assured me they wouldn't send any undercover cops but took my name, phone number, and address again anyway. "Who are you kidding?" I thought. "It will be a free Rush concert in a deserted inner-city mansion. Of course narcs will be there."

On the afternoon of the party, I helped the band remove the mattresses and set up a wooden stage in the huge back room, testing out the Marshall amplifiers, multicolored spotlights, and strobes. Then we set up incense burners throughout the house and went across the street to eat at Arby's. At nine o'clock, people were streaming toward the house from every direction. Carloads of college students came from Webster, Wash U, Florissant Valley, and St. Louis U, and street people were pouring in on foot. A motorcycle gang on choppers pulled into the rear parking lot, and unmarked police cars delivered the narcs. I propped open the front and rear doors of the house and stationed my brother George to block access to the stairs leading to the second floor, telling him nobody goes upstairs except in an emergency.

Rush cranked. The throngs flowed through strobe-lighted rooms, black-light halls, and clouds of marijuana smoke and incense, drawn toward the increasing din of Rush's acid rock music. Mounds of beer and wine bottles sprouted outside the front and back porches, and the audience screamed with delight as Gene led his band through its anti-establishment repertoire at a deafening pitch. Thunderous bass vibrations echoed off the vacant old Victorian homes next door, and strobe-light reflections bounced off the walls. Passing motorists stopped to join the revelry, partygoers walked across the street to use the pay phone to call friends, and the crowd swelled.

Three-hundred-pound "Tiny" from the motorcycle gang stood outside the first-floor toilet, good-naturedly charging people $1 to enter, and then *$5 to come out.* Even the narcs got into the spirit, ignoring the harmless lawbreakers and dancing, singing, and trying to pick up hippie chicks incognito. George let one band groupie on a bad acid trip upstairs to lie down, but for the rest, the celebration was controlled rock concert frenzy.

In through the front door, out through the back, tugging on wine bottles and sharing joints and swaying to the Rush vibes on the way through. Still thinking their cover was not blown, the narcs were the last to leave and even thanked me for the outstanding party.

When the academic year ended, I packed for my Fulbright year in Germany and took one last slow walk through the mansion, remembering the Rush practice sessions, the soup kitchen hot dog lines, the party, and countless visitors, known and unknown, sprawled out over the floor in sleeping bags and wool blankets in one room after another. A little creativity in solving my own housing needs had also provided shelter and refuge for many, many others. That simple idea would pay off a thousandfold over the next decades, for me and for scores of globetrotting mathematicians and graduate students who would find shelter at one of my unconventional hostels.

After Madison and Stanford, that year at Wash U was the third pivotal academic experience in my life. It reinforced a lifestyle that seemed perfect for me—a mixture of solitude and open hospitality, with minimal material possessions, and with the main focus on learning and passing on scientific insights to the next generation. I had also seen firsthand that year that a life in mathematics did not mean giving up physical adventures. For the first time, I saw how incredibly important unstructured time is for me, and as I prepared for the Fulbright experience, my mind was made up to set my sights on an academic career that could continue my mathematical carpet ride.

7

THE FULBRIGHT INTERLUDE

The ten-hour flight to Frankfurt, courtesy of my Fulbright award, was my first intercontinental civilian flight, and very relaxing, especially compared to those previous bare-bones MAC flights. And at the end of this flight would be a wonderful year of studying mathematics at the University of Göttingen, not some involuntary combat assignment. Yes, life was very good indeed, and my main concern for the year was that my conversational German needed a lot of work. I had always done well in languages—Latin, German, Russian, and a tiny bit of Japanese—but the majority of it had been written, not conversation.

My German grammar and vocabulary were fine, and I had studied literary German—*Faust* and even *Das Nibelungenlied* in archaic Middle German. But my speaking skills were practically nil, and I could barely order a restaurant meal smoothly. The Fulbright administration was aware of this common shortcoming for American students, so the award also included a two-month intensive course in conversational German the summer before university classes began, at a Goethe Language Institute in Germany.

After a three-day orientation at the Fulbright Kommission headquarters in Bad Godesberg, the chic diplomatic suburb of Bonn, they sent me to a Goethe Institute in the tiny pre-Roman riverbank village of Boppard, whose river dock sign proudly proclaimed that it was *Die Perle des Rheins*, the pearl of the Rhine. The students at the language institute were from all walks of life and ages, including a few pensioners, and most were developing or sharpening their language skills to work in German factory or service jobs. Although there were a few other Americans, the majority came from other parts of Europe and the Middle East, from Sweden to Spain and from France to Turkey and Italy. Our only common language was German, the Institute instructors spoke only German, and they lodged us in private homes scattered throughout the village. No two students with the same mother tongue shared the same *Hausfrau*. My own housemates were Gabriel, a career diplomat from Bucharest, and Pierre, a student from Paris.

Goethe Institute classes reminded me of those at West Point, with about a dozen students in a small classroom. The highly motivated and animated instructor's main goal was to get us all speaking German immediately. After an initial oral proficiency exam, they separated us into different groups, and they put me in a section of *Mittelstufe II*, top tier of the middle level, probably because my vocabulary had impressed the graders. Certainly my conversation had not. My class had one other American, Cynthia Rostankowski, a tall, slim, and somewhat formal woman from Milwaukee with waist-length auburn hair, a husky voice, and very good German. I learned *auf Deutsch* over morning coffee break that Cynthia was also a Fulbrighter and, coincidentally, was also headed to Göttingen for a year before starting in the philosophy PhD program at Stanford.

She told me there was also another American graduate student at Boppard headed for graduate work at Göttingen. Jonathan Knudsen was sharpening his German in the Oberstufe, the top tier of the Goethe Institute language courses, and we struck up a conversation one morning during the break. He was a bit pudgy, with shoulder-length sandy brown hair, sparkling blue eyes behind granny glasses, and an infectious impish grin.

"What's your field?" I asked him in German.

"History," he answered, with only a hint of an English accent. "I'm a PhD grad student at Berkeley. My thesis is on eighteenth-century German culture, and the Max-Planck-Institut für Geschichte at Göttingen is *the* place to go for my research."

"Hey, I'm headed to Berkeley next year too! You'll have to tell me about it some time. But what about Göttingen? Been there before?" I asked, continuing in German.

"Nope," he said. "But I studied a year at the University of Munich and have an idea what to expect. German universities are a hell of a lot different than ours."

I had figured that university life at Göttingen would be similar to my experiences at Madison, Stanford, and Washington University. Not like the special courses set up and staffed by American professors teaching in Europe during students' junior year abroad, but like normal university classes, except in German. His answer had surprised me, and I asked him to elaborate.

"Well," he said, "I'm from a working-class family in Detroit and had the standard American public high school education. Maybe even subpar, being that it was inner-city Detroit. After that, just another typical Michigan college student from a ho-hum high school. But here, even the word *Student* has a pompous ring to it. In fourth grade, the teachers single out the top fifth of all German pupils for admission to a *Gymnasium* or *Lyceum* for nine years. Super high schools, where they get intense doses of classical Latin and Greek, Euclid, and Herodotus. When and if they pass the *Abitur*, the single comprehensive final exam at the end of their studies, then they may apply to go to a university. From what I saw in Munich, I'd say those that finish their *Abitur* already have the equivalent of a bachelor's degree from a good American college the day they enter university. Those poor fourth graders who are superb in math or history, but not both, and all the late bloomers, never even get a chance to go to university."

"Then the bottom line is it's just like one of our top colleges, no?" I said.

"Not at all," he answered. "For one thing, there are no campuses. University departments are spread all over the city, in old buildings and new, with almost no green space. No student center, no intercollegiate teams, no school spirit. Nobody working his way through college or scraping by to pay tuition. All German universities are state institutions, with essentially no tuition. Not only that, but all German university students get nonrepayable government grants for living expenses, as well as discounts on food and public transportation. The result, of course, is that the student population in German universities is a boringly homogeneous and conceited lot."

"At least there will be some superb competition," I said.

"Yes and no," Jonathan said. "Sure, there will be extremely smart people in some classes, but they simply don't do homework exercises. After the nine years of intense studies at the *Gymnasium*, the tables are turned and there is no pressure at all at the university. Exactly the opposite from what we had. University exams for most courses are voluntary, and the official student transcript is a *Studienbuch*, a small brown book with the student's photo ID on the inside cover and the course entries filled in by the student himself! German students rarely ask questions in class and almost never challenge an instructor's logic. They spend more of their energy espousing radical left politics and drinking beer."

"I don't get it," I said. "The product is excellent. German university graduates are tops, across the board. At least that's what my colleagues at Wash U told me."

"Sure," he said patiently. "That's because the system only takes the cream of the crop, at an early age, and runs them through nine years of challenging elite secondary education. They work far harder in high school than we ever did, but after that, Easy Street at the university. You'll see."

Jonathan, Cynthia, and I agreed to keep in touch when we got to Göttingen but went our separate ways during the Boppard period. We all agreed it was better to mingle with new friends who were not native English speakers.

Boppard nestles on a stretch of the Rhine famous for its scenic hills and valleys, its castles and vineyards. When I left St. Louis, I had already planned to buy a Volkswagen camper to explore the backroads of Europe without needing lodging. I had planned to study at Göttingen on my own dime anyway, and now with the Fulbright, I could use part of that money to buy a secondhand car. The third weekend at the Goethe Institute, I caught the train to Frankfurt, hopped a bus to a VW dealership, and bought a used green Volkswagen Kombi. Since that particular camper van model was made only for export to the US, with running lights and other accessories not legal in Germany, no local person could own it, and I negotiated a very good price. On weekends, while my Parisian housemate joined his friends speaking French at riverside cafés, I invited Gabriel to join my excursions, trading transportation for the opportunity to learn from his superb German vocabulary and grammar, albeit delivered with a heavy Romanian accent.

After the two-month language course finished, I toured England, Scotland, and Ireland for three weeks in my camper, accompanied by a German woman friend I had met at a stage play during the Fulbright orientation at Bad Godesberg. She and I had an agreement to speak only German until we crossed the Channel, then we would switch to English. Hampered by my halting German, I thought that the conversational tables would turn at least for a short while. But as we crossed the invisible border, I was shocked to hear beautiful fluent BBC sentences coming out of her mouth. She actually spoke *English* better than I did.

When we returned to the Continent, I dropped her off in Bad Godesberg and drove to Göttingen. Renowned for its literary and scientific history, especially in physics and mathematics, Göttingen is the quintessential old European university city, with its sixteenth-century stone-and-timber *Marktplatz* and *Ratskeller* surrounded on three sides by a wide stone wall with a walking path on top, dating back to the twelfth century. I looked up Jonathan and met him for coffee in the city center.

"Isn't this city remarkable?" he said, beaming, continuing our agreement to speak German. "Just look at all the history and mathematics and literature around us. Even the street names say it all—*Gaußstraße, Goethe-Allee, Brüder-Grimm-Allee.* And the physicists—*Keplerstraße, Planckstraße*, you name it. Inspiring, at least for a historian."

"For me too," I said. "Glad it wasn't leveled like Berlin during the war. Guess because it had no ball bearing factories or other war industries."

"And," Jonathan smiled, "because some of the top Allied generals directing the war had been students here."

Jonathan had already been there two weeks and had found an apartment near the center. The Fulbright award also provided living expenses, and since there were no dorms, I sublet a room in a three-bedroom student apartment in the nearby hamlet of Nikolausberg. My new housemates took me out to celebrate, plying me with beer, pot, and, as they told me the next day, a good dose of LSD. It was my first acid trip, and although they had meant well, at 3 a.m. I was still wide awake and on a bad trip when they all fell asleep and left me to hallucinate. I lay there for hours, seeing alternating bursts of hideous demons and black caves. At dawn, still crashing between this world and hell every few heartbeats, I pulled on a light jacket and hiked for hours through the woods and hills until my head was clear and then found my way back to the apartment. After that experience, I decided to steer clear of the more serious hallucinogens, at least without an experienced guru guide.

When the semester began, there was no formal registration process. I simply chose my own courses from the posted departmental listings and entered them in my *Studienbuch*: Differential Geometry, Probability, two courses in Topology, and, just to keep the linguistic lobes in my brain active, a course in conversational Chinese. In the corridors of the seminar rooms in the Mathematics Institute were photographs and portraits of many of history's very best mathematicians who had taught there—Klein, Riemann, Hilbert, and Gauss—still inspiring young scholars. In the older lecture rooms, the professor wrote in chalk on a wide dark-green 10-foot-tall canvas that reminded me of an old-fashioned window shade, which was wrapped around wooden rollers at top and bottom. As he wrote, the instructor used a metal hand crank at the bottom to roll the front canvas upwards, bringing clean new writing space from below. When the first lines the lecturer had written appeared again, rising at the bottom, the lecturer erased them with a large damp sponge and continued alternating writing and rolling. It was an infinite blackboard!

After the first week of classes, I realized that Jonathan's description of university life was spot on. *Herr Professor Doktor* lectured stiffly to small groups of long-haired *Studenten* in blue jeans, who listened politely but almost never asked questions or did homework. One of the Topology courses was way over my head, and I struggled to follow the lectures, but I finally managed to do a few of the assigned homework problems that my classmates had not even tried. The class in Chinese, on the other hand, was another kettle of fish. Mandarin is tonal, like Vietnamese, and my limited experience with that language had already clearly demonstrated that my atonal shortcomings in music carried over to languages. But since the instruction was in German, I figured I'd be learning on both ends. I tried my best, and would have failed miserably in any American university, but in this *laissez-faire* German university system, I was just another face in the class, and Chinese was just another self-entry in my *Studienbuch*.

I remembered that in all my previous academic experiences, what worked well for me was to balance the intellectual challenges of mathematics with the rigors of a full-on contact sport. Göttingen had no university rugby team, but I learned that it did have a judo club, and I decided to join that. I thought my experience wrestling at the US Military Academy and hand-to-hand combat in the Ranger Pits might give me an edge, and indeed it did. The same emphasis on balance and surprise moves and go-for-the-jugular mental attitude transferred nicely to judo, and I took to the sport immediately. Since the university judo club only included *Studenten*, I also joined a city judo team where, by contrast, I could meet people from ordinary working-class families. Even their German was different.

Weekdays I usually studied in the university's superb math library, followed by supper at the university cafeteria *Mensa*, and then watched a spaghetti Western in which John Wayne spoke dubbed German without a trace of an accent. Weekends I traveled with the university or city judo clubs to local meets or explored the nearby Hartz Mountains in my camper. Göttingen was very close to the East German border, and on many of those excursions, I caught a glimpse of the barbed wire and minefields that separated East and West. I wondered what life on the "other side" was really like and daydreamed about trying to visit there and beyond, perhaps even to one of the world epicenters of mathematical probability at Moscow State University.

I had been drawn to probability theory at Stanford. Unlike most of the rest of mathematics, probability lends itself to colorful gambling and coin-tossing interpretations I could share with friends, and its many counterintuitive surprises often stump even the experts. But visiting Moscow was perhaps only a dream.

In the eight straight years of US Army propaganda films and war games, I had been fed nothing but anti-Communist accounts of the "enemy Russkies" and the evils of Soviet society. On my Hartz excursions, I could see in the distance where the Communist Bloc had split rural villages right down the middle with a desolate war zone no-man's-land. Thinking about what great contributions the Russians had made to the world's science, arts, literature, and mathematics, I knew there must certainly be another side to the story, and I hatched the idea to try to penetrate this Iron Curtain in my camper during our two-month semester break. Over beers one evening, I described my plan to Jonathan.

"Look," I said. "I know it looks impossible, but I'm *curious* what it's really like over there. We're only fed propaganda, same as them. I want to see for myself. And from a professional standpoint, Moscow State is still the epicenter of mathematical probability. Ever heard of Kolmogorov? In the 1930s, he was the first person to finally put probability on a formal axiomatic logical basis. The school he founded at Moscow University has become the world's mecca of mathematical probability. Many of the most important theorems in the field bear the grand master's name: the Kolmogorov Consistency Theorem, the Kolmogorov Three-Series Theorem, the Kolmogorov Zero-One Law, and the Kolmogorov Strong Law of Large Numbers. I want to at least try to see the place where all this happened."

"Sure, I've heard of Kolmogorov," he said. "I'm a *historian*! But are you totally daft? Aren't you following current politics? Last month was the worst spy scandal in English history. They evicted 105 Soviet agents! The whole East-West espionage community is still in chaos. And now a Communist-fighting Vietnam veteran who once had a Top Secret clearance wants to traipse on in? In February and March? Are you crazy? That weather even stopped Napoleon in his tracks."

I thanked Jonathan for his concern but started researching the idea in earnest anyway. I drafted a triangle-shaped route that went due east from Göttingen through East Germany and Poland, then turned northeast to Moscow, southwest all the way to Athens, and then back up through the Balkans to West Germany. All that on a shoestring budget. Although I heard rumors that it was theoretically possible to get permission to drive a private car into Russia, I could not find anyone who had even heard of such a trip. Moreover, I wanted to camp along the way, instead of staying at the expensive and rigid Intourist-approved hotels. I also wanted a travel companion to help with the driving and expenses and rounding up supplies. Since many borders have different requirements for different nationalities, it would be best if my companion held a US passport and was fluent in German so I could keep up my *Deutsch*. I put the word out among my university friends and at the International Center, and for a long time, there was no response. Potential companions were either German citizens or didn't have the time or money. Then Cynthia, the philosophy graduate student I had met at Boppard, came to see me.

"I'd like to join you," she said. "I've got the money, can drive a van, and am even taking a class in Polish because of my ancestry. That might help us getting through Poland. And I fully agree we should only speak German the whole two months."

I liked her spirit and personality. Everyone knew Cynthia was a devout Catholic, and that could pose problems along the way, especially in the anti-religious Communist Bloc. But she was smart and friendly and easy to get along with and, as far as I could tell, very well organized. I had her test drive the camper van, a challenge that intimidated most of my friends. But she drove with confidence, a little too much confidence, it later turned out.

"Any special requests?" I asked her.

"Just two," she said. "I'd like to rent a room once a week so I can wash my hair. And I'd like to visit a place of worship every week. It doesn't have to be a Catholic church, or even Christian, but I haven't missed a single Sunday mass since I was a little girl."

We shook hands on it and started making plans. Jonathan told me I was being unrealistically optimistic, but I mailed off a travel visa inquiry to the official travel agency Intourist, the *only* travel agency in the entire Soviet Union. No response, so I sent another letter. Finally they answered. Camping in the Soviet Union was explicitly forbidden, except for two months at one site near Odessa that was open only during the summer. I wrote back offering to park my camper in front of a police station every night. *Nyet*. I next offered to sleep *in jail* every night, figuring that would allow the authorities to keep a pretty good tab on my whereabouts. *Nyet*. I tried every cost-cutting idea I could think of, and Intourist finally told me we would have to book their two best single rooms in each hotel for the whole trip and pay for everything in advance. Take it or leave it. Everything also meant all meals, official Communist Party tour guides, and gasoline coupons. The gas coupons could only be used at a few authorized gas stations, which were sprinkled sparsely along approved routes. Once inside Russia, neither coupons nor gasoline could be purchased, so it was necessary to carefully calculate the expected total gasoline consumption in advance and add a good chunk for margin of error. "Good thing I know a little algebra," I thought.

The gas coupons, worthless outside Russia, could also not be redeemed again at the border for cash, and Intourist simply pocketed the hard currency equivalent of the overestimates. Any deviation from the approved schedule would be penalized with a heavy surcharge. For example, if for some reason a traveler had to spend three extra nights in Minsk and was scheduled to visit five Soviet cities after Minsk, the surcharge amounted to payment in full for each of the fifteen hotel night changes called for in the new itinerary. The Soviet authorities were clearly not encouraging this sort of trip.

The week before our Iron Curtain trip was to begin, Cold War relations worsened. In January 1972, US fighter-bombers escalated attacks into North Vietnam, and in February, Nixon was scheduled to make his historic first visit to Russia's ancient enemy, China. But amazingly, Moscow finally sent us permission to visit the Soviet Union in my van and returned our passports. Our official visas were loose documents slipped inside the passports, affixed with our photos and the required assortment of bureaucratic stamps and signatures. And the visas specified our exact required itinerary, right down to the precise stretch of road each calendar day.

We still needed visas to get us through Communist East Germany and Poland to reach our goal. With our official West German automobile and student documents, we didn't expect any problems getting through East Germany, but standard tourist visas for Poland normally took months to obtain. We heard that a three-day transit visa, which only permitted a sprint across Poland to the Russian border, was much easier. We applied for the Polish transit visas, hoping to convert them to full-fledged tourist visas once we were inside Poland. The immigration bureaucrats inside Eastern Bloc countries were said to be much more friendly and flexible than those on duty at or outside the border, whose staff had been carefully screened to eliminate potential defectors.

When the semester ended in mid-February, Cynthia and I packed the van, gassed up, and drove to the first border crossing. West Berlin was a political island, with the border circling it heavily guarded by East German troops. Barbed wire and minefields were on three sides, and the Berlin Wall on the fourth side separated the parts of the city under Soviet and Allied control. There was only one way to reach West Berlin from the rest of West Germany by land, and that was by passing through Checkpoint Alpha on the West German–East German border, driving through a 100-mile sealed autobahn Corridor, and exiting the Corridor into West Berlin through Checkpoint Bravo. Once inside West Berlin, the only land exits were to return back west through the Corridor or pass through the Wall into East Berlin via Checkpoint Charlie.

Our sprint through the Corridor was smooth, but crossing through Checkpoint Charlie with a private auto was not. We crossed on a bitterly cold, gray Friday afternoon, and the Communist border guards noted that our international *Zollnummer* license plates were valid in every country in Europe—in every country *except* East Germany, they said with a frown. If we wanted to proceed, we had to rent and affix temporary East German plates. My hands grew numb from the cold, screwing and unscrewing the metal rectangles. Then the East German chief customs inspector ordered us to unload the van completely and lug everything into the bleak border building. In we marched, trip after trip, carrying clothes, sleeping bags, blankets, tent, tent heater, benzene stove, pots and pans, first aid kits, car tools, snow chains, water and gasoline canisters, maps and books, fire extinguishers, backpacks, and suitcases.

As we emptied our pockets on the long counter and sorted through and explained everything, a guard drove the van to an adjacent garage. There a soldier-mechanic put it up on a ramp and probed every cubic centimeter, behind the dash, and inside the exhaust pipes, spare tire mounting, and upholstery. He inspected nooks and crannies in the camper I had no idea even existed. After the hour-long inspection, Cynthia and I each exchanged the required 5 West German marks at the official one-to-one "our mark is as good as theirs" rate for 5 East German marks. The highly illegal black market exchange rate then was about 8 East German marks for each West German mark.

We signed the necessary documents and drove through Checkpoint Charlie. With these temporary documents, we could now go anywhere in East Berlin we wanted for twenty-four hours but could not leave the city, so we drove directly to the Intourist office to try to get a transit visa for permission to cross East Germany to the Polish border. The Intourist agent started to tell us that a transit visa was almost impossible, but when we showed her our Soviet visa allowing us to cross into Russia with the car, she was clearly surprised and issued us the visa. But to continue on into East Germany proper, she explained, we had to first cross back temporarily into West Berlin and surrender our original twenty-four-hour visa at the border, and then return through Checkpoint Charlie the next day, using our new transit visa that would be stamped with Saturday's date.

Cynthia and I hatched a plan to simply leave East Berlin a few minutes before midnight, do a quick U-turn in full view of Checkpoint Charlie, and then return a few minutes after midnight. In the meantime, we would eat dinner and take in a movie. An unexpected surcharge for the movie tickets put the price slightly above our legally converted 10 East German marks, so I pulled out 10 West marks to make up the difference. The man behind me immediately thrust a 20 East mark bill into my hand with a wink and took the West mark note. I paid for the tickets with the 20 East mark note, got change in East marks, and forgot all about the 10 East marks I already had.

The film was *Sweet Charity*, a dubbed Shirley MacLaine film selected to depict the decadence of American capitalism. After it finished, we waited until just before midnight and then drove back to Checkpoint Charlie. The border guard listened as I explained that I would just turn around 20 feet inside West Berlin and cross back into East Berlin, neither stopping nor leaving his sight. I pointed past the gate, and my hand drew a U-turn diagram in the air. He looked skeptical—after all, he had no guarantee we would not disappear into West Berlin—and ordered us to bring all our gear inside again, the car up on the ramp. Who knew what goods we could be smuggling back? After changing the icy license plates once more, punch-drunk with cold and exhaustion, I emptied my pockets again on the long plywood counter. Immediately the guard zeroed in on the 16 East marks in my wallet.

"You exchanged only 10 marks here at the border, *Ja*?" he demanded in German. "Then where is your official receipt for changing the other 6 marks? The banks have been closed, so it was impossible for you to change money legally. This is very serious. It is proof that you have engaged in black market currency transactions."

He called in his supervisor, and that gave me a few minutes to think. The Gestapo-like boss glared at me and demanded to know how I had obtained the other Communist currency. I tried to look like a gullible tourist.

"We went out to dinner and when the waiter gave us the bill, I asked him whether we should pay in East or West marks," I said, "and the waiter told me West marks. He gave me change in East marks."

The two guards shook their heads and looked at each other, a look that said, in any language, "How could anybody be that stupid? No sense in putting an American village idiot behind good East German bars," they mumbled, and released us and our East German marks with a stern warning. We reloaded the van, crossed the border, and immediately made the U-turn. Since it was well after midnight, the entry date now matched our transit visa. Although the van remained in motion, and in sight as promised, the East German border police once again ordered all our gear inside, the car back on the ramp, and our pockets emptied. Again I fumbled with the rented license plates in the frozen slush, and when we finally got through, we immediately drove to a quiet street adjacent to a park and slept until dawn.

The next morning we headed east. Unlike the Berlin autobahn Corridor, that sealed-off stretch of highway between Checkpoint Alpha and Checkpoint Bravo, the autobahns inside East Germany led in many directions. To make sure motorists were on approved routes, at each highway interchange, uniformed soldiers with loaded automatic weapons inspected our documents. After spending one night inside East Germany in an approved inn in Leipzig, we finally left the German Democratic Republic to enter Poland. The grim German Communist border police at the Görlitz checkpoint reclaimed the rented license plates and, just after midnight, motioned us through the barriers.

Ready for a new gauntlet of Communist immigration officers, we were caught completely off guard by the Polish border police. Sloppily dressed and good-natured, they beamed with delight when they saw Cynthia's surname Rostankowski. They then joked about German superiority and stiffness. "*Bei uns ist alles besser*," they mocked, in Polish-accented German.

Everything is better in Germany. They told us we had no travel restrictions at all in Poland and could camp in the Volkswagen wherever we wanted. Westerners were forbidden to drive at night in East Germany and the Soviet Union, but not in Poland. Since our transit visa was valid for only three days, we decided to drive all night to reach the visa office in Warsaw early the next morning.

A half hour into Poland, on the nearly deserted frozen roads, we saw a sight we'd never seen in East Germany even during the day—a hitch-hiker! With long hair! Of course we stopped and picked up the young man, who spoke a little English, as he told us, since he was a rock musician. We reached his home in the countryside about 2 a.m., and he insisted we come in to meet his family. After he woke everyone up to meet these unusual voyagers who had helped him, they spread out a meal of black bread and pickled turkey, while he put on a Blood, Sweat & Tears tape.

We had not been on the road another thirty minutes when we picked up a second hitchhiker. This one spoke no English or German but also insisted, with waving arms, that we come in to meet his family. He woke his sister from her bed in the living room, and at 4 a.m. the whole family helped spread out another feast. Cynthia and I communicated through his mother, who had learned some German as a forced laborer in Auschwitz, and she told us she wanted us to stay with them several days. We explained that we needed to reach Warsaw as soon as possible to convert our transit visa into a longer-term visa. They seemed vaguely familiar with the problem and wished us luck.

When we reached the visa bureau in Warsaw later that morning, the only question the immigration clerk asked was, "How long do you want to stay? A few days, a few weeks, perhaps a few *months*?" What a difference from the East German Communist bureaucrats, and even their own Polish colleagues in East Berlin! Poland was like a breath of fresh air—we sipped coffee in the Old City in Krakow, feasted on $2, four-course goose dinners, bartered hard currency for gasoline in the countryside, and visited Chan's American fiancée, who was teaching in the English-language school for diplomats' children in Warsaw. Cynthia and I also would often go our separate ways, reconnecting over evening meals to recount our individual adventures and discoveries.

* * *

The Soviet border visa deadline came all too soon, and our entry visa was valid only for the morning of February 23 at the Brest checkpoint. After clearing the friendly Polish checkpoint, we drove under the border pole, and a three-man Soviet border team greeted us by name. We were the first English-speaking people to cross the border in months, said the captain, and all those came in Intourist buses. He was middle-aged, with a broad face and a Cossack fur cap, wearing a snug-fitting brown army uniform and high black leather boots. As he explained the border-crossing procedure in broken English, his thin black mustache twitched, and his dark eyes squinted from the glare of the snow.

First, he said, a soldier-mechanic would examine the van after Cynthia and I brought all our gear and luggage into the inspection station. That sounded familiar. Then a propaganda specialist began inspecting all our books and printed matter. We knew ahead of time that *Playboy* and *The New Republic* were forbidden capitalist propaganda, but this interrogator was an English specialist, and the assortment of German, Polish, and Chinese magazines and books in our luggage baffled him. Americans studying Polish and Chinese in Germany? Yes. He even questioned two long-forgotten German movie ticket stubs in my Levis jacket pocket. A capitalist lottery? No. My math books got the green light, but Cynthia's two volumes of Coplestoni's *History of Philosophy* were another matter. They could not decipher the complex sentences and would not risk that the books contained anti-socialist teachings. We waited hours for a new interpreter, who finally released the suspicious works.

In the meantime, the soldier-mechanic had inspected the van, parked it behind the border office, and reported back to the Cossack captain, who was supervising the inspection. The captain then took me outside, alone, and motioned me to get in the rear of the van. Climbing in behind me, the Cossack captain did a full body search—luckily it was too cold for a strip search—and fondled me for several long minutes. Swallowing my pride, I told him to just let me know when he finished, and I endured the affair in silence. My lack of reaction, negative or positive, apparently discouraged him, and soon he motioned me back to the office. Homosexuals have a terrible life behind the Iron Curtain, I had heard.

Back in his drab border office, the captain informed us that our universal international automobile insurance was not valid in the Soviet Union. We were required to purchase special Soviet insurance. There were two options, one covering only liability, and another, at twice the cost, a comprehensive policy that also covered collision. At the East German border, Cynthia and I had opted for the cheapest insurance, but for some reason, this time we flipped a coin, and we purchased full coverage for $35 cash, a small fortune in hard currency. That would turn out to be one lucky toss!

At last the border team released us, and we drove toward Minsk. It was sunny and cold, with 2-foot snowbanks lining the road, and the asphalt covered in places with ice. Even though this was the main east-west highway from Paris to Moscow, we saw almost no cars, and only a few trucks, and made good time. We kept to the letter of our travel visa requirement to be only on approved roads and to use those only on approved dates. The visa did not permit even stopping along the way, as we soon found out. On a Sunday morning, Cynthia wanted to attend her weekly church service, and outside a small village we could see a Russian Orthodox church less than 100 yards off our approved route. I pulled slowly onto a snow-covered side road, but before we had even started the short stretch to the church on foot, the village commissar was standing in front of the van, blocking our way. We could not stop on this road, he told us, but must stay precisely on the approved road from checkpoint to checkpoint. For this violation alone, he could already throw us in jail. But he let us go with a warning, and we got the point. An hour out of Moscow, I let Cynthia drive, while I climbed into the camper bunk and, pulling a sleeping bag over me, drifted off.

* * *

Slamming into the ceiling of the van woke me from a deep sleep. The camper finally came to rest right-side up in 2 feet of snow after doing a 360-degree roll over a 10-foot embankment. Gasoline fumes permeated the cabin, and Cynthia, trapped in the driver's seat, struggled with her seat belt like a fly in a spider's web.

"*Black ice*!" she said, partly in shock. "I hit a stretch of black ice. Can't undo my seat belt. No control—nothing I could do."

The windshield was destroyed, and I crawled over the jumble of camping gear and glass, pried open her seat belt release, and hauled us both out to safety. We heard voices. Up the snow-covered slope, three heads in thick fur caps peered down at us.

"*Vsyo v poryadke*?" one yelled. "*Nuzna pomoshch*?" Was I okay? Did I need help?

"*Da*," I answered. "*Da*!"

As my head began to clear, I realized that here we were, two Americans, hundreds of miles behind the Iron Curtain, somewhere between Smolensk and Moscow, during the height of the Cold War, in a broken-down hippie van.

But the truck drivers who witnessed the accident were friendly, curious about my long hair and broken Russian. They scrambled down the slope, watching for sparks or flames, and, together with their truck's front-mounted winch, a dozen of us wrestled the van slowly up the embankment onto the main road. The roof was partly caved in, and the workers helped me wedge the broken windshield into place temporarily, with gaps around the edges where the frame had buckled. The engine compartment looked intact, so I tried the ignition, rather than just abandoning the car. To my surprise, the Volkswagen started right up! Maybe we could make it to our next visa checkpoint in Moscow on time, but that would mean two hours of driving with the Siberian arctic winds whistling through the broken windshield. We decided to try anyway and piled on extra layers of clothes. As I drove, I kept from freezing by bouncing in my seat and fuming about the accident.

When we reported the accident in Moscow, the Intourist agent told us that our special insurance would cover every expense, but it was our responsibility to get the repairs done. We should get the crucial windshield replaced here in Moscow and, when we returned to West Germany, have the roof and other cosmetic repairs fixed at a VW dealership and send them the bill. But there were no Volkswagen dealers or spare parts in the entire Soviet Union! We first tried the American embassy, but they told us they couldn't help. Then, since we were both official West German residents, we caught a bus to the West German embassy and noticed two embassy Volkswagen vans parked outside, which gave us some hope. The embassy staff directed us to their Russian mechanic, who spoke passable German and, they told us, was often happy to moonlight. The mechanic told us his spare Volkswagen parts all came from Finland, which had normal trade relations with the Soviet Union, and he would try to order a replacement windshield. Once they air-freighted it to Moscow, he could make the repairs himself.

During the week waiting for the windshield to arrive, Cynthia and I enjoyed Moscow as much as we could in a city that was paranoid about KGB retaliation for fraternizing with foreigners. We took in a performance of *Swan Lake* at the Bolshoi, caught a show at the Moscow Circus, and wandered the subways to marvel at the magnificent architecture of the French-designed metro stations. While Cynthia went off to explore local churches and galleries, I had my own itinerary. The Red Army Museum did not appear on most tourist programs, but their doors were open to the public, and I am probably one of the few Western visitors who saw its gory Vietnam display, complete with the bullet-ridden and bloodstained uniform of an American Army sergeant.

I especially wanted to visit the mecca of theoretical probability, and I walked an hour through frozen streets to Moscow State University. The campus consisted of a single immense building with only one visible entrance. Just inside the towering entrance door, two rows of guards checked my ID and frowned *nyet*. One guard took pity on my blue face and shivering hands and let me warm my hands by their heater for five minutes before ushering me back out into the cold. As I walked out the door, I turned to glance back over my shoulder into the long wide corridor behind the guard desk, where scores of students were changing classes and exchanging books and new ideas in animated conversations, just like college students anywhere. Many years later, one of those very students was to become a coauthor of mine, and he and his family among my closest friends. But for now, armed Soviet guards separated me from those Muscovite university students.

Our Moscow visa expired on a Friday, and that same afternoon, the windshield finally arrived. The embassy officials were determined to get us out of their jurisdiction and had apparently pulled strings. By the time the mechanic and I rubber-hammered the windshield into place, it was pitch black, and Cynthia and I headed south from Moscow to our next approved stop in Orel. We were risking getting caught driving at night, which was illegal, but arriving on the wrong date was also a serious offense. Driving at night seemed the lesser of the two evils. With so few private cars on the Soviet highways, police cars were rare, and we were lucky. Even internal borders could be dangerous, we learned.

After Orel, our next approved stop was Kiev and then the post-card-scenic Black Sea resort and port city of Odessa, with its French architecture, mild weather, and noticeably warmer hospitality. A fellow Intourist hotel guest saw me checking in and invited me to his room to share a bottle of Moldavian wine. I had learned that Odessa had a reputation for openness, partly because of its history as a resort and seaport, and as home to many famous artists, scientists, and the wealthy merchants who built splendid palaces throughout the city, but this was completely unexpected. Such bold and friendly contact with a Westerner would have been risky in Smolensk or Moscow and had never happened to me before behind the Iron Curtain. I was curious. Over wine, my host slowly explained, in broken German and English and French, that he was a gynecologist from the republic of Moldavia, attending a conference in Odessa. He stressed that his motherland was not really a part of the Soviet Union, at least not voluntarily. He then invited me to a Russian war movie that evening, an action-packed epic of the battle of Stalingrad that clearly showed how the Russians won World War II single-handedly. I figured it was no more biased than our John Wayne war movies, and I enjoyed seeing this different slant. During the entire rest of the trip, no other Russians ever invited us to their apartments, or even to join them at a café table.

We exited the Soviet Union March 6, on schedule, at the tiny border outpost on the Danube delta in the Romanian village of Albita. The Soviet border officials confiscated our disposable visas, leaving no evidence of our visit in our passports. During the relatively informal Soviet exit inspection of our luggage and car, they ordered us to put our remaining rubles on the counter. Taking Russian currency across the border, even a single copper *kopeck*, was strictly forbidden, and neither the money nor our remaining gas coupons could be converted back into hard currency. But the Soviet border desk did include a small food counter, and the guard cut a thin slice of cheese worth exactly the value of our remaining pocket change. The cheese could leave the Soviet Union.

Romania, having just opened its borders to the capitalism of Pepsi-Cola, welcomed us with open arms. As our passports indicated, we had exited Poland several weeks earlier at the Soviet border and now mysteriously reappeared in Romania. But the Romanian border officials knew the drill and gave us a two-week visa on the spot, without restrictions. We drove at a leisurely pace, through the Germanic villages of Transylvania and the diplomatic sections of Bucharest, where we linked up with my Boppard friend Gabriel, who treated us to a traditional roast pork dinner at a family restaurant. After Romania, our van slogged through the muddy potholed main roads of hardline Bulgaria, a miniaturized version of Mother Russia, complete with repressive bureaucracy and even the Cyrillic alphabet. Bulgaria made us even more eager to begin the leg through Istanbul into Asia Minor.

On St. Patrick's Day, we turned back north en route to Greece, where the martial law of a right-wing military dictatorship had inspired the recent movie *Z*. Colonel Papadopoulos had just removed from power the other two junta colonels from the 1967 coup and assumed complete control of the country himself, explaining that "present-day Greece is like a patient in a plaster cast which will be removed only when the patient is politically cured."

A few miles before the Greek border, I picked up two pairs of hitchhikers headed for Athens. As we approached the border, I asked if any of the four riders was carrying any contraband like pot. I told them I had nothing against recreational use of hallucinogens but insisted that anyone with drugs cross the border separately. They all swore "no drugs," but when the Greek soldiers and military vehicles came into sight, I felt strangely apprehensive. After an interrogation in the Greek customs building, the senior inspector pulled me aside. A civilian about sixty years old, he had a pleasant smile and the patient, penetrating eyes of a guru.

"You are the driver, yes?" he asked, in good English.

I nodded.

"Well, you should know that that young man over there," he motioned subtly toward one of my passengers, "is carrying drugs. Not much, probably only a little hashish, but that is a very serious crime here in Greece. Serious for him, and serious for you, the driver. Many years in jail. I also know you know nothing about this, so I'm going to let you all pass. Be more careful in the future. The drugs are in your car."

I was shocked and started to ask him, in a stammer, how he knew.

"I just do," he said, and pointed to his piercing eyes. "It is my job. Now go, and enjoy Greece!"

I thanked him, and we again got underway. A mile down the road, I confronted the culprit, who turned white as a sheet. The inspector had not said a word to him. I ordered him out of my van with his dope, and he was still trembling as we drove away.

Inside Greece we saw few signs of the military juggernaut, and we camped freely at the base of Mt. Olympus and even inside Athens. After a week of relaxing on Crete, we headed north, around sealed-off Communist Albania, and into Yugoslavia, where we were forced to pass through the planet's last epidemic of smallpox. Already the disease had infected more than a hundred people and killed dozens. Roadblocks along the route slowed our progress while inspectors checked and rechecked our international immunization documents. One skeptical country doctor at the third roadblock, an *ad hoc* health hazard border of sorts, re-vaccinated me on the spot. We drove up the Dalmatian coast, through Trieste at the northeastern tip of Italy, then finally back to Göttingen. We arrived back on a sunny April afternoon, exhausted and grimy from the last long haul. I dropped Cynthia and her gear off at her apartment and headed back to my little rented room in Nikolausberg, where I immediately fell into a bone-deep sleep.

The next day, I went over to Jonathan's house to say hello and let him know we'd made it back, then checked the judo training schedule and fell back into the rhythm of my Göttingen life. Cynthia and I met from time to time to reminisce about our epic journey and remained close until the end of that year, when she went back to start her PhD at Stanford and to eventually get married and start a family in California.

* * *

In the spring semester, I entered the new courses I had selected in my official *Studienbuch*: Mathematical Statistics, Topological Groups, a Probability seminar, and Combinatorics, the study of patterns in finite sets. Our Combinatorics instructor was Professor Dr. Ulrich Krengel. He was a superstar, a mere six years older than I, who had already won a full professorship and was director of the Institute of Stochastics, one of the three subfields of mathematics at Göttingen. Professor Krengel invited our class to his home for a reception, a rare event in the usually stiff atmosphere of German academics. He was already famous for his research in ergodic theory, and a few years later, he would make another discovery that would lead him and me to collaborate and become lifelong friends, with many reciprocal visits. But for now, I was just another graduate student among many.

I continued with both judo teams, making trips to compete against city teams in the Hartz Mountains and in the West German Collegiate Championships in Berlin. Even though I was the lowest-ranked competitor by two colors, I had an effective and unusual foot-stopper technique, and I managed to place fourth in the heavyweight division. After evening judo practices, I had started frequenting an underground beer hangout, the *Junges Theater Keller*, mainly to feast on their delicious and cheap *Bockwurst*, which fit both my continually healthy appetite and my budget. After I returned to my apartment, I always hung my clothes outside to air out, recalling Jonathan's warning that "these German students smoke like chimneys."

At the *Keller* I became friends with the doorman, a left-wing Polish-German named Hans who brandished a beret and a Che Guevara button on his threadbare gray sport coat. Hans was one of the unlucky fourth graders who had not made the super high school cut. The school secretary told his mother that it was not because of his abilities—he had excelled in school—but that the head administrator said that Hans was too *nervous*. So he could not attend a German university; but Hans had persevered and was then studying at the *Pädagogische Hochschule*, the local teachers' college. He and I spent hours in heated debates about military service and university elitism and sex, and capped off our new friendship with a trip in my VW camper to the annual spring gypsy festival of drinking, flamenco dancing, horse racing, and religious ceremonies at Ste. Marie de la Mer on the southern coast of France. I visited my woman friend in Bad Godesberg, my West Point classmate and Bahamas partner Chan—now a captain stationed at the American Army base in Fulda—and my German Military Academy counterpart Peter Hupfer, stationed near Munich.

The carefree Fulbright year at Göttingen, with its *Freunde, Kultur, und Mathematik*, was coming rapidly to an end. Hans told me about a low-budget chartered EgyptAir flight that took German social workers and students to Nairobi, and that triggered the idea for one last adventure trip I wanted to make before returning to California for what I knew would be years of intense academics at Berkeley. During my outdoor boyhood adventures, I had always daydreamed about *real* wilderness—the jungles and savannas of Africa. Now that I had all that recent experience with crossing Communist borders, I reckoned I could easily handle less sophisticated crossings. What I was about to learn is that if you *really* want to know what it's like to travel, you should cross Third World borders *on foot*.

During the rest of the semester, I spent hours researching the needs of a backpacker-hitchhiker in East and Central Africa and turned up good potential campsites along a circular route from Mombasa to Malawi to Murchison Falls. I calculated rough road time distances and researched visa and currency requirements and common medical and health problems, including the dreaded freshwater bilharzia. I even learned a little Swahili. But somehow or other, once again I completely overlooked making a careful review of current political events in East and Central Africa, especially in Malawi, with its new president-for-life Dr. Banda, and in Uganda, with its "charismatic" new leader Idi Amin.

During past travels abroad, I had sent postcards to my brother Russ, and my latest card from Göttingen, describing my plan to visit Africa, was his last straw. His dissertation advisor at St. Louis University approved an unprecedented two months' leave in exchange for Russ drafting an urgent National Science Foundation research proposal. I promised Russ that the trip would be a walk in the park compared to my trip behind the Iron Curtain. I sketched out a tentative itinerary, beginning with the cheap EgyptAir charter flight, from Munich to Cairo to Nairobi.

Russ flew to Frankfurt, where I met him and drove him back to Göttingen to see the city for a few days, recover from jet lag, and help me organize our gear. The night before we boarded the train to Munich, a *Bundespost* messenger delivered a telegram from my father. At age twenty-nine, my dear friend Gary Jackson had died in his sleep. His father had tried to reach me and finally contacted my father. The funeral was already over—no further details. Russ put his arms around me, and I wept.

"Gary and I dreamed about this trip," I told Russ. "He'll be there with us in spirit."

At the Munich airport, we went through the heightened security checks that had been put in place for the upcoming 1972 Summer Olympics, soon to be the scene of the infamous massacre. Our refueling stop in Cairo was scheduled to be on the ground for only two hours, but immigration officers immediately confiscated our passports, issued us temporary IDs, and announced that the layover would instead be twenty-four hours. The main terminal swarmed with nervous Egyptian Army security troops armed with automatic weapons and manning makeshift sandbag bunkers and checkpoints throughout the corridors. Middle East tensions were always high, and we didn't know the cause of this one, but Egypt had severed diplomatic relations with the United States after the Six-Day War and had still not renormalized them. As American citizens, we felt especially vulnerable. But we were also exhausted after the long charter flight and soon fell asleep on the airport cots.

When I awoke, I asked the guards about our restrictions and was surprised to learn that our temporary IDs even permitted a short excursion to the pyramids at Giza. The next day, we reclaimed our passports and reboarded the plane, relieved to leave the insanity and perils of the Middle East. Africa would be serene by comparison, we assured each other, and I imagined an Eden where animals roamed freely and man lived in harmony with beast. There would be the occasional lion and bull elephant to contend with, perhaps, but at least wild beasts were predictable and killed only when hungry or threatened. An hour out of Nairobi, the cabin loudspeaker in the rattling old EgyptAir DC-10 crackled overhead.

"Ladies and gentlemen, this is your captain. I have just been notified that we will have to make an unscheduled stop at Entebbe Airport in Uganda. We do not expect any problems, and the government of General Idi Amin has given us its assurance the delay will be short."

When we landed, Entebbe was pitch dark, hot, and humid. Airline officials offered no explanation for the delay and led us to the concrete terminal building, under escort by a handful of heavily armed airport security troops in sloppy uniforms. The Jewish passengers on our flight were tense.

"Only last year," one told us, "Amin was a close ally of Golda Meir. Our Israeli military trained Uganda's police and even Amin himself. Meir sent captured Arab tanks from the Six-Day War as presents here to Kampala, and Amin owns one of our $3 million Israeli executive jet planes. But after a trip to Libya, Amin suddenly reversed his position and last spring ejected all Israelis from Uganda."

Russ and I listened but figured that Amin's year-old coup was simply another dime-a-dozen African changes of leadership. Much to the relief of our more politically savvy fellow passengers, we soon re-embarked on the EgyptAir flight for the hour-long flight to Nairobi International Airport, 15 kilometers (9.3 miles) east of Nairobi, and landed there in the late afternoon of June 26. From there Russ and I caught a lift to Central Park in downtown Nairobi, which our underground travel guide assured us was a convenient bivouac site. Right there in the center of Nairobi, lone tents and campfires lay scattered among a half-dozen Land Rovers and safari trucks, in the African equivalent of a circle of covered wagons. Dead tired, we pitched our tent under a *baobab* tree and fell asleep instantly.

After two days acclimating to the altitude, we laid out our gear on the ground and then managed to squeeze it all into our backpacks: flashlights; emergency food supplies of peanuts, raisins, and dry biscuits; a tent; sleeping bags; medical supplies, clothes, and cooking gear; plus compasses, maps, and a heavy-duty 5-liter yellow plastic jerry can of disinfected fresh water. Thus loaded, we started hitchhiking to our first destination, the tropical warmth of Kanamai, a small camp on the Indian Ocean coast, between Mombasa and the coral reefs of Malindi Marine National Park. Traffic was light, with almost no passenger cars, but truck traffic was moderate, and in two rides over six hours, we reached Kanamai just before sundown. After a week exploring Mombasa and skin diving the coral reefs in Malindi, we started thumbing south, toward Tanzania. Traffic was extremely sparse, mainly a few heavy trucks, with the occasional van or Land Rover. We accepted every lift, whether it was the roof of a loaded safari vehicle or the bed of a dilapidated cattle truck littered with manure. When the cattle truck hit cruising speed on the potholed road, the swirling wind vortices spinning off the cab pasted us from all sides with bits of flying dung.

"This just in," droned Russ in a deep monotone, mimicking the 6 o'clock news, "Today in East Africa, the shit hit the fan."

We crossed the Tanzanian border without incident and caught a lift to the next village. There a British expatriate in a Land Rover sized us up and then offered to exchange Tanzanian shillings for part of our dollars and pounds sterling, at extremely favorable black market rates. Socialist Tanzania, just like the Soviet Union, maintained rigid control over its currency, and it was illegal to enter or leave the country carrying Tanzanian banknotes. Our share of the transaction more than covered all our expenses in Tanzania, so when we arrived at the Zambian border a few days later, we still had a few shillings left over.

At midafternoon on a Monday, sweating heavily under our backpacks, we arrived on foot at the Tunduma outpost on the Zambian border. In the small wooden shack, two tall border guards in dirty khaki uniforms stood behind a rough wooden counter. Outside, a barren 50-meter strip of no-man's-land lay between the armed Tanzanian guards and their Zambian counterparts. Both countries' wooden red-and-white striped counterweight traffic poles were in the raised position.

Russ and I had rehearsed the border crossing several times, since a thorough check of our currency documents would have aroused suspicion of our black market money transactions.

There were no money-changing booths at the border, and, unlike the tiny kiosk inside the Russian-Romanian border outpost, where I had been permitted to spend my last kopeck on cheese, the Tanzanian border shack simply had a large glass candy store jar on the counter. There was no candy, just a jar with a few small coins and crumpled *Shilingi Tano* 5-shilling notes. The guards smirked and motioned that we should drop all our Tanzanian money into the jar.

Here we were, two young fellows traveling the world on a student budget, and maybe it was the heat, but the sight of this involuntary border guard tip jar somehow rubbed us the wrong way. There were still several hours before sunset, so we trudged back to the last Tanzanian settlement and spent our remaining shillings on a large sack of warm jelly donuts at an outdoor clay-oven bakery stall. With bulging bellies and powdered sugar and jelly dripping from our chins, we walked back to the border at 5:30. The guards watched glumly as we continued filling out the exit paperwork. They began asking questions. Were we brothers? Did we have the same father? They were checking, rechecking, and stalling for half an hour. Finally, just at the stroke of 6, they stamped our passports with a Tanzanian exit visa dated August 7, and let us pass.

We shouldered our packs and walked out the door as the Tanzanian guards looked at each other and grinned. Across the wide strip of no-man's-land, the Zambian red-and-white border pole barrier was dropping, and the Zambian guard called out to us.

"The border closes at 6 p.m.," he shouted. "Reopens tomorrow."

As we were turning back toward the border shack, the Tanzanian guards halted us with upraised palms.

"You may not reenter Tanzania without an entrance visa," they said, still smirking, and then a singsong sarcastic, "*Good-byeeee*."

We were now trapped between borders without water or a toilet. I told Russ we should carry our packs halfway between the two countries' border poles and start setting up camp as noisily as we could. The Tanzanian guards had no jurisdiction there, but a tent and campfire in the restricted border zone might well cause them considerable trouble with their superiors. When they saw us pounding our tent stakes into the hard clay, the Tanzanian guards called us to come back over the line to talk. Leaving Russ and the tent in the neutral zone as collateral, I negotiated with the guards and soon struck an agreement. We could cross a few meters back into Tanzania, off the record, and get drinking water from the outpost, in exchange for pitching our tent out of sight behind the border shack. The next morning we walked into Zambia at 9 o'clock, where the border guards stamped our passports with an August 8 entry visa. Officially, for that fifteen-hour stretch between the Tanzania exit and the Zambia entry stamps, we were neither in Tanzania, nor Zambia, nor anywhere else.

After three days trying to hitchhike in Zambia, we had not caught a single lift, and we decided to catch a public bus to Malawi. We had used them before and knew what to expect. The battered old heaps were always crammed—with people, pigs, and chickens, with their accompanying lice and fleas—and suitcases and straw baskets full of everything from fruit to firewood stacked in the aisles and roped on the roof. Each bus carried a driver, a bus mechanic with his metal toolbox, a ticket conductor, and the captain of the ship, a dignified older man Russ and I called the Superconductor, in an immaculate gray wool uniform. With delays and breakdowns, the buses covered about 100 miles from sunup to sundown, for about $1 US. We rode for twelve hours, packed into a crowded, scorching converted school bus, with knees crammed into the backs of the metal seats in front, jolting over the potholed road in a vehicle with broken shocks. At dusk the bus halted at government roadhouses that reminded me of Pony Express stations, where we passengers could rent a floor mat for the night, in a room of thirty hacking, scratching bodies, for the equivalent of 2 cents US. Then, just before dawn, the Superconductor made his rounds with his carved wooden walking stick, prodding us all back on the bus by first light. If a parcel fell from the roof while the bus was underway, its owner could choose between continuing on without his possessions or being dropped off and abandoned with them alongside the road.

Our Malawi-bound bus crossed the Zambia-Malawi border not just once but many times. The winding dirt road between Zambia and northern Malawi predated the modern straight-line boundary, and the road and our bus crossed the border again and again—into Malawi, then back into Zambia, back into Malawi, back into Zambia . . . Each time we left Zambia, Malawian border guards ordered all passengers out of the bus and into a shack for interrogation. The government of Malawi, that is, the self-proclaimed president-for-life Dr. Banda, a former physician who had not set foot in Malawi for forty years prior to taking office, feared infiltration of liberal revolutionaries from Zambia. The guards usually ignored Russ and me—the only two whites on the bus—but at the last crossing, a worried but friendly inspector gave me his own cap and implored me to hide my long hair constantly while in Malawi.

After exploring Livingston Falls and camping on the Zomba Plateau, we turned back toward our final objective, the game reserves of Uganda. Passing through Nairobi again, we camped another day in the City Park. Around the campfire that night, we heard rumors of trouble in Uganda with the "Asians." Descendants of the laborers from the Punjab and Gujarat districts in India, who had been brought in by the British at the turn of the twentieth century to build the Mombasa-Nairobi railroad, the Asians had prospered throughout East Africa. They now owned four out of five businesses.

Ninety-eight percent of the educated elite, including virtually every doctor, lawyer, teacher, businessman, and accountant, was Asian. The vast majority of native Africans in the cities and villages worked for this racial minority as domestic servants and store sweepers. Kenya had begun addressing the problem by gradually phasing black Africans back into mainstream jobs, and the Kenyan government announced future African-only job restrictions years in advance. An Asian postal worker in Kenya knew he had twelve years to find a new occupation. But as far as any of the other campers in Nairobi knew, the violence in Uganda had been exclusively intertribal, with no threats to the Asian community or the relatively few whites visiting or living there. Russ and I weighed the information, reread the descriptions of Uganda's incomparable wildlife, and decided to follow our original plan to head for Kampala and Murchison Falls.

We arrived at the Ugandan Malabar border outpost, where the Nairobi–Kampala highway A104 crossed the border, just before midnight on August 18. Inside the dimly lit wooden immigration shed, the customs officer looked confused and exhausted, as if he had slept in his dirty khaki uniform for a week. His hands trembled, and he kept peering out into the dark behind us, muttering something in broken English about some new required currency declaration documents, but then he quickly processed our visa paperwork and stamped our passports.

As we stepped out into the night on the Ugandan side and our eyes adjusted to the dark, we made out small groups of Asians and a few Africans in the shadows, speaking in hushed voices. As we joined one group, a tall, safari-jacketed Asian man was explaining that Idi Amin had issued a presidential decree that all Asians must leave Uganda within ninety days and could take with them only $100 each and a transistor radio. He told the press that they were economic saboteurs engaged in "smuggling, black marketeering, encouraging corruption, running monopolies, and currency frauds." He claimed that God led him to this decision in a dream, and when asked by a *Time* reporter if he had these dreams often, Amin had replied, “Only when it is necessary.” The decree was putting nearly the entire middle class and educated elite of Uganda into permanent exile.

The Malabar checkpoint where we crossed was only a few yards from the Nairobi–Kampala train tracks, and it also controlled rail traffic. The daily passenger train was stopped dead in its tracks, its engine shut down, and Indian families, mostly women and children, many of them wealthy third-generation citizens of Uganda, were being expelled from the train and herded into refugee collection points.

“We’ve passed the point of no return,” said Russ. “We’re already in Uganda. It’ll look fishy if we turn back now—we might as well go for it.”

We shouldered our packs and caught a ride into Kampala. Compared to Nairobi, Kampala’s streets were narrow and potholed, its buildings small and unsophisticated. We set up camp in the Kampala City Park, and when we awoke, the city around us was locked in a giant traffic jam. But it wasn’t the bottleneck in the streets that alarmed us—it was the pedestrians. Instead of Nairobi’s friendly and businesslike sidewalk traffic, the streets of Kampala were swarming with Asians and Africans in disheveled clothes, scurrying in every direction, lugging Oriental rugs, stereos, and heavy suitcases. When they spoke, it was in quick whispers, eyes full of fear and uncertainty. Truck drivers seemed uncertain whether to simply abandon their cargo, and the fruit and curry stands were deserted. Russ and I were still naive about the politics. Around the campfire, we talked with a young Brit.

“We know Amin was a heavyweight boxer and took over the country in a coup last year,” we said, “but it was bloodless, no?”

“Yes,” said our fellow camper. “It was bloodless—except for Uganda’s anti-coup General Hussein, whose severed head Amin kept in his icebox. And many say Amin practices ritualistic cannibalism. After he took office as president for life, he dissolved parliament, abolished political activity, and gave the army almost unlimited powers of arrest, search, and seizure. He even gave his troops retroactive immunity for anything done, or *not done*, to maintain public order or security. *Watch your backs!*”

That convinced Russ and me to get out of the city as quickly as possible and head to the game reserves at Murchison Falls. With Uganda’s commerce in a complete gridlock, the roads were almost deserted, and hitchhiking would be impossible. We carried our packs to the Rhino Safari Company, another Asian business, and rented a battered Isuzu sedan for the jaunt up to Murchison. When they learned we didn't have any currency declaration forms, the rental agents told us that could mean serious trouble with the authorities, and they urged us to go directly to the Bank of Uganda to get it straightened out.

When we left the safari office, the tension on the streets was still mounting. At the Bank of Uganda, when we reported that we hadn't been given currency declaration forms at the border, the clerk froze and called his supervisor. A bank officer appeared immediately, with a security guard in tow, and the two of them escorted us to an office on the second floor with more bank officers. The currency declaration form, they told us, was an irreplaceable document—unlike a passport, whose numbers are recorded several different places and which can be reissued after verifying other basic records like birth certificates. On the other hand, it is impossible to confirm the amount of money carried into a country after the fact. The currency declaration form provided the only real proof a traveler had not engaged in black market currency transactions. The bank officers were growing impatient. Perhaps they should let immigration officers handle this, one said. Then the one rechecking our passports noticed Russ's birthplace was Wisconsin.

"I was a student at Madison," she said with a smile.

"So was I!" I answered, and tried to think of some way to prove it. "Remember Lake Mendota in the fall? The leaves, the water, the clear skies?"

She beamed, told us how much she missed the university, and took us to an office where she convinced an administrator to issue us currency declaration forms.

"Don't lose them," she warned. "There are no replacements. You were extremely lucky this time."

Just before leaving Kampala, I bought a copy of the national newspaper, with 3-inch headlines that read "*ALL ASIANS MUST GO*," to take back to Wes Clark, who was teaching political philosophy at West Point. An hour before sunset, on a rutted dirt track far north of Kampala, the road was blocked with a rough wooden pole—the bush equivalent of the official red-and-white border poles. Our map showed us to be about 10 miles from a small ferry across the Blue Nile, and as we were studying it, a bushman appeared from one of the half dozen mud-and-wattle thatched huts in the small clearing next to the road. In poor but perfectly understandable English, he told us he was the local official, responsible for overseeing traffic on this road. Pole down, as it was now, meant there wasn't enough time to catch the last ferry, so no vehicle could proceed past this point until the next day. A backroad near the Nile was no place to be stranded after dark, he explained, and offered to let us set up our tent next to his village.

After pitching camp, I needed to relieve myself. Passing water is never a problem, but solid wastes accumulate over time, and I realized that squatting in the bushes could not be a village's long-term solution to sewage disposal. As I watched the village activity, I noticed that people from all the huts were occasionally visiting the same tiny adobe hut. After someone came out, I poked my head in. Just as I hoped, it was the village outhouse.

The hut, made of solid, sun-baked adobe, with a thatched roof, had no door at all, and in the cement-like clay floor, a hole the size and shape of a football. I dropped my pants and carefully straddled the opening, imagining the concoction of exotic parasites and microbes below. "What would Russ, the PhD microbiologist, make of it?" I thought, smiling. Back at the tent I told Russ about the outhouse, and he went to use it. A few minutes later, he emerged from the hut with a stricken look on his face.

"Get the flashlight," he said.

In an instant, I knew what had happened. Before the trip, Russ had ordered a custom-made heavy leather wallet, large enough to hold both our passports and other travel documents. Its thick rawhide belt loop attached to his sturdy leather belt, and once it was buckled in place, wild horses couldn't separate him from that wallet. Ah, but the Great African Bush Crapper could. Squatting over the hole, with his pants down, he saw the wallet suddenly slip off his open belt and disappear into the void below. All the critical papers—our passports, our currency declaration forms—had plummeted down the shithole.

The flashlight showed us to be worse off than we'd expected. The hole, 8 to 10 feet deep, had been built to last generations, and as the wallet fell, it had spun open, flinging passports and IDs left and right. We could see them in the flashlight beam below, embedded in the worst mass of pathogens a microbiologist could imagine. Russ and I stepped outside for fresh air. With a good pickax, we could break open the adobe floor, but we probably didn't have enough money to pay for a new outhouse, and besides, maybe the village elders would prefer us to rebuild it ourselves. And we couldn't walk away. The US embassy in Kampala could replace our passports, but not the currency declaration forms. And without those, we could be thrown in prison at the border, or worse yet, simply disappear in the swirling muddy Nile.

One of the villagers noticed us walking in and out of the outhouse, and came to see what the problem was. We showed him. Then he called his friends, and when they all stopped laughing, one came up with a solution. We would break open the thatched roof, instead of the floor, and use a fishhook attached firmly to the end of a long fishing pole to snag our papers. The roof would be easy to repair.

Our first attempts pushed the papers farther into the filth, but, one by one, we retrieved all the important documents. Once we had them out on the ground, I handled them using two twigs as chopsticks and spread the documents out on the back dash of the car to bake in the equatorial sun. That night our tent started shaking violently, and we awoke to a thunderous snorting and foul breath. A small herd of Cape buffalo was lumbering through the campsite, uprooting our tent stakes and nearly trampling us. We only dozed, half awake, until dawn, thrashing in the confines of the collapsed tent. What a night. After two afternoons in the sun, the hardened wastes on our passports scraped off easily with my Swiss Army knife, but Russ still wouldn't touch them for several more days. He didn't fancy becoming Plate 27 in the tropical parasite section of the next edition of the *Microbiology Handbook*. He might make it yet—our old passports still have those brown stains.

But the next few days more than made up for all those slight inconveniences. The Murchison wilderness was nearly deserted, and as we explored the refuge in the Isuzu, we came across lions mating in the track and outran a rhino we had unwittingly spooked in the elephant grass. Sitting under a flame tree, on a knoll surrounded by lush rainy-season-green grasslands, Russ and I gazed out over the hills around us, dotted, as far as the eye could see, with herds of wild elephants. We started counting and estimated there were more than a thousand wild elephants in view at that one instant, far more than we saw in the Kenyan and Tanzanian wilderness areas, and far more than have ever been seen in Uganda since. After Amin's Asian purge decree and the resulting complete collapse of the economy, desperate ivory poachers and hungry villagers would soon decimate the herds.

On the dirt tracks we had several minor breakdowns, but each time Russ managed to jury-rig the Isuzu enough to continue. During one monsoon rain, the key broke off in the door lock as we tried to unlock the car. We jimmied open the window, and he hot-wired the ignition for the rest of the trip. Our plan was to pass through the chaos in Kampala as quickly as possible, return the Isuzu, and leave Uganda immediately.

When we returned to the safari company, the Asian manager asked where we were going next. He seemed impressed at our resourcefulness in keeping the Isuzu running.

"Nairobi," we said, "tomorrow morning."

His eyebrows raised, and he told us he had a great deal on a car for us. But we said we had had enough trouble with his last car, and besides, we wanted to try out the East African trains.

"Look," he insisted. "The whole country is falling apart here. We'll give you a new Toyota to drive to Nairobi, a luxury model, and the same rate as the Isuzu."

We thanked him but said no. Then he begged us, again and again, and told us to stop by the next day before we left Kampala. He guaranteed us he would make us an offer we couldn't refuse. That night Russ and I talked it over and concluded that the Asian company was desperate to move everything of value they could out of the country. A valuable car would be a huge coup. The next morning, Russ and I walked to Rhino Safari, bluffed that we had decided to go by rail, and flashed $5 train tickets.

"Look, my friends," the manager pleaded. "I'll be honest with you. We need to get this car to Nairobi. You can take it *for free*. We'll fill it with gas and write up a false contract saying you are making a circle route through East Africa, will return the car here, and have left a $2,000 cash deposit. Then you will certainly not have any trouble at the border."

Russ and I conferred again and agreed to do it, but only if we could use the car a few extra days and could drop it off at the airport.

"Whatever you want, my friends," he said. "It takes eight hours to drive to Nairobi directly, but if you want, you can take three days."

He called his assistant and led us to a spotless new white Toyota. Our last week in Africa, after all those manure-riddled cattle trucks, dilapidated buses, and smoke-spewing flatbeds, would be in luxury. The manager himself typed up the bogus deposit and rental agreements and walked us to the Toyota, where he opened the trunk.

"Here's a new jack," he said, trying to push it into the customized recess in the trunk built for a factory-equipped jack. It didn't fit. "If you have any trouble at the border, call this number," he said, and handed us the business card of their sister company, the Rhino Safari Company in Nairobi. In other words, *Don't call us*.

He handed us the keys, and we loaded our backpacks and headed for the Nairobi road, intent on crossing the border as quickly as possible back into the relative safety of Kenya. As we approached the frontier, two armed border police motioned us to a halt and demanded our papers. They slowly inspected our passports and finally the false rental contract. We tried to look calm and prayed they could read. Mumbling to one another under their breaths, they turned the documents over and over, one hand holding the papers, and the other next to the trigger. At long last they ordered, "Okay—you go!" and waved us through with their carbines.

Once back in Kenya, we relaxed and explored the countryside, making side trips to snow-capped Mt. Kenya and camping along the sea of pink flamingos at Lake Nakuru. We arrived in Nairobi two days late, and the guy behind the rental desk said he had no record of the Toyota. He went to get the manager, who brought us into his office, alone, and shut the door.

"Listen," he said. "We need that car back in Kampala. The Uganda office has been phoning every day to see if it has arrived."

"Well," I said. "Your agent in Kampala promised us we could keep it until Friday and return it to the airport."

"That Toyota is probably pretty dirty," he said. "You don't want to be driving a car like that around. Bring it in and we'll give you a clean one to use until Friday."

Russ and I glanced at each other. Apparently we had just smuggled something very valuable out of Uganda for this company, and it wasn't the car.

"Seems like a lot of bother to me," I shrugged.

I guess he figured we were getting suspicious and said we could keep it until Friday night and that he himself, the president of the company, would pick it up at the airport. Russ and I drove back to our campsite in the Nairobi City Park, borrowed tools from one of the Land Rovers, divided up the car, and began going over it with a fine-toothed comb. We took apart the dash and upholstery, probed the gas tank with a long wire, scrutinized the crankcase and tires for recent tampering, and ripped off the door panels. As we worked, I told Russ how the East German soldier-mechanic had practically disassembled my Volkswagen van at Checkpoint Charlie, and I tried to recall in detail the potential hiding places on his checklist. My own area of responsibility included the trunk. I removed the case containing the jack and spare tools and ripped out the trunk liner. Hours later we gave up. Perhaps our hunch was wrong. The prospect of spending our last few days in Africa covered in grease, instead of tracking hippos, sounded like a loser, so we replaced the panels and trunk liner and tools and drove out to the game areas.

Friday night the president of Rhino Safari was waiting for us at the airport, along with two of the biggest Asians I have ever seen, who reminded me of sumo wrestlers. The three of them had driven way out here to the airport, on a Friday night, to pick up one car. When I handed him the keys, they immediately walked to the trunk, opened it, and three heads disappeared inside. Ten seconds later, the heads reappeared, smiling, and they shut the trunk. Now we knew where the contraband was hidden—in the new jack, the jack that didn't fit. In my hurry to inspect the deep recesses of the trunk, I had overlooked the obvious and now remembered the manager at Kampala trying in vain to force the jack into the tool compartment.

On board the EgyptAir flight back to Cairo and Munich, Russ and I wondered what might have happened if we had found the mysterious contraband. We had given our true names and passport numbers to the agent in Kampala, and the East Asian mafia could easily have tracked us down to recover their fortune. On the plane, we exchanged travel tales with several fellow passengers, who reminded me of the clean-cut CIA type who had chastised Gary Jackson and me in Cuzco about our prospecting misadventures.

"You two are damned lucky to be alive," one told us. "Especially driving that luxury car. Ugandan police routinely arrest the driver of a car they like and motor off with him in the trunk. The victim is usually never seen again, and they often leave his shoes behind as a curious grim warning. Just last February, two Asian brothers from Kampala were killed over a car. Soldiers shot the first brother in a scuffle at a traffic roadblock, when the illiterate guard who stopped him distrusted the papers and accused him of stealing the car. They cut his brother's throat when he came to recover the body."

"And you were very lucky crossing those other borders," said another. "It's not like that trip behind the Iron Curtain you told us about. There you might have wound up behind bars a few years, but there was always strict inventory accountability. In Africa people like you can just *disappear*—no paperwork, no passport numbers recorded—just more food for the Nile crocodiles."

When we landed in Munich, Russ and I took the train back to Göttingen, appreciating the cleanliness, punctuality, and orderliness of the German rail system in a whole new way. On the way back, I told Russ how much our trip reminded me of that Andes expedition with Gary—especially the physical adventures and our failure to do even the most basic research about potentially dangerous political events. I told him how much I was going to miss Gary, and the next day I placed a phone call to one of my West Point classmates who had been at Gary Jackson's funeral.

"Yes, I was there," he said sadly. "Apparently Gary's new religious group convinced him he had special protection by God, after all his ordeals, and that he didn't need his medicine. He stopped taking it and died two nights later. The funeral was hard for me to take—those people were happy and smiling, saying things like, 'If only we could see him now, with his wings.' His parents were in shock—he was their only child, you know."

Russ comforted me again and soon flew back to St. Louis, while I prepared to return to the States and enter my new role as a PhD mathematics student in Berkeley. That was my last real trip with Russ, since he was soon to marry a St. Louis girl, buy a house, settle down, and start a family. During my remaining days in Göttingen, I filled a steamer trunk with my few possessions and shipped it by freighter to Jonathan, who was already back in Berkeley. I then had a VW dealer estimate the cost of repairs to the camper roof. The total was much higher than I expected, enough to pay for shipping the van all the way to Chicago. To my pleasant surprise, the Soviet insurance paid in full, so I skipped the repairs and drove it to the German docks. I had no idea that beloved dented camper would be my ticket to travel and adventure for ten more years.

On the flight back to the States, I reflected on my Fulbright year. Mathematically, even though I had not published or proved any theorems, I had experienced European mathematics firsthand as a graduate student at one of the best universities, had made what would turn out to be lifetime mathematics contacts, and had rekindled my love of probability theory. I hadn't made it to Kolmogorov's seminar rooms, nor had I done any mathematics during the trek across East Africa. But those experiences that year living in Göttingen, together with the Iron Curtain and Africa trips, had greatly expanded my comfort zone, setting personal benchmarks for travel risks and deprivations, much as Army Ranger School had set personal benchmarks for physical endurance and mental toughness.

It would turn out to be the foundation of what was to become a lifetime of living and traveling and doing mathematics abroad, lecturing in four languages in fifteen countries in both industrialized and developing nations. But now, looking forward to the comparatively safe and serene Berkeley campus, I was about to embark on a new mathematical voyage of the mind that would test the limits of my endurance in a whole different dimension.

8

BERZERKELEY

I crossed the Nevada-California state line at Lake Tahoe and wound down California Highway 50 into the 90-degree Central Valley, thinking back to my trip six years earlier after the Andes expedition with Gary, when I drove the T-bird convertible cross country from West Point. So much had changed since then. This time I was in a battered Volkswagen camper, and my goal was radical Berkeley, not conservative blueblood Stanford. America's obsession with Vietnam was beginning to wane, and now, instead of the radio alternating between "Ballad of the Green Berets" and "Unknown Soldier," I was smiling to the irreverent lyrics of one of 1972's Top Twenty hits, Chuck Berry's "My Ding-a-Ling." I crossed the scorching onion fields east of Sacramento, and the van smelled as if I had collided with a hay wagon of Lipton Onion Soup Mix.

Suddenly the coolness of San Francisco Bay, thick with the scent of eucalyptus and salt air, brought my overheated body back to life. I exited the freeway at University Avenue and drove up Hearst to Northside to Jonathan's home. He pulled out my footlocker, still sealed with freight and customs stickers, and invited me to crash in his spare room while I looked for my own place. After a week of checking the bulletin boards at Safeway and the co-op, I'd found a small apartment in the cellar of a huge house on Cedar Street, just above Euclid. The flat had a low ceiling, well below code, but it was quiet and was so high up on the hill that the skyscrapers of San Francisco and the Golden Gate Bridge were visible from my basement window.

I walked down Euclid and through campus, pausing in Sproul Plaza to recall the news clips of only a few short years earlier, when reporters had broadcast grainy, jerky footage of helicopters tear gassing anti-war demonstrators. The atmosphere now was completely different. Low-key but highly educated police officers chuckled in amusement at a suntanned student who, except for his backpack, was walking toward the Student Union completely naked. I continued south onto Telegraph Avenue, where street artists, Hare Krishnas, aging hippies, and panhandlers mixed with Bible thumpers and soapbox politicians. Sandalwood incense from the head shops, music from used record shops and sidewalk guitarists, People's Park, cafés, and the famous used bookstores Moe's and Cody's—I'd never seen a place with so many free spirits from all walks of life. I loved it.

The thought of living in this permanent circus sideshow captured my heart, but I didn't know how I would survive financially. I still had the $10,000 I'd saved in Vietnam since the year in Göttingen was paid by the Fulbright award, and I could count on the $200 a month from the GI Bill. Tuition for out-of-state students, however, was triple that for California residents, and for a walk-on like me, that could quickly devour everything. I had anticipated this, so fifteen months earlier, just before leaving St. Louis for the year in Germany, I had traded legal advice on California residency from a Los Angeles attorney in exchange for my promise to ship him out-of-stock Mercedes parts from Germany. Based on his tips, I drove from St. Louis to Barstow, the nearest city in California, and took the California driver's license tests using Jim Eberhardt's home address in Felton, a tiny village in the Santa Cruz Mountains. Then, from Germany, I had filed a California state income tax return and voted in the next Felton dogcatcher election by absentee ballot.

Now, as I was starting the graduate student registration process in Sproul Hall, came the acid test. A sign said, *If you have been outside California for more than 3 of the past 12 months, go to Window C.*

"Do you have a California driver's license?" asked the clerk at Window C.

"Sure," I replied casually, as I slowly opened my wallet.

"Did you vote in a California election during the past year? File a state income tax return? Do you have utilities receipts?"

"I didn't bring any electric bills," I said, "but I have the rest." I handed her a manila envelope.

After glancing at the Santa Cruz County voter's receipt and photocopy of my California tax return—bottom line zero taxable income—she stamped my tuition fee form CALIFORNIA RESIDENT. I figured that little stamp doubled my student financial life expectancy.

Now I could concentrate on academics. Berkeley had taken a chance admitting me to their mathematics PhD program, perhaps encouraged by a letter of reference from Professor Hillier, my Stanford advisor, or perhaps based on my Graduate Records Exam score in mathematics. There were other walk-ons besides me, but as far as I knew, I was the only PhD candidate admitted to the program who did not have any formal degree in mathematics, and the only Vietnam veteran. I had never heard of any other West Point graduate who even tried to get a PhD at Berkeley in math. Since Berkeley consistently earned first rank in the National Research Council's standings of mathematics departments, I knew that competition would be stiff. Berkeley's crop of pure and applied postgraduate math majors were the best of their generations. They'd been undergraduate math majors at Harvard, Chicago, Cal Tech, and Princeton, or superstar math students at smaller colleges and universities. My temporary goal was to last at least one academic quarter—just ten short weeks plus exams, a little shorter than Beast Barracks had been, and one week longer than Ranger School.

Next stop was an appointment with my faculty advisor in Evans Hall, the uninspired ten-story gray cement box facing Hearst Mining Circle and the Berkeley Hills to the east, with a spectacular view of San Francisco and the Golden Gate Bridge to the west. Mathematics laid claim to the top four floors, with Economics and Statistics below. I walked down the halls, lit by fluorescent lights, stopping to read the bulletin boards covered with seminar and conference announcements. What an adventure and privilege this would be, whatever the outcome.

My first academic advisor, Professor Michel Loève, was an old-world French mathematician whose blend of enthusiasm and demand for rigorous thinking reminded me of my first calculus teacher, Nohel at Madison. Loève's two-volume probability text, dedicated *To the students and the teachers of the School in the Camp de Drancy*, was considered the first comprehensive treatment of modern probability. Known by many experts as the bible for probability theory, it had even been translated into Russian.

"You have a very unusual background," said Professor Loève as he looked through my folder. "I figure you lost about four or five years of mathematics in the Army."

Loève knew firsthand about losing time away from mathematics. Born in Jaffa and educated in Alexandria and Paris, Professor Loève had somehow survived imprisonment in the internment camp at Drancy, a Nazi facility for confining Jews en route to the extermination camps. Loève told me that my year in Göttingen had helped, but now I really had my work cut out for me. The requirements included language exams—two out of three from French, German, and Russian—two research seminar talks, three oral exams, and the dissertation. He said he would recommend courses to help bring me up to speed, but most of it was up to me.

I signed up for Loève's undergraduate course in Measure Theory and a graduate course in Probability and rented a university gym locker. I knew the mental ordeal ahead would require frequent cardiovascular flushings to cleanse my brain and relax my body. With the first day of classes, I settled down to a rigorous schedule, studying seven days a week, twelve to sixteen hours a day, with the few remaining waking hours practicing judo, playing racquetball, and motorcycling in the East Bay's Tilden Park. I'd left my Beesa with my brothers in St. Louis and shipped only the Triumph 650 to Berkeley. On Sunday morning, I allowed myself the luxury of reading the color comics in the *San Francisco Chronicle*. No dating, no fancy restaurant meals, no trashy novels, no watching football on TV, no running around making friends. Two years of monastic living should about do it, I figured, just to make it through all the requirements except for the dissertation.

My classmates, most of them six or seven years my junior, had been undergraduate math majors, and many had won summer math internships and undergraduate research fellowships. For me, because my basic math vocabulary was so deficient, it often took days before I even understood the words in a homework problem. But I reminded myself of the miseries of Ranger School and kept chipping away hour after hour, day after day. I assumed that we were supposed to solve every one of the eight new probability problems assigned each week, and even after racking my brain the whole week, there were always one or two I couldn't crack.

"What do these scores mean?" a classmate in Probability asked the professor six weeks into the term, after he'd handed back graded homework for the first time. "How should we be doing?"

"Oh, you're doing very well if you get 40 percent," he answered. I just shook my head. My scores were running about 80 percent. I was glad I didn't find out earlier, or I might not have pushed so hard. Unlike West Point homework and the master's-level classes at Stanford, these PhD-level Berkeley homeworks were not problems every student was expected to be able to solve, but the professor had never bothered to tell us that.

At Stanford I had found it very useful to think about math problems while motorcycling. Leaning my Triumph into the hairpin turns on Old Tunnel Road, I felt overwhelmed by the beauty and power of this whole new level of mathematics. I struggled to try to develop some intuition behind these powerful concepts. Kolmogorov's Zero-One Law, for example, said that certain types of events were either guaranteed to happen or would never happen. If you were flipping coins, fair or not, then you either were certain to get an infinite number of heads or certain not to, no matter what coins you used. Almost every waking hour I struggled just trying to understand the basic concepts, but I never thought of quitting mathematics. Perhaps I would fail out of Berkeley and have to restart at a different university and lower level, but not quit. I felt it in my blood.

My perseverance with the homework paid off, and I passed Measure Theory with an A and Graduate Probability with an A-minus. I had never been that mentally exhausted in my life, but somehow I had survived the first term in the PhD program of the best university mathematics department in the country. My brain felt numb, and I knew that I needed more of a cure than a few hours of racquetball or motorcycling.

I packed my VW van with camping gear and headed south along scenic Coastal Highway One, following the same route Jon Steel and I had taken on motorcycles in 1966, across the border into Baja California. After a week of relaxing alone in the desert, beachcombing along the turquoise Baja shores, and feasting on fresh fish tacos, on New Year's Day 1973, I turned back north. Crossing a small valley on the main highway between Ensenada and Tijuana, I saw a lone middle-aged Mexican man standing on the road, frantically waving his hands to flag me down. I pulled over to the side.

"*Accidente*," he shouted. "*Hombres muertos*!"

That part of the highway crossed the valley on a tall earthen levee, and I could see far down the road ahead of and behind me, and the desert floor in the distance below, off to both sides. The only movement was shimmering waves of air that rose above the baked earth and disappeared into the desert landscape on the horizon. The man motioned me out of the car and down the slope, toward the ravine off the shoulder that was out of sight from the road above. I had taken four or five steps when shadows behind me suddenly caught my eye. Two men emerged from hiding in the depression on the opposite slope of the road and were walking toward me. My first thought was they were going to rob me, so I wheeled around and crouched in a defensive hand-to-hand combat stance, hands raised, ready to parry and chop. To my great surprise, the two men staggered past me, down to the edge of the slope where the other man stood. One of the two newcomers spoke some English.

"Accident," he said. "Come here."

A car had gone over the edge of the 20-foot drop-off and smashed headfirst into the gully, throwing two riders through the windshield onto the desert rocks. I squinted in the bright sun to search for signs of life, but nothing moved. Now I smelled the alcohol on the men standing beside me and realized what had happened. The five drunken *amigos*, celebrating the New Year, went over the cliff in their car. These three standing beside me, limp and loose from intoxication, had walked away from the crash.

I scrambled along the ridge to a spot where I could climb down and ran to the motionless figures lying on the ground. The first, a handsome, well-dressed Mexican youth of about twenty, had no obvious external injuries but was bleeding from the nose and ears. I detected a weak pulse and screamed, "He's alive!" I sprinted to the next victim, who lay covered in blood, with bits of lung from a massive chest wound spotting his white shirt. I tried to find a pulse, but my hands trembled, and his hand hung limp.

Their three companions had slowly staggered down the slope behind me, and when they reached the wreck, I slapped them across the face to sober them up. Then I ordered them to help me carry the first young victim to a place we could scale the slope and reach the van. I held the boy's head level, while they followed behind, dropping an arm or a leg every few steps as they stumbled, then catching up again. Our ascent took twenty minutes. Finally we laid the unconscious victim on the bed in my camper.

Returning down the slope with these three drunk and exhausted helpers, I figured, would take at least another half hour—thirty minutes that could mean life or death for the young man in the camper bed. I had to make a snap decision and decided to rush this first victim to a doctor. Leaving the other man to a certain death, we started up the highway. As we sped along at 60 miles an hour, the VW's top speed with that load, the English-speaking fellow thanked me for stopping.

"*Gracias*," he said. "No other car would stop. Mostly *turistas* on this road."

He hesitated and then pointed to the bleeding youth in the back.

"He is my brother. *I* was driving the car. It's *my* car. This very serious crime here in Mexico, *señor*, you must understand that. My friends will say the dead man was driving, that I was not even here. Only four people in the car. I will show you the hospital but then disappear. If you tell police I was here, they will know I was driving, *comprende*? *Por favor, señor!*"

I told the two drunks in back to help keep the boy on the bed breathing, but they lit cigarettes and stared back at me through bloodshot eyes. I couldn't both drive and give artificial respiration, and none of them was sober enough to drive. When we reached Tijuana, the streets were jammed with the holiday turmoil of New Year's Day celebrations: horns blaring, bells ringing, people shouting and waving flags. Shreds of red firecracker casings littered the sidewalks in front of giant tequila bottles on billboards piercing the blue sky. If I honked, or screamed and waved my arms, I would fit right in with the rest of the partying. Nothing I could do would draw attention to our emergency, so we crept along slowly in bumper-to-bumper traffic. Finally my English-speaking guide pointed to the next intersection, told me to turn right, and again begged me to lie to the police.

"*Por favor, señor.* For my life! Four. *Cuatro.* Please!" He pointed halfway down the crowded block to a plain brick building with a large red cross in a white rectangle, then pushed open the sliding cargo door and disappeared into the holiday throng.

I pulled up in the clinic's entranceway and ran inside shouting, "*Emergencia!*" The man on duty walked slowly outside and looked in the side window of the van. I pushed him toward the open sliding door. He calmly stepped inside and lifted the boy's wrist. Suddenly the medic's face lit up, and he yelled something in Spanish, apparently shocked to find a pulse. As I watched in horror, with both hands he pushed down hard on the boy's chest, there was a quick convulsion, and blood and a lump of lung appeared in the boy's mouth. *Didn't he know that CPR technique was never to be used on a victim with internal injuries?* The boy was dead now.

Within five minutes the police arrived and shoved the two drunks and me into the back cage of a paddy wagon. Then it hit me. If the two Mexicans claimed this gringo ran their car off the road, accidentally or not, I was in serious trouble. Under the codified system of Mexican law—like the Japanese law I had warned the R&R troops in Tokyo about—I was automatically guilty until proven innocent, and the crime was homicide.

When we arrived at the jail, the police confiscated our belts so we couldn't use them as weapons or to hang ourselves and pushed us into separate metal CONEX cargo container cells. I paced back and forth as I waited, just as I had done in the Wellesley jail cell, out of earshot from the others. Thirty minutes later, my cell door opened, and a police lieutenant introduced himself with a smile and warm handshake. He spoke perfect English.

"Thank you," he said. "Thank you, *caballero*, for trying to save that man. No one else would even stop on that road."

He handed me my belt and led me outside, never asking my version of the accident. I told him that one more victim was still out there beside the wrecked car and gave directions and approximate distances. The lieutenant thanked me again and escorted me back to the paddy wagon, where his deputy now invited me to sit up front in the cab. One of the policemen who had manhandled us at the hospital offered me a cigarette.

When we got back to my van, a dusty black funeral parlor hearse was already loading the boy's body. Death was an everyday affair here, and they didn't waste time. I borrowed a bucket of water and sponge from the medic to wash the blood out of my car. As I wiped down the vinyl camper bed, three street kids appeared out of nowhere and swarmed around the van, claiming someone hid drugs in it while I was in jail. That was a distinct possibility, I realized, either to smuggle the drugs across the border or to win the $80 reward the authorities offered for information. The kids volunteered to help me search the van, but if there weren't any drugs stashed there already, I figured there might be after these street urchins made their pass. I kept them away from the car, made a cursory inspection myself, and then drove to the border, numb with the thought that the end of the day could find me in jail again, this time on drug-smuggling charges. But somehow it all seemed insignificant in comparison with the needless loss of that young man's life.

A long automobile queue waited at the border. The border police singled me out almost immediately and directed me to a special inspection area. "This is it," I thought wearily. But as soon as the inspector asked his first question, I realized this was just a random search. Well, not exactly random—I was a long-haired gringo, traveling alone in a beat-up Volkswagen van.

"What was the purpose of your trip to Mexico?" he asked.

"Camping," I said.

"*Alone?*"

"Yes."

He raised his eyebrows and took a long look at me and then the van. "What's in the footlocker?" he asked.

"Camping equipment."

"You know, *señor*, I believe you," he smiled. "But I just *have* to look—otherwise it would bother me all night."

I flipped open the lid for him to see, and he waved me through with wishes for a happy New Year.

I crossed over the border and, my hands still shaking, pulled off at the first exit in Chula Vista. I made a collect call to my brother Russ, who was still studying microbiology in St. Louis. I had seen dying men in Vietnam, but always with a medical corpsman or field doctor at hand. My own rudimentary knowledge of first aid had never mattered.

"R," I said shakily, "if I were studying medicine instead of mathematics, that guy would still be alive. What is a single life compared to a hundred theorems?"

"Look, T, try to relax," he said calmly. "If he was bleeding from the nose and ears, there's not much anybody could have done. It wasn't your fault that medic was incompetent. Without your help, that boy wouldn't have made it to the clinic in the first place. You're no medical doctor. Check into a motel, buy a fifth of Seagram's, and call me in the morning. In the meantime, I'll talk to the emergency room doctors here to see what they say."

When I talked to Russ the next morning, he told me the ER staff agreed—the chances of that boy surviving, mentally intact, were slim even with proper treatment. When my hangover faded, I pointed the van back to Berkeley.

* * *

Having survived the first academic term, I now set a new goal to pass one of the PhD oral exams by May. Three outcomes were possible: fail, pass at master's level, and pass at PhD level. I needed to pass at PhD level to remain in the program, and I chose to attempt the Probability oral exam first.

The orals, more affectionately known by graduate students as the "anals," were comprehensive exams designed to test aptitude for a dissertation. They were the most terrifying intellectual experiences of a graduate student's life, far worse than the written SATs or GREs. PhD candidates in mathematics had to pass three exams, including two of Algebra, Analysis, and Geometry, plus one elective. Each exam subjected the student to a horrific hour of humiliation, standing at a blackboard while two or three of the world's experts in that field peeled open the analytical halves of their brains, like onions, layer by layer, to determine the exact depth of knowledge and intuition. You were on trial for your academic life, pleading your own case. Unlike written exams, orals allowed total flexibility. The examiners could instantly switch lines of attack as soon as they saw you could answer a question and probe instead for something *simple* you didn't know, which always happened. It felt like pithing, the pricking of a live frog's brain in zoology lab with a needle-tipped probe until you found the spot for the primal screech.

To prepare for the orals, graduate students formed study groups and role-played mock trials, shared lists of old test questions, and took tranquilizers months in advance. Some even visited the faculty examiners' offices with flimsy excuses, making mental notes of the relevant algebra or geometry texts on his bookshelf and then rushing to Moe's Bookstore to buy used copies. Then they worked through the books' exercises again and again, first to find correct solutions, then for speed. But in spite of all these measures, there were still nervous breakdowns and vomiting at the blackboard.

The next five months I continued my seven-days-a-week work regimen, this time preparing for my first oral. Judo, racquetball, and strenuous hiking kept me fit and able to sleep without drugs. My plan was to stop studying two days before the exam, and the day before, to rise before dawn and relax in Tilden Park, sitting in the grass and mending clothes I'd saved for the occasion. After a 7 o'clock movie, I would then easily fall asleep without the customary pre-oral dose of Sominex. That way I would be clear-headed and well rested on the morning of the exam.

My plan worked fine, until the movie. I wanted to take in a simple Western, and a friend recommended Clint Eastwood's *High Plains Drifter.* I went into the movie relaxed and already nodding off, but after two hours of watching men being bullwhipped and burned to death, I left the theater in jitters. I stopped by Jonathan's house and staggered into his kitchen. He took one look at me, told me I looked like a deer in the headlights, and sent me home with a half pint of brandy in a mason jar. That knocked me out immediately.

My Probability oral examiners were Loève, the world probability expert, Haskell Rosenthal, a Banach space theorist recently interested in probability, and a physics professor. University statutes required an outside examiner as a partial check against inbreeding and deterioration of standards.

Rosenthal spoke first. "I'm not a probabilist and have only a few questions, so maybe I'll go first." After the others nodded assent, he continued. "Suppose you have a converging sequence of Lebesgue-Stieltjes integrals . . ."

All the other Probability oral exams I had ever heard of had started with a few basics—the definition of *expected value* or *statistical independence*—to give the candidate a few seconds to say a few words about something easy he definitely knew and to get used to the sound of his own voice. But Rosenthal's question did not use standard probability terminology, and it threw me off balance. For twenty minutes, I squirmed like a live victim on a meat hook. Slowly I collected my wits, translated his question into more familiar probability terms—*characteristic functions*—and finally answered his question. The hour was already a third over, and I had not really shown anything deep. I glanced out the window for one blink of my eye toward the Berkeley hills, wondering why I was even here. Then Rosenthal finished, and Loève dove in. Luckily for me, he used probability language I was familiar with, and I quickly answered his barrage of questions. His go lasted nearly until the end of the hour, leaving the physicist time for only one question.

"What does *almost surely* mean?" he asked, referring to my repeated use of that very precise mathematical expression, which appears uncharacteristically sloppy to most other scientists. The tension broke slightly, as Loève, Rosenthal, and even I smiled as I explained the definition. It simply means with certainty, with probability one.

I left the room feeling I had probably failed because of the first twenty minutes. I had an appointment with Loève several hours later to get the results, and when I walked in, Loève congratulated me. I had passed at the PhD level, barely. "One down, two to go," I thought, and awarded myself a weekend of celebration in San Francisco, smoking dope, making love, feasting on Dungeness crabs at Fisherman's Wharf, and listening to rock music. On Monday morning, I started an intensive four-month preparation for the Analysis oral. While half of Berkeley danced in the streets over Nixon's resignation and then rioted over his pardon by Ford, I studied Banach spaces and operator theory.

During the summer quarter, I chose to forgo formal classes in order to concentrate on the remaining two oral exams. To break the monotony and refresh body and soul, I signed up for sailing lessons at the Berkeley Marina with the University Sailing Club. I spent several afternoons a week helping repair fiberglass leaks in the Tiburon sloops, replacing anchor lines, and taking as many lessons as I could schedule. The rigging exercises came easy for me, since sailors use the same figure-eight and end-of-the-line bowline knots we had learned in Ranger School mountaineering.

The Sailing Club members had a reputation for being crack sailors and tough taskmasters. Slowly I advanced from novice to certified sailor and finally to instructor, and put my new students through the same rigorous exercises, man-overboard drills, putting the boat in irons during high winds, and righting a capsized centerboard sailboat. The strenuous exercise and fresh salt air kept me energetic and alert and improved my concentration on mathematics the other eight to ten hours a day.

Three months later I passed the Analysis oral, also at the PhD level, and with less pain than the first oral exam. Then in my final exam, the Algebra oral, one of the examiners asked what I knew about "groups of order 2p." I answered that every group of order 2p was either cyclic or dihedral, and he asked me for a proof. That theorem and proof were not in any of the syllabuses but had just struck me as beautiful, so I had taken the time to become familiar with them, and I was able to write down the complete argument on the blackboard. They were so surprised that one of the examiners blurted out to the other, "How did he know that? Did you teach that?"

"No," the other said, "and he wasn't in my class anyway." I passed the final oral with flying colors.

I stopped by to tell Jonathan and raise several glasses of wine with him.

"Congratulations!" he said. "And you can shake my hand too. My thesis is all but done, and it looks like I've landed a tenure-track job in the history department at Wellesley!"

"Congratulations back!" I said. "But did you have to pick the one college in the whole United States that I'm officially forbidden to visit?" I told him about being shot at by the Wellesley police and banned from campus for life. And sure enough, Jonathan went to Wellesley and spent his whole career there, later becoming full professor and department head.

The "Bear of the Orals" was now finished, and by the end of the second academic year, I had also given the two required seminar talks and passed the two language exams. German had been easy after the year in

Göttingen, except for not knowing some of the *English* mathematical terms. The Russian exam was more of a challenge, but with the textbook from my Intensive Russian course at Stanford and the phrase book I had carried behind the Iron Curtain, the essential grammar slowly came back to me.

After those two years of intense concentration, I needed a solid break away from Berkeley before beginning the "dissertation ordeal." I decided to hit the road in my Volkswagen van for the three summer months, just enjoying life as a drifter, working odd jobs, exploring the deserts and Great Plains, and enjoying sunsets over a campfire. And I wouldn't even have to sleep under bridges—I always had my beloved home on wheels.

My friend John Oneal had just returned from a nine-month pilgrimage in India, following his guru Sant, and I invited him to join me in the cross-country trek. John had finished as a Star Man in the West Point Class of 1968 and also chose Stanford for his graduate school scholarship in political science. After spending the two academic years 1968 to 1970 in Palo Alto, he did his stint in Vietnam as the war wound down. Like me, John also left the Army early to return to graduate school, but not by finding a logical loophole, as I had done. Just the opposite: he was one of the first West Pointers ever to be released from the Army as a conscientious objector, and, unlike other COs, he filed his petition for release only *after* finishing combat duty in Vietnam. Because he had been raised in an Army family—his father was still a colonel in the artillery—his decision had been doubly difficult, but his application, based on John's belief in the philosophies of Far Eastern religions, even came with his father's blessing. Now he was back in the PhD program at Stanford, where his dissertation in Political Science was soon to win a national award.

We loaded the van and mapped out our route, past Yosemite and along the Grand Canyon. Passing through the Texas Panhandle, we looked up Abe Dean, who had survived his open-cockpit flying missions in Vietnam and was now raising Quarter Horses at Hay Camp Ranch. That, and constructing a country club for oil- and cotton-rich Texas farmers, complete with its own airstrip for their private planes. A severe drought was now threatening his golf course, and he desperately needed help. I promised to return after I dropped John off in Lawton, Oklahoma.

"You know Mike Snell was killed in Vietnam when we were there?" Abe said. "In June."

"No!" I said, flashing up an image in my mind of his laid-back Texan West Point friend with the wavy black hair. "I thought he'd already finished his tour before then."

"He did," said Abe. "But somehow he started loving the Army and volunteered for a second tour. He was killed in a firefight while pulling two of his soldiers to safety. I named one of my two sons after him."

John and I got back on the road to Lawton, and during those long drives through the desert and long chats over campfires, I came to like and admire him more and more. He was an amazing man of contradictions—conservative Okie, conscientious objector, curious scientist, dope-smoking hippie-in-disguise, astute financial investor, and unusually gifted storyteller. That trip was the beginning of a deep lifetime friendship, helping compensate a little bit for the loss of Gary.

I bid farewell to John at his parents' home in Ft. Sill, Oklahoma, just outside Lawton, and returned to Hay Camp to help Abe clear land and haul water. Then I drove east to paint houses with my brother George in St. Louis and then west again, arriving in Lake Tahoe several weeks before the start of fall quarter classes in Berkeley. I found a wilderness campsite on the lower Truckee River, where I was sure the Forest Service would never check, and drove into South Shore to apply for a job at the California/Nevada Employment Office, which literally straddled the state line. The east side of the huge room had flyers and clerks helping job hunters find work in Nevada, and the west side of the same room handled California. On the California bulletin board, I saw an ad looking for a dishwasher in the restaurant of the Elm Lodge Inn and drove over to apply in person.

"Holy shit," the manager said, looking at my application. "You have more degrees than the *cook*! And he's a mathematician too."

In addition to my bachelor's degree from West Point and the Master of Science from Stanford, I had also automatically picked up a Master of Arts in Mathematics from Berkeley as a tiny reward for passing the orals. I was curious about this cook and sought him out during a break from washing dishes. He was a thin, middle-aged, nervous man with a warm smile, comfortable in his rumpled white chef's uniform.

"Yep," he said, "I was a mathematician. Went to Paris, to the Sorbonne, to get my master's. While I was there, I decided to learn to cook in my spare time. I paid a dollar an hour—one helluva lot in those days—just for the privilege of watching. I had to stand in a corner of the kitchen, out of the way, and couldn't ask any questions, just watch those chefs work. Fell in love with it. Finished my math degree finally, but my heart was in cooking, so I studied to be a chef. Even got a few medals."

He proudly showed me an old photograph in his wallet, of him in his formal black chef's uniform, medals on his chest.

"Want a *steak*?" he asked.

My dishwasher's pay was for minimum wage, plus all I could eat, *except* steaks, the manager had stressed. The chef knew the rules.

"Sure," I said with a grin, and he threw a New York strip on the grill.

The poor man had found his niche here, in a low-key restaurant off the beaten track that was tolerant of his alcoholism. Every now and then, he would re-create a Paris delicacy from the old days. The manager would list an English translation on the daily Elm Lodge menu specials and stack the tidbits in the freezer. When a customer ordered one, the old chef winced as the kitchen staff threw it in the microwave.

Two weeks later, I returned down Highway 50 again to Berkeley, eager to pick up mathematics once more. Completion of the orals was only the first step toward a dissertation, and it was actually the next step that most graduate students failed. But whether I obtained my PhD or not, I vowed, I would never abandon mathematics completely as that Sorbonne chef had done.

The PhD oral exams had reminded me of plebe year at West Point. Being grilled by an upperclassman while standing up against a wall in his room, or by world-class mathematicians while up at the blackboard, both were designed to eliminate weak candidates. For those who passed, either plebe year or the orals, internal motivation had to quickly fill the void left after surviving the weeding-out phase. Just as I had been free to choose my lifestyle after my release from the Army, during the remainder of my quest for a PhD, I was now free to choose my own mathematical directions and set my own pace.

My next administrative advisor was Professor Steve Smale, whose solution of a major part of the Poincaré Conjecture had won him a Fields Medal, often said to be the mathematical equivalent of a Nobel Prize, except that it was awarded only once every four years and given only to a person under forty. Like me, Smale had begun his education in a one-room country schoolhouse, but unlike me, Smale was extremely political. During his senior year at the University of Michigan, the administration put him on probation for his radical political activism. As a faculty member at Berkeley, he helped organize the national Days of Protest against the Vietnam War and held a press conference, critical of US policy in Vietnam, on the steps of Moscow University. I wondered if the same guards had let him warm his hands. Smale was radical even for Berkeley, and together with other activist colleagues, he published a short-lived anti-authoritarian departmental "counter newsletter" whose name they derived from *functor*, the mathematical term for a "morphism between categories." Title of the newsletter? *Up Against the Blackboard, MotherFunctor!*

I signed up for his course on Mathematical Economics. Waving his hands in the air, his crop of unruly curls a holdover from his radical days, Smale announced the first day of class that there would be no homework or exams the entire term, a final paper was voluntary, and all students would get an A regardless. As my administrative advisor, he immediately signed every bureaucratic departmental form I brought him, almost without reading it, and the grapevine said Smale believed that the only requirement for a PhD should be a good dissertation—nothing else. That, of course, was my ultimate goal.

In addition to the academic pressures, a critical obstacle to survival as a walk-on mathematics graduate student at Berkeley was money. Unlike West Point, where every student had a full government scholarship that included not only room, board, and tuition but also a clothing allowance and small salary, the Berkeley math department offered only enough graduate teaching assistantships to support roughly a quarter of its PhD students. Since the average time to completion of a dissertation was about eight years, among those who made it, many were facing years of study without any financial support.

To make ends meet, graduate students graded papers, relied on spouses' incomes, lived in subsistence-level student communes, and took part-time jobs. My friend Maurice drove a delivery truck for the *San Francisco Chronicle*, David wrote calculus books, and Tom smuggled marijuana from Colombia by cruising up the coast solo in his tiny Tiburon sloop. The Coast Guard figured no boat that small could make it five miles outside the Golden Gate.

I took jobs most graduate students wouldn't touch with a 10-foot pole. I worked as a process server for a private-eye company in Oakland. As a newcomer, I got stuck with the worst cases, the files with old addresses and notoriously successful subpoena dodgers. The new California law required only that the server see the target person, not physically *touch* him with the papers, as the law had required in the past. That allowed me to serve papers to delinquents who stood cursing, laughing, and giving me the finger from behind locked glass doors. My long hair and motorcycle also helped catch a few culprits off guard, including a used-car salesman, and for each summons I successfully served, they paid me $3.50.

But many of the addresses were too old, many of the targets, including one particular ambulance driver, were too elusive, and many of the summons addresses were too risky. The detective agency issued me sealed documents, with names and supposed addresses printed on the cover, and I had no idea of the legal contents. I once served papers to an eighteen-year-old street tough playing basketball with his friends by rolling them up and pushing them through a cyclone fence. It was too easy. The target was expecting a pro football draft letter and happily ran to the fence to get the envelope. When the papers he opened turned out to be a lawsuit filed on behalf of a girl he had shot with a shotgun, I fled on my Triumph and quit the process server business the next day.

I also applied for teaching jobs other PhD students wouldn't even consider. San Quentin Prison advertised for a college-level math instructor to teach inmates, and selected me—from a pool of millions of applicants, I'm sure—to replace an instructor who was taking early retirement. Just as I was about to start teaching, the previous instructor reenlisted for three more years, and my job was placed on indefinite hold. But it wasn't a complete loss, since San Quentin had already gotten me a California Community

College Lifetime Teaching Certificate—registration number 33355—much to the envy of fellow graduate students who had been trying to get one for years. It was like the bureaucratic catch-22 for US Immigration Green Card status. You needed a job offer to get the certificate and needed the certificate to get a job. "How can you possibly be jealous of that?" I joked to my friends. "Getting *life* at San Quentin."

I also managed to land another job shunned by most other graduate students, who felt it beneath them to teach anything below college level. I applied for, and won, a university position as Community Teaching Fellow (CTF), where I traveled four days a week to a public elementary school in a nearby Richmond ghetto, for a reversal of *To Sir with Love*. I was the only Caucasian under that roof—including teachers, students, and administrators—and my job was to use abstract mathematics to help poor kids, mostly fifth and sixth graders, who were growing up in a gang-ridden war zone and desperately needed a boost in their self-esteem.

Many of these inner-city children had failed repeatedly and were convinced that they would continue to fail. A significant number did exactly that, on through high school, if they made it that far. Many were unresponsive to normal teaching methods, and remedial arithmetic programs conducted by the public schools didn't work, since those systems used standard learning material and standard tests. No matter how hard they tried, these ghetto kids were continually playing catch-up with middle-class WASP, Asian, and Jewish kids whose parents drilled them on their multiplication tables at the dinner table and helped with their homework. It wasn't that the ghetto kids weren't bright. It was that they lacked self-confidence, and to restore that was more important than teaching them specifics.

The CTF program used a "discovery" method, asking students questions, posing mathematical games and riddles, and leading them to discover mathematics on their own. We avoided standard grade school mathematics topics and instead exposed them to the Game of Nim, the Towers of Hanoi, Cake-Cutting Problems, the Prisoner's Paradox, and other elementary examples of abstract mathematics that their usual classroom teachers couldn't solve. I asked the questions, posed the problems, and let *them* come up with the ideas. If it wasn't a fun problem, then that was *my* fault. They would try one solution idea after another and get insights one by one, and on the way discover for themselves how creative and analytical they really were. I worked with the whole class, never with specially selected students, for only forty minutes each day. It was a tremendous opportunity to begin to repay society for its gifts to me.

I decided on an informal approach and the first day introduced myself as "Ted." The students couldn't understand my Midwestern accent—*Tudd? Taad?*—until I wrote it on the blackboard. From then on they called me *Mr. Tay-ed.* At least it was better than it would have been had they known my correct surname, *Mr. Heel.* But my kids liked the disguised math problems I gave them so much that I could use the threat of not letting them come to my class the following week if they misbehaved.

There in inner-city Richmond, violence was an everyday occurrence, even at school. Other teachers came into my classroom and frisked students up against the wall. Twelve-year-olds threatened to blow my head off with a shotgun, while others begged me to demonstrate judo throws after class. I once made the mistake of calling the parents of one hyperactive youngster to ask them to speak to him about his classroom shenanigans. The poor boy came to school the next day with multiple bruises and sat painfully and quietly through the hour. It took weeks before his spirit returned to normal, and after that lesson, I handled all disciplinary problems myself.

When the 1974 teachers' strike broke out in Berkeley public schools and turned bloody, the city made desperate appeals for substitute teachers. Many math graduate students were knee-jerk union supporters, regardless of the issues, but I talked to the striking teachers. Their main beef was salary, and they complained that the average Berkeley high school teacher's pay for the nine-month school year was only $16,000. But that was $5,000 more than I had earned as a full-time university lecturer in St. Louis and was six or seven times the minimum wage. I decided to substitute teach just so the students wouldn't have another math-phobic babysitter for a month, and the strikers—and some of my math friends—were furious.

"Motherfucking scab!" yelled one of the striking teachers, giving me the finger when I was signing up to teach.

"Look," I said to the heckler. "Those kids are missing an education, just because you want more money. I worked my butt off in a Richmond primary school to help prepare some of these same kids for high school, and I'll be damned if I'm going to let you kill their chances. If they don't finish high school, I might end up teaching them in San Quentin. I love mathematics, and I'm going to help them enjoy it too. And unlike you, my friend, I'm doing it without pay." I pointed to the line on my work application where it stated all my earnings were to be donated back to the school. Quiet.

The school district administrators assigned me to Martin Luther King School, and I phoned the principal to get directions. He warned me not to park on the street or my tires would be slashed. When I arrived on my motorcycle to park in a guarded lot, two strikers shoved me back and forth, nearly knocking over the Triumph. Luckily for all of us, the strike soon ended.

During those first two years at Berkeley preparing for the orals, I had lived in the little basement apartment on Cedar Street, but even that was not cheap and cost me most of my income from the GI Bill. I thought back to my $15-a-month mansion in St. Louis. If I could find inexpensive living quarters here in Berkeley, it would significantly extend the educational buying power of my diminishing savings account.

Every day, as I cut through the wealthy neighborhood north of campus on my shortcut from Cedar Street downhill to the math department, I passed a large vacant house, partially hidden by shrubbery and large trees, near the intersection of Leroy and Ridge. What caught my eye were two large official signs, posted on the front door and porch, warning, Misdemeanor *to Occupy*. The rambling three-story house looked solid, so I figured the signs would soon disappear and I would see some sort of activity. When that didn't happen after several months, I crept up to the front window, peered in, and was shocked. There I saw solid redwood paneling, beam ceilings, hardwood floors, and built-in, recessed, hand-carved redwood bookcases and fireplace benches. The natural beauty and elegance of the interior were overwhelming. Real estate agents later told me it was original classic Mission Revival architecture.

Although the house was physically beautiful and sound, it reeked with a foul odor, and neighbors told me they had made numerous health hazard complaints to the Berkeley Housing Department. They said that both the neighborhood association and City Hall were pressuring the owner to sell, rent, or at least clean it up. Such a gorgeous house, in that beautiful neighborhood just one block north of campus, and vacant for so long—it didn't make sense.

When I had a free afternoon, I bicycled over to City Hall to research the property and tax records for 1776 Leroy Street. The owner, I learned, was one Mortgage Loan Servicing Corporation, whose office was an hour away in Palo Alto. I phoned them to make an appointment to talk about the property, borrowed a sport coat and shoes, packed a briefcase with several heavy algebra books, and drove to Palo Alto, where I parked my battered VW van a block away, out of sight from their office.

"That's a beautiful home," said the vice president, as he pointed proudly to an old photo of the house in his real estate scrapbook.

"I guess you haven't seen it in a long time," I said. "It doesn't look like that anymore. Why hasn't it been restored or sold?"

"To tell you the truth," he said, "we don't own it. We just manage it for a group of seventeen independent investors, scattered all over the Bay Area. It's next to impossible to get them to agree on anything. The house next door on the corner is also part of the estate."

"The one with the fire damage?" I asked. I pictured the other house, twice as large as the one I was interested in, with blackened holes in the roof.

"Yeah," he said. "Those two houses have been a pain in the neck for us. Lawsuits and insurance claims, neighborhood complaints, you name it. The price tag for both together is $100,000. We just want to get rid of them."

"A hundred thousand is about what my partner and I had in mind," I bluffed. "Tell you what. I want to check out the foundation and sanitation problems and get a feel for the neighborhood. Give me permission to enter and occupy rent-free until I make a decision. In the meantime, I'll start an initial cleanup. The neighborhood association will be glad to see that."

"Fine," he said. "I'll have my secretary type up the papers."

"And since I plan to do some minor repairs," I said, "of course I'd like a right of first refusal."

If a serious buyer came along, a right of first refusal would grant me the right to match that offer and buy the property myself. Usually such an option costs a tidy sum, but I was gambling that the vice president was delighted someone finally showed interest in the property.

"Of course," he answered.

Two hours later, I returned to Berkeley with a key to the house, written permission to occupy rent-free, and a signed right of first refusal. When I opened the front door, the stench buckled my knees. I covered my face with a handkerchief and walked from room to room. There were fifteen rooms, just like the Lindell place, but here each was strewn with half-filled bottles of urine and rancid wine and mildewed, rotting mattresses. Human excrement and wriggling maggots filled the toilets in all five bathrooms, and even the bathtubs were splattered with feces. It reminded me of the septicemia patients on Ward 16 at the Long Binh hospital, except this smelled much worse. I opened all the windows on the second floor and left it a few days while I advertised to sublet my apartment on Cedar.

The day I started work on the Leroy house, I skipped breakfast and used a tool I had jury-rigged from a large crescent wrench and oversized screwdriver to turn on the water to the house at the city water meter on the street. Wearing a surgeon's mask and rubber gloves, and armed with two galvanized buckets, a water dipper, and a small shovel, I started at the main bathroom on the second floor. Using the dipper, I first transferred the raw sewage from the toilet bowl into the bathtub. Then I cleared the toilet passageway by hand, primed and filled the tank, and soon had that toilet flushing normally. For the next several hours, I used this one toilet to flush the filth from the other toilets and bathtubs, until, one by one, I cleared all five toilets and bathtubs.

Opening all the windows, I pitched out mattresses, ragged sleeping bags, newspapers, rugs, and wine bottles. Everything that I could move, I heaved out the windows on the south side, forming a mound of refuse 8 feet high. After spraying industrial-grade disinfectant throughout the house, with double doses in the bathrooms, I arranged to have the debris hauled away. Then I left to let the house air out for a few days.

Within a week, I had furnished three rooms with Goodwill furniture and donations from friends and was enjoying the restored charm of a Mission Revival architectural masterpiece. It was a mathematician's paradise, with the look and feel of a German hunting lodge and two working fireplaces, redwood benches, and hardwood floors. It was a spectacular place to just sit and think, and only a short ten-minute walk from one of the best mathematics libraries in the world. I was in heaven.

Neighbors stopped when they were walking by to tell me how much better it smelled and to thank me for ending the eyesore. The mailman told me he had avoided the house for a whole year because of the vicious Dobermans that had been chained to the porch, and more recently because of the odor. I even had a visit from the Berkeley police.

"The Gypsy's doing time in Folsom Prison," the officer said, "and soon as he gets out, this is the first place he'll come."

I asked the neighbor across the street about this Gypsy fellow.

"Oh, *that* one was an operator," she said, shaking her head disapprovingly. "Two years ago he saw the house was vacant, broke in through a window, and re-keyed the door locks. Then he just set up shop, rented out rooms to transients for $45 a head, and carried on a major drug trade. Sometimes he had more than two dozen derelicts and drug addicts living there. Finally the cops arrested him and took him away. But the only way they could get rid of the rest of the squatters was to have the city shut the water off. Those vagrants lasted over two weeks without plumbing, can you imagine that?"

Unfortunately, I could. I decided to take my chances with the Gypsy, and sure enough, several months later, he appeared at my front door. Fresh out of jail, he looked pale and thin, with sunken eyes and close-cropped dark hair. He was much smaller and more docile than I had pictured, and his Free Box clothes hung in folds. After I showed him there was none of his "furniture" left in the house—my guess is he was looking for some of his stashes—he left quietly and never returned.

He didn't return, but others did. One Saturday night, there were three separate and unrelated break-ins at 1776 Leroy. As soon as I would fall asleep, it seemed, I'd be frightened awake by another suspicious creak upstairs and have to go up and run off another intruder or two. Finally I fell into a sound sleep, until I was startled by another squeak of a door. This time I was both scared *and* angry, so I picked up a fish gaff I had found while beachcombing on Point Reyes. The short club, with a five-inch metal spike attached perpendicularly to its tip, looked like a meat hook on a baseball bat and was made for impaling large gamefish. Fishermen used it to haul the struggling victim on board, and this one had old bloodstains and smears of dried fish entrails.

I switched on the light in the front hall, coughed, and noisily opened and closed the front door, as if I'd gone out. Then I hid in the shadows in the front hall and waited. After a few minutes of quiet, the prowler began moving around on the second floor, walking from room to room as if he owned the place. I crept up the stairs and waited silently in one of the darkened rooms. As the man walked down the hall past my doorway, I sprang out, grabbed his collar from behind, and shoved the bloodstained spike of the gaff around in front of his face.

"All right, motherfucker," I said. "Spread-eagle on the floor, *now*, or I jam this in your brain."

He nearly fainted and dropped face down on the floor, trembling from head to foot.

"Don't hit me, man," he pleaded. "I'm scared!"

"I'm scared too, you sonofabitch," I said. "This is my house. What the hell are you doing here?"

"Don't stick me with that, man," he said. His eyes fixed on the wicked spike on the gaff.

I let him up.

"Why didn't you just come to the front door?" I asked. "If you need a place to crash or food, just say so. Why break in and scare the bejesus out of both of us?"

He apologized, and I asked him why he had picked *my* house. I told him it was the third break-in that night.

"The word is out on Telegraph Ave, man," he said. "You need a place to stay, or drugs, just go to 1776 Leroy. Easy to remember. Just go up the fire escape and in the back window." He pointed to an open window in a dark bedroom.

I calmed him down and led him out the front door. He wanted drugs, not a place to sleep. The next morning I dismantled the fire escape, which put an end to most of the break-ins. Most, but not all. Two months later, faint sounds of a radio came from a secluded back room below the floor where I lived. That particular basement room had its own outside entrance, with no access to the main house. I knocked on the door. It opened slowly, and a hippie couple appeared. Behind them I could see sleeping bags stretched out on the floor and a radio and electric fry pan plugged into the wall outlet.

"I live upstairs," I said. "How long have you been here?"

"Two weeks," said the youth. "But we're heading for Santa Cruz tomorrow. Please don't call the fuzz on us, okay?"

I assured him I wouldn't, and the squatters were soon gone. Most of my time in the Leroy house, however, was a mathematician's dream come true. I read and studied mathematics in front of a blazing fire in the recessed stone-lined redwood fireplace and, for breaks, walked over to the math library or down to La Val's on Euclid for a pizza. I was still recovering from my self-imposed reclusion of the orals years and had become friends with Jack Miller, the fellow who had sublet my apartment on Cedar. A crack IT troubleshooting expert, Jack had studied undergraduate physics at Ann Arbor and was taking a break for a few years before starting back on his PhD. He and I had hit it off immediately, discovering our common love of hiking, backpacking, and racquetball, and soon became good friends. To help kick-start my release that fall from the seclusion of my pre-thesis years, I invited a girlfriend from my Göttingen judo team and Jack, who was still new to town, to join me for Thanksgiving in the Mission Revival mansion. No telling how long I could hang on to that place, and I was going to enjoy it while I could.

Sure enough, several months later, a real estate developer discovered the property, started escrow proceedings, and tried to get me evicted. I consulted a lawyer in the university legal aid office, and she told me she had heard about this buyer's Gestapo tactics—buying old houses, intimidating the tenants into leaving, then restoring the houses and quadrupling the rent. After weeks of harassment and interruptions to my thesis research, the lawyer said it was now time to play my trump card—the right of first refusal. A company in Oakland was conducting the title search, and I phoned them to ask its status.

"One of the most complicated searches we've ever done," they said. "The fire, the lawsuits, the seventeen different owners. That file must be 2 inches thick. Finally should be done in about two more weeks, though."

I waited a week and then drove to their office to hand-deliver a certified copy of my right of first refusal. They stared at it in shock. When I got back to Berkeley, my phone was ringing.

"Why didn't you tell us about that?" asked the developer's lawyer angrily. "We'll give you $100 to sign a quit-claim deed." I guess he knew just how destitute math graduate students really were. I told him I was actually thinking about buying the place since it looked like a good investment to me.

Good investment? No, it was more like a spectacular investment. Both huge houses, on that prime location one block from campus, for $100,000 total? But my own top priority was finishing my thesis, not real estate. I called my friend Jim Eberhardt in Santa Cruz, who drove up the next day, took one look at the properties, and offered me $5,000 cash for the right of first refusal, under one condition: that I remain in the house to oversee repairs and work crews.

"No deal," I told him. "My dissertation is number one. I don't want to be tied to this house."

Jim borrowed my phone and called the two real estate companies in Berkeley with the largest ads in the Yellow Pages. He told them we had a right of first refusal on the house at 1776 Leroy. The Mason-McDuffie agency had a man there in twenty minutes.

"My God," the man gasped, as soon as he arrived, "this is an original Mission Revival!" He asked to use my phone, and soon two more Cadillacs were circling the block, looking for parking.

"What is a house like this worth?" Jim asked the Mason-McDuffie guy.

"Well, as a house, you could sell it immediately for about $90,000," he said. "But this is a Mission Revival, and you just don't put a price on a house like this. You wait until someone comes along who wants one and is willing to pay for it."

Jim and I stepped into the den to talk. The smaller house alone was worth far more than the asking price for both properties. But Jim didn't want to get involved in a project requiring such extensive repairs without an on-site partner, and I wasn't willing to give up mathematics research to remodel houses. I finally settled for free rent for two additional months, moving expenses of $350, and $1,000 for the quitclaim deed waiving my right of first refusal. For me, that was a veritable windfall and gave me time to find my next lodging.

Thinking back to my success finding the Lindell mansion in St. Louis, I placed another "wanted-to-rent" ad, this time in the *Berkeley Gazette*, using the same wording from my ad in the *St. Louis Post-Dispatch*. After a few dead ends and crank calls, a woman phoned. Her voice was cracking with age but strong and clear.

"I have a cottage that needs some repairs," she said. "It's two blocks west of Telegraph, on Blake Street—2222 Blake Street. Come to the back door. I'm in a *chair*."

When I arrived, Olga was waiting on her back porch in her wheelchair. She looked even older than I had pictured on the phone, with deep wrinkles, thick glasses, a flowered print dress, and her hair in a white bun.

"I'm ninety-four years old," she said. "I live here alone. Back there is the cottage." With her gnarled hand, she pointed to a tiny, brown-shingle cabin behind me, surrounded by 5-foot weeds and blackberry brambles. "I haven't been inside in two years. Here's the key. Go take a look."

From the outside, the cottage looked quaint, rustic, ordinary. As I stepped through the door, her words "needs some repairs" sprang back at me. Someone—drug addicts, I later learned—had stripped it completely bare. Not only had they made off with all the interior doors, the plumbing, the toilet, and the proverbial kitchen sink, they even tore down all the old lath board and plaster interior walls to rip out the electrical wiring and outlets. Except for debris, it was an empty shell, with pine two-by-four supporting studs marking the former locations of the kitchen, bathroom, and bedroom, just as the fossilized ribs of a dinosaur skeleton mark the body cavity. A gaping hole in the floor revealed the last location of the commode. The reconstruction would be a challenge, but at least the structure was dry and free of hygiene problems, unlike the Leroy house had been, and didn't need sterilization.

I walked back to the main house, where Olga waited. I told her it would be quite a job and asked her what she had in mind. She shifted the conversation to the university and asked about my education and current study program. Then she slowly came back to my question and told me that if I repaired the cottage, I could live there rent-free for five years. *Five years free rent in Berkeley!* I accepted on the spot.

I returned the next day and began making plans for the renovation, taking notes as Olga described the original rooms and colors. As I walked through the cottage with a tape measure and clipboard, I saw through the holes that the floor was made of two layers of hardwood, separated by a thick sheet of black felt. I had never heard of such construction, and I asked Olga about it. She told me her father had been a German immigrant, a craftsman, and had built the cottage as his violin-making workshop. He imported his violin wood from the Black Forest and seasoned it there in the cottage. The layer of felt regulated temperature and humidity, she said, when the daily fog rolled in from San Francisco Bay.

Using my $1,350 proceeds from the Leroy house settlement, I drove down to San Pablo Avenue and bought secondhand toilet, sinks, and plumbing from Sunrise Salvage. Then I installed new electrical wiring and outlets, drywall, kitchen-counter tiles, a Sears water heater, and, in the front room, a cast-iron potbellied stove. I had never done this kind of renovation before but taught myself as I went, helped by advice from friendly contractors, including a city planner who knew Olga personally. After twelve days of intense labor, I had another mathematician's paradise.

As a writer's retreat, it was even better than the Leroy house had been, hidden behind the main house, quiet as a cemetery, and surrounded by weeds and wildflowers, with a few hardy cannas, Peruvian lilies, and hydrangeas poking through the mass of vegetation. I threw one last party at 1776 Leroy, sending friends home with all the furniture I could not use at Blake Street, gave the redwood fireplace mantel one last kiss, and moved to Olga's cottage.

Some afternoons we talked for hours. Her full name was Olga Pausch Grace Todd Martz, she told me, and she had married five times. I asked her why only four surnames.

"My fourth husband did terrible things," she said. "They sent him to San Quentin. I haven't spoken his name since."

Her first husband, she told me, was a US Navy lieutenant who had served as military attaché in the court of the last emperor of China. "I was married in the bridal gown designed for the emperor's wedding," she told me. "When the emperor got engaged, my fiancé stole the plans for the dress, had an exact duplicate made, and switched the gowns just before the royal wedding. It has gold thread on white silk and special stitching reserved for the imperial family."

She told stories of traveling alone in Europe as a teenage girl and said no one ever molested her, that people called her a "spirit child." Over the next few months, I began to understand why. Our Blake Street neighbors were convinced she was psychic and kept their distance, but her stories only kept me entranced. Olga told me tales of her first husband's mission, in 1913, to return the remains of Admiral John Paul Jones from an unmarked grave in France to their current resting site in a crypt in the United States Naval Academy chapel in Annapolis, where Jones is revered as a father of the US Navy. During the transatlantic shipment, a flag was draped over the casket—not the Old Glory with fifty stars we see covering the coffins on the news today, but the appropriate flag for Jones—an original 1776 flag of the thirteen colonies. Navy regulations required her husband to burn the flag after the reburial ceremony, but he burned only a small swatch, reported that he had burned the flag, and then stored it in his sea chest, convinced it would someday be of historical interest. Olga had donated the flag to the Berkeley American Legion Post in the 1930s, but it had long since disappeared.

She was a remarkable woman and fiercely independent. Olga boiled tea over open gas jets on an ancient stove without sides that was less sophisticated than the Coleman camping stove I carried in the van. Twice a week, the Center for Independent Living's Meals-on-Wheels program delivered hot food to her door. The rest of the week, she made simple sandwiches from the groceries that the Center delivered to her back door and from the treats I would bring her.

When I first moved in, Olga could use a four-leg walker to slowly maneuver down the three back porch steps to reach her beloved garden. One day, when I returned at dusk from a three-hour motorcycle ride, I found her lying face down in the garden. Olga had fallen from her walker, and, unable to get up or even crawl, she weeded a patch of garden as far as she could reach. Neighbors didn't hear her cries for help, she said, and she didn't know when I would return, so she figured she might just as well weed. If I came home before she died, fine, and if not, well, her Peruvian lilies would be weeded. There in the yard where she had fallen, it looked like a giant cookie cutter had cut a swath in the shape of the wings of a snow angel.

Olga never ventured outside again. She realized she didn't have much time left and made arrangements to leave the house and cottage to the university. Then she located a distant cousin in Iowa whom she had never met and, piece by piece, had me mail the cousin all her jewelry, gold earrings, pearl necklaces, and silver brooches. As a present, Olga gave me a rectangular gold tie pin set with tiny emeralds and diamonds, but I told her I couldn't possibly accept it. Instead, I told her, I would put it on my dresser to absorb its beauty for a week before mailing it and keep only the memories. I built her a special mailbox on her front windowsill where the postman could put her mail, and she could open it from her wheelchair inside the house.

When I introduced her to the wonders of Oscar Mayer hot dogs, my staple food dating back to my days in the Lindell mansion in St. Louis, she thought it was a miracle. There was a hot meal she could boil on her little stove, and if that was too much trouble, she said, it even tasted good cold. Olga painted verbal pictures of Berkeley's horse-and-buggy days and addressed the birds at her bird feeder by name, telling me that this one's nest was over on Parker Street, that one on Dwight Way. I never doubted a word she said.

One afternoon a young woman knocked on my cottage door, in tears and shaking hysterically. I recognized her as one of Olga's housekeeping workers from the Center for Independent Living.

"Please tell Olga I can't come back," she said, her voice trembling. "Don't tell her this, but I'm afraid of her powers. Tell her something else. Tell her I moved or something."

I waited for the explanation I knew was coming.

"Yesterday when I came to work," she sobbed, "Olga looked me straight in the eye and said, 'You've been raped.' I *had* been raped, hitchhiking up Highway One from Santa Cruz. But I didn't tell anyone, not *anyone*!" the girl said. "I can't come back. I'm sorry."

Olga had her eccentricities all right, but then I guess so did I, and we got along very well. I felt completely at home in her little cottage, creative and comfortable in that inner-city Walden. It was the solution to my rent problems and the perfect place to continue pursuit of my mathematical dreams. Besides, I figured I could use a little psychic help.

9

THE APPRENTICESHIP

At least the Berkeley math PhD orals were relatively quick and clean. Either you passed them within two years and could stay in the program, or you didn't and had to quit. You could repeat the two required language exams until you passed, with no limits on the number of attempts or the number of years it took. And the two required seminar talks were not graded. The next real hurdle after the orals was the innocuous requirement to "find a thesis advisor."

The doctoral thesis advisor is a mentor, a mathematical guru who can guide you past the knowns of coursework and graduate texts into the unknowns of research and intuition. He helps guess where the frontier might be expanded and how to approach it. He is the benefactor Carlos Castaneda sought in Don Juan, the highest level of teacher. Thesis advisors are like fathers—a good one can help you develop your talents tremendously, and a bad one can kill you. In fact, the German word for thesis advisor is *Doktorvater*, a father figure who will guide you through the doctorate. But unlike the rest of life, the doctor father has final say over whether you ultimately succeed or not, and without his final signature, you are doomed.

In mathematics the mentoring system is like an artisan's guild, where each craftsman passes on techniques to his apprentice, who adds his own discoveries and then passes on the accumulated knowledge to the next apprentice, generation after generation. A person with a PhD in mathematics can generally trace their academic ancestry exactly, from PhD to PhD, down through the ages, back through such masters as Gauss and Riemann.

For many PhD students, finding and satisfying this mentor became a dreadful trial, a purgatory that the majority of the mathematics doctoral students at Berkeley did not survive. The math department kept the discouraging statistics under wraps, but we could see the evidence around us. Classes shrank. Vaguely familiar faces attended the seminars ever less frequently, year after year after year. Finally, many just gave up searching and slowly faded away.

Others' exits were less clean. A disgruntled forty-year-old math PhD student at Stanford, also named Ted, bludgeoned Professor Karel deLeeuw to death in his office with a 3-pound sledgehammer. After he served seven years in jail for second-degree murder, his math career was over. DeLeeuw, a much-loved teacher, wasn't even the killer's advisor but simply had the misfortune of having his office door open in the same hallway when the murderer could not track down his own advisor. One of my eight classmates in Professor Bremermann's Biomathematics class blew his own head off, in his dorm room, with a 12-gauge shotgun. After the funeral, I tried to help his brother understand the pressures and frustrations of the thesis process. Finding an advisor and thesis topic often went on for years, and even having both in hand was still no guarantee of success.

I started the search for my own mentor and thesis topic by taking classes and seminars in three different fields—Biomathematics, Automata Theory, and Probability. Biomathematics uses differential equations and other mathematical tools to model processes such as population growth. After only one semester, I somehow found it too nebulous, too imprecise for me. Automata theory, on the other hand, the mathematical foundation for digital computers, is pure abstract algebra, and I found the subject very attractive. I went to see the professor during his office hours, without a sledgehammer.

"Are you in the market for any PhD students?" I asked.

"Yes, I am. And I only ask one thing if you want to work with me. That you understand there is *no hope whatever* of getting a university job after you finish."

I knew that the current job market for fresh PhDs in mathematics was one of the worst in history. That didn't bother me, but his negativism did. An attitude like that could affect my own enthusiasm and dreams for a mathematical career, enthusiasm and dreams that would be crucial in motivating me through the trial by fire of creating new mathematics. Maybe there would be academic job opportunities if I finished a thesis and maybe not, but for the time being, I needed those dreams. Scratch Automata Theory.

My next probe, into Probability Theory, was a wonderful and fortuitous fit. Many of the most fundamental theorems in probability—the law of large numbers, the law of the iterated logarithm, the central limit theorem, and many of the most basic unsolved problems—can be expressed in terms of coin tossing that I could easily explain to my non-mathematician friends. The law of large numbers, for example, generalizes the well-known fact that in tossing a fair coin, half the tosses will be heads in the long run. The law of the iterated logarithm, a much deeper result, tells how fast the average goes to one-half in terms of a very uncommon function depending on the logarithm of the logarithm of the number of tosses. The central limit theorem, the basis for much of applied statistics, explains why in many real-life datasets such as coin tossing results or test scores, the limiting distribution is the famous bell-shaped curve of Gauss, not a triangular or rectangular or parabolic curve. This field had long intrigued me, dating back to my exposure to graduate probability at Stanford and Göttingen.

After a quarter-long probability seminar on abstract gambling theory, I approached Professor Lester Dubins, and to my amazement, he agreed to take me on as his thesis student. At that time, I did not know how many others he had accepted or who had failed to meet his standards. He did not pass judgment until the mathematics was in, and perhaps something about me had piqued his interest.

Dubins's own PhD advisor, in 1955, was Segal at Chicago, whose 1940 advisor was Hille at Yale, and so on back through the ages—Hille, 1918, Stockholm—Riesz, 1912, Budapest—Fejer, 1902, Budapest—Schwarz, 1864,

Berlin—Kummer, 1831, Halle-Wittenberg—Scherk, 1823, Berlin—Bessel, 1810, Göttingen—Gauss, 1799, Helmstedt—Pfaff, 1786, Göttingen—Kaestner, 1739, Leipzig—Hausen, 1713, Halle-Wittenberg—Wichmannshausen, 1685, Leipzig—Mencken, 1668, Leipzig. It was an illustrious unbroken line of mathematics doctoral mentors, fifteen straight generations of PhD, spanning more than 300 years. If I had consulted the grapevine at the time, I probably would not have had the courage to solicit him as my mentor.

Lester Dubins was a Berkeley legend. His muscular, lanky, 6-foot frame, his shock of medium-long white hair and white moustache, and his piercing, brilliant dark eyes reminded me of Albert Einstein and Mark Twain. In his fifties and single, he lived alone in an unfurnished apartment on the South Side, without even dinner plates or salt and pepper. Still living the life of a twenty-year-old mathematician, Dubins debated new theories in coffee shops and described deep discoveries and conjectures at the blackboard with colorful examples about roulette and "casino functions," scribbling inequalities and graphs that invariably sloped downhill to the right. He was oblivious to the mundane concerns of home ownership, regular meals, and family responsibilities that devour the lives of most middle-aged men. A maverick in his mathematics, he often disagreed with mainstream trends, even on the fundamental definition of probability itself. Dubins and a small group of like-minded scientific rebels felt that the basic premise of probability should be "finite additivity," an axiom that did not require endless operations such as infinite flips of a coin. And he was a maverick socially.

"You're Dubins's student?" asked a professor from Hawaii. "What a character. Once, three of us—two young grad students and the grand old master—were sitting in a coffee shop on Telegraph, discussing finite additivity. Right then, a cute young chick, maybe twenty, comes into the café and sits down by the window. We're all silently checking her out—dreaming away—but keep talking math. A few minutes later, Dubins excuses himself politely, walks over to her table, and strikes up a conversation. Then he sits down with her, and twenty minutes later, they both get up and walk out the door to his car. You remember his beat-up old Cadillac? Well, it's parallel parked right in front of the window, and the two of us young guys at the table are just kicking ourselves. They get in the car, and what happens as he pulls out? So excited he rams into a car coming down Telegraph. Not just any car, a *cop* car! That's typical Dubins!"

But inside a seminar room, it was we who crashed and burned. Dubins's questions, uncommonly formal and courteous for Berkeley—"Mr. Hill" this, and "Mr. Pestien" that—immediately cut to the core. His strong, polite voice interrupted at the first hint of sloppy logic, and twice I saw speakers leave the room in tears. Once he abruptly canceled the talk of another PhD apprentice of his five minutes into the lecture, when the poor fellow couldn't give a concrete example of the new theorem whose proof had taken him six months to work out. The next day that student, who had come to Berkeley from India specifically to work under Dubins, quit and went to work for another advisor. Dubins never meant harm in his questions and was charming socially, but his standards of clear logic and irrefutable proof were without equal. He would simply not allow careless reasoning and obscure arguments in his seminars.

His integrity was complete and unwavering. You didn't invite Dubins out to dinner and ask him how he liked the restaurant unless you were ready for the polite but unadulterated truth. If he didn't understand something, mathematics or not, he asked immediately, while others just nodded in feigned comprehension. I admired both his mathematics and his integrity. He was never intentionally rude, but only mindful of logic and demands on his time. Under his tutelage, I buckled down to identify a research problem in probability theory—with luck, one I could hope to crack in three or four years. Some advisors rushed their students to completion, but others, like Dubins, demanded a significant mathematical breakthrough for the thesis, and that typically took years.

Meanwhile, the distractions of Berkeley were overwhelming, not only the street artists and the Hare Krishnas and foreign film festivals, but also the radical city politics. Urban guerrillas were just surfacing—*Venceremos*, Weather Underground, the Black Liberation Army, and the Hells Angels. On election night of my second fall quarter, November 6, 1973, the so-called Symbionese Liberation Army (SLA) had assassinated educator Dr. Marcus Foster in neighboring Oakland with cyanide-tipped bullets.

Three months later, the same group kidnapped Patty Hearst at gunpoint from the Berkeley apartment near Telegraph that she shared with her boyfriend, a former math teacher at a private school on the San Francisco Peninsula. The SLA guerillas used Ms. Hearst to extort money from her father, media mogul Randolph Hearst, demanding that food be distributed, beginning February 19, on every Tuesday, Thursday, and Saturday, for four weeks, with distribution centers at Glide Memorial Church, Nairobi College in East Palo Alto, and the San Francisco Mission District.

The Hearst Corporation and the authorities knuckled under, and workers doled out truckload after truckload of turkeys and cheese—$2 million worth—as the media showed propaganda clips of converted hostage Tania *née* Patty holding a rifle in front of the SLA's battle flag emblazoned with a seven-headed cobra. In May the whole television world witnessed the fiery gun battle in Los Angeles when police killed six members of the SLA. Armed urban guerrillas seemed to make the news every night.

* * *

One afternoon an Iranian classmate I had met in Helson's course on Linear Operator Theory visited my cottage, and his eyes widened in disbelief when he saw on my bookcase, next to Rudin's *Complex Analysis* textbook, my .38 Special Smith & Wesson revolver.

"Jesus, where'd you get this?" asked Massoud, as he turned it over and over in his hand, testing its grip and heft. "The police are really paranoid about handguns, what with all the terrorists around here. There are hundreds of mathematicians in Berkeley, and I bet you're the only one with a gun."

"Maybe," I said. "But most of them are city people. In the country, we grew up with guns. Double-barreled 20-gauge shotgun in our kitchen closet, Sears, Roebuck single-shot .22 rifle leaning against the side door, air rifles and pistols hanging on hooks in the back hallway. Did a lot of plinking, at tin cans and varmints. You didn't in Persia?" I knew he hated the word *Iran*.

I took the revolver from him and demonstrated how to flip open the cylinder. "Want to try it sometime?" I said. "I've got a .22 rifle too." I could see the excitement burning in his dark eyes.

He pleaded with me to go as soon as possible, and since we had no classes on Tuesdays, we agreed to meet the following Tuesday morning.

Massoud was a character. He was short, lean, and built like an acrobat, with the classic dark features and prominent nose of a Middle Eastern warrior. "No way Persians look like Arabs, man!" he would insist, with the fiery eyes of a revolutionary. When he wasn't pressing out hundreds of push-ups or thousands of skip-rope reps, he read Marx and *The Economist* and *Le Monde*, agonizing over the plight of oppressed peoples in the world, especially in his own homeland under the Shah. He played tag with neglected neighborhood kids, rewarding them with a cookie every time they could touch him as he darted to and fro like a fox terrier.

Massoud's low-rent, ground-level apartment on Hearst Avenue was the local mecca for Persian dissidents, university scuba divers, and the odd mathematician. I had often stopped by on my customary late-night, two-hour walkabouts through Berkeley. And even at 1 a.m. the door would be wide open, the aromas of chicken simmering in tomatoes and onions, or of freshly poached—in both senses—Lake Tahoe crayfish were pouring out to mix with the cool fog-and-eucalyptus night air. My father had spent that half year in Iran helping a small, rural food-canning factory and had told me many stories of the remarkable Persian hospitality. I saw evidence of it right here in Berkeley. As soon as I would stick my head in Massoud's door on one of those late night walks just to say hello, we'd soon be jabbering mathematics or planning our next abalone dive, feasting on another of Massoud's midnight meals. It was going to be a pleasure to show him a little about guns.

When the day arrived, he and I drove my van to the old-fashioned gun shop on the corner of College and Ashby. The two middle-aged proprietors behind the wood-and-glass counter wore flannel shirts, string ties, silver-and-turquoise belt buckles, jeans, and cowboy belts. Here, at the epicenter of liberal California, these two chaps stood their ground, surrounded by rifles, pistols, ammo, and leather holsters. To most passersby on trendy College Avenue, they must have looked like space aliens. The smells of wood stocks and leather and gun oil brought back many fond memories of learning to care for my first rifle as a boy, and less fond memories of rifle inspections at West Point.

The two men sized us up when we entered the shop, mumbling something about the latest news on urban guerrillas and anti-gun activists. I asked them for two boxes of .38 Special wadcutters, and one of the men put a box of the cheap target ammunition on the glass counter. Since I spoke their language, they relaxed slightly but still kept an eye on Massoud.

"Say, I'm new to California," I said. "We just want to do some target practice. What's the penalty here if we get caught shooting tin cans alongside a country road?"

"Don't do it!" the older guy warned. "It's illegal as hell here, and they can confiscate your car, as well as the guns. And the police are trigger-happy these days because of the SLA and *Venceremos* gangs. There's a shooting range 14 miles from where you're standing, up in the Oakland Hills."

I jotted down his directions on the ammo box and thanked him for the tip. Massoud carefully cradled the revolver and the ammo. Even at a firing range, he would have fun.

We drove up past the East Oakland Hills where the road narrowed to a winding, eucalyptus-shaded lane, and the Volkswagen van ground uphill in second gear. *Ten Miles to Firing Range*, read a sign. Then, *Six Miles to Range*. At that pace, the signs seemed hours apart. At the *One Mile* marker, we could hear firing in the wooded valley below, and finally we came to the gate. *Firing Range Entrance*, it said. *Closed on Tuesdays*. Massoud exploded and kicked the locked padlock. Why all the shooting, then? Was it for the benefit of some privileged members?

"Look, Massoud," I said. "Let's just go back down the road a half mile, walk into the woods, and try out the revolver. With all that noise on the range, they'll never hear us. Probably just some rich gun club guys anyway—they won't give a damn."

We backtracked just out of sight from the gate, parked the van on the ridgeline, and hiked into the woods with the .38, two boxes of ammo, and a dozen paper pie plates for targets. I tacked the paper plates to the trunk of a tree to absorb stray shots and prevent ricochets, and after slowly squeezing off 50 rounds, we collected the brass casings and bullet-ridden plates, leaving only the white paper bits the bullets had pasted to the bark. I told Massoud to walk slowly through the woods toward the van, and I followed a stone's throw behind, carrying the revolver, and watching him closely through the undergrowth. If he pulled out his handkerchief, that meant he had run into the authorities, and I would dump the casings and revolver in the bushes and try to escape.

We reached the van without incident, and I opened the driver's door and placed the .38 on the floor, between the two front seats. I then stepped back out, without bothering to shut the door, and walked across the road to where Massoud stood surveying the valley below. Just as he stood pointing to a good potential campsite on the next ridgeline, around the bend came a posse of Oakland Police, motorcycle and squad car lights flashing. As they screeched to a halt in front of us, I whispered to Massoud to do the talking and to turn on the heavy accent. The motorcycle cop reached us first.

"Did you guys hear any shooting?" he shouted, glancing around.

"Yaa–here–onder hill . . ." Massoud said, and pointed down the valley to the firing range.

"No, not down there. *Up here*," said the cop.

"Onder-hill," said Massoud slowly, his accent thicker than ever.

The cop shook his head angrily, muttered, "Damn foreigners!" under his breath, and barked orders to the squad cars. They jumped out, shotguns and revolvers in hand, formed a line at the edge of the road, and swept off into the woods on foot, 50 feet from where we had just exited. Massoud and I glanced at each other and slowly ambled back to the van. The driver's door was still open, the revolver in plain view. It was pure luck we had been standing across the road when the posse arrived and that the cops were running off into the woods to catch or kill the culprits instead of leaving one behind to question us. Driving slowly back down the range road, our eyes were glued to the rearview mirrors, expecting to see flashing lights any second. The return 14 miles seemed like 40.

In Berkeley we breathed a sigh of relief but wondered how the Oakland police had pinpointed us so quickly and precisely. Tuesday, we later found out, was Police Practice Day at the range. The officers on the range below had immediately heard our .38 firing on the hill and radioed in the coordinates. Excellent coordinates, at that—the posse had pulled up within 100 yards of the bullet-ridden tree. But by now, the poor motorcycle cop was probably trying to explain to his shift boss exactly why he let go, scot-free, two foreigners in a beat-up Volkswagen van located exactly at those coordinates while his team rushed off into the bush and came back empty-handed. That close call gave us something to laugh about as we both returned to our more sedate and cerebral mathematics lives. We promised to try it again sometime.

I continued to dive into the mathematical probability of "gambling theory," of which Dubins was one of the founding fathers and leading experts. A typical example of his is the problem of a gambler in a casino with $1,000, whose goal is not to make a fortune or to beat his friend but to keep playing indefinitely. Although often expressed in terms of betting and casinos and roulette, the mathematical theory of gambling is an abstraction of a very wide class of important problems involving elements of decision making under uncertainty. Suppose, for example, that you have isolated a rare microbe you hope will eventually provide a cure for cancer or Alzheimer's. Your objective is to keep this organism alive indefinitely. Every morning you must make a decision—to add water, or remove waste, or inoculate against disease, or perhaps do nothing—and every decision you make involves some risk. Your goal, as was the case for the casino gambler, is to find a strategy for keeping the process alive.

One day in the Dubins seminar, a young German professor visiting from the University of Bonn ended his talk with an example that showed that there are generally no good strategies for the decision maker that depend only on the current state—for example, the amount of money or microbes. In formal terms, good stationary strategies don't always exist, and in order to keep the process alive, you are forced to vary your action, even with the same number of dollars or microbes remaining. Otherwise the process will die out with certainty. General strategies, of course, can be extremely complicated, depending on the whole history of the process and what happened after all your previous actions. If possible, you would like to find a fairly simple strategy to keep the process alive. The last part of the talk contained further negative results, and in the question period afterward, I asked the speaker what possible *positive* results one could hope for in the simplest case.

He didn't know the answer, but Dubins spoke up. "For finite sets," he said, "it is thought that perhaps good Markov selectors exist. But it's still unknown."

That is, Dubins suspected that there are always good strategies where the decision you make each day depends only on the current state and the time. I found this problem very appealing. To prove something new about probabilities on general finite sets struck me as both basic and interesting. I set myself the goal of solving this little problem to show Dubins I could do research and then to move on to a thesis-level problem.

Weeks ran into months as I struggled with the question. I read the latest research papers on the subject, struggled through the first three chapters of the classic Dubins and Savage research text *How to Gamble If You Must: Inequalities for Stochastic Processes*, and filled reams of scrap paper with arrows and dots and equations and conjectures. When I found counterexamples—proofs by example that a certain conjecture is not true—I kept records of them and strove to understand why the result failed. I worked until late at night, on weekends, and during holidays. When I finally made tiny headway, for spaces with only three states, I went to see Dubins during his office hours and described my findings. He saw immediately that I was far from a solution but encouraged me to continue. More months passed, and I began to feel discouraged that I had not cracked this small homework exercise. What would Dubins think about my ability to solve a major dissertation problem if I had so much trouble with this little question?

Thesis advisors had to submit periodic progress reports on their PhD advisees to the departmental administration. Following new university guidelines on freedom of information, the math office automatically sent copies of these reports to students. One afternoon, in my pigeonhole mailbox in Evans Hall, there was a sealed white campus envelope, and inside that, a Xerox of my latest progress report.

Mr. Hill has begun working on a problem which could make a fine PhD thesis, signed by Professor Lester Dubins.

PhD thesis?! Apparently Dubins also considered the problem basic and interesting, but unlike me, he had more correctly estimated its difficulty. This new information, that the Markov selector problem could be my dissertation, rekindled my excitement, and I redoubled my efforts. There would be no partial solution to a problem like this. It would be all or nothing, but I felt it would be worth the gamble. I decided to celebrate this small bit of encouragement.

I phoned Massoud and told him I needed a little break. Did he want to risk another outing with the .38 and try out the .22 rifle? I already knew his answer in advance and had dug out a topo map of the East Bay and Sacramento River Delta. The map showed a railroad tunnel near Martinez that was several miles from any county road. I figured it would be secluded enough to do some shooting. We drove Massoud's beat-up 1966 Ford panel truck and took the .38 Special, the .22 rifle, and Omid, a Persian friend of Massoud's who had just turned eighteen. Omid also wanted to experience boyhood Americana.

The forty-year-old map was still fairly accurate, and only a dirt road led to the railroad tracks near the foothill. We parked the truck, took out the guns and ammo, and took turns making tin cans dance in the California sunshine, using the ridge as a backstop. Even a simple .22 Long Rifle bullet can travel well over a mile in the air. After an hour we tired of the target practice and followed the railroad tracks on foot to where they disappeared into a tunnel.

The topo map indicated that the tunnel, only one track wide, was about three-quarters of a mile long. The rails looked rusty, and having seen no sign of trains all afternoon, we wandered in, aiming toward the small beam of light from the other end of the tunnel that floated in the darkness ahead of us. As we started picking our way along the rough stones and rusty iron spikes between the railroad ties, our eyes slowly adjusted to the dark.

"I got caught in a train tunnel just like this once near West Point," I told Massoud and Omid as we slowly picked our way along the railroad ties in the shadows. "I was off limits, camouflaged in black parka and dark green fatigues, exploring the banks of the Hudson, when I came across the spot where the West Shore Railway cuts through Academy grounds. Right under the parade ground! None of us had ever heard of it. I couldn't resist checking it out. The jagged hole had been dynamited out of the Hudson palisades' gray granite bedrock and was barely wide enough for a single boxcar. Since I'd never heard about the tunnel before, I figured it was no longer in use.

"I was several hundred yards into it when suddenly I heard a noise like low rolling thunder, and a huge black mass blocked out the light at the far end. I looked back to see if I could sprint to my end of the tunnel, but no way I could make it. I figured I had two options—lie low between the tracks or flatten myself up against the rough tunnel wall. I prayed none of the boxcars had boards or pipes sticking out sideways, and I slammed up against the wall, facing away from the tracks in case the steel wheels kicked up stones or sparks.

"I was expecting the horrendous noise as the freight flew by, but not the gale-force blast. The train was sucking air through the narrow shaft, forming a gigantic wind tunnel with me in the middle. I pressed the wall as hard as I could as the freight came within inches of my back. Seemed to last a lifetime. When the last boxcar passed, I ran for daylight. Legs were wobbly, but the engineer hadn't seen me, dressed in black in the shadows along the wall, and I made it back to the barracks in one piece. Put my sedate life as a cadet into a whole new perspective."

I had barely finished my story, about two-thirds of the way through the Martinez tunnel, when Omid screamed, "*Train!*"

Massoud and I glanced at him, thinking he was joking. But when we looked where he was pointing, we saw a locomotive that would be on us in about twenty seconds. "Oh, shit," I thought, "not again." We had to act fast. "Split up 10 yards apart," I yelled. The noise from the train was already loud. "In case one guy gets hit, it won't cause a chain reaction. Face to the wall. Don't look over your shoulder. That's what worked for me last time." I took a breath, and we all shook hands. "Goodbye," I said, "and good luck."

We ran to the wall on the right side of the track, which looked to be a few inches wider than the left, and split up. The freight thundered down on us. Again the deafening roar and wind tunnel blast of air, but even stronger than in the West Shore tunnel, since this train was moving faster and the tunnel was longer.

Again I held my breath and prayed that no loose cargo jutted out, prayed I wouldn't faint, prayed no stones would be kicked up, prayed for the buddies I couldn't see along the wall. I closed my eyes tightly as the freight thundered past, belching out smoke and cinders. Finally the caboose roared by, and we raced for the end of the tunnel, still clutching rifle and revolver. Outside the late-afternoon sun cast long shadows, and our limbs and voices were trembling. Instead of returning through the tunnel to get to Massoud's van, we all agreed to scale the ridge and climb down the other side.

After an hour of scrambling through dry weeds and loose gravel, we finally reached the crest. A swarm of police cars now surrounded Massoud's van far below—Railroad Special Police, County Sheriff, and California Highway Patrol. They had binoculars and a bullhorn.

"You up on the ridge," cracked the bullhorn. "Wave your arms if you were in the tunnel."

We waved. They couldn't hear us that far away.

"Wave your arms if no one was hurt."

As we learned later, the train engineer had seen us this time but had no chance of braking. He had radioed in to the railroad police to send a squad car and to alert the coroner. He figured we were dead men, and the morgue would have a messy job.

Again we waved and started our descent.

"Move down here with your hands up."

They had seen the rifle. I quickly removed the bolt from the .22, and held it in my left hand, over my head, the rifle in my right. They probably had not spotted the revolver tucked in my belt, and that was more of a problem. Handguns are easy to carry and conceal—they're the weapons of choice in most robberies and murders—so ownership of a revolver like this was much more tightly controlled than that of a rifle. And I had serious doubts about the history of this particular .38 in my belt. I had gotten it from my friend Jim, who was still doing part-time police work in Santa Cruz, so it was probably okay. But then again the ammo we had been using all day had been stolen from the Navy Military Police.

"*Stolen*?" I'd said, when Jim mumbled the word when he gave me the bullets.

"Well, sort of," he answered with a smile. "You know, when ammo reaches a certain age, it's supposed to be destroyed. We take it out to the demolition range, rig it with a little C-4, and blow it all up. Looks like the Fourth of July. I just pulled a few cases out of the pile before we set it off and fudged the reports. Same explosion, same hole in the ground, and nobody the wiser. Just don't get caught with that ammo."

The bullets, long and shiny and brass-tipped, looked like copper-colored versions of the Lone Ranger's silver bullets. These weren't wadcutters for tin cans or paper targets—they were designed for tearing through flesh.

Knowing Jim, I figured the revolver might also not be 100 percent legal, so during our descent, at a point where the brush and a 2-foot drop into a dry streambed put us out of sight from the cops for a few seconds, I dropped the Smith & Wesson in the weeds. A minute later, the police point men met us with their guns drawn. One grabbed the rifle and bolt, and while the rest spread-eagled us up against separate squad cars and frisked us for weapons, he radioed in the serial numbers of the rifle. I knew the rifle was clean.

After two independent body searches of each of us, they started the interrogation. We could sense a mixture both of relief and anger in their questions. The only plainclothesman, a handsome black man in his thirties who reminded me of Shaft, led the questioning. He was wearing the badge of a railroad special agent.

"How the hell did you do it?" he blurted. "Last time I got called out here, three twelve-year-old boys got caught in that tunnel. Two survived. But they were a hell of a lot smaller than you. And on the next ridge over, I went in to get a man's body, and the biggest part of him I found was a foot, and that was in his shoe."

I described how we faced the wall and had no idea how close the boxcars had come.

"Good thing you didn't lie between the rails," he continued. "That worked fine in the old days, but these new engines ride 4 inches above the tracks. You'd have been hamburger." He started to relax a little. "Damn. I'm in bed with a beautiful woman on a fine Sunday afternoon, and I get called out to this shit. But I'm glad as hell I didn't have to go in there and scrape you up with a putty knife."

"So are we, sir," I said. "Sorry for the trouble we've caused you."

When his part in the investigation finished, the regular cops took over. They quizzed us about trespassing and shooting, the Symbionese Liberation Army, and *Venceremos*. One officer pointed to a metal electronic switch box along the tracks, about 3 feet high and a foot square at the base. Colored electrical wires poked out gaping holes in its sides.

"You do that with the rifle?" he asked.

"No, sir," I said. "Our .22 would never make holes like that. Somebody's used a high-powered rifle and steel-jacketed bullets."

They knew that, but for some reason, one of the deputies wanted to throw the book at us. He handed me the rifle and said I could put it back in the van. I knew that if I opened the sliding door and they saw something suspicious, they'd have probable cause to search the van, so I slipped the rifle through the half-open passenger's-side window. The deputy frowned, and moved up for a closer look at the front seat. He saw the .38 ammo, reached in, and pulled it out.

"What is this for, then? Thought you said you were shooting a .22 up here."

"We were shooting a .22. But we also had a revolver, and that ammo you're holding is for the .38 I dumped in the bushes up there." I pointed toward the base of the ridge.

He recoiled instantly, pushed me back up against the van, and spread-eagled me to pat me down once again. Handguns upped the ante. I told him I would show him where the .38 was, but he told me he wouldn't let me anywhere near it and ordered me to draw a map in the dirt. I used a twig to sketch the streambed and bushes, and he shouted to the other cops to keep the three of us separated and under close guard. In five minutes he came back with the .38 and called in the serial numbers, as I sweated it out. Luckily the central police computer cleared us again, but now the same deputy and another officer were examining our ammo on the hood of their squad car.

"Strange-looking loads," said the other cop. "What are these red marks for?"

In his rush to uncover evidence of a serious crime, the deputy had ripped open the cardboard ammo box without even looking at it. *Not for Civilian Use*, it read. *For Use by Military Police Only*, stamped in letters I could read 10 feet away. In our situation, it might just as well have been stamped *Stolen from the Military Police*. The red dots on the bases of the cartridges were an additional clue to someone in the know.

"Oh, those red marks just mean they are *reloads*," said the deputy with authority.

I sighed silently with relief as they handed the ammo back to me. Then began the business of deciding what criminal charges to press. It would be trespassing at least, but the deputy was pushing for a felony.

"Look," he said. "Southern Pacific has been holding up interstate trains in that tunnel for three hours now while we've been clearing it. I say we nail these guys for interference with interstate traffic of trains. That's a federal offense."

But the other cops were more sympathetic, especially the special agent. He waited patiently, then spoke. "Hey, look, nobody was hurt," he argued. "No property damage, no larceny. And it was obviously unintentional. Let's just write them up for trespassing on railroad property."

Luckily for us, the special agent's opinion carried a lot of weight in that crowd. Finally the other officers yielded to his recommendation and charged us with trespassing, a misdemeanor that carried a maximum penalty of six months in jail. I flashed back to the Wellesley College incident, where I also ended up in jail after nearly being killed, not by a train, but by police bullets. This time around, however, I could not plead Army officer status in bargaining for leniency. To make matters worse, Omid did not have his Green Card yet, and even a couple of days in jail could get him deported. Along with Massoud, whose anti-Shah reputation was widely known, they would instead send him back to face SAVAK, Iran's notorious secret police. My father had recently told me that he had learned that his personal interpreter Behruz, a beloved friend of the family, had been tortured to death by SAVAK.

I told the officers that it had been all my idea, that Omid had just turned eighteen, and that I wanted to take the rap. It hadn't worked with the Wellesley police, and it didn't work here either. The deputy wrote out a summons, giving us a date to appear at the Martinez courthouse for trial. The official charges listed only trespassing on railroad property.

Two months later, Massoud, Omid, and I appeared in court. Just before our case came up, two huge bailiffs burst through a side door of the courtroom, struggling with an even larger man in waist chain, handcuffs, and leg irons. The convict looked like a pirate, a mountain man with long, shaggy red hair and beard, barrel chest, and massive shoulders and forearms. His eyes blazed with the defiance of a cornered grizzly as the officers wrestled him into a side alcove. My two Persian friends gaped in shock and sucked in deep breaths. This was their first experience with the American judicial system. The clerk read our names and the charges, and we stood up.

"Your Honor," I said, "With your permission, I would like to act as spokesman for all of us. My friends are from Persia, and I was just showing them some typical American boyhood experiences."

"What about the *trespassing*?" said the judge.

"Well, Your Honor, we didn't see any signs and didn't cause any harm," I said.

"What about the *guns*?"

I choked slightly. The judge knew more than we'd hoped. "Just doing some target practice, Your Honor. My friends had never fired a revolver before."

"What about the *interstate train tunnel*?"

"We didn't know it was still in use, Your Honor," I said. "Otherwise we never would have gone in it. We almost got killed."

He asked if we had anything else to add, and I said no.

"I find you guilty of trespassing, which is a misdemeanor," said the judge. He paused for a few long seconds to let it sink in and to give us time to sweat out the thought of a six-months-long jail sentence for me and deportation for my friends. I glanced at Massoud and Omid, who were staring tensely at the shackled mountain man, imagining themselves soon to be in the same boat.

"I fine you each $15," said the judge. "But don't you Berkeley boys come back trespassing in my jurisdiction again, do you understand?"

"Yes, Your Honor," we said in unison, and rushed out of the courtroom to pay our fine at the court clerk's desk. The poor mountain man would not be as fortunate.

As we drove back to Berkeley, we talked about our good fortune to be alive after the brush with the train, to be in America, and most of all, to not be in jail. True, we had been convicted of a crime, but it was only a misdemeanor. As the excitement of our adventure wound down, our conversation turned to the high attrition rate among math grad students and the prospects of Massoud and I ever finishing, now that we were still breathing.

I'd had firsthand experience with high casualty rates before, in Beast Barracks at West Point, in Ranger School, and in Vietnam. The results were depression, sometimes death, and either way it meant devastating changes in somebody's life. Many of our fellow doctoral candidates were child prodigies, superstars in science high schools, award winners in the best undergraduate colleges in the world. During the first two years in graduate school they continued to excel, but suddenly, and unpredictably, they faltered when required to be creative. The pre-PhD academic sieve, Graduate Record Exam scores, the orals, the seminar talks, and the language exams did not test for imagination, and for the first time in their lives, brilliant minds bogged down. Many drifted in and out of graduate school for five, ten, fifteen years, surviving on welfare, odd jobs, and support from their families. Two-thirds of the PhD students in our department failed to ever complete a dissertation.

The attrition in the Berkeley mathematics PhD program was becoming personal. While some friends did finish their PhDs—Sherman from San Francisco's Chinatown, and James from middle-class black Oakland, the first in his family to even graduate from college—many more dropped out. Tom, who day-sailed the marijuana from South America, suddenly quit and returned to his father's tool business in Los Angeles. Then his friend Allan, who worked with me in the Richmond ghetto school, also dropped out. Maurice had failed his orals the first time around, switched examination subject areas the maximum allowable number of times, failed again, and filed requests for delays and additional examinations based on his unusual dual major in mathematics and paleontology. After he exhausted all official remedies, he appealed to last-resort Committee Omega, the secretive "supreme court" of the Mathematics Department. When Committee Omega refused to grant him further special exemptions, Maurice divorced his wife, sold his house in Pinole, and moved east. Thirty years later, he sent me an email that he was still working on his PhD in mathematics, in his third or fourth university program. He passed away while still working on it.

Massoud was also bogged down, picking up two additional master's degrees in Electrical Engineering and Physics, as he rammed his head against the mathematics thesis wall. It became clear it would be at least ten years before he finished . . . if ever.

As a sort of consolation prize, the university administration designed a new formal degree, the Candidate in Philosophy Degree, which ranked between a master's and a PhD. If a student passed the orals at the PhD level and completed all the coursework and seminars and language exams required for a PhD—everything but the dissertation—he was awarded this new Cand. Phil. degree. It was meant as formal recognition of the significant accomplishments necessary to survive up to the final dissertation-writing phase, and to soften the blow of possibly never finishing. In effect it was a formal version of what graduate students at other universities generally refer to unofficially as an ABD—All But Dissertation.

The new degree, complete with sheepskin bearing official seals and the chancellor's signature, came as a complete surprise to those of us in the PhD program. Since Doctor of Philosophy is called a PhD, I christened the Candidate in Philosophy a "PhC." From a graduate student's perspective, the degree was completely worthless. Job advertisements only listed requirements for a master's or doctorate, and outside of Berkeley, almost no one had ever heard of the degree. For the math department, however, it brought the same university resource allocations as any other formal degree and helped cover up the costly and embarrassingly high attrition rate of its PhD students. I now realized that, statistically speaking, in my future job applications, there was a good chance that the box marked "highest degree earned" would most likely be the universally unknown PhC. But for now, I was determined to keep pushing.

Dubins was the kind of professor who would gladly talk mathematics with anybody, anytime, but he had little patience for vague generalities. A visitor without solid ideas met only awkward silence. So while other graduate students met weekly with their thesis advisors to brainstorm about their thesis problem, some several times a week, my appointments with Dubins were sometimes months apart. In our initial meetings, he made sure that I understood the unsolved problem precisely. *In every finite-state gambling problem, are there always epsilon-optimal Markov strategies?* That is, are there always good strategies for keeping the process alive that depend only on the time and state? Yes or no? The answer required either a proof or a counterexample, no more, no less.

Other advisors pointed their students to mountains of research papers and monographs, to 1,000-page abstract texts like Dunford and Schwartz. They helped their students read through the known results in the literature and understand basic ideas, and sometimes, in the process, even ended up solving the thesis problem themselves. In those cases, some advisors published the new result under their own names. Others published it jointly with their student. It even happened that advisors essentially wrote the candidate's *whole dissertation*, just to chalk up another PhD student on their own *curriculum vitae* and move that student out the door in order to start working with a new apprentice.

With Dubins things were different. No known results would help solve the Markov problem, and Dubins left it completely up to me to decide what, if anything, to read and how to attack the problem. Time did not matter to him. When a PhD student from Israel solved a new stochastic dynamical programming problem, he took it to Dubins to ask if it could be the basis for a thesis.

"No," said Dubins. "No. Publish the result. It certainly warrants that. But for your thesis, solve something more significant."

The student took the very same solution to another math professor, a distinguished member of the National Academy of Sciences, who accepted it immediately as a thesis and signed off. That professor's philosophy was that academic life is hard enough as it is, and obstacles like dissertations should be negotiated as easily and as quickly as possible. Dubins felt otherwise. A friend of Massoud's who had already finished his PhD orals and master's and was looking for an advisor, went to see Dubins. The student asked him how much longer a dissertation would take.

"For a good thesis," Dubins said, "about eight or nine more years. The dissertation should be a substantial result, and to predict the time necessary for that is impossible. It's like guessing how long it would take to write a good symphony."

That student too went to work for a different advisor, but I stuck with Dubins and the Markov problem. It was an indeterminate sentence, unlike the nine weeks in Ranger School and the year in Vietnam, and although I had been working hard for over two years now, my dream of becoming a globetrotting career mathematician still seemed a very long way off.

When I bogged down on my thesis, hitting one logical dead end after another, I turned to the soothing remedy of my boyhood: hiking, alone, as far as possible from civilization. For me, nothing refreshes body and soul better than raw nature. I bought topographic maps of the Bay Area and ran my finger along the remote stretches of beach at Point Reyes National Seashore until I found a spot that was miles from the nearest road or trail. I drove to Point Reyes, left the van at the last parking lot, and starting hiking south along the beach, which ended at the horizon with a reddish-brown sandstone promontory. The dunes ahead of me rose gently to the left, ending in hillocks of wiry European dune grass. On the right, the sand banks were flattened smooth by the choppy green waves of the Pacific. The bright sun made me squint, and the cold salt air whipped along the beach toward me, its cargo of fine sand stinging my face like tiny hornets.

Hiking in dry sand seems to use ten times the energy of hiking on flat ground, and as I walked, I tried to find an explanation from basic physics, estimating the foot-pounds of work needed to move sand out of each footprint. A half hour out, other beachcombers' footprints turned back toward the parking lot. An hour out, the bluff appeared just as distant as when I'd started, and piles of driftwood and decaying sea kelp now dotted the sands. The sun-bleached logs increased in size as I crunched through the coarse sand, and the chalk-white torsos of giant sequoias reminded me of the marble columns at the Parthenon. Mounds of flotsam contained broken pieces of hulls, and long beams of teak washed ashore from shipwrecks, along with crates stenciled in red or black with Japanese ideographs. I had hiked many remote beaches in many countries and never seen anything like this.

I had underestimated the distance, and ran out of water. Turning back, I stooped to pick up a heavy, hollow glass sphere, the size of a basketball, transparent jade green with Japanese markings branded into its side. It was the float from a fisherman's net, I later learned, that had probably drifted all the way from Japan. Back at the Point Reyes parking lot, I saw a fisherman loading his tackle box and asked about the unusual size and variety of the driftwood and debris on that beach.

"This formation is unique," he said, pointing to the promontory. "That triangular ridge juts out into the Humboldt Current, perpendicular to the San Andreas Fault. It's like a grappling hook, sticking out there to snag jetsam coming down the coast from the Bering Strait and Japan. And the point causes enormous riptides. I lost a boat here once. From the sea, this beach looks flat and ordinary. But when the radical currents ran me aground and I radioed to the Coast Guard for help, they told me they wouldn't come near this beach. Said that a few years back they lost an 80-foot Coast Guard ship, right here."

I returned to my little thesis cottage from these jaunts exhausted yet rejuvenated and dove back into my thesis investigations. My social life at Berkeley at the time, in sharp contrast to my student years at West Point, Stanford, and Göttingen, was virtually nil, and I still viewed those Berkeley years as a kind of voluntary solitary confinement. I had made a few close friends, Jack and Massoud in Berkeley, and there were Jim and his wife Linda in Santa Cruz and John Oneal working on his PhD in political science at Stanford. But my siblings and most of my other friends were now married and lived thousands of miles away. Jonathan had taken up his new job at Wellesley, and Jon and Laurie Steel were in England, where he was studying to become a veterinarian. Al was now working at a law firm in Atlanta after graduating *cum laude* from Harvard Law School in 1973, and Wes had decided to stay in the service and was a rising star in the Army.

My estrangement from my parents had also steadily increased over the years. From time to time, my father tried to lure me back into the family fold. He tried putting stock in my name and sending presents of Persian carpets or my great-grandfather's silver coin collection. I thanked him but returned each gift, not wanting to be obliged to him in any way. Finally he found something I couldn't resist, a 1788 copy of Nicolas Pike's *New and Complete System of Arithmetic*. When he didn't get that back by return mail, my father knew he had found my Achilles' heel and began a thirty-year quest for Early American mathematics books, which he began sending me, volume by volume, whenever he found them. Over the years, we maintained minimal but cordial contact, primarily through this growing collection, which provided a neutral scientific topic of conversation.

I joined the university racquetball club and won a spot on the intercollegiate judo team. The only real interpersonal relationships I had during those years were with ninety-four-year-old Olga and two women friends from days past, an American Airlines stewardess from my Stanford years, and an old friend of John's from Oklahoma who had given up teaching high school mathematics in the Midwest to come to South Shore Lake Tahoe to work as a blackjack dealer. Both were independent, patient, and understanding, and our infrequent liaisons brought back fond memories of the free-love Sixties.

* * *

During one afternoon visit with my stewardess friend, we were listening to the radio when Steppenwolf's "Magic Carpet Ride" reminded us both of the delights and therapeutic values of travel. As a full-time employee of a major airline, she enjoyed almost unlimited free travel, and I pipe-dreamed about a job perk like that. We talked, at first jokingly, about whether I should marry a flight attendant to obtain the "immediate family" travel privileges. She was not interested in such an arrangement but agreed to help me research it. Even if I didn't finish the PhD, maybe I could at least obtain lifetime free travel. And, thinking back to my military MAC flights to Peru, Australia, and Japan, I figured there was always a chance that overseas travel might spark my mathematical creativity. Perhaps I could at least guarantee the globetrotting part of my dream, and I could definitely use the diversion from my thesis grind, without guns and without brushes with the police.

How could I find a willing stewardess accomplice? Since it had worked so well before, when I was looking for something as unlikely as free housing, I decided to simply run an ad in the newspaper. First I rented a post office box at the Alcatraz Station in Berkeley, using my middle name Preston, just in case the airlines did not see eye to eye. Then I called the *Berkeley Gazette* classified ads department and explained that I wanted to run an ad offering cash to a flight attendant in exchange for matrimonial flying perks. The *Gazette* was the most liberal of the local newspapers and routinely ran offbeat ads covering everything from encounters with space aliens to man-seeking-donkey sex ads. I figured there would be no problem.

"No sir," said the ad editor. "We can't run an ad like that. It's out of the question. Good-bye."

Next I called the *Oakland Tribune.*

"We will not run a classified like that," the man said. "No way. The airlines are not going to like that, and we don't need any legal hassles."

I told him I had checked the legalities, which I had, and that it was all on the up-and-up. If he had any doubts, I said, he could easily get an independent opinion from the *Tribune* attorneys.

"We don't need that kind of trouble," he said. "Sorry."

I had put off the conservative *San Francisco Chronicle* for last, figuring those odds would be the worst, but eventually the *Chronicle* was the only newspaper left on my list. I phoned their classifieds department.

"Sure," said the person who answered, after I explained my request. "Just read me the ad you want to place." I read the ad slowly, as she copied it down. "For personal classifieds," she said, "you have to come in and pay the bill in person, in advance." Her voice was matter-of-fact, a canned response.

I jotted down the San Francisco address, grabbed my checkbook, and jumped in my van. "Act quick, before they change their minds," I told myself. It was rush-hour traffic on the Bay Bridge, and finding an open slot in the choked parking lots cost more than an hour, but I made it to the classified ads desk just before closing time. The clerk at the counter read my ad and grimaced.

"We can't run an ad like that," she said.

"But I just called your office here, and they said it was A-okay," I said. "I drove all the way over from Berkeley. Who makes the final decision on classifieds?"

"Well," she said, staring at my application, "since you want the ad to run ten days, including two weekends, it has to be approved by the editors of both the *Chronicle* and the *Examiner.* On Sundays we have a joint edition, you know."

I told her I would appreciate it if she would let the editors rule on it, especially since I had called first and been given the green light. She agreed to send my request up the chain, told me she was pretty sure it would not be approved, and asked me to phone back in three or four days for the decision. I thanked her and drove back to Berkeley, figuring I had wasted the whole afternoon. The next day my phone rang.

"May I speak to Preston, please?" said the voice.

"Speaking," I said. It had to be the *Chronicle*—no one used my middle name. I figured it would be the kiss-off.

"This is the *Chronicle* classifieds," she said. "I'm calling to confirm your ad."

I did a double take and asked her to read back the exact wording. They had probably confused my ad with another.

"Certainly," she said. "The ad is to run in the personal classifieds for ten days starting Saturday, August 23. It reads, *"Grad student desiring flight privileges will pay to marry stewardess. Preston, P.O. Box 3205, Berkeley 94703."*

I reconfirmed the wording and thanked her. But why in the world had the *Chronicle* accepted the ad, and so quickly? The answer came less than an hour later. My phone rang again, and another voice asked to talk to Preston. I figured that by now the editors had discovered the mistake and wanted to cancel the ad. I was wrong. They wanted the story.

"This is Mike Grieg," the voice said. "I'm a reporter for the *San Francisco Chronicle*, and I'd like to interview you concerning your ad to marry a stewardess."

I asked how he got my number and told him that the classifieds had assured me my personal data would be kept confidential. The ad did not include my phone number, but the application form did.

"I apologize," he said, "and I promise I'll respect your privacy completely. No one else has this number, and no one else will call. Take my word for it. It's just that one of the editors thinks this might make an interesting story. We will not give out your phone number or any other personal information. I get a story out of it, and your ad gets more exposure."

I agreed to the interview, and we talked at length. Mr. Grieg had already done a fair bit of research, talking with marriage lawyers and airline representatives.

"What was the airlines' reaction?" I asked.

"Pretty good, surprisingly enough," he said. "They think it's good publicity for them. Apparently no one has tried this before. They said it was 'creative.' If my story gets approved, it'll be in the paper next week. Good luck on your marriage!"

My ad appeared on schedule, with a paragraph in the "Fantasia" section and a short blurb in Herb Caen's column. On Friday, August 29, 1975, the "Top of the News" section on the front page referred to an article on page 17, entitled "He Wants Bride He Can Fly Away From." UPI picked up the story, datelined San Francisco, under the less flamboyant title "Man Would Pay Stewardess to Marry Him," and AP followed. The *International Herald Tribune* brought my quest to the European audience. Even the airlines jumped on the bandwagon. The September 1975 issue of American Airlines' employee newsletter *American Newsline* ran an article in the *It's AA Funny Life* section, arguing that the ad proved the monetary value of travel privileges.

Stephen Cragg, an associate producer at KGO-TV, wrote to Preston's PO Box to invite me to be on the *A.M. San Francisco Show* to talk about my "inexpensive travel plan." He guaranteed that I would not have to be identified if I didn't wish to be. I phoned him to tell him I had all the exposure I wanted and didn't need any more publicity. He said they would guarantee anonymity, that I could wear a mask, or they would shoot from behind, or use silhouettes. I told him that I really *did* just want free travel, not fifteen minutes of fame, and to my way of thinking, excess publicity would lessen the chance of pulling it off. I thanked him and declined his invitation.

A handful of responses to my ad began to fill the post office box. As with my classified ads for housing, about 90 percent were solicitations for money in one form or another. I sorted out the rest, narrowed the field, and set up anonymous interviews in public places. Some respondents really wanted to be married, others wanted to have kids, others were just curious. I reduced the list to three finalists. One was a woman based in Oakland who wanted to take her nephews on world trips and would claim she was marrying a man with two sons, who would then also have flight privileges. I liked that idea. The second was a stewardess based in New York, who was also a successful author, and who told me that she wanted to write a book on the "marriage," and if it worked out, she would pay *me*! The third was a flight attendant out of San Francisco who simply wanted money for car payments.

By sheer luck I learned that the first lady already had legal problems with the airlines, having logged in a bogus marriage and maternity leave, so I dropped her. The second wrote me that her editor said the idea was not a book-length story, and she dropped out. The last applicant was all set to go through when her current boyfriend accidentally found out about it and drew a line in the sand. She phoned me in tears to call off the marriage. By several weeks after the ad had appeared, the responses had dried up completely, and the marriage scheme fell through. There would be no free "magic carpet ride" after all, at least of the free stewardess air travel kind. I had lost a little time and energy on this project, but it had been an interesting diversion. Now it was back to the mathematical drawing board.

The next week, I scheduled a meeting with Dubins.

"I tried a conditional compactness argument," I told him, "but it doesn't work. I found a counterexample for four-point spaces."

He sat silently, his eyes almost sad. He had heard these "no progress" reports many times, from many would-be mathematicians. It was simply another good idea that didn't work—the daily disappointment that not only scientists, but also inventors and composers and poets, must learn to live with.

"But I have three more ideas," I said, and Dubins's eyes flashed in surprise. "I'll check them out and let you know what I learn."

My remote walkabouts seemed to pay off, and the thesis ideas kept coming. Each idea so far had led to a dead end, but at least I discovered more branches of the logical maze to explore. And, as Edison had explained when his assistant remarked that he was getting nowhere with his search for an incandescent bulb filament, I knew "two hundred things that won't work." Then one night, working by the glow of the pot-bellied stove in Olga's cottage, I stumbled onto a new type of strategy for keeping a gambling process alive, an alternative to Markov. Instead of depending on the time and state, this new measure-selector depended only on the current state and how many times you'd been at that state before, not on total elapsed time. I could prove the optimality of these new strategies, which I called "tracking," and reported the result to Dubins, who had me explain it in a seminar talk.

Ten years later, mathematicians at the University of Bonn asked me about the name "tracking." They had studied my paper and understood the results but were curious about the name I picked. "It's like hunting in the snow or sand," I told them. "When you return to a particular spot, you may not know how many total steps you've taken, but you can see at a glance from the tracks how many times you've been there before." The tracking strategy was a good partial breakthrough but still did not answer Dubins's Markov strategy question, and I went back to the drawing board again. I scribbled conjectures and examples on the back of computer printout paper, chatted with Olga, and attended seminars and colloquia. My tracking-selector result led me to the discovery of a generalization of the classical decomposition theorem for finite-state Markov chains but still did not shed any light on my all-or-nothing Markov selector dissertation problem.

I sandwiched in more returns to nature and added a new remote beach hike just south of Pelican Point, near Half Moon Bay. This trek offered even more solitude than Point Reyes and spectacular views of the cold, green-blue Pacific crashing against towering golden sandstone bluffs. To reach the deserted beach, I had to rappel down a 20-foot cliff and cling to crevices in the walls along narrow, wave-swept ledges. Several outcroppings could be negotiated only by finger and toe holds at ebb tide and, at high tide, were sea tunnels filled with waist-deep swirling cold seawater at the trough of a wave and with thundering deep whitewater at crest. For those tunnels, I stripped to shorts and boots, carried my pack overhead safari bearer style, and tried to time my entry to reach midpoint at maximum ebb. Often as not, the unpredictable waves thrashed me anyway.

Hiking alone one day on that stretch of beach, I picked up a shiny metal object, bobbing at the water's edge, in one of the small hidden bays where sea otters feed. It was a marine canister of some sort, about 7 inches long and 2 inches in diameter, sturdy, with solid caps of glistening, sea-resistant brass. Along the olive-drab center tube were stenciled numbers and words in Cyrillic text. From the little Russian I remembered from my class at Stanford, my trip to Moscow, and the Russian language exam, I could make out the words for "gas" and "marine." I tossed the canister into my backpack, along with the ropes I brought to rappel and the abalone shells I found.

Back at my cottage in Berkeley, I tried to decipher the rest of the inscription with my Russian-English lexicon, but the terms were too technical for my standard dictionary. The nomenclature suggested it could be of military origin, which gave me an idea. Why not call the FBI in on the case? My thesis progress was nil, and at this stage, every new little diversion was still welcome.

In the mid-1970s, the FBI was in full force in Berkeley, brought in en masse to deal with the urban guerrilla problem. The city teemed with agents, about as incognito as the narcotics agents at my party in the Lindell mansion. Although most Berkeley citizens disapproved of the SLA's kidnapping and murder tactics, they did support the free speech and anti-war movements and generally distrusted and feared the FBI, which was viewed as a secret police, an agent of the evil Nixon-era federal government. They said the FBI was our own American SAVAK.

The city Pacific Telephone book listed the new Berkeley FBI field office in bold print, and I phoned, half expecting them to dismiss me as a prank caller. To my surprise, the agent who answered the phone promised that their Soviet specialist would get back to me, and an hour later, a man identifying himself as the resident Russian expert called. He did not want to discuss much on the phone and made an appointment for the next afternoon to meet me at my Blake Street cottage.

The next day, exactly on schedule, I answered a knock at the door and opened it to see a James Bond–like man in his early thirties. Tall, athletic, and handsome, with neatly combed short dark hair, he was wearing a sport coat and tie. In Berkeley during those years, he might just as well have been wearing the navy-blue nylon windbreaker you see at crime and air crash scenes, with foot-high white letters reading FBI. Not wanting to upset my neighbors, a typical healthy mixture of Berkeley flower children, students, illegal immigrants, potheads, and militant pacifists, I ushered him into the front room and quickly closed the door.

The Soviet expert introduced himself, and I put another log in the pot-bellied stove before handing him the canister. He turned it over and over slowly in his hand and then from his coat pocket took out a small Russian-English dictionary, exactly the same paperback edition I used myself that was there on my shelf. It was probably a Soviet marine canister, he told me with an air of authority, designed to hold some sort of gas. He asked if he could take it back to the FBI laboratory for analysis. I said sure, and we pored over the topo map of Half Moon Bay on my desk to pinpoint the spot where I found it.

"Did you see any marks in the sand there?" he asked.

"What do you mean?" I said. "What kind of marks?"

"Scrape marks. Like from a rubber boat coming ashore."

I blinked in disbelief and couldn't suppress a big smile.

"Are you kidding?" I said. "I know the FBI is paid to be suspicious and skeptical, and we certainly want someone in your job who takes it seriously, but do you really believe the Russians might be making secret amphibious landings at Half Moon Bay?"

He wasn't the least bit defensive and launched into a detailed description of the political and industrial espionage taking place in Silicon Valley and the rest of the Bay Area.

"My job is to try to uncover and intercept as many of these operations as I can," he explained, "and I'm leaving no stone unturned. Many of these so-called students at the university are really Soviet moles, and even many of our professors are passing sensitive information. The Russians are *already* here," he said with a frown, "and if we don't do something about it quick, they'll destroy our society."

I listened patiently. "Look," I said, pointing out the window. "See that van? I've driven through Russia in that Volkswagen. I've been there—Moscow, Kiev, Black Sea—even visited the Soviet Army Museum. Do you really think they would let me—a former captain in Vietnam with top secret clearance—make a trip like that if they still hope to bury us? I don't."

He sat in stunned silence as I described my trip behind the Iron Curtain, visiting a country he had studied for many years and had been taught to distrust but had never seen. We chatted for two hours, and I found him intelligent, well educated, and very likable—the perfect secret agent. As he left, he promised to return the canister after the FBI made its lab tests.

A week later, the FBI agent phoned to tell me that their investigation had concluded that the canister was standard marine equipment, military or civilian, probably used for launching flares. That his office was not sure *exactly* what it was, or perhaps was not willing to tell me, surprised me. He asked to meet with me again to return the canister. I told him he could just leave it in my mailbox, but he insisted on seeing me in person.

Again I escorted him quickly into my living room. He handed me the canister and thanked me and then took a large manila envelope from a briefcase.

"Would you mind looking at a few photos?" he asked. "We suspect that some of these people are Communist operatives and want to know if you recognize any from campus. Perhaps mathematicians."

He slowly shuffled through the large 8x10 glossies, this one of a man bending over a drinking fountain in a park, that one of a man walking on the sidewalk with a newspaper rolled under his arm. I could only guess at how many thousands of dollars these clandestine pictures had cost the taxpayers.

"Probably not mathematicians," I said with a grin. "Look at those three-piece suits."

Again we chatted for an hour, but this time it felt different. There was something else on his mind, something he was not telling me. Finally he got up to leave, took a few steps toward the door, and then turned to me.

"I was wondering if..." His voice trailed off. He hesitated and then said aloud to himself, "No." Another pause. "Oh well, it won't do any harm to ask. Our office is charged with determining which foreign nationals are really bona fide students, and which are not. One of our methods is to secretly sponsor parties and open houses for the campus International Center. We foot the bills and try to mingle to check out some of the so-called students. Trouble is, we don't know enough advanced chemistry or sociology, or mathematics in your case, to be able to tell who's bluffing."

I understood exactly. If a self-proclaimed mathematician announced that his thesis topic dealt with groups of prime order, this could well make it past an FBI agent with a general liberal arts degree, but it wouldn't fool a specialist. There is only one group of each prime order, the trivial cyclic one.

"What we'd like you to do," he said, "is attend some of these parties, socialize, and mingle with the foreign students. Uncle Sam will pay you. What do you think?"

I told him I'd love to go to those parties, *especially* if there were some beautiful spies at them—but not under those circumstances. I respected his dedication to our country and his opinions, I said, but we were living in different worlds. He said he understood, we shook hands, and he left. After

I had reported the mysterious Soviet canister, the Berkeley FBI office must have pegged me as a friend, and those days their "FBI friends in Berkeley" list was rather short.

* * *

As I kept chipping away at my dissertation problem, I continued to teach part time whenever I could. My love of teaching also helped keep things in perspective, as every new classroom experience reinforced the fact that I absolutely loved the mix of research and teaching. I hoped I would be able to do both if I ever finished and landed an academic job.

One day, while proctoring a calculus final exam in the Hearst Women's Gymnasium on the southern edge of the UCB campus, I spent my first fifteen-minute break exploring the sprawling complex, which was normally off-limits to male students and professors. I wandered up to the outdoor swimming pool on the second floor. Built like a Roman bath, its terraced stone seats, cement columns, huge bas-reliefs, and tiled pool reminded me of the outdoor pool at Hearst Castle, but much more modest. Along the diving board end of the pool was a narrow cement storage building, and inside, lifebuoys, water polo nets, and lane float markers lined the long dark corridor. Halfway down the musty corridor, as my eyes slowly adjusted to the darkness and chlorine fumes, I spied something that brought instant memories of my teenage years canoeing the Canandaigua River below our house in Alloway.

Chained to the wall on the left side of the walkway, with the classic upswept curves of an Indian birchbark, was a classic Old Town canoe, handmade of spruce and canvas. Both of its cane seats had gaping holes, and the dust of many years covered the ribs. The padlock on the chain looked rusted through, but I tested it, and it was still solid. I thought back to the countless afternoons I had spent in a canoe just like that, gliding silently over huge snapping turtles hiding in the mud and rushes, and past bloated carp, thrashing and spawning among the lily pads in the warm backwaters of the cove below the Giesy farm's lower heifer pasture. And now this canoe also reminded me of myself, lost and forgotten in the dark bowels of the university, gathering mold. We both pined to be outside on the water again, in sunlight and fog, exploring new streams and hidden inlets.

During my next proctoring break, I sought out a custodian in the gym.

"What's the story on that old wood canoe in the pool building?" I asked. "Think they might want to sell it?"

"Hell, son," he said, "that thing hasn't been used in at least ten years. You ought to just take it."

I told him I'd rather not and asked who might know about it. He suggested the Department of Physical Education, over in Harmon Gym, and I phoned there. The Head of PE had no idea the university even owned a canoe and referred me to the director of the Women's PE program, since I found it in the women's gym. I phoned her, introduced myself, explained that I was a graduate student in mathematics, and asked about the canoe.

"What about it?" she asked.

"Well," I said, "obviously it hasn't been used in years—the seats and a couple of ribs are broken. Do you think the university would sell it?"

"No," she said, her voice cold. "That canoe has been part of Women's Physical Education for many decades. It's not for sale."

"But it needs repairing," I said, "and should be put back on the water. If I restore it, for free, would you let me use it now and then?"

She said no, that it had historical value. I offered to leave a deposit of $1,000, in cash. I told her that if she had ever been in a canoe like that one, she would understand how I felt.

"It's not for sale or rent or loan," she said, "with or without a deposit. We're not interested. That's final."

"Perhaps the old custodian had been right," I thought. "I should have just taken it." Now the director knew my name and department, but I still wanted to restore the canoe, with or without her blessing, and get both of us back on the water again. It would be a welcome relief from the long hours poring over student exams and struggling with my dissertation. And besides, as a boy, my best ideas often came when I was walking in the woods or paddling a canoe like this. I decided to return to the pool storeroom after hours.

First, I did a walk-by, just after sunset. The outdoor pool, built on the roof of the women's gym, was barely out of sight of the University Police

Station, across from an athletic field. I ran through a Ranger checklist. There were no access roads on the west side of the gym. Just outside the fence, at the far end of the pool, two 40-foot magnolia trees obscured the end of the building, casting shadows from a bright security light in the corner. It would be an excellent commando refresher exercise, climbing the drainpipe to the second story, up the chain-link fence, and over the barbed wire.

I waited several months, and shortly after midnight on a cool, foggy Berkeley night, I arrived at the gym with a heavy beach towel and short metal file. If caught during this initial sortie, I'd claim I was just sneaking in for a secret swim. That explained the towel. The file? "In case I got stuck on the barbed wire, officer."

Shinnying up the drainpipe was easy, and I had plenty of experience scaling cyclone fences, so in less than thirty seconds, I was at the top, two stories above the ground. I draped the towel over the barbed wire and slipped over onto the pool deck. In the moonlit fog, the pool looked even more like a Roman bath, and the air was saturated with the scents of eucalyptus and hemlock. I found the storeroom passageway and groped along the corridor in pitch dark until I felt the canoe chain and worked my way down to the padlock. In twenty minutes, I had filed through the hasp loop, and using a mixture of spit and dirt, I molded the brown wad into the gap cut by the file. Even in daylight, it would take a sharp eye to see that the rusty lock had been sheared.

I walked to the other end of the pool and, using the towel, unscrewed the scorching security light bulb until it went dead. Then I sat down to enjoy the cool evening and wait to see if any alarms were raised. After a half hour there was no sign of curious policemen or security guards, so I reinstalled the bulb and made my way back over the barbed wire and cyclone fence and down the drainpipe.

I waited another month and removed the tire cover from the front-mounted spare tire on my Volkswagen van. Just maybe some game show whiz police lieutenant would make the connection between the symbol I had painted on the tire cover—an Indian teepee on a knoll—and T. P. Hill. Then I splashed mud on the rear of the VW to partially obscure the license plate and drove around Berkeley for a few days, to make sure the police would not stop me for having an illegible license plate. I spread newspapers on the floor of the cottage and went to Ace Hardware to buy sawhorses, paintbrushes, and red marine paint.

For the second canoe sortie, I needed an accomplice, and Massoud was the natural choice. I casually mentioned to him several times in the library that I planned to liberate a canoe, and then, late one night at the country-rock It Club on San Pablo, I waited until he polished off three Heinekens. I didn't even need to question his manhood, which is a guaranteed way to get a male Persian to do just about anything.

"Say, Massoud," I said, "you remember that canoe I was telling you about?"

"Yep."

"I need a little help getting it—might be a little adventure in it. You interested?" I reminded him he could be in danger if we got caught—deportation to the Shah's Iran—and told him I would understand if he decided it was not worth the risk.

"Sounds good," he said. "I'm Persian, man. It'll be an unbeatable combination, a Persian and a Ranger. When you want to get it?"

"How about right now?" I said.

"Okay," he said, "let's go." He paused. "I know what you're doing, man."

"What's that?"

"Well, I figure you took one look at that Candidate in Philosophy degree you got and decided to make sure you pick up something useful before you leave Cal!" he said with a laugh. "It's not worth much, but at least it's not signed by a Hollywood actor, like our master's sheepskin." Our MA diplomas had been signed by the president of the California Board of Regents in 1974, Governor Ronald Reagan.

At 2 a.m. we left the bar, and I stopped at my cottage to change into old pants. Massoud mumbled something about Persians again, and how they didn't need to change pants for something as easy as this. We parked the van under the tennis court complex next to the gym and walked quickly to the drainpipe. Massoud had figured it for a simple walk-up. Just walk in, pick it up, and walk out. Now he stared at the barbed wire, drainpipe, and cyclone fence.

I brought two towels and a rope, "to get in and out, Your Honor." No burglary tools. We scaled the fence easily, except for the seat of Massoud's best pair of pants. I unscrewed the security light, crept to the pool house, and removed the severed lock. We fastened the rope to the bow of the canoe, carried it out to the edge of the pool, and hoisted it over the barbed wire. I held the rope, with the canoe dangling at its end, while Massoud climbed over the barbed wire and shinnied down the drainpipe. At his signal, I lowered away and then hurried back to where the canoe had been locked and left a 3x5 notecard: *This canoe has been liberated by T. P. Hill, Mathematics Department, telephone 642-3158.*

Massoud was stunned when I told him.

"That's crazy, man. What the hell did you do that for?"

"In case we get caught between now and when we get the canoe back to my cottage," I said. "Just trust me."

He rolled his eyes and shook his head, as we lugged the canoe to the dirty van and lashed it to the top. Taking backstreets to my cottage, we laid the Old Town upside down on the sawhorses, and I drove Massoud home. He was still complaining about the note. I told him not to worry and returned to Blake Street, where I parked the van in front of Olga's house.

Carrying only a towel this time, I returned to Hearst Gym on foot, reran the drainpipe-cyclone-fence-barbed-wire obstacle course, and retrieved the 3x5 card, prepared to eat it if caught. The next day, I admired my new canoe and started repairing the seats and cracked ribs and gunwales. When Massoud came by to see the progress, he slapped me on the back.

"Man, you find a tunnel, you have to explore it. The railroad special agents catch us, and we wind up in court. Now you find a canoe, and you have to liberate it, just 'cause it's there. There's a Persian saying for somebody like you," he teased. "We say, *You're the type of man that if you found a free rope, you'd hang yourself.*"

I laughed. I had painted the Old Town with red marine lacquer and after giving it three days to dry, loaded it onto the van's dented roof and drove to the Sacramento River Delta Wildlife Conservation Area. Sliding the wood canoe softly through the slick, muddy silt at the edge of a narrow estuary, I jumped in and paddled back in time. It was pure bliss, total freedom, like cruising country roads on my motorcycle, but more primal. As

I zigzagged through the tidal flats, reeds rustling and bullfrogs croaking around me, the canoe and I were exploring prehistoric San Francisco Bay, out of sight of Pacific Gas and Electric power lines, 7-Elevens, and other evidence of man's intrusion.

As we glided in silence, it slowly dawned on me why I felt so attracted to theoretical mathematics and nature, much more than human culture. Music and poetry and art are created by and for man, but in my view, mathematics and nature stand alone, completely independent of the very existence of *Homo sapiens*. As I drifted along through the bulrushes, thinking of mathematics, my heart soared, as it never would with *Swan Lake* or Picasso. I felt alive again, creative, energetic as never before.

But perhaps Massoud was right. Maybe subconsciously I did want to make sure I took something tangible from Berkeley. I dubbed the Old Town my "PhC Canoe."

10

EUREKAS

By my fourth year in the doctoral program, I had made only minor progress on my dissertation problem. Counting Madison, West Point, Stanford, Göttingen, and now Berkeley, I was entering my thirteenth year in college and was beginning to have serious doubts about whether it made much sense to push on. Most of the other graduate students had simply faded away, and it would be easy for me to do the same. I had no wife and family suffering through the ordeal, waiting for the payoff, and I had no pressures from family or friends. I reread Castaneda, who abandoned his remarkable apprenticeship with the Yaqui Indian sorcerer Don Juan after five years. But I still loved mathematics and reminded myself of the absolute *privilege* of just being at Berkeley, of going through this academic hell, and studying under a mentor as demanding as Lester Dubins. After all, this was completely voluntary.

I continued to attack my thesis problem from every classical and offbeat angle I could dream up. Scores of hopeful ideas had not panned out, and a few led to secondary discoveries related to Markov chains. I kept chipping away, developing intuition, learning new tools, keeping track of examples and counterexamples and methods that didn't pan out. Dubins listened patiently to my progress reports but still left it to me to come up with ideas. Instead, he continued to lead by example. Anyone who followed his seminar lectures or was lucky enough to take part in his chalkboard and café conversations or who read his publications knew his inimitable mathematical style. He preferred to study the most basic of problems, not the intricate and technical questions that often dominate mainstream mathematics. He emphasized clarity and elegance of argument and would work on a broad range of problems from lattice theory and geometry to abstract gambling and classical probability, as long as the problem was clean and clear. Yes, I had an inspiring mentor, but the big breakthrough that would satisfy him, and me, seemed as distant as that Grand Bahama landfall when the offshore wind and ebbing tide kept Chan and me out to sea in that rickety boat.

I worked mainly in Olga's violin-making cottage, usually until well after midnight. I slept late and began each morning with a grilled turkey burger on a toasted English muffin, dipped in soy sauce, and for a dose of sugar and caffeine, washed it down with a Dr Pepper. Before the cool, damp morning fog broke, I started a wood fire in the pot-bellied stove and relaxed in my rocking chair, mentally reviewing the overall strategy and logic of my latest idea. Then, after several hours of work at my desk, I'd go check my mail in Evans Hall, perhaps attend a seminar, and return for several more hours of work before a motorcycling or racquetball break.

If I needed still more escapism, I took in one of the new genre of Blaxploitation *Shaft* or *Cleopatra Jones* movies at the Roxie Theater in Oakland. After the movie, I returned once again to the cottage for more head-scratching, scribbling ideas on the backs of the reams of used computer printout paper I salvaged from the waste bins in the basement of Evans Hall.

Practically every day saw a tiny new hopeful idea and almost as often, a new hidden stumbling block. When I sensed burnout late at night and was too wired to sleep, I donned my Vietnam jungle boots and a black parka and scaled the cement-and-barbed-wire security fence at the university track on Bancroft Avenue to run 3 miles on the dark track, as I joked to myself, *behind enemy lines*. For variety I added slipping over the Strawberry Canyon cyclone fence in the middle of the night into the dead-silent Cal football stadium, as I had done at Madison and West Point.

Then, one overcast afternoon I was sitting outside, relaxing in the overgrown garden surrounding Olga's cottage, when it all came together in a blinding flash. *Eureka!* The crucial insight I had sought for so long suddenly fell into place, like the final keystone of a Roman arch. All those reams of handwritten conjectures, examples, and counterexamples I had amassed in stacks of paper on my floor finally paid off. My brain had at last distilled them down, understood exactly where each failed attempt had gone awry, and added to my own personal knowledge of the intricacies of the problem. Many people assume that mathematical insights are simply manna from heaven, and they completely underestimate the vital importance of two things: persistence and optimism. The key insights are often unexpected, and perhaps even undeserved, but almost never occur to anyone before they have invested huge amounts of energy and intellectual effort.

I ran inside to my desk and jotted down a few notes and then spent the next several weeks sketching out the general skeleton of the argument and then all the details of the long logical tree. I checked and rechecked each syllogism, comparing each conclusion against my list of counterexamples. I had followed false leads before, but this *felt* right. When I knew the logic was correct, I went to see Dubins and told him I could prove the existence of epsilon-optimal Markov strategies for all finite-state spaces. That is, in every gambling problem with limited resources, whether it is a casino or microorganism, there are always good strategies for keeping the process alive that depend only on the current state and time.

He raised his eyebrows in excitement. He canceled his afternoon appointments, and we walked to the café on the corner of Hearst and Euclid for coffee. He listened intently, ignoring his coffee, as I described my new insight with gestures in the air and scribblings on a paper napkin. Unlike most mathematicians, Dubins did not nod in polite agreement with the arguments. His eyes told me he already realized that the subtleties of the proof were far beyond comprehension during a coffee talk, and he would not pretend otherwise. My argument was inherently complex and remained so, even after we sorted through it together at the blackboard, piece by piece, month after month. I gave a seminar talk outlining the main ideas, and then Dubins asked me to give two formal lectures to a larger audience, including professors from the Berkeley Mathematics and

Statistics Departments and visiting professors to whom he had announced the result. After the first talk, a professor from Israel came up to me as I was erasing the blackboard.

"Very nice result," he said, with a thick Eastern European accent. "That question has been around almost twenty years, and even Dubins himself worked on it. Do you realize you are only the third student to finish under him?"

Dubins had never told me he had worked on the Markov problem, or I might never have attempted it. But only his third student after all those decades?

"How do you know that?" I asked.

"Because I was his second," he said, and stuck out his hand. "David Gilat, nice to meet you."

I recognized his name immediately, since I had read several of his papers in the field, and we immediately struck up a friendship.

Now came the task of putting my arguments into written form, checking and polishing every claim, every comment. Dubins, as I now knew, was notorious for his insistence on absolute perfection in writing. He drove his secretary crazy, having her type and retype even the simplest business letter again and again, replacing this word or that phrase with a slightly more appropriate one—tedious work in those days before computerized word processing.

Once I tried to draft a letter for him myself. Since I was no longer formally enrolled in classes, in order for me to continue receiving GI Bill payments, the Veteran's Administration needed a letter from my thesis advisor stating that I was working full time on my dissertation. To save Dubins the trouble of composing the letter, I drafted a simple note to the VA, in his name, stating, *I, Professor Lester E. Dubins, hereby certify that Theodore P. Hill is working on his PhD thesis full time.* I took the letter to Dubins.

"I can't sign that," he said. "I can't *certify* what you're doing." He took my draft to his office, agonized over the wording a few weeks, and eventually found a phrase he could live with—one that satisfied both his unwavering integrity and the Army's rigid requirement for documentation. I never saw the final version of the letter, but whatever he wrote satisfied the VA bureaucrats, and my monthly $200 GI Bill checks kept rolling in.

I wrote out in longhand the complete arguments of my thesis, polished it, and rewrote it again several more times before I gave it to Dubins. Week after week I heard nothing from him, and finally I realized that he would never get to it, especially in handwritten form. I even gambled and paid to have it typed, which other grad students did only after their advisors had given their blessing to the dissertation. But Dubins never even read the typed draft. Instead, we met once a week, when he tested my ideas orally, almost at random, questioning this lemma and suggesting changes in that notation. After five or six more complete drafts, he suggested I start dating the different versions, and I knew then that just the write-up alone would be another long process. Dubins placed no value on personal considerations like time or money. He weighed only the intrinsic logic and esthetics of the final written word. *That's* why he had told Massoud's friend the dissertation process could last eight or nine years.

"Your PhD thesis should be the best written piece of mathematics of your life," he once told me.

Not the best discovery, hopefully, but the best written. It was the one time that your mathematical writing was scrutinized, at every step, by a mentor with a lifetime of experience and a clear vested interest in the result. If I succeeded, and the long line of mathematics descendants increased, his name and my dissertation would be recorded on the same page of the mathematics genealogy.

Over the next year and a half I revised, changed notation, and reordered fifteen complete handwritten drafts. His suggestions were sometimes amazingly penetrating and at other times were redundant and frustrating. There was never a hint that the process might be nearing an end. The manuscript filled only eighty handwritten pages, which would be about twenty pages in print, but the rewriting ordeal was discouraging. Often I worked all night on new revisions he wanted and early the next morning caught him by surprise when I delivered a complete new version of the manuscript. Twice I fell asleep on the floor outside his office door, and he had to step over me just to get in. But still he gave no hint that the end was in sight.

I finally reached the breaking point and asked the department secretaries to fill out the dissertation forms that required his signature. I toyed with the idea of walking into his office with the forms, along with my loaded .38 Smith & Wesson, the one retrieved from the bushes by the railroad special detective. I wouldn't make any threats but just lay the revolver quietly on his desk and ask him to sign the forms. Let him figure out if I was contemplating homicide or suicide, or both.

Again I fell asleep at his doorstep, and this time when he woke me I said, "Professor Dubins, I'd like to make an appointment to see you this afternoon." Never had our meetings been that formal, and he must have sensed a change.

"Of course," he said. "You've been working all night again, haven't you? Tell me when you want to meet, and I'll call you to wake you up, if you like."

His phone call woke me from a deep sleep.

"This version looks very good," he said. "Why don't you have the forms typed up, and I'll sign them."

Eureka again! I felt like the happiest man in the world. Publication of a Berkeley PhD thesis is virtually guaranteed and with it, the thrill of immortality that also rewards authors of fiction and poetry. The sublime pleasure of *creating* mathematics intoxicated me, and to have met Dubins's standards at long last, without even using the .38, was no longer a pipe dream.

I waited until the final signatures on the dissertation were affixed and then celebrated, first by taking my two closest math grad student friends James and Sherman out to lunch, and that evening by smuggling beer and vodka into the gymnasium for our weekly Tuesday night round-robin racquetball tournaments.

It slowly began to sink in. This was formal acknowledgment from experts at one of the world's leading universities confirming that I had discovered and proved interesting new mathematics. I already knew that would be one of the highlights of my life, come what may. I celebrated with solo hikes at Half Moon Bay and Point Reyes, canoeing in the delta, and motorcycling through Tilden Park, letting the idea of reaching that milestone in life sink in.

Next I turned my attention to finding an academic job, preferably one that combined teaching and research. The employment situation for new math PhDs in 1977 was the worst in recent history. One of my office mates, the last student of famous Polish logician Alfred Tarski, applied to 300 colleges. The other applied to 250, which meant both advisors had to send out mass mailings of hundreds of letters of recommendation. But Dubins was an old-school academic who still wrote out mathematics in longhand and refused to sign a form letter. That effectively eliminated the shotgun approach. He told me to narrow my search. I researched the job listings published by the American Mathematical Society—excluding Wellesley College, figuring there was a chance their college administrators might know about my police record—and pared my list down to seven universities. I brought Dubins the names.

"How many of those ads *specifically* require a letter from me?" he asked, and I scratched three more names off the list, knowing full well that implicitly *every* place expected a letter from the thesis advisor, whether their ad mentioned it or not. I mailed out the remaining four applications, including Cal Poly, the University of Hawaii, and Georgia Tech.

At that point, I fully expected to become an itinerant mathematician, job-hopping from junior college to junior college across the country and around the world, or driving a truck and doing mathematics at night. Maybe I would even become the new mathematician chef at the Elm Lodge Inn in Lake Tahoe, while doing probability research in my spare time. We all heard stories that so-and-so *didn't get a job*, meaning he didn't get a faculty job at a good college, but I was prepared, and even expecting, never to land a job as assistant professor at a research university. I felt that getting a PhD from Berkeley was reward enough, and society didn't owe me anything more, including a PhD-level job. Berkeley had taken a chance on me as a walk-on, and I had made it through the sieve. To have satisfied some of the best mathematical minds that I had made an original and significant contribution to mathematical probability was already a thrill, and if I ended up teaching high school or even doing manual labor, so be it. A ditch digger with a PhD from Berkeley in theoretical mathematics—why not?

Typical academic jobs for fresh PhDs range from teaching junior college, where an instructor's main duty is teaching twelve to fifteen hours a week, to the standard publish-or-perish assistant professorship at a research university, where the teaching load is only five or six hours a week but there is high emphasis on publishing new research and bringing in grants. In between is a wide spectrum of temporary visiting professorships, postdoctoral positions, and lectureships. The absolute plum, a tenure-track assistant professorship, gives the applicant six guaranteed years of faculty employment at the same university. After six years, his research, teaching, and service are evaluated, and the candidate either gets tenure—that is, the virtual guarantee of a lifetime job—or is denied tenure, in which case he is forced to leave that university. No extensions, no exceptions, no partial rewards. Either lifetime job security or dismissal.

None of the four universities I applied to even responded to my job applications, and I later learned that good research universities at that time were receiving between four and eight *hundred* applications for each available position. Dubins had not gotten around to sending in his tailor-made letters by the announced deadlines, and the hiring committees simply rejected my application as incomplete, jumping on any excuse to narrow the applicant pool. So, applying another strategy, I decided to pay my own way to attend the annual meeting of the American Mathematical Society in St. Louis to deliver a paper and possibly turn up some leads.

After my talk, Bob Kertz, a professor in the audience from Georgia Tech, asked to talk to me about some of my discoveries. He knew Dubins's work on gambling theory very well and had written several papers on it himself. He was even familiar with the epsilon-optimal Markov problem. Engrossed in a conversation about research, we completely forgot about lunch and then drove down the tree-lined avenues of Forest Park to get something to eat at a new fast-food restaurant. The location looked very familiar.

"I used to live here," I told him, as we started eating.

"In St. Louis?" he said.

"No, I mean right *here*," I said, and pointed to the ground under us. Developers had leveled the beautiful old mansion at 4000 Lindell to put up a McDonald's.

As we drove back to the conference, I asked Bob if Georgia Tech was interviewing at the meeting.

"Yes," he said, "we are." Then he hesitated and smiled. "You just got interviewed."

Four months later, Georgia Tech called and offered me a nine-month visiting position. I had no other job offers, so I called the Director of Mathematics, Professor John Neff.

"I'd love to come to Atlanta," I said, "but just for nine months seems counterproductive—both for you and for me. As soon as I get there, I'll have to spend all my time sending out job applications again, instead of collaborating on research." I thought for a second. "What if I come half-time for two years?" I figured any new researcher worth his salt could survive on half salary, especially a Ranger used to living in condemned houses.

"*What?*" he said. "I've never heard of such a thing. I'll talk to the hiring committee."

Several days later, Neff phoned back. "The hiring committee liked your attitude," he said. "They recommended we offer you a two-year visiting position, *full-time*. The second year has to be gentlemen's agreement, though, since in Georgia, officially it must be either a one-year contract or tenure-track, nothing in between."

I accepted, delighted that at least one research university was willing to take a chance on this unusual candidate, this thirty-three-year-old Army Ranger rugby-playing University of California PhD. The Berkeley doctoral program had taken a chance on my unusual background, and I was one of the one-third who finished. Now Georgia Tech was taking a chance on me, and I was determined to show them that they too were not making a mistake.

That last year in Berkeley, I had fallen in love with a twenty-six-year-old Dutch woman from The Hague. Noreen was touring across America by Greyhound and Amtrak, and from the moment we met, we became inseparable. She was gorgeous, spoke four languages, and had traveled even more than I had. This exciting new relationship was such a distraction that I had to send her away on a five-day Greyhound trip up the coast to Mendocino while I worked on preparing a seminar talk on my thesis research. All too soon, she had to fly back to Amsterdam, but we talked on the phone and wrote frequently.

I was hoping to convince her to join me in Atlanta, but she gave me a firm "*Helemaal niet*—no way!" She had spent time in Atlanta, and compared to most of Europe, Atlanta was still a cultural backwater. I had a bit of trepidation myself moving to the Deep South, with vivid memories of my first trip with Gary Jackson to segregated Florida and Ranger School at nearby Ft. Benning. But I had never expected to land a job offer, even a temporary one like this, at a research university, and I was ready to go anywhere to give a career in mathematics a shot. Noreen and I talked it all over when I flew to Holland to celebrate my new degree and job, and we decided to settle into a long-distance, part-time-lover, and full-time-friend relationship that would last decades.

When I returned to Berkeley, I bade a tearful farewell to Olga. We both suspected it might well be the last time we would see each other, and indeed, she did pass away peacefully in her sleep some months later. I loaded my books into my trusty VW, lashed down the red Old Town canoe on top, and drove across country to Atlanta. Most colleagues had lived in cheap apartments during their graduate student days, but when they arrived at Georgia Tech and started receiving a professor's salary, they immediately upgraded to a standard suburban house in Cobb County or modern flat or condo in Buckhead or on Buford Highway, a half hour or hour from Georgia Tech. But I figured that since I had been quite content living in condemned houses near campus as a grad student, I shouldn't have to change simply because I now had a decent job. My blissful years in the Lindell mansion in St. Louis, the fifteen-room Leroy house, and the tiny Blake Street cottage in Berkeley had taught me the sublime pleasures of a simple life and the rewards of being creative and flexible in my private life as well as in research.

So just before I left Berkeley, I mailed in another "situations wanted" ad, this time to Atlanta newspapers, again saying I was a teacher looking for a cottage or servant's quarters in need of repairs. When I reached Atlanta, I stayed a few days with my old West Point and German Military Academy Exchange friend Al Lindseth, who had recently taken a job in a law firm there. I drove to the newspaper office to pick up the responses to my ad, and, as I'd expected, most were the usual mix of letters from crackpots and fringe religious groups. Three of the responses, however, were worth checking out, and all three were *rent-free*.

Two were in wealthy neighborhoods northwest of Atlanta. The first was a two-story wooden-frame servant's quarters that needed lots of work just to make it habitable. It had the only bathtub I've ever seen with just one water pipe leading to it—cold water only. But the structure was in very poor shape, needing major roof, plumbing, and carpentry repairs, in addition to painting inside and out. I realized if I undertook that project, it would leave me no time to do research, so I passed it up. The second offer was an Atlanta business executive's modern guest cottage in woods a short walk from his mansion. In lieu of rent, he wanted me to tutor his two teenage sons in mathematics three hours a week and drive them to an occasional Boy Scout meeting. But their school vacations didn't coincide with my Georgia Tech breaks, which would have meant giving up some of my precious travel time, so I also turned down this offer. The third response came from a single mother in Midtown who had a servant's quarters behind the main house. The building looked to be in fine shape.

"What are you thinking in terms of rent?" I asked.

"Well, there's a hippie couple living in it now," she said. "I'm sure they aren't married, and that's okay with me, but they smoke pot a lot, and I can smell it from our porch. I don't want my little girl to be exposed to that." She nodded down to the child clinging to her side. "So you can have it rent-free—all you have to do is tell them their time is up. They've been here over a year, and I just don't want to tell them myself."

"Thanks," I said. "I understand. But I don't want to be the one to evict them either. Sorry."

I didn't want my creative lifestyle to come at the cost of someone else landing on the street. After the rent-free options dried up, I found a small cabin off Ponce de Leon about 2 miles from campus for $150 a month and lived there a few months while I got my feet on the ground. I kept looking for something closer in, and one day, just 100 yards north of campus, I spotted a beat-up, vacant clapboard house, with a *For Rent* sign, at 543 Ninth Street. I pried open a window to get a look at its condition and phoned the owner.

"I'm calling about your house for rent on Ninth Street," I told him. "What are you asking for it?"

"Three-fifty," he said. "The front part goes for $275, and the back studio has a shower and separate entrance, and for that I get $75. And for that price you have to keep the house in the same good condition it's in. How does that sound?"

"Listen, sir," I said. "When is the last time you were in the house?"

"I run a small grocery down in south Atlanta near the federal penitentiary," he said. "I don't get up there that often. Why do you ask?"

"Well," I said. "I figure you haven't been here for a while. In order for me to keep it in the condition it's in, I'd have to run around kicking in walls every week. Instead of that, I'll actually make a few improvements and keep the winos and vagrants out. I'll give you $150 a month."

I guess he liked my answer, because he laughed and agreed to my offer. The single-story house, typical of that lower-middle-class neighborhood, was 40 feet long but only 12 feet wide, built to fit on a lot 20 feet wide, with 4 feet on each side before the neighbor's property began. The front door opened into the living room, and straight back behind that, one after another, were a breakfast room and kitchen, a bedroom, and a second bedroom with its own back entrance and shower. This construction, called a shotgun house, was common in poorer neighborhoods in the South. In theory, as my friends explained, you could kick in the front door of one of these houses and take out everyone in the whole house with one blast from a shotgun.

I made a sleeping platform, a thin sleeping mat on pine boards set on cement blocks, to try to replicate the exquisite physical pleasure of sleeping on a hard surface that I had learned during my four months on tatami mats in Japan. I furnished the rest of the house with tables, lamps, and chairs I could scrounge, some donated by colleagues and others scooped up in rich neighborhoods on the monthly large-item pickup day, just a block or two ahead of the city garbage truck. The house was perfect for my purposes—a short ten-minute walk across campus from my office, in a very quiet working-class neighborhood, and in good enough condition to keep the rain out but bad enough to discourage break-ins. Also, its decrepit condition meant I did not have to worry about collateral damage, so I figured it would make an excellent place for parties.

A short walk away from this low-rent neighborhood was a wonderful new academic world. For the first time, I had a private office, technical support, a decent full-time salary, and, most essential of all for me after all the years in the Army, essentially no boss. At Berkeley most of us graduate students had immersed ourselves in our thesis research and were completely unaware of the other essentials of academic life: the committee meetings and grant proposal writing, the interviewing of new potential colleagues, the internal politics. This was on-the-job training again, but unlike

Ft. Devens, I had no First Sergeant to teach me the ropes. At Berkeley I had taught undergraduates, usually under the supervision of the professor in charge of the course, and I had done independent research under the supervision of my mentor Lester Dubins. But now I was suddenly expected to be a *leader* in both teaching and research. In his book *Academic Duty*, Stanford University President Emeritus Donald Kennedy wrote, "In a sense, universities are societies without rules." That suited me perfectly. I was free as a bird to find my own style of research and teaching, as long as my publications and student evaluations were up to par.

In Berkeley Dubins's research seminar ran Wednesday afternoons at 4 o'clock, year after year. Faculty visitors, new graduate students, returning alumni, and whoever happened to be in town Wednesday afternoons could count on an hour of lively discussion on the latest discoveries in probability or the subtleties of unsolved problems.

Using the Dubins Seminar as a model, I immediately organized a weekly Georgia Tech Probability Seminar. Canvassing my new colleagues, I found a half dozen who were interested in probability, statistics, or measure theory and were delighted at the idea of meeting once a week to debate and ponder the latest developments in the field. With that core, I invited graduate students and visitors, drummed up speakers, and set the research wheels turning.

After one of these seminar talks, I asked my new colleague Bob, who had "interviewed" me in St. Louis, about a new inequality that had just been announced in the *Notices of the American Mathematical Society*. The fundamental result, informally called a "prophet inequality," compared the theoretical winnings of an ordinary gambler with the winnings of an opponent armed with complete knowledge of the future, hence the term "prophet." The inequality said that if the variables are independent and positive, then the average payoff to a prophet is never more than twice that of a gambler. This amazingly clean and counterintuitive result caught all the experts by surprise, but the *Notices* did not include a proof. Bob and I immediately got hooked and struggled for our own proof, after numerous concrete examples convinced us of its truth. We presented our findings in the seminar.

One of the two discoverers of the original prophet inequality, Göttingen professor Ulrich Krengel, had been my instructor in the class in Combinatorics during my Fulbright year in Germany. I remembered him well, and the clarity and depth of his lectures and the exceptional hospitality at the reception in his home for faculty, visitors, and graduate students. The *Notices* announcement also mentioned that Ulrich would speak on the prophet inequality at the next International Congress of Mathematics in Helsinki. Since I already planned to attend, I wrote him a short note congratulating him on the discovery and asking to meet with him to discuss our own findings. He responded immediately. He did not remember me but wanted to hear everything we had learned about prophet inequalities and looked forward to meeting me. My research was off and running.

The teaching part of my new position required more deliberate thought. I view teaching as a privilege, especially in a good university with sharp and eager minds, and Georgia Tech left it up to us instructors to organize our courses any way we saw fit. I thought back over my long career as a student, from the extremes of West Point to Berkeley, and tried to identify which teaching methods I had found most effective. Standard university undergraduate math courses, like those I'd taken at Madison and helped assist in Berkeley, were usually organized around weekly graded homework assignments, one or two midterms, and a final exam. In my own experience both as a student and as a teaching assistant in calculus, graded homework assignments had always seemed counterproductive. The good students worked the homework out in great detail and then wasted time writing it up neatly, while the poor students either copied from them or didn't even bother to submit anything. From the other end, the instructors or their assistants spent huge amounts of time grading, and most teachers will tell you that grading is the part of the job they most hate.

I compared that system with the one I'd seen at West Point, where instead of graded homework in math, we had regular and frequent tests, standing at the blackboards or sitting at our desks. To me, it was clear which system was more effective, at least for lower-division undergraduate mathematics—no graded written homework but regular frequent quizzes. Even though I'd never heard of that system used in any civilian college, that's the way I decided to organize my undergraduate courses. For classes that met three times a week, I'd first break the term up into two-week blocs. The first day of each bloc, I'd tell my students the mathematical goals of that two-week period, and I'd post *suggested* homework problems, not to be turned in. Then I'd give four lectures on the topic, spend one lecture hour going over questions on the suggested practice problems, and the last day of the bloc, I'd give an in-class, full-hour exam. That meant one one-hour exam every two weeks. That was the plan.

For classes that met five days a week, as many undergraduate math classes do, it was a trifle more intense. My first teaching assignment at Georgia Tech turned out to be two classes of thirty students each: a freshman calculus course and a junior-level, calculus-based probability course. Each met for an hour every day Monday to Friday. I told the students on the first day of class that there would be *no* required homework, *no* quizzes, *no* midterms, and *no* class attendance. They looked at each other in silence, wondering what this new unknown professor was up to.

"During the next ten weeks," I told them, "I only ask that you think for me one hour a week. Every Friday, except the first and last, there will be a one-hour, in-class written exam, starting next week."

Shock set in. When I told them I would drop their two lowest scores, to cover bad days and fraternity parties and grandmother funerals, I sensed a slight sigh of relief. The key to making my system work, of course, was organization. I knew from my lectures as the R&R liaison officer in Tokyo that a one-hour lecture can convey a good amount of information, but to be effective, it has to be well organized, interesting, delivered at a good pace, and, most important of all, it had to have a beginning, a middle, and an end—in other words, every good lecture is a good *story*.

In my math lectures, I also continually reminded my class that mathematics is very much alive, and every week I showed them easy-to-state questions that still no human being could answer. How many sevens are in the decimal expansion of *pi = 3.141 . . .* are there infinitely many pairs of prime numbers that differ by 2, such as 3 and 5, 5 and 7, and so on?

"That's where your generation gets the baton," I told the students, who were mostly engineers. "And to accept the challenge, it will help you to master some of these basics. Most of you are not mathematics majors, and the math department does not require you to take this course. It is the experts in your own fields that have found these tools useful."

I saw to it that the hour-long tests were all graded by Monday, either by an assistant or by me, and I made all the old exams available in the library, in later years online. After three or four weeks, my students loved the system. There were no surprises, they knew exactly how they were doing each week, and, as I had told them, it would be very easy for them to prepare for the final exam, since they had all those hour exams to look at.

My system was hard work, not only for my students, but also for me. The amount of time it takes to prepare a one-hour lecture can vary from a few minutes to a few hours, depending on the level of the subject, whether the instructor has taught it before, the quality of the course textbook, and, of course, on the individual teacher. Some professors always took the time to deliver excellent lectures, and others did not. It is also hard work to make up a good exam, which requires creativity and hours of trial and error.

On some first shots, the statement of the tentative question is too complex, or the solution is too difficult or too easy. All the new ideas have to be covered, and the exam has to fit into an hour and still give the student time to think. I put a lot of effort into writing good exams, and it cost me time in the short run. But in the long run, it really paid off, since the students had both time and space to record their answers, they found the questions fair, and the exams were easy to grade. To complement my effort to produce polished exams, I hired the very best graduate students to grade them and paid the graders extra out of my own pocket. My students loved this system and gave me high teaching evaluations, even though I was one of the tougher graders in the department. Later on, I tailored this approach to upper-division and graduate classes as well, and the higher-level students also came to appreciate it. Of course, it helped that I actually loved teaching and found it fun to give lectures and interact with the students.

Just before the end of my first fall quarter, John Neff, still head of the department, came to see me during my office hours. A tall, thin chain smoker with stooped shoulders and a quick wit, he told me that the hiring committee had voted to convert my two-year visiting position into a tenure-track assistant professorship. They felt that my research leadership, including the Probability Seminar and joint publications, together with my high teaching evaluations, justified such a promotion.

"I'd love to be put on tenure track," I told him. "But you and I agreed on a two-year contract, and there are other visitors here who desperately want the job. I started the Probability Seminar and collaborations because I wanted to and don't want that misread. I'm very grateful for the visiting appointment you gave me and will be glad to stick with that."

"Okay," he said, and shrugged his stooped shoulders, thanked me for my time, and left.

"What an idiot I am," I thought as he disappeared down the corridor. Most visiting professors would kill for a tenure-track appointment to avoid the semipermanent limbo of a long succession of temporary jobs that usually led to an exit from academia.

A few days later, Neff again came to my office. "The hiring committee won't take no for an answer," he said. This time I accepted.

Eureka number three! I had landed a tenure-track job, which meant a guaranteed six years to pursue mathematics, without interruption, at one home institution. True, it would be at a technical university, dead center in the genteel, conservative New South—about as spiritually distant from the campus and streets of Berkeley as one could get in North America. But I was confident I could adjust, just as I had adjusted to the Army and then civilian life again, and the thrill of being *paid* to teach and create mathematics overwhelmed me. Most of my artist friends had to wait tables in order to pay the rent.

In the first week of January 1978, as the department completed the paperwork to convert my appointment from visiting to tenure-track assistant professor, Dr. Neff once again walked into my office and this time closed the door behind him. His sports coat reeked of tobacco.

"May I ask you something?" he asked.

"Sure," I said, sensing something amiss. He'd never closed the door before.

"Do you have the PhD degree?"

"*What?*" I said, reeling in shock. "Remember when you hired me, I asked should I bring my PhD diploma or a certified letter. You said no—that no piece of paper I could walk in off the street with would be sufficient proof of having a doctorate. Instead, you told me, my credentials would be checked directly from university registrar to university registrar, so I left it up to you. What's going on?"

"Well," he said, "there seems to be a problem. When we gave you the original visiting contract, our hiring clerk checked your degree record, and it looked okay to him since he saw another degree above your two master's degrees. But now that we're initiating the tenure-track paperwork, the dean's office is double-checking every detail, and your highest degree seems to be something called a 'Candidate in Philosophy.' It's not a PhD, I understand, and we should have caught it when we first hired you, but nobody here has ever heard of any degree in mathematics higher than a master's *except* the doctorate. I called Berkeley to check, and it's not clear you have a PhD. If we had seen this was a Candidate in Philosophy degree, we would have noticed the trouble immediately and straightened it out last fall. But now even your present contract is in jeopardy since a doctorate is required. Can you try to sort it out? I talked to an administrator in the Berkeley math department named Nora Lee. Here's her number."

That was a stroke of luck. Nora was not only a senior member of the mathematics administrative staff at Berkeley, but she also happened to have typed my thesis, and we were personal friends—I once helped move her daughter's player piano in my van. I phoned her immediately.

"Hey, Nora," I said, "I thought I had everything signed, sealed, and delivered before I left campus. Now Georgia Tech tells me there's a problem. Don't I have a PhD?"

"Well, you do and you don't," she said.

"*What?*"

"The California regents has to approve all degrees, and the official date of conferral for your PhD was last December 11. But a legislative emergency came up, and the regents adjourned for Christmas Recess before passing the degree resolution. When they reconvene next week, they'll award you the degree *retroactively*. So officially, today you don't have a PhD, but next week your degree will date back to last December. Unless a meteor hits Sacramento in the meantime."

I went to the director's office and explained.

"Hmm," he said. "*Berkeley*! Always did think they were a little crazy out there. Probably the LSD in the drinking water. Let's try this—I'll hold up the paperwork in my office for two weeks on some pretense, and then we'll check again. A *PhC*? What will they think up next out there in *la-la-land*?"

His stratagem worked, and soon my coveted tenure-track job was official. I relaxed and began to adjust to my new surroundings. "Georgia Tech is different from other universities," senior colleagues had warned me several times. "The administration here is *very* autocratic. If someone yelled, 'Right *face*, forward *march*!' half the campus would march off." I politely thanked them for their friendly advice and suppressed a smile. They intended the warning for a Berkeley hippie-era PhD. Most of my new colleagues did not know I was also a graduate of Beast Barracks, West Point, Army Ranger School, and Vietnam. "You have no idea what 'autocratic' means," I thought to myself.

But since the warnings came from all directions—young colleagues, old colleagues, Yankees, Californians, and Southerners—I figured there must be *some* truth to it. "Just great," I thought. My key to a college education, free from my father's financial yoke, had hung on surviving America's most regimented undergraduate program—West Point—and if my new colleagues were right, my key to life in the utopian world of academics now hung on surviving one of America's most authoritarian university administrations. But I put those thoughts out of my mind. For the time being, at least, I had finally *arrived*.

Slowly I adjusted to Atlanta's ways and learned to carry shoes and a shirt with a collar in the trunk, in case I wanted to go into a club. Al and his wife, Carroll, had continued their Atlanta welcome and often invited me to dinner at their home in Midtown. After dessert on one of those dinners, Al and I reminisced about the time he and I and two girls from Buffalo spent the weekend in Alloway under the watchful eye of that cowboy NY State Trooper, and my visit to the Lindseth wheat farm in North Dakota, when he and I raised clouds of dust on the dirt roads racing his '66 Corvette and my '56 T-bird. We caught up on each other's families and about Vietnam and our careers. Al was about to make partner in the Atlanta/Washington law firm of Sutherland, Asbill, and Brennan and was already becoming one of the nation's leading experts in school desegregation litigation.

"I have a landmark school busing case coming up here in Atlanta," Al said. "Wanted to ask you something." He brought a book from his study. "In desegregation trials, the first crucial step is to *prove* the city is segregated. Just like there are established standards of proof in mathematics, the courts also have standards of proof. Now, to prove to *you or me* that Atlanta is segregated, we could just give a cabbie $100 and tell him to show us all around the city, and we'd be convinced. But that isn't a mathematical proof, or a legal one.

"Courts rely on testimonies of expert witnesses and their statistics. In all the other major school desegregation trials the past ten years, coast to coast, the courts have relied on the same expert witness, a professor of sociology from Madison named Taeuber, who developed the so-called Segregation Index everyone is using. His testimony has never been successfully challenged, and in our trial, he will also be a star witness—for the other side. I've read all his books, and everything seems to boil down to this one single formula."

He opened the text to a bookmarked page and handed it to me.

"His Segregation Index looks reasonable to me," he continued, "but since all his testimony hinges on that one formula, I'd like to understand it better. Does it look okay to you?"

Al's clear-headed logic, born of solving North Dakota farm machinery problems and honed at West Point and Harvard Law School, always impressed me. He excelled in engineering and mathematics at West Point and was now applying that same analytical power to questions in law. In this case, he had done homework that all the big-shot lawyers had missed, or had given up on, and had distilled the crux of the segregation issue down to one clean line of text. Now it was up to me to see if I could help. On the surface, the formula looked perfectly reasonable. To determine the segregation index of a city, you went down each street, say north to south, and used a bogus survey to record each house as white or minority, just based on who came to the door. Once all the houses on the street were polled, you calculated a numerical rating for that street and went to the next street. At the end, you combined all the street ratings for the final segregation index. The possible ranges of the index were from 1, the lowest segregation, to 100. For example, if you were looking at a checkerboard with a third of its squares black and the rest white, and all the black squares were clustered into one corner, you would expect an index near 100. If the black squares were sprinkled sparsely throughout the checkerboard, you would expect a low index.

I used the same approach I had learned in my apprenticeship under Dubins. First, reduce the problem to the simplest possible case and work back up. I sketched out some checkerboards with only two streets and two avenues and calculated the segregation index for different proportions and spatial distributions. It looked okay. Then I worked up to the three-by-three case, which looks like a tic-tac-toe game. A half hour later, I stumbled onto something.

"Look, Al," I said. "In this hypothetical city, if you calculate the index starting with the streets first, you get a high segregation index. But if you use the *avenues* first, you get a low one. A mathematician would say this numerical index is not 'rotation invariant.' Shouldn't matter if you go north-south first or east-west, should it?"

Al was excited about the discovery and called me at the office the next day to describe an even more extreme example he found. I was out of town during the trial but heard that the *Atlanta Journal Constitution* reported that Mr. Lindseth's cross-examination completely destroyed Professor Taeuber's testimony. Al phoned me and summarized the critical part.

"I just played dumb," he said, "and told the professor I didn't understand his Index. I asked him to please calculate it for me on a sample city I had drawn on a large mock-up. While he was explaining his formula to the court, I just sat back and kept my mouth shut. Then suddenly the judge piped up and said he had scribbled down his own calculation going the other direction first and got a totally different answer. That meant that the sacred Segregation Index was faulty, at the very least. That was it—best thing that could happen in court—when the judge makes your point for you."

"Exactly the same thing in math classes," I told him. "The best lesson of all is when the students discover the keystone idea by themselves."

After a year at Georgia Tech, I had met only a few colleagues and graduate students, and there were no social events to get acquainted. Most of my colleagues lived far from the inner-city campus, which was surrounded by housing projects and other shotgun houses in my Home Park neighborhood. Remembering the formal open house parties my father had hosted every year in Alloway to share his good fortune with his friends and coworkers and Professor Krengel's hospitality in Göttingen, I decided to advertise an Open House Party, beer and wine and snacks provided, to welcome new faculty and grad students. My Ninth Street shotgun house was only a block off campus and just dilapidated enough that I didn't need to worry about cigarette burns or spilt wine and just undilapidated enough so that once I had furnished it with Salvation Army auction furniture, partygoers would feel right at home after a few free belts.

A tall handsome graduate student from Greece came to see me in my office hours.

"Professor Hill," he said, "the graduate students are really looking forward to your party. Would it be okay if I brought some hardcore movies? I have lots of 8-millimeter John Holmes films and a projector."

It was certainly a novel and unexpected offer. I asked for more details. He bought the blue movies wherever he could find them in the US, he told me, repackaged them in plain boxes, and took them back to Greece, where he told customs inspectors they were home movies. Then he sold the movies on the black market at a huge profit—enough to pay for his trips to Athens. I thought it over and told him yes but that he would have to set up the screening in the back room.

The night of the party, it seemed like the whole department turned out. I met the guests at the front door and gave them the layout: "The first room here is the living room, the next one back has snacks and drinks, the one behind that has music for dancing, and the last one has blue movies." And nearly every one of them immediately marched straight through the house to the flickering lights in the standing-room-only back room.

During the academic term, I continued to pour time and energy into classes and research, with much of the same intensity as in graduate school. But now "research" took on a broader meaning, involving coming up with a steady stream of new and interesting math problems to tackle, finding solutions, and writing up and submitting the papers for peer-reviewed publication, a process that sometimes lasted over a year. In addition, the deans and vice president for research expected all tenure-track faculty to submit proposals for outside funding—grants and fellowships from government and industry agencies.

I'd never written a grant proposal before nor received any guidance on it, so I went to see our department technical expert, Annette Rohrs, who had been helping me far beyond the call of duty from my first days in the department. She could produce any kind of technical paper or chart or talk slide I asked for, and when she made drafts of slides for my professional talks, she would set aside time for me one on one, reserve a room, and actually project each of the transparencies, showing me different color options and symbol choices! Her expertise, work ethic, and can-do attitude were legendary in our department and even recognized at the institute level, when she won the award for the best staff support person in the whole university. When I asked Annette about how to write a grant proposal, she got permission for me to see several successful proposals and walked me through the whole process.

In some senses, writing a grant proposal is much harder than writing a research paper, since the proposal must describe ideas that are not yet fully formed and must be of a much broader scope, encompassing perhaps a dozen concrete ideas in several different areas. To make it even worse, the proposals are sent out for review to the world's top experts, who have been in the business for decades. A certain amount of gamesmanship was involved, first in finding attractive topics and then in describing methods of attack on those problems that looked plausible but not already finished. The best part of grant writing, I came to learn, was that it forced us researchers to sit back and plan our long-term research strategies from initial pipe dreams to concrete techniques.

A successful grant proposal brought in funding, which supplemented the standard nine-month salary with a month or two of summer salary to work on research with no teaching duties. It also enhanced the reputation of the institution and brought in cash in the form of payments for overhead. Most active researchers had to cram their research work into those summer months when they had no teaching or committee duties, and many relied on that extra summer support to help pay for their families' expenses. My simple lifestyle gave me the flexibility to get research work done in addition to the teaching during the academic year, but I still needed the kinds of physical outlets I had cultivated in Berkeley. So, to balance the periods of intense intellectual concentration, I took up whitewater canoeing and racquetball and taught some of my new colleagues how to rappel on the cliffs along the Chattahoochee River just north of the I-285 Perimeter. Although I softened the old Ranger sergeants' instructional techniques for the "civilians," I still retained their demand for discipline and safety—didn't want to have to give a colleague casualty report to the department head.

I was surprised at how cold Atlanta could be in the winter, with temperatures low enough to freeze and burst water pipes and with its high incidence of slightly warmer but more havoc-wreaking ice storms. By March I longed for a spring break in the sun, with a bit of physical adventure to balance the intense intellectual work, much as I had used sailing and hiking and motorcycling in graduate school.

I decided to return again to the remote reefs and tiny uninhabited cays ringing Grand Bahama Island, where I had first experienced the wonders of the undersea world with Chan. I had visited Grand Bahama a few times since then with different people, and during those trips, the survivalist mentality and preoccupation with food instilled in Beast and Ranger had always risen to the surface. With all the exercise and camping in the bush, the next meal was always in the back of my mind. On my second trip to Grand Bahama, I was snorkeling alone on a reef in 4 feet of water when I saw my first lobster hiding under a shelf. "That guy looks delicious," I thought, and I was surprised at how close I could get to him. But when I tried to grab it, I learned why Caribbean lobsters are called *spiny* lobsters, and even the antennae stung my fingers. The next trip I brought gloves, finally caught one, and had a hamburger place grill it up for me. I felt some sort of primal caveman satisfaction catching my own supper and was hooked. The first big conch I picked up was clearly the same delicious animal locals were selling out of the backs of their trucks and serving with peas and rice in the restaurants. I knew it was delicious but not how to get the animal out of its shell, and I tried everything from slamming it on the cement to running it over with the rental car. No luck with either, so I took it to a local fisherman, who showed me how to knock a small hole three rings from the pointed tip, dislodge the conch there, and slip it out of the main orifice with a dull dinner knife. He made it look easy, but it took me forever to learn. Now I was set on catching all my suppers, but sometimes I got a little carried away.

On one trip, I roped an adventurous colleague into joining me, with promises to train him in the fine points of skin diving and to bring him back in one piece. While exploring a small coral cave on West End, I spotted a sleeping shark, its vacant eyes staring out of the depths. All I could see in front of me was a larder full of fresh shark steaks. I let myself drift into the cave with the ocean swell and managed to slip a makeshift lasso around the shark's midriff. I swam back out with the slack end of the line and gave it a tug from behind a coral head. The shark suddenly spooked and bolted right past me, and I suddenly realized it was much larger than I had guessed and was a potentially dangerous lemon shark, not the passive nurse shark I had taken it to be. My diving buddy, a Georgia Tech mathematician whom I was just introducing to this world of diving, stared at me in disbelief after we returned to shore empty-handed.

"Why the hell did you have me go along?" he said. "I wasn't any help out there."

"Because," I said, "having two of us in the water lowered the odds of me getting attacked to fifty-fifty, and for a Ranger, that's an acceptable risk." I grinned.

He was less enthusiastic than I about our little adventure and soon quit the annual dive trips. But the exercise and sun and sparkling clear water with reefs full of seafood were just what I needed after a long, cold winter of teaching and research, and I started making the self-guided dive trip an annual spring event, each trip trying out another companion or two from on campus and off. The vast majority lasted only a single trip. For some it was just too strenuous, and for others camping in the bush was too uncomfortable.

But when I brought Vince Ervin, a math graduate student at Georgia Tech from Australia, he took to it instantly. Of medium height, lean, and superbly fit, he had spent his boyhood at the edge of the outback in Victoria and was quick to learn how to handle the new physical and mental challenges inherent in skin and scuba diving. Smiling through his bushy beard, he was instantly addicted to the adventure and beauty and thrill of catching our own supper each night. On each trip, we continued to learn something new. How to spot an octopus by its garden, and how to hook it. How to pry a triggerfish out of its hole, how to "tickle" lobsters into leaving a coral hideout, how to clean and cook whelks. The inhabitants of Grand Bahama are not divers or even swimmers, so we always had the reefs to ourselves, which also meant we had to learn by trial and error. Vince was a natural and helped lead the annual dive trip team for decades to come.

* * *

My original plan when I first got the visiting offer from Georgia Tech was to immerse myself completely in academic research and teaching for those two years to see whether I liked it and whether I was any good at it. I now knew that, so far anyway, I *loved* it, and apparently the department liked what I was doing as well. My PhD thesis on Markov strategies was accepted for publication in the prestigious *Transactions of the American Mathematical Society*, and I also was awarded my first federal research grant from the Air Force Office of Scientific Research.

But now that my academic career was well launched, I was a little worried about settling into a year-in, year-out routine that I believed would eventually stifle my creativity. I saw that for some of my colleagues, research and teaching had quickly become chores, and I didn't want that to happen to me. And besides, despite my short intermittent business and vacation trips, I was getting the travel bug again, itching to experience a new environment and think nothing but mathematics over a longer period of time.

So when I got the research grant, which covered two months' summer salary for two years, I did a few calculations and figured out that, if I kept to my simple living style, I could easily stretch that four-month salary to last me a whole year. Since my grant permitted me to work on anything I wanted and my "laboratory of the mind" was infinitely portable, I decided to take a chance and apply to Georgia Tech for an unpaid year's leave of absence. This would give me *fifteen* straight months off—two summers and the nine-month academic year in between. My plan was to spend the summers back in Berkeley, and in between I would return to the most beautiful island I had ever seen, the Garden Island of Kauai. I'd spent two glorious weeks there while working on my thesis and had promised myself to return some day for a full year. Much to my surprise, Georgia Tech approved my leave request, and at the end of the spring quarter, I sublet the house, packed camping gear and a few books and papers into the VW, and took my favorite route across country to Berkeley by way of Denver, Dinosaur National Monument, Flaming Gorge, Great Salt Lake, and Lake Tahoe.

Kauai's natural beauty is legendary, even in the Hawaiian Islands, where ancient tradition cites it as the birthplace of the rainbow and home of the leprechaun-like Menehunes. Mount Waialeale's rainfall is the highest on earth, and only several miles downwind lies a volcanic desert, dotted with immense cacti and sliced through by ancient streambeds. On Kauai I shared a house in the tiny village of Kalaheo and made friends with one of my housemates and his adopted family, the Olivers.

I spent half of each day hiking the mountain swamps and seaside cliffs or skin and scuba diving the coral reefs, and the other half immersed in the beauties of abstract mathematics. No distractions of nightlife or bookstores or academic duties interrupted my quiet times, and the only post-secondary school on the island was a two-year junior college.

During that year, I discovered a new basic prophet inequality, talking to Kertz weekly by phone at prearranged times. I also discovered one of my favorite and most abstract mathematical results, a meta-theorem or theorem about theorems, which says that many theorems about independent random variables can be immediately extended to variables that are dependent. After its publication in the *Annals of Probability*, this idea led other researchers to general theories about "decoupling," or removing independence requirements, of many types of random processes. On that island, there were no science libraries or fellow mathematicians to test my ideas, and I am convinced that the intellectual isolation of Kauai was instrumental in triggering my idea for the meta-theorem.

At the beginning of summer, I flew back to San Francisco and rented a small, unfurnished apartment in Berkeley off Sacramento Avenue. I rejoined the Dubins Seminar and spoke about the Kauai meta-theorem to a handful of the world's foremost experts to learn whether it was already known. To my delight, it was not, and their feedback reinforced my confidence in my own mathematical intuition and my success with this new remote-island "self-sabbatical" experiment.

Late one night, I needed a study break, and, as usual, a walk through the dark wooded campus was just the ticket. Suddenly I found myself at the scene of the canoe heist again, staring at the drainpipe and barbed wire. "A criminal always returns to the scene of the crime," whispered the rational part of my brain. "I should get out of here right now." But I kicked off my sandals under the magnolia tree and climbed, digging my big toes into the gaps in the cyclone fence. Without the towel for protection, picking my way over the barbed wire took longer than before. Once inside I moved silently around the pool, feasting again on the fragrant, cool, damp Berkeley air and charged by the thrill of another little illicit outing. At the far end of the pool, a door to the main building was propped open, and through the doorway I saw a dimly lit stairway. My curiosity again got the better of me.

I descended the concrete and steel stairs silently on bare feet, pausing before each landing to peer carefully around the corner with one eye before proceeding down to the next level. On the second floor, my eyeball periscope came face to face with four other eyeballs, less than 6 feet away—uniformed security guard eyeballs. I had no choice but to continue my descent smoothly, my head pulling the rest of my reluctant body along behind it like a caterpillar. I sized up the situation immediately. One of the security guards, a senior officer in charge, was inspecting and quizzing the other, a young trainee. Both their jaws dropped as I rounded the corner.

"Wha' the hell?" the senior guy blurted. They glanced at me and then at each other. "Who the hell?"

The human brain is often quite remarkable when survival is at stake. I had an instant inspiration, totally spontaneous. The inspecting officer's face looked vaguely familiar, not surprising on a village-sized university campus of 25,000. Cutting them both off in mid-sentence, I slapped the inspecting officer playfully across the chest with the back of my hand.

"Hey, man, you don't remember *me*?" I said.

For a second he stood there dazed, and before they could answer, I reached out to shake the younger guard's hand.

"Name's Ted," I said. "How's it going?"

Then I shook the older guy's hand, and both mumbled their names. I forced a big grin and pointed to their clipboards and pencils.

"What're you guys up to?" I asked, before they had a chance to ask me that question.

"Security inspection," said the senior guard. "We're checking windows and entrances."

I wanted to answer, "Well, I'm off to clean the pool..." or whatever they thought I should have been doing. But there I was, in an old Navy T-shirt and jeans, *barefoot*, without the faintest idea of who they thought I could be or where I should be working. If I had known, I could have just marched off cheerfully in that direction.

As they continued testing window locks and putting check marks on the clipboards, I tagged along, making small talk, and silently wondering whether jail time could count toward the six-year tenure period at Georgia Tech. Then I had another idea. We stopped on the ground floor near a door with a horizontal panic bar, which opens under pressure from the inside. I pushed on the bar and sprung open the door, half expecting an alarm to go off. Nothing. I pulled it shut again and pointed to their clipboards.

"Maybe they should put alarms on these doors," I suggested, and the senior guard jotted it down.

As we continued on their rounds, down the long corridor paralleling the length of the pool above, I padded along barefoot, making polite conversation. Inside, my brain raced.

"Why all the security these days?" I asked.

"They're doin' a lot of renovation on this building," the senior guard said, "and there's been a shitload of burglaries of expensive construction equipment. We ever catch somebody in here, we're gonna nail 'em for all the thefts in the last six months."

I gulped. At the end of the corridor, the senior guard said he had to take a leak and started toward the men's room. The usual Pavlovian response kicked in, and the other guard followed. I nodded and muttered something about relieving myself too, pretending to follow them into the toilet.

As soon as both guards stepped through the door in front of me, I turned and bolted down the hallway, sprinting silently on bare feet as fast as I could go, crashing out through the same panic-barred door I'd tested earlier. I dashed into the night and across campus and home.

Several hours later, I returned to campus in my van with a change of clothes, this time wearing shoes. Massoud was still grinding away at his dissertation, and I had promised to pick him up after a late night hitting the books. Across the parking lot, police squad cars ringed the gym, and I tried to imagine the look on the senior guard's face, literally caught with his pants down, when I suddenly disappeared and the trainee asked him who I was. Hopefully neither of them got in much trouble.

* * *

When I finally returned to Atlanta, grad students and colleagues alike told me they were glad I was back—the department was still talking about my fall quarter party. I immediately announced another open house and especially encouraged new graduate students and faculty to come. But I emphasized that it was also open to people from all departments and their spouses and friends. The annual free beer, free food, and blue-movie parties became a department tradition.

The dean hired Les Karlovitz, a ham-fisted, hard-drinking Hungarian-American, as new head of the math department. He had previously been a program director at the National Science Foundation and was respected as an excellent analyst. At his first visit to the fall quarter open house party, Les walked up to me and smiled with a beer in his hand.

"At my first dean's meeting," he said, "I arrived early, along with the heads of the other departments, before the dean arrived. Three of us were new, and the old-timer department heads introduced themselves and asked us which units we represented. When I said 'mathematics,' one smiled enviously and said, 'Oh, that's the department with parties with porno movies!'"

"Why do people always assume we mathematicians are boring?" Les said, and patted me on the back.

My first PhD student, Martin Jones, was a perfect counterexample. Martin arrived in Atlanta with an impressive and diverse background—master's in mathematical logic, accomplished flutist, and former tennis pro and Pan American Team kayaker. Georgia Tech had a few professors who were notoriously lax in signing off on dissertations, and Martin could have signed on with one of them, but when he asked to study under me,

I immediately accepted. He chose to work on a difficult unsolved prophet inequality. The problem resisted Martin's attacks for months and then for nearly two more years, with no sign of cracking. He came to see me.

"I'm discouraged," he said. "I have no idea when, or if, I will ever finish the PhD."

"Look," I told him, "This is a tough dissertation problem, a beautiful one. I know there are other advisors out there where you can finish in one year, guaranteed. If you want to change advisors, I'll understand. Think of it like this. Today you are within one year of getting a PhD if you switch advisors. I'll understand. No hard feelings. See if that helps. Now go to the gym, hit the Nautilus, take a sauna, and think it over."

Within two months, Martin found his own keystone, reminding me of my discovery in Olga's cottage in Berkeley.

Within several more months, he and I verified every step in the argument, and a leading research journal accepted his paper for publication. I signed his thesis, and the unbroken chain of PhDs in my mathematical family tree now stretched from Mencken in seventeenth-century Leipzig down through the ages to Dubins at Chicago, then Hill at Berkeley, and now Jones at Georgia Tech. It reminded me of the Long Gray Line of West Point lore, with the image of a continuous line of cadets stretching back into the fog of centuries past.

* * *

After the idyllic year on Kauai, I had returned to campus completely rejuvenated, full of energy and new research ideas and, most surprising of all to my colleagues, actually looking forward to organizing research seminars and explaining the paradoxes and principles of probability to the new cohort of students. I was happy to be back and raring to go. But instead of considering this a once-in-a-lifetime experience, it occurred to me that perhaps this could become a regular part of my academic career—taking a yearlong leave without pay after every two years. I had no personal or professional *impedimenta*—no wife, house, mortgage, kids in school, fancy stereo, or even a TV. My colleagues joked that I could be at the airport in two hours with everything I owned. Also, my particular brand of mathematics research, inspired by Dubins and honed over the previous few years, was paper-and-pencil theoretical probability. No computers needed, no thick files of experimental data. I reckoned that for a one-year absence, about fifteen research articles and a few books would suffice. With my thrift store lifestyle, I could easily survive on half or one-third salary, about the amount awarded in two summer research grants. So, from my own personal standpoint, the goal was certainly attainable.

Now the big question was, would Georgia Tech go for it? In most other colleges and universities, professors are not free to come and go at will, even on unpaid leave, since most departments need to have their basic core courses covered. As a polytechnic university, where all students were required to take basic calculus courses, Georgia Tech had a large math department—fifty full-time professors of various ranks. But the key difference was that when someone like me took unpaid leave at Georgia Tech, the *department* kept his salary and could spend it any way they liked. They could use it to hire two junior lecturers or for travel or computer equipment or even pizzas. Of course, if too many professors wanted to go on leave every third year, that would cause a severe teaching shortage. Luckily for me, no one else did. When I went to see our new director with yet another leave request, I felt sheepish.

"Ted," he said with a grin, "if you didn't go away without pay like this, we couldn't make budget. Leave approved!"

I had not known about this unusual leave policy when I first took the job, and it was a wonderful serendipity to discover the ultimate professional freedom in this ultraconservative institution. *Eureka iterum.*

11

THE GLOBAL MATH GUILD

After my gregarious friend Jim Eberhardt had become a multimillionaire in his thirties buying and selling undeveloped land in the Santa Cruz Mountains, he still spent one weekend a month in a patrol car as a lowly deputy sheriff. I knew he had a bachelor's degree from San Jose State in law enforcement, but that was long ago.

"Why in the world are you still doing that?" I asked. "It isn't worth your time."

"Oh, yes it is," he said. "I meet lots of people on those weekends. One thing leads to another, and some of them need land. Plus there's often a little Code 3 chase adventure, and I like the camaraderie. Just like my time in the Navy. And, believe me, it never hurts to be carrying around a badge in your wallet when you travel. You'd be surprised how many tickets get torn up and how many doors it opens. Remember that trip I took to Germany last month?"

"Sure," I said. "But don't tell me a California police badge helps in Europe."

"Absolutely," he said. "We stayed at an inn in a small Bavarian village, and the first thing I always do is march right down to the local police station, introduce myself, and show them my badge. Hell, I don't even speak the language, like you do. But immediately they accept me as one of the international fraternal order of police, and before you know it, I'm having coffee and pastries and trading stories. And the local police always know where the best action is, whatever you're looking for."

* * *

Like Jim's experience with his police brotherhood affiliation, I discovered early in my career that one of the beauties of being a member of an academic community is that you are automatically linked to a network of colleagues all over the world. From little-known, remote Third World colleges to leading centuries-old universities, as a "card-carrying" college professor, I found warm welcomes on campuses wherever I went. At each of those academic nodes lives a subcommunity of math "artisans," much like the guilds of olden times. This global network is dynamic, with new nodes continuing to appear regularly and the experts and expertise within each node changing with the times. New discoveries are communicated around the network through papers, journals, conference presentations, personal visits, and now, the Internet. And I was lucky enough to learn at the beginning of my career, through my own travels and colleagues' travels to visit me, just how rewarding it can be to get to know other academic mathematicians face to face, both personally and professionally.

I had already gotten a student's view of the international math guild during my Fulbright year at Göttingen and had made a few connections at conferences, but my first in-depth experience with it as a professor came a decade later. In the spring of 1982, I started planning my second fifteen-month leave from Georgia Tech. Although I had loved the Eden-like isolation of Kauai, this time I wanted cutting-edge mathematics as well as a change of culture. I decided to spend my next long leave at a European university, with the challenges of both a new language and different scientific traditions. From my thesis research, I knew that one of the strengths of Dutch mathematics was Markov decision theory, the field of my Markov strategy dissertation, so I started looking at universities in the Netherlands. I was prepared to pay for the sojourn myself, as I had on Kauai, but I also applied for several grants to try to cover some of the costs. I was fortunate enough to win a postdoctoral research award cosponsored by the National Science Foundation and NATO, which paid for a twelve-month visit to the mathematics department at the *Rijksuniversiteit* in Leiden, a major center of science and mathematics since the sixteenth century.

In preparation for the year in Holland, I hired a Georgia Tech graduate student from Amsterdam to teach me Dutch. It was more difficult than I expected, especially the pronunciation. As my German Military Academy friend Peter insisted, "Dutch is not a language, it is a sickness of the throat!" But I worked hard and surprised my tutor with the time and energy I put into the project, especially since there was no language requirement in my fellowship. My tutor assured me that very few foreigners, including his own American wife, ever learn more than a few words of Dutch, and my efforts would be well rewarded. He was absolutely right.

Departmental secretaries at Leiden had put me in touch with a Dutch mathematician there who was about to go off for a year's sabbatical to Cal Tech and had an apartment I could sublet. When I arrived in Leiden, several weeks before the fall term began, I spent three nights in the university's International Center and then moved into his furnished apartment near Leiden Central Station. I settled in to my new living quarters and started to get acquainted with the town. I didn't know a single person in Holland apart from Noreen, who now had a new boyfriend and little time for me. It clearly would be another lesson for me in dealing with solitude, since this time I was completely alone in a non-English-speaking world, and my Dutch was far weaker than my German had been during my Fulbright year in Göttingen. Luckily I was used to eating alone most evenings, but it was hard to break through the social barriers and meet ordinary people. The Dutch seemed even more reserved and private than the Germans, especially in traditional cities like Leiden.

The weeks before classes began were very hard. My first coping mechanism was to take long bicycle rides through the surrounding polders, using this new solitude to immerse myself in the Dutch language and culture. Reading and rereading *Asterix* and *Lucky Luke* comic books in *het Nederlands* until I could finally connect the visual clues with the written words, I slowly began to understand the several layers of humor. I went to American and English movies with Dutch subtitles and practiced conversation in the weekly market. Almost every day, I bicycled for hours through flower fields and along the North Sea dunes. As I pedaled, I carried on a running two-way conversation with myself in Dutch, happy to have a companion at exactly my low level of fluency.

"*Nu, Ted, waar ga je heen fietsen morgen? Ik weet nog niet, misschien langs de duinen.*" Hey Ted, where will you go biking tomorrow? I don't know yet, maybe in the dunes.

As in Göttingen, I again found it liberating to have my thoughts and ideas unconstrained by my native tongue. And it helped immensely that in Leiden, completely unlike freewheeling Amsterdam, hardly any English is spoken on the street. But even though I began to speak passable Dutch, shopped at the weekly market, lived in a standard apartment building, and dined at local cafés, I was still a complete outsider—treated with politeness but always at arm's length.

Once the academic year began, however, the Leiden University Mathematics Department was a completely different story. The main institute on *Wassenaarseweg* was twenty minutes by bike from my apartment, and the second I stepped into the building, my new colleagues welcomed me as one of their own. They immediately introduced me around, gave me my own office, and took me to their café for coffee and *stroopwafels*. Yes, I spoke *Nederlands* with a strange Anglo-German accent, but I was one of the clan. I belonged!

Monday through Friday, I went in almost every day to use the library and exchange ideas with colleagues and graduate students. However, unlike American universities that are essentially open 24/7—at least to students and faculty—the main doors at Dutch universities, like those in Göttingen, were locked after 6 o'clock and on weekends, and even full professors didn't have keys. Dutch academic mathematicians and students worked hard, but only from nine to five, five days a week, unlike American universities, where scholars were coming and going at all hours. As in most European universities, there were no fraternities, sororities, or athletic teams, and after dark the university was like a cemetery, as the students and faculty retired to their homes or favorite beer cellars, cafés, and theaters.

Within two months of my arrival in Leiden, I had organized a weekly Probability Seminar, again following the Dubins Seminar model, and delivered my first mathematics lecture in heavily accented Dutch. My new colleagues applauded the mathematical results and my Dutch rendition of them. They understood every word and told me with friendly smiles that I had made some very *interesting* grammatical constructions. The Dutch are exceptionally multilingual, and I'm sure every one of them spoke much better English (and French and German) than I did Dutch. But my new colleagues clearly appreciated my effort, and that was the beginning of a lifetime of collaboration with Dutch mathematicians and my love affair with the Dutch culture and spirit.

Spending the whole academic year 1982–1983 at a major university, but without any teaching duties, was perfect for research. Again following Dubins's example, I began to look at research questions outside Markov decision theory, questions that were just plain *fun* to think about and that I could share with my nonmath friends. In 1961, while I was still a freshman at Madison, Dubins and his fellow Berkeley mathematician Edwin Spanier had published a widely cited paper entitled "How to Cut a Cake Fairly," addressing the basic question of how an object, such as a cake or inheritance, can be divided among several people with possibly different values in such a way that each person is guaranteed to receive a portion that he considers a fair share. The classical "one-cuts, the-other-chooses" solution works fine for two people but not for three or more. Dubins and Spanier found an elegant and practical "sliding knife" fair-division algorithm for any number of players.

In that article, they also discussed the Problem of the Nile, an ancient fair-division problem from Egypt that asks whether *land* can also be fairly divided. Unlike cakes, land cannot be cut and moved around, and the location of the pieces matters. I reread the Dubins-Spanier paper, remembering with a chuckle my own unorthodox cake-cutting strategies at West Point, and I decided to tackle the fair-border aspects of the Problem of the Nile. None of the known fair-division algorithms were helpful, since the usual partitioning schemes would often cut a desired territory so it could not be connected to the country that wanted it.

I had found a good working schedule—going in to the office, talking to colleagues and working on my problem, having lunch in the cafeteria followed by coffee, working with my Dutch host Professor Hordijk, enjoying a solitary evening meal, and then working more at night in my apartment. Weekends I continued bicycling and carrying on my auto-dialogues in Dutch. After a few months, I finally found a solution to the border problem using a famous existential convexity theorem discovered in 1940 by the Russian mathematician Aleksandr Lyapunov, and everything fell into place. I wrote it up, and after its publication in *The American Mathematical Monthly*, that success led me to a long series of fair-division publications, with applications in estate settlements and testing of statistical hypotheses. Twenty years later, when the Institute of Mathematical Statistics elected me as IMS Fellow, the citation included my work in fair division.

As these discoveries became known, other mathematicians took note. The University of Nijmegen, on the German border in southeast Netherlands, invited me to speak on the topic of fair division. My lecture was very well received, and afterward several Nijmegen graduate students contacted Wouter Klootwijk, science editor of the Dutch national newspaper *de Volkskrant*. Mr. Klootwijk arranged to interview me for two hours in an Amsterdam café, where he explained that the Dutch are constantly embroiled in land division disputes. When a farmer dies, he passes on his valuable flower fields and dairy polders to his children, who typically do not have enough cash to buy each other out. Some fields are closer to markets, others have better drainage, and not everyone agrees on the relative values of the different parcels. The problem is so pervasive, he said, that the Dutch government set up a special federal agency, the *Ruilverkavelings-Commissie*, whose mission is to mediate land division disputes. So when some guy announced to mathematical audiences in Holland that he could prove that fair land divisions always exist, the public took note.

I explained to Mr. Klootwijk that my solution was only theoretical and of little use in practice. It only proved logically that fair boundaries exist, not how to find them. He then asked me if there was a way to divide a halibut fairly among three fishermen, as his weekend hobby often required. I showed him how the elegant Dubins and Spanier's "sliding-knife" algorithm was perfect for that problem.

"Pass a knife slowly over the fish from head to tail," I told him, "as all three fishermen are watching. As soon as one fisherman is satisfied with the portion from the knife to the top of the head, he says stop. The fish is then cut by the knife at that position, and the declarer gets that portion. The remaining fishermen, who have not said stop, agree that the cut piece is less than one-third the value and are perfectly happy to divide the remainder, either using the same procedure or by simple cut-and-choose. No matter what the values of each participant are, this technique guarantees that each fisherman will receive a portion that he himself values as at least one-third of the fish. Elegant and practical, and it works for any number of people."

Mr. Klootwijk was delighted and told me he would use it on his next weekend fishing trip. And *de Volkskrant* published his long article in their Saturday science section, including an exact photocopy of my published fair-land-division theorem—the only time a newspaper ever printed a theorem of mine verbatim.

* * *

From my Leiden base, I also made excursions to other nodes in the global math network. I visited my academic brother David Gilat at Tel Aviv University and made an excursion by bus to Jerusalem, where I didn't know a soul. A month earlier, Bob Kertz had written me that when I was in Israel, I should stop to see a certain Professor Ester Samuel-Cahn in Jerusalem, a member of the Norwegian Academy of Sciences who had written him of her interest in the prophet inequalities we had been studying. Today we would just Google the name and find photos, websites, publications, and even short biographies. But back then, even email was not in widespread use, and we just took chances on making personal contacts. After spending the night in a bed and breakfast, I explored the Old City and in the afternoon walked through ancient neighborhoods to the Mount Scopus campus of Hebrew University and went to her office. A matronly, gray-haired woman opened the door, and I introduced myself, explained that I was a visiting mathematician from Atlanta and had been told she was interested in prophet inequalities.

"Not really," she answered politely, in a thick Scandinavian accent. "But why don't you come in and show me your ideas at the blackboard?"

I picked up the chalk, thinking Kertz must have confused her with someone else. I'd quickly write out a few definitions and theorems and then thank her for her time and excuse myself. After I had written the second line of equations, she jumped to her feet and shouted.

"Oh—pro-*fate*! *Prophet* inequalities! You are *Hill*! Come here!"

Professor Samuel-Cahn took me by the arm and led me to her desk, where she then pulled open her briefcase to show me the stack of papers she was taking home that night—reprints of my articles with Kertz. Her Norwegian background was the cause of our original miscommunication. Unlike English, in most European languages, the words *profit* and *prophet* are pronounced quite differently—*pro-feet* versus *pro-fate*—and she had interpreted my English pronunciation in the most logical way for a mathematician—*profit* inequalities, about which neither of us knew a thing. We spoke until late in the afternoon, when she had to return to her husband and four children. But we had made an excellent connection and started planning a sabbatical visit for her to come to Georgia Tech. Another link in the network.

"Should I call you a taxi?" she asked.

"No, thanks," I said. "I walked here from the Old City, and it was interesting for me. First time I've ever seen olive trees up close. I'll just go back the same way."

"You *walked* here from the city?" she gasped. "Those Palestinian neighborhoods are very, very dangerous. You were incredibly lucky." She thought a minute and added, "But I guess you'll be okay again—anyone can see you're not Jewish. Please call me when you get back to your room."

* * *

Returning to Atlanta in the fall of 1983 after that year in Europe reaffirmed my decision to take frequent extended leaves, with or without financial support. Again I had arrived back on campus completely refreshed, full of energy and new ideas. My long absences also offered one other major advantage—they kept me out of academic politics. Georgia Tech's autocratic administrative structure rubbed against my grain, just as the Army had, but Director Neff and his successor had ruled quite fairly. The next change of administration, however, put a new director in charge of mathematics, and this one had a very different style of interaction, automatically following orders from the dean without question.

When I returned from Leiden, it was time for me to prepare and submit my case for promotion to associate professor with tenure. The tenure decision is perhaps the most vital event in an academic career. The tenure review committee not only examines internal performance like teaching and service to the community but also solicits input on the candidate's research from experts around the world. Even with my footloose and fancy-free academic lifestyle, taking unpaid leaves all the time, it would be good to have a long-term home base, and I took the process seriously. With research grants from both the Air Force Office of Scientific Research and the NSF, a postdoc award to Leiden, publications in leading research journals, and great teaching evaluations, my academic life had been going very well—I even did well on committee service, when I was in residence. I was confident it would go well.

Normally a senior faculty member presented the case to a departmental review committee. The committee's vote was then submitted to the director, who in turn sent his recommendation to the dean, and so on up the chain of command all the way to the university president. However, after the departmental review of my case, the full professor who represented me came to my office looking very somber.

"Everything was going great—your case was very strong, and we were about to vote when the director interrupted our meeting," he told me. "He ordered us not to take a vote on your tenure. He's not even supposed to be present in our deliberations, since he has his own formal input at the director level. Interfering with our decision was unethical, especially after he told you to prepare a case for tenure, and he sent out letters for outside evaluations. Nobody on the committee dared say a word—he controls our salaries, and teaching loads, and everything else. We've heard that because of the economy and current budget crunch, the provost has instructed department heads to delay all permanent budget decisions, and that includes tenure. Except, of course, when it was already in progress. So the decision about your tenure is on indefinite hold for now, although we did vote to promote you to associate professor. This should not have happened to you, Ted, and I'm very, very sorry."

I was stunned and angry at this unexpected blow and realized that what bothered me wasn't so much what the director had done, since he was known to be unpredictable and temperamental, but the fact that senior full professors had failed to speak up when they knew he'd abused his power. "If I ever make full professor somewhere," I promised myself, "and someone treats junior faculty like this, I will speak out, come what may." I had no idea at the time that in a few short years, I would have to make good on that promise.

I thought it over for a couple of days and then made a decision. Life is short, and I'd left the Army partly to get away from the rigid chain of command decision-making process. Much as I'd had a great career at Georgia Tech until this happened, I didn't really care for living in Atlanta, so I decided to put myself on the market to at least check out possibilities at other universities.

Since Hawaii was always in my dreams, I applied for a job at the only academic research node on the islands, the University of Hawaii in Honolulu. My research and teaching record was now well established, and they immediately offered me a tenure-track associate professorship in mathematics. In late June, after classes had finished, I packed my belongings into a used short-bed Chevy van I had bought to replace the dying VW, and Jack Miller flew out from Berkeley to join me in the cross-country road trip. When we got to California, I spent two months as an official visiting scholar in the Berkeley math department, then sold the Chevy in Santa Cruz and flew to Hawaii. I had left Atlanta planning never to return but before I left I had arranged another unpaid leave of absence from Georgia Tech. That would give me a yearlong safety net—a Right of Return—just in case.

On Oahu I stayed at the YMCA for a week until I found an apartment a short bike ride from the main campus in Manoa Valley. For $800 I bought a used VW Rabbit with 140,000 miles, a huge odometer reading for an island less than fifty miles in diameter. Waikiki was ten minutes away by car, but ten minutes in the other direction put you in dense jungle. I kept two sets of diving gear in the trunk of the Rabbit, and my university office was only an eighteen-minute drive from the renowned coral reefs at Hanauma Bay.

Compared to my years at the universities in Göttingen and Leiden, this new academic experience "abroad" was a much easier adjustment in some respects, with its typical American university semester system and, of course, lectures in English. I loved the informality of classes in Manoa—we taught the same calculus-based probability course as at Georgia Tech but in shorts and aloha shirts. On the other hand, the *Haole go home!* and *Kill Haole!* graffiti scrawled on restroom walls, off campus and on, came as an unpleasant surprise.

A more important unpleasant surprise was that I found the research environment in Hawaii to be as laid back as its classroom attire. In Atlanta I'd been working in an ideal professional environment while living away from nature. Here in Manoa, on the other hand, I was surrounded by the jungles and beaches and coral reefs but not by an ideal research environment. *Which was more important for me?* As I learned, I was not the first mathematician to struggle with this decision. In the early 1960s, UH hired the famous Hungarian mathematician Paul Halmos to build up its math department, but he'd left abruptly after only one year to return to his tenured position at the University of Indiana. In his memoir, Halmos lists his main reason for leaving—the reputation of UH was not high, even in Hawaii. Conscientious island parents sent good students to college on the mainland, so even the local pool of good math students was going elsewhere. Much as I liked my colleagues and the beauty of the Manoa Valley campus—packed with flowering plants from islands all over the South Pacific—the university was geographically very isolated, and the math department lacked the vigorous *eureka* spirit I had loved in Atlanta.

When my Georgia Tech friend and colleague John Elton cracked a problem in fair division we'd been working on together that year, I realized that for me, a vigorous research environment trumped living in a tropical paradise. I could always visit Shangri-La on my own. So, like Halmos, I left after one year in Manoa and returned to Georgia Tech but, unlike him, without any guarantee of tenure. I decided to take my chances on surviving petty academic bosses by focusing on teaching and research and avoiding departmental politics whenever I could. Shortly after I returned to Atlanta, however, my tenure was approved after all, and I was now a permanent member of the Georgia Tech community, a fixed node in the global math network. My work in probability theory was getting more recognition, and

I was fortunate to win a steady stream of research grants, which, in turn, supported my continued international activities.

My work on optimal stopping, including my dissertation, also led to an invitation to visit one of the "inner circles" of the guild of mathematicians, the Mathematical Research Institute known as Oberwolfach, located near the tiny village of that name in Baden-Württemberg. The event that took me there was a workshop on "Gambling and Optimal Stopping," where I was to meet some of the leading researchers in that field. Optimal stopping, like fair division, is one of my favorite research topics, since in both subjects I can share some of the main basic ideas with non-scientist friends, and at the same time I can delve as deeply as I want into purely mathematical questions. The theory of optimal stopping addresses the common situation in science—and the rest of life—when there is an element of chance involved and a crucial problem is deciding when to stop. That could mean waiting to buy or sell Google stocks or your house or car, proofreading a paper or debugging a large software program, deciding when to switch to a new medication, updating eBay auction bids, or interviewing for a new secretary or spouse. At some point you need to stop, and your objective is to do it in a way that maximizes your profit or satisfaction.

As a concrete example, suppose I will let you throw a pair of dice up to five times, and you can stop whenever you want, at which time I will give you the number of dollars showing on the last roll. If you roll a twelve the first time, clearly it's optimal to stop right then, and if you throw a two, not to stop. But what if the first roll is a ten? Stop or not? There is an optimal rule, and it can be calculated. This mathematical theory, also known in the literature by the colorful names of Secretary, Marriage, Dowry, or Best-Choice Problems, has a long history complete with excellent rules of thumb, counterintuitive surprises, colorful paradoxes, and famous unsolved problems, and I was about to join some of the world experts in that field.

Oberwolfach occupies the estate of a former hunting lodge deep in the Black Forest. Founded during the final stages of World War II by Hermann Göring as a secret mathematics research center, it was originally designed to bolster Nazi war efforts by developing mathematical tools that could lead to superweapons. Its remote location was chosen to avoid Allied discovery and air raids. At war's end, many Allied occupiers wanted to destroy all

Third Reich institutions, but luckily for us mathematicians, a young British Royal Air Force officer recognized the potential of this isolated retreat, and the unique facility was saved. Since that time, it has far outstripped its unsavory origins and is now one of the most beloved mathematical institutes in the world.

The Institute is not open to the public or even to the general mathematical public. Workshop organizers submit names of suggested participants, but attendance is only by personal invitation of the institute director. One of perhaps a dozen such mathematical retreat centers worldwide, Oberwolfach is certainly the best known, though most mathematicians never have the good fortune to visit it even once in their lifetimes.

The trend toward extreme specialization in today's research world makes it even more important to nurture personal contacts among scientists, and the goal of Oberwolfach is to bring together mathematical researchers in one focused field for an intense week of lectures, spontaneous chalkboard discussions, and social interaction. The weeklong workshops run throughout the year. Ours, in the second week of June 1986, brought together thirty-six researchers from ten countries. Its library is considered one of the ten best mathematical libraries in the world, and the seminar rooms are clean and modern. There was no big city such as Munich or Berlin nearby to distract workshop participants, and the only time most of us left the main building during that week was for the traditional Wednesday afternoon group hike through the Black Forest.

The living area of the retreat center was specially designed to encourage interaction among participants. There were no spouses or children, no visitors, and no pets or other distractions. Each of us had a Spartan room with bed, desk, and bathroom, and no doors had locks. For relaxation, the main building had billiards and ping-pong but no TVs. We dined three times a day, family-style, in a large dining hall with huge picture windows looking out over the wooded hills. Before each meal, the waiters randomly distributed napkin rings with our names, and we sat next to strangers at almost every meal. I already knew a few of them—Lester from Berkeley, David from Tel Aviv, and Ulrich from Göttingen—but most were people whose names were familiar only from their mathematics papers, and now we could put faces and personalities behind those theorems. Evenings, in the lounge overlooking the black pine forests, the staff laid out mineral water, wine, fruit, and cheese, and the lively exchanges continued without interruption.

At one evening meal, I sat next to Ramakrishnan, who had done his graduate work in Calcutta and was now at the University of Miami. His meal was different than mine. The Oberwolfach staff knew every person's dietary restrictions, and Rama was a vegetarian. Our conversation drifted from gambling theory to life in India and Florida and the wonderful mathematical monastery we were visiting. I asked him if he wanted to play a little ping-pong after dinner. His eyes lit up, and he eagerly accepted as we finished our desserts.

"I'll meet you there in a few minutes," he said. "I have to stop by my room and pick up my paddle and my ping-pong shoes."

The personal paddle I could understand, but *ping-pong shoes*? I now realized that he was a serious player, certainly way out of my league, and I was in for an exhibition. Rama, I learned later, had been one of the top-ranked players in Florida. To make things mildly interesting for him, I made up new rules that might give me a chance to score at least a point or two. First I said players had to switch hands before each return, since I was pretty good with my left hand after playing years of handball. When that met with little success, my next rule was that the ball had to bounce off the floor once before a return shot was made. No matter what I came up with, Rama won hands down. When he made one serve that just nicked the table for an automatic point, I muttered something about him being very good indeed but also very lucky. With a wide smile, he set me straight.

"You're right, that is indeed a low-percentage serve," he told me. "But I practiced it for years, and I can nick the white line nearly half the time. When I'm behind, I often use that shot to rattle an opponent into blaming my blind luck and then losing his cool." It definitely worked on me.

Another participant at our workshop was Isaac Sonin, a mathematician from Moscow on his first trip out from behind the Iron Curtain. In 1986, the Communist Party was finally beginning to let a few scientists attend foreign conferences, but as insurance to guarantee his return, the Soviet authorities essentially held his family hostage in Moscow. Isaac had crammed for weeks, trying to learn enough English to be able to communicate, but the result was largely incomprehensible until he stepped up to a blackboard and wrote in the universal language of mathematics. His infectious smile—almost as wide as he was tall—and his enthusiasm and spirit broke all barriers. Everyone loved him. Twenty-five years later, I was a guest at his home near the University of North Carolina at Charlotte, one of the first universities to recognize the spectacular advantages of hiring top-notch ex-Soviet scientists fleeing after the breakup of the CCCP.

With all our different native tongues, one evening the subject of the meaning of the word *professor* came up. In countries such as Germany, there was only one "professor" in each department, referred to as *Herr Dr. Professor so-und-so*, and the rest of the faculty had various lesser titles, equivalents of the American titles of lecturer, assistant, or associate professor. In Latin American countries, on the other hand, the word *professor* simply means "teacher" and may mean anything from a university PhD to an informal secondary school tutor with no degree at all. The British system has readers and tutors as well as professors, and I told my colleagues the story of my recent visit to Cambridge, where my former Ranger buddy Jon was still studying veterinary medicine.

"Great to see you, T," he'd said. "Now shake my hand and congratulate me."

I gave his hand a firm crank and asked him what the occasion was.

"Just got my *bachelor's*," he said with a chuckle. "When they asked me to fill in a form listing my previous degrees, I figured they might be skeptical of the West Point degree, but certainly they would recognize the master's degree in aeronautical engineering from Stanford. Nope. They told me to write down 'no degrees,' and now, three years later, I just got my *BA*! Cambridge and Oxford don't recognize degrees from *any* other universities, except each other of course. I understand the same thing happened to Wes Clark on his Rhodes scholarship in Oxford."

My new friends were skeptical about this tale. Then I spotted our fellow participant Doug Kennedy, an Irish mathematician who had won the Gold Medal in Mathematics at Dublin, taken his PhD at Stanford, and was now on the permanent faculty at Cambridge.

"It depends who you ask," Doug said with the sparkling twinkle in his eye that, for us, soon came to be the trademark of his sharp wit. "Formally,

Cambridge does not recognize my Stanford doctorate or any other university's degrees except Oxford. So when they hired me here on the faculty, they awarded me an official Cambridge master's degree so that I could wear an academic gown and vote in departmental matters. Some of the older staff still refer to me as *Mister* Kennedy."

These chance after-dinner encounters led to new collaborations and several lifelong friendships—but of course, that was the idea. Three of the participants in that workshop later spent sabbaticals collaborating with me at Georgia Tech, and over the years, I published joint research papers with seven mathematicians from that Oberwolfach meeting.

One of those was Doug. Between the conference lectures, he and I had come across interesting new research questions in optimal stopping. When the workshop ended, Doug invited me to visit Trinity College to collaborate in person. I decided to combine the Cambridge trip with a stopover in Amsterdam, and Doug told me the cheapest way to get to Cambridge from Amsterdam was with Suckling Airways, whose sole aircraft, an eighteen-seater prop Dornier 228, flew low over the Channel with spectacular views of the white cliffs of Dover. The Cambridge airport runway was tiny, and since this was an international flight, upon landing we passengers had to pass through Immigration. On my first visit there, I arrived on a Sunday, and no Immigration officials were in sight. Instead there was an ancient Xerox machine, and next to it a sign that read,

PLEASE PHOTOCOPY YOUR PASSPORT,
FILL OUT THE FORM, AND DEPOSIT THEM IN THE BOX.

"Now that's my kind of border crossing!" I thought, thinking back to my East African and Iron Curtain misadventures.

Like Oberwolfach, Trinity College is sacred to mathematicians—not because of workshops and group hiking excursions, but because of its unparalleled tradition in mathematics, stretching back four hundred years to Isaac Newton. Unlike Oberwolfach, visitors to Trinity usually work one on one with their hosts and sometimes lodge in the fifteenth-century Trinity College rooms. Over the next several years, I visited Doug three or four times and each time stayed in a different set of antique Trinity rooms. Each day the "bedmaker" assigned to my room tidied up and collected the order form for the next morning's breakfast. And each morning at 8 o'clock, there was a sharp knock on my door, and my bedmaker entered with a heavy antique silver tray holding the toast, baked beans, and cooked tomato I had checked on my breakfast request form the previous day. Bedmakers, unique to Cambridge, were initially used by the college authorities to check that undergraduates returned to campus after nights on the town and returned alone. Also, by a 1635 law, they had to be at least fifty years old and, by tradition, were selected for physical characteristics that would not tempt the young male students.

Checking me in at the Porter's Lodge one visit, Doug looked at the books and said, "We're in luck—the Judge's Room is available." I had previously stayed in the Judge's Valet's Room, among others, and those had served me just fine. But the Judge's Room, in the north end of the Master's Lodge, is a huge corner room with towering windows looking out over formal English gardens and the River Cam. Next to the cut-stone fireplace, I wrote letters at the massive mahogany writing desk that had certainly seen the handwritten pages of many famous poets and mathematicians over the centuries.

Doug and I would work together during the morning and then dine in one of the commons areas overlooking the punting on the Cam. Trinity Fellows are allowed to dine "in Hall" four times a year, and on each visit, Doug invited me to High Table. There, in Henry VIII's abbey with stained-glass windows and vaulted ceiling, Fellows gather in their black academic robes to share a formal dinner. High Table is one long, massive, bare wooden table, located on an elevated platform where the altar normally would be, and looks down over the tables of the lowly undergraduates. With its daily engraved menus and heavy sterling silverware, the setting was reminiscent of the formal evening meals in Washington Hall at West Point, except that now *I* was sitting on an elevated platform looking down on the students. Seating at High Table is by seniority, and I later learned that the white-haired scholar at the head of our table was 97 years old, taking good advantage of his lifetime High Table privileges.

After evening High Table, a few of the Fellows would retire to the Combination Room for a traditional ritual of Stilton cheese and unlimited free port. Doug told me that Fellows often decided whether or not to attend the after-dinner gathering depending on what vintage port was printed on the menu. Sitting at that table of ten distinguished black-robed academics in candlelight that night, under a portrait of Sir Isaac Newton, I learned that even Nobel Prize winners can be as silly as the rest of us after a few rounds of free drinks.

The nights in Trinity College were the most magical, since I was often completely alone in that wing. The castle-like stone buildings were cold, quiet, and musty, and it felt like a bed-and-breakfast museum, or, I imagined, like it must be to spend the night alone in Shakespeare's rooms. I gazed up at the towering carved wooden headboard and closed my eyes in awe. These Trinity chambers had been home to princes, poets, and prime ministers, as well as spies and a few mathematicians. It was under this very same roof, I mused, that Newton had invented calculus and discovered his method for solving equations that, four centuries later, is still one of the most widely used tools in applied mathematics.

* * *

My next invitation to visit an "inner sanctum" came from Scandinavia. In 1992 Finnish mathematicians invited me to give five lectures on fair division and optimal stopping at their annual national Stochastics and Statistics Summer School. Realizing that such a sparsely populated country had difficulty attracting visiting lecturers, they had established a tradition where all probability and statistics PhD students in the country come together for one week each summer at some idyllic spot in the Finnish countryside. There they hear six state-of-the-art research lectures from each of five visitors chosen for both their research and their lecturing reputations. That summer my lectures took place in Mukkula Manor, a mansion on a fifteenth-century Finnish country estate.

As at Oberwolfach, all participants dined together in the evenings, and I got acquainted with the other lecturers whose names and theorems I knew, and with the Finnish graduate students, one of whom would later marry an Atlanta colleague of mine from Stanford. Instead of Black Forest hiking excursions, after the daily lectures at Mukkula, we flushed our brains by alternating sweat lodge sessions in the Mukkula Pier sauna with dips into the bracing waters of Lake Vesijärvi.

Whenever I returned to my Atlanta home base, I happily plunged back into teaching, research, and campus life, but I also started making plans for my next leave of absence. Piet Holewijn, the professor of probability at the Vrije Universiteit (VU) in Amsterdam, learned about some of my research discoveries and arranged a grant for me from the Dutch equivalent of the US National Science Foundation, the Nederlandse Wetenschapelijke Organizatie. They invited me to visit the VU for six months in 1993 to work with Frans Boshuizen, one of Piet's PhD students who needed mentoring for his thesis. Although I had visited Amsterdam dozens of times in the past while passing through Holland and living in Leiden, this was the first time I ever lived there. My guest quarters near the university were only a short tram ride from the Centrum, and Amsterdam soon became my favorite city in the world. Of course it helped a lot that I now spoke passable Dutch, which I never would have been able to do had I not experienced the isolation of Leiden. As a city, Amsterdam simply cannot be beat. Bicycle paths have special stoplights and even *curbs* separating them from automobile traffic. There are foods and ethnic groups from all over the world, street markets, seventeenth-century architecture, Rembrandt statues, and networks of narrow canals teeming with boats boasting Orange soccer banners and Heineken kegs. You can walk from the Jordaan to Leidseplein and Rembrandplein in twenty minutes, much of it on pedestrian-only streets, and on the way stroll through the Red Light District and enjoy hashish in one of the city's coffeeshops or magic mushrooms at a smartshop.

The Dutch mathematical tradition in Amsterdam is renowned and a little less formal than in Leiden, where one of the most respected professors still came to the office every day in a three-piece suit with a gold pocket watch on a gold chain stretching across his vest. My new Dutch graduate student Frans, on the other hand, was as informal and extroverted as he was eager and brilliant, with excellent English and a wonderfully wicked sense of humor. He would later come to work with me in Atlanta on a Fulbright scholarship, as subsequently did his wife José. They became my first two Dutch PhD students, as well as lifelong friends, and still visit me frequently in California twenty years later with their two children.

The six-month stint at the VU sped by, and I had already decided to do something completely different the next three months by venturing into a Third World university. Over the years, starting with the expedition with Gary prospecting for gold in the Andes, I had picked up bits and pieces of Spanish and loved the language. From my previous experiences with German and Dutch, I knew that total immersion was the best way for me to really learn a language, so I asked Latin American math grad students at Georgia Tech where was the best place to learn Spanish. They said every Latin American country had its own distinct accent and that the "cleanest" two were Colombia and Costa Rica. I had often heard of the natural beauty of Costa Rica, stretching from its tropical jungle Caribbean coast across the volcanoes and jungles and cloud forests to its pristine, arid Pacific coast. So I scheduled the next three months of my unpaid leave in Costa Rica.

"Why Costa Rica?" friends asked.

"Three reasons," I said, with a smile. "I've never been there before, I don't know anyone there, and I don't speak the language."

I arranged to take an intensive Spanish course at a language institute near the main campus of the Universidad de Costa Rica in the San José suburb of San Pedro. No one at Georgia Tech had contact with any mathematicians in Costa Rica, so I mailed off my resume to the Departimento de Matemática at the university and soon received an enthusiastic response offering me shared office space in the department and assistance with housing. A Berkeley PhD opens many doors automatically, my hosts later told me. The Universidad sent me housing information, but I could see that their tips were aimed for visitors accustomed to the usual middle-class *Nordamericano* lifestyle—dishwashers, televisions, and modern living room, dining room, and bedroom. But if thrift store furniture and condemned houses had been good enough for me in Berkeley and St. Louis and Atlanta, why not here in Costa Rica too?

When I arrived at the San José airport, I caught a taxi to San Pedro, found a room for the night, and the next day started looking for a place to live. The *Ballanato*, a small *taverna* two blocks south of campus, was known as the local mecca for Costa Rican artists, writers, and poets living on the fringe, as well as the occasional rogue mathematician. My first night there, I joined a table with a statistician, a poet, and Roki, a sixty-ish fellow who looked like an old man of the mountains and whom the others insisted was a *brujo*, a sorcerer. When I told them of my search for an apartment, Roki arranged to show me a flat near campus. He said I could have it for three months for $100 total, and he would show me the apartment the next morning at 5 a.m. I thought I must have misunderstood his Spanish and made him repeat it several times.

The sun was just breaking over the thick grove of golden bamboo along the creek on campus when Roki led me to an apartment building in a run-down barrio just north of campus. As we walked up the stairs to the third floor, the other apartment entrances looked ordinary, with flower pots and doorbells and *bienvenido* doormats. But at his apartment, heavy iron bars secured the door, which was daubed with black magic *Helter Skelter*–like symbols. Inside I held my nose as cockroaches scurried across mildewed sleeping bags and dirty newspapers. Empty wine jugs, moldy orange peels, and stumps of scented candles littered the floor. Coarse, threadbare blankets hung over the windows to keep out the prying eyes of nosy neighbors. I pushed a blanket aside and glanced out into the courtyard. The other apartments in the building looked poor but tidy, with open windows, clean curtains, and tropical flowers in window boxes. But Roki's apartment, with its painted black walls, bizarre symbols, and generally disgusting condition, seemed like a hellhole in this otherwise poor but normal neighborhood. But it was no worse than the Berkeley Leroy house had been, and here, at least the ceramic tile floors would clean much more easily than wood. "Like Yogi Berra said," I thought, "it's déjà vu all over again." Besides, it was actually fun to take up the challenge again after the spic-and-span cleanliness of my Amsterdam accommodations.

I told Roki I'd take the apartment and paid him in cash on the spot in exchange for a receipt he scribbled on a scrap of paper. When he left, I began the exorcism. As I had learned to do in the past, everything I could lift I chucked out the window into the alley two stories below—every rag, blanket, candlestick, beer bottle, and even the wooden furniture, whose pores oozed the stench. I swabbed ceiling and walls and floor with a heavy cotton mop dipped in Central American basic industrial-strength disinfectant and painted over the obscenities and occult symbols twice—three times in some places.

I propped the windows open, and when it had all dried out two days later, I returned with a futon and secondhand furniture and kitchen utensils I bought from barrio street vendors. Then I settled in to my latest simple home away from home.

After my morning Spanish classes, I walked to the university for the $2 fixed-price lunch at the student cafeteria and then to my mathematics office on campus, where I practiced my Spanish with my new colleagues, most of whom spoke almost no English at all. I tried to describe, in my very broken Spanish, the experience with my apartment. At first they thought they had not understood me correctly, and when I repeated my story more slowly and with much gesturing, they raised their eyebrows and looked at each other. Who was this Roki fellow with the suspiciously cheap apartment? Was it safe for me? They told me they were concerned and would do some detective work, an easy task in a provincial university village like San Pedro. I'm sure they were also wondering a little bit about the crazy gringo mathematician in their midst who would take up such an offer.

Roki's father, they reported the next day, alternating very slowly between broken English and simple Spanish, was not just one of the richest men in Costa Rica, he was one of the richest in all of Central America. His *brujo* son had somehow secretly acquired keys to a half dozen apartments in his father's apartment buildings and used the flats as hippie pads to recover from his drinking binges and to lodge his short-term lovers, usually runaway hippie women and black magic nymphets. As far as my new colleagues could tell, though, I was in no physical danger, but they shook their heads nonetheless.

In preparation for that trip, I had used flash cards to memorize two thousand Spanish vocabulary words. The daily all-morning language lessons in San Pedro, 8 a.m. to noon Monday through Friday, exhausted both me and my instructors, who were unprepared for a student with such an impressive vocabulary but absolutely no grammar or conversational skills. They spoke only in Spanish by institute policy, and the first week consisted largely of pantomimes and endless repetitions of *¿Como esta?* and *¡Buenos dias!* I had arranged for the most intensive course, one-on-one instruction, and each week I had a new tutor. The instructional strategy was to force me just to talk, talk, talk. Every day they demanded a new story from me—forget correct grammar and pronunciation. Their eyes widened at my fractured descriptions of the *brujo's* flat, which took me two days to tell in detail. I struggled through my Spanish lessons four hours every morning, ate lunch on campus or in the village, and made my office rounds before memorizing useful new words I had encountered during the day.

One month into the intensive language course, just to keep me talking, my new instructor asked about my education. To him, Berkeley and Stanford meant nothing, but when I mentioned West Point, his eyes lit up. The presidential election in Costa Rica was two weeks away, he told me very slowly, and one of the two *candidatos*, Figueres, was a West Point graduate. Then, as I understood him, and made him repeat over and over until I was sure, he told me that Figueres had been caught cheating (*copiando*) at West Point.

"*Eso es imposible*," I said. If he got caught cheating, then he did not graduate.

But my instructor insisted and said something about *muchos cadetos* and a year *en exilio*. That night it dawned on me. Figueres had obtained his appointment to West Point via the political connections of his father, "Don Pepe" Figueres, then president of Costa Rica, who, ironically enough, was best known for abolishing the Costa Rican army. The son might have been one of those caught in the huge cheating scandal at West Point in 1976, exactly when Figueres was a cadet. Over a hundred cadets were found guilty of cheating on exams for the still-dreaded Electrical Engineering EE304, Juice Class. The Cadet Honor Committee recommended mass expulsion, and the superintendent concurred. Congress and the Pentagon, however, overrode that decision and instead expelled all the convicted cadets for a year but allowed them to return, if they chose, after a "year of reflection." Was a West Point cheater about to become the elected president of Costa Rica?

Election Day in Costa Rica, always a Sunday, is a national holiday as festive as Mardi Gras, the Super Bowl, and New Year's Day all rolled into one. Bars close three days before the election, *and three days after*, my language instructor explained, so the losers do not drown their sorrows in a drunken stupor. On Election Sunday, February 6, 1994, I walked to the Plaza de Cultura, the central square in San José adjacent to the Teatro

Nacional and the Gran Hotel de Costa Rica, to watch one party's cheerleaders wave green-and-white party flags at their red-and-black counterparts in passing convertibles. Horns were honking and loudspeakers blaring patriotic music and political propaganda. As I stood in front of the Gran Hotel, wearing khakis, my Teva sandals, and a black backpack, a motorcade with flashing lights and sirens approached the hotel. A police cordon held back the crowd.

"*El candidato*," shouted a bystander. "*Figueres!*"

Out of Partido Liberacion Nacional's green and white–bannered Winnebago stepped four gigantic bodyguards and a thin man of medium height and close-cropped, salt-and-pepper hair. I recognized Figueres from the campaign posters. Seeing the banners on the hotel balcony, I now realized that the Gran Hotel was his campaign headquarters. Figueres disappeared into the hotel behind me, and police and private bodyguards took up positions between the support columns. They stood stiffly, feet apart, with hands on riot clubs and eyes scanning the dispersing crowd. I waited a few moments. Then, on impulse, I walked up to the guard at the door and, in passable Spanish, explained that I was a professor from America, visiting the Universidad de Costa Rica. I then slipped in "Berkeley" and "Stanford." No response. But when I mentioned "West Point," the guard immediately lit up, proudly announced that his party's candidate was a West Point graduate, and asked me what I wanted.

"To wish him luck," I answered in Spanish. After all, Figueres too had survived Beast Barracks and bracing, and even Juice Lab, one way or the other.

To my great surprise, the guard opened the door, let me pass without even looking in my backpack, and pointed to the elevator, where two more guards stood. These guards were not swayed by my little speech and were wary of this hulking *Nordamericano* in sandals and backpack. I could ring up the candidate's suite and wish him luck, they said, and pointed to a house phone on the wall in the lobby.

I dialed again and again, but the line was busy. My persistence and informal attire soon attracted the attention of another party official, who could see which room number I kept dialing on the wall phone. He walked up to me and asked me what I was doing there. This time the West Point password clicked again, and he led me to a middle-aged woman in a business suit, who spoke perfect English.

"I think we can get you up to meet the candidate," she said. "We are very proud that he graduated from West Point. I am his campaign manager."

She led me to a tiny elevator and accompanied me up to a small briefing room, where Figueres was addressing a small group of well-dressed, inner-circle supporters. As he walked through the room shaking hands, I clasped his and said, in English, "West Point Class of 1966—good luck in the election." He stopped and thanked me, then retired to a back room.

When I left the hotel, the election was underway. By Costa Rican law, no preliminary results may be broadcast until every vote is in, so with two hours until the polls closed, I went to a nearly empty movie theater to sharpen my vocabulary skills watching a Spanish-subtitled version of Schwarzenegger's *The Terminator.* After the movie, I walked to a bus stop and waited. A young couple sat holding hands and kissing on the bench and told me no buses were running because of the election holiday.

"Who won?" I asked in Spanish. *¿Quien ganó?*

"Figueres," they said.

When I tried to explain that I had just met him, they thought I was using the wrong verb—that I meant I had just *seen* him. Slowly I explained again, holding out my hand and shaking it. "And I haven't even met the president of my own university," I thought, as I slowly walked back to my *barrio.*

By the ninth week in Costa Rica, I gave my first mathematics seminar in Spanish at the university, relying heavily on well-rehearsed overhead transparencies and the infinite patience of my audience. It surprised me how few of them spoke English until I learned their backgrounds. During the Cold War, Communist countries had wooed the best and brightest of Latin American students with full scholarships. Nearly all the Costa Rican math professors with PhDs had studied behind the Iron Curtain: Edwin Castro at Bucharest, William Alvarado at St. Petersburg, and others at Leipzig and Moscow. My hosts knew firsthand from their own immersions in German, Romanian, and Russian just how challenging it was to give a talk like that, congratulated me heartily, and marched me to the *ballanato* for the requisite celebratory tequila.

After I returned to Georgia Tech, the Costa Rican connection blossomed, and I helped my new colleagues found a Central American Mathematical Society, which would host conferences in different countries—Costa Rica, Guatemala, and Nicaragua. Often I was the only American attendee, valued as much for making it possible for them to list *Los Estados Unidos* as a participating nation to the government sponsors as for my math ideas. At my first such conference in Costa Rica, I stepped off the recycled Blue Bird school bus that took me to San Ramon, carrying only a small overnight bag and my overhead transparencies. One of the mathematicians from San Pedro asked me where my blanket was. I looked around and saw that he and all the other participants had blankets under their arms. It surprised him when I told him that in America, conference participants were not expected to provide their own bedding. He and two friends took me to a local market to buy a wool blanket before the opening session.

Another year the annual conference was held in a 350-year-old active convent in Antigua, Guatemala. The whole conference cost $100, including registration and conference brochures, four nights' accommodation, all meals, coffee and cakes in the morning, and afternoon tea. Nuns rang the bells for the main meals and maintained complete silence while we conference participants ate in the same dining hall. My old friend, political scientist John Oneal, wanted to see Guatemala again and simply signed up, paid the fee, and accompanied me to the meeting, even though he didn't attend any lectures. They welcomed him with open arms and even mentioned his name in the closing ceremony.

At the annual meeting in Managua, Nicaragua, in 1995, I was the only participant who arrived four days early, to practice my Spanish and enjoy the culture. My *Berkeley Travel Guide* described Managua as "grimier than grimy, uglier than ugly, hotter than hell," and we conference attendees slept on hard wooden bunks in the Olof Palme Centro de Conventiones near the university. The Centro's rough clapboard barracks reminded me of those at Camp Buckner at West Point, but with much tighter security. Razor wire fences encircled the sleeping quarters, and at night knife-scarred security guards patrolled the conference compound with snarling German shepherds and sawed-off shotguns. I was not surprised to learn later that shortly after our meeting, the Olof Palme was looted and abandoned for more than a decade.

On my arrival, the convention center was nearly deserted, and I was the only one eating in the camp mess hall. The mess hall waiters wore food-stained khaki shirts, with loaded well-worn revolvers in dirty brown leather holsters, as they served lunch at the long rough-hewn wooden tables. I got to know the one who served at my table, a handsome young man in his twenties who spoke no English. Javier was patient with my broken Spanish and told me he had a wife and two small children. My underground travel guidebook described the central plaza at Managua as a must-see and said the city's best view of Lake Managua and Volcan Momotombo was from the balcony of the national cathedral. Problem was, like many of the other buildings, the cathedral had not been rebuilt after the devastating 1972 earthquake. Half the spiraling stone staircase had dropped out in the tremors, and the main support timbers sagged. Worse yet, the guidebook warned, the area around the cathedral was thick with *ladrones*—thieves and thugs. At lunch one day, I asked Javier if he wanted to make some extra money on the weekend, showing me the city as my *guardaespaldas*, my bodyguard. I liked that Spanish word—a person that guards not your body but your back.

"*Si, Señor! Si!*," he said, apologizing and explaining that it was forbidden for him to take his pistol into town but assuring me he would guarantee no harm came my way. We agreed on a price and set Saturday noon to meet.

As my *guardaespaldas* and I wound our way through the crowded ramshackle markets and poverty-stricken ruins of the city center, he warned me where to watch for pickpockets and when to clutch my backpack to my chest. When we arrived at the cathedral, I pointed to my guidebook and told him I wanted to see the view from the top. He told me it was too dangerous, *muy peligroso*, even for him, both because of the stairs and the *ladrones*. He had never been up there, he said, and did not know anyone who had. I told him I wanted to risk it, as I might never be back, and he could help me by standing guard at the entrance below. But Javier refused to let me go up alone, and seeing I was set on it, insisted on joining me, stood tall, pointed to his chest, and reminded me he was my *guardaespaldas*.

The next Monday in the mess hall, he told his *amigos* what had happened. We had hugged the wall, he told them, where enough of the spiral stairs were still intact, and inched our way slowly up to the fourth-floor balcony.

"The view was incredible," he told them in Spanish. "My client and I worked our way to the edge of the terrace. No guardrail remaining after the earthquake, and four stories to the ground. When we got to the edge, I heard a noise behind us and turned just in time to see four *ladrones* coming out of the staircase, right at us. I started to get my knife out and quickly glanced to my side," he told them. "I couldn't believe my eyes—the *gringo* already had *his* knife out!"

Our weapons and combat-ready stances told the thugs we were not the easy pickings they had hoped for, and they backed off. As we descended to the relative safety of the open plaza, I felt sorry for the people of this friendly country, who had to endure such hardships every day.

When the conference began, I was about to give my first formal conference talk in Spanish, and I should have remembered the old Ranger motto, "Expect the unexpected." I gathered up my intensely rehearsed transparencies and was getting ready to go to the podium when all the electricity went out, not just on the campus where we were staying, but in the entire capital city. This was no surprise to anyone but me. My hosts immediately wheeled out candles, kerosene lamps, a large paper tablet, and a magic marker they had waiting in the wings. I barely managed to stumble through that talk, despite my diligent preparations.

In spite of their daily survival challenges, however, the intrepid Nicaraguans still devoted incredible energy and resources to two of their most cherished activities—mathematics and music. During the day, we conference attendees scribbled on wobbly blackboards and, if lucky, projected slides of formulas and equations on rough plaster walls. At night local village choirs and violinists serenaded us under the stars. Our hosts' incredible hospitality, and their determination to do mathematics in the midst of all that poverty and misery, made a deep impression on me.

The new connections with the Central American math network grew. They asked me to be part of the Scientific Organizing Committee for the next meeting in Costa Rica and elected me foreign editor for their new journal *Revista de Matemática*. My PhD student Martin Jones later spent a year at the Universidad de Costa Rica as a visiting professor, and I arranged for the head of our department and his associate chair to visit the Costa Rica Institute of Technology. We started attracting some of their top graduate students to our PhD program, including their very best student, known to all as "Newton," who eventually earned his PhD in mathematics at Georgia Tech. In addition to students, we also began hosting more and more Latin American professors.

One of these was Victor Perez-Abreu from the Centro de Investigación en Matemáticas (CIMAT), Mexico's national mathematics hermitage on a mountain overlooking the city of Guanajuato in central Mexico, a UNESCO World Heritage Site. Victor had lived in my house during his semester in Atlanta, and we became friends, conversing both in his fluent English and my halting Spanish. When he became director general of the Centro, Victor invited me for a three-month visit. Unlike Oberwolfach, CIMAT has permanent faculty and, at 7,000 feet, an invigorating high-altitude desert climate. The main structure, which reminds me of our Southwestern pueblo cliff dwellings, is a huge clay-red labyrinth of nine stories of split-level floors, with water dispensers at every level, in lieu of elevators. The research center looks down on the Spanish colonial city, across the valley to the prominent bluff *Bufa*, and over to an eighteenth-century church and silver mine, both with flying buttresses, on the mountainside at the same altitude. The offices and seminar rooms have the latest computers and lecturing equipment. The graduate students are flown in for interviews and represent the best young mathematical minds in the nation, and the professors have doctorates from all over the world. CIMAT even has company cars for the use of the faculty, something I have never seen anywhere else in the world. Just outside this modern research center, donkeys carry bundles of sticks for firewood.

During my stay I lived in CIMATEL, the center's three-story, stone-and-timber guest quarters, a short but invigorating nine-minute walk away. Its fifty rooms have tile floors, window boxes, and beds hard enough for my taste, comparable to the tatami mats in my apartment in Tokyo. For once I did not have to sleep on the floor. When I first arrived, students attending a conference occupied most of the other rooms, but when they left, I was the only guest. When I returned from my office or from a trip down to the city center, the silence was as complete as those during my midnight college stadium adventures, except this time I had a key. Standing in the center of the rectangular courtyard and gazing up at the night sky, absent any hint of air or light pollution in the high desert climate, was like standing in a giant rectangular planetarium. There were more stars than I had ever seen, tiny crystal lights everywhere. In our rooms, hot water was turned on for one hour every day, and Institute cooks prepared food to order. Breakfast ran until almost noon, with lunch at a civilized 3 or 4 o'clock in the afternoon. I gave five lectures in perfect broken Spanish, as I had promised, and later arranged for Lisa Bloomer, another one of my PhD students, to spend three months in residence. It was the first time in her life, she later told me, that she had been out of the American Deep South.

* * *

Often my off-the-beaten-track travels were also catalysts for new mathematical discoveries. During one six-week visit Down Under, I lectured at six Australian universities in the math network. At each campus, my new colleagues and friends invited me to give a lecture and engaged me in lively mathematical discussions. Afterward they treated me to hard cider in the campus pub and invited me to their homes for traditional Aussie barbies. After each visit I rented a car, loaded my camping gear, and hit the Outback. Each university paid me a modest honorarium, but for me it was another mostly self-paid carpet ride where the main attraction was the math hospitality at all these new nodes. My Aussie skin diving and whitewater companion Vince Ervin, now a Clemson math professor, encouraged me to visit his parents' sheep station near the tiny village of Pyramid Hill in northern Victoria. Vince's father gave me a tour of the station, and, as we walked through the dusty wooden sheds, he described the annual sheep-shearing operations.

"After shearing," he said, "we bale it and send the raw wool to market." He pointed to heavy gray bales stacked in the corner.

"Do some kinds of sheep have more valuable wool than others?" I asked.

"Not really," he said. "The main factor on price of wool is how clean it is, not the breed of sheep. The main cost is removing the dirt and sand and burrs. So if some sheep are rolling around on the ground all day and others are not, the buy price difference is huge."

"How do they judge the quality of the bales, see how dirty they are?" I asked. "Rip them apart?"

"No. The buyer inserts a hooked, thin metal probe into the bale and pulls out a sample tuft. Based on that, he estimates how much it will cost him to clean that batch of wool and gives us a price."

It struck me later that this could be viewed as a mathematical game. One player, the seller, tries to arrange his various grades of wool to maximize the probability that his opponent, the buyer, will draw a high-quality sample. The buyer, on the other hand, tries to outwit the seller by somehow drawing a *low-quality* sample, on which he could base a low price.

The next night, at my solitary campsite in the bush, I started thinking more about this game. Unable to solve the problem, I looked at a simpler question. What strategies are possible for the seller? Then it hit me that I, a supposed expert in mathematical probability, did not even know the answer to a basic probability question, namely, *What distributions can you obtain by mixing a given starting distribution?*

For instance, starting with 10 gallons of 80-octane gas and 10 gallons of 90-octane, you can mix everything together to obtain 20 gallons of 85-octane or just mix half of each, resulting in 5 gallons of 80-octane, 10 of 85-octane, and 5 of 90-octane. You can never get any amount of 75- or 100-octane or ever get more than 10 gallons of 90-octane. But exactly what else *can* you get?

Each night in my tent, I reviewed what little I knew, and after my weekly lectures, I asked my hosts. No one knew. Passing through Berkeley on the way back to Atlanta, I asked the world's real experts, and when *they* didn't have an answer, I knew I was on to something. For two solid years, I worked on that problem with my Georgia Tech friend John Elton, during which time we produced at least fifteen drafts and revisions. The final result, published in the *Annals of Probability* under the title "Fusions of Probabilities," remains one of my most satisfying research accomplishments in abstract probability theory and was my first paper to be translated and published in a Russian scientific journal. And it all came from visiting an Outback sheep station in Australia!

* * *

My travels over the years during my self-sabbaticals gave me the opportunity to enjoy the hospitality of many remote nodes in the global math network. But between trips, when I was in residence in my home base in Atlanta, I wanted to reciprocate and establish a hospitality node of my own at Georgia Tech. A combination of my simple lifestyle philosophy, some creative housing research, and the good fortune to be in the right place at the right time led me to find the perfect residence. Over the course of twenty years, a condemned house run by a freewheeling ex–Army Ranger bachelor mathematician would become a home away from home for scores of mathematicians from all over the world, who affectionately dubbed it "The Hill Hotel."

I rode my German Army counterpart Peter Hupfer's motorcycle near Göttingen during a weekend break from university classes in 1971. Seen in the rear was my Volkswagen camper van, which I would soon use to penetrate deep behind the Iron Curtain. [17]

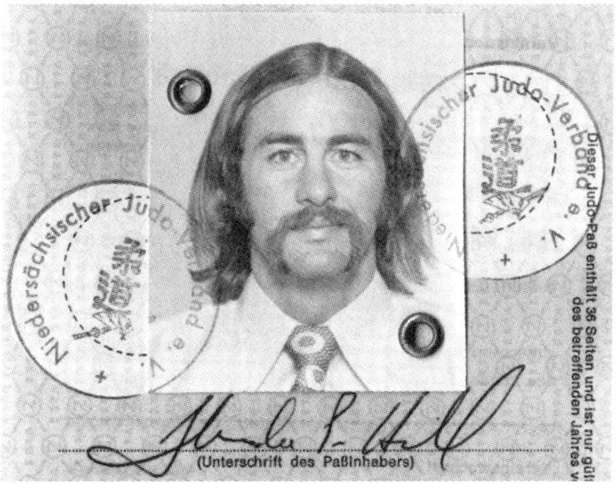

German bureaucracies required official stamped photo IDs for almost everything. This Judo ID allowed me to compete in local meets and would permit me to participate in the German National Judo Championships in Berlin in 1971. [18]

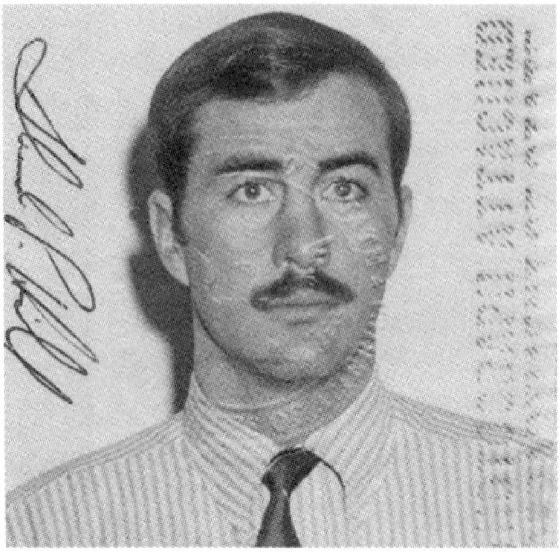

During my 1972 road trip into six Communist countries in Eastern Europe, my passport carried an Army photo that showed me with short hair and a trimmed regulation mustache, but when I crossed the border, it was with shoulder-length hair. [19]

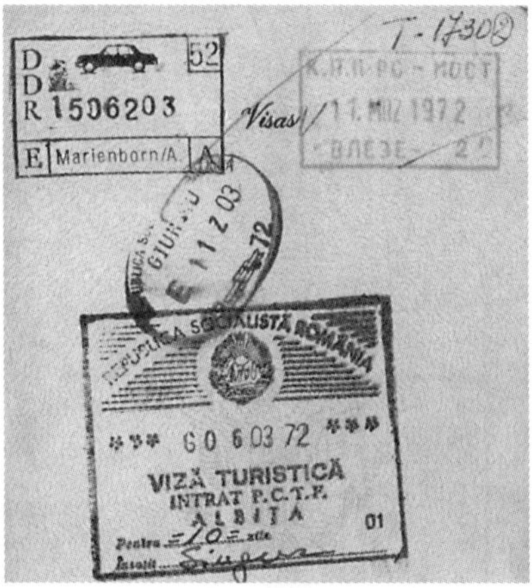

When I reached the Iron Curtain, Communist border agents stamped my passport with the silhouette of an automobile to make certain I did not leave without the van. The stamp for entering Romania from the Soviet Union at Albita had no counterpart from the other side, since Soviet authorities there removed all evidence of my visit to Russia. [20]

During the decades of the Cold War, Checkpoint Charlie was the single crossing point from free West Berlin into the East Bloc. The thorough and intimidating vehicular and personal inspections were intended to discourage visitors, but we pressed on anyway. [21]

Hitchhiking in East Africa in 1972 was a matter of luck and patience, and many of our lifts were in the beds of open trucks. Here I enjoyed the view as this flatbed inched its way up a mountain in Tanzania. [22]

When we reached the top of the mile-high Zomba Plateau in Malawi in July, my brother Russ and I were the only campers, and we set up our lone tent near the Haile Selassie Overlook. [23]

On August 18, 1972, during the weeks of dictator Idi Amin's infamous and disastrous purge of all Asians from his country, my brother Russ and I unwittingly entered Uganda on foot. [24]

OFFICE OF VIRGIL S. HOLLIS ○ MARIN COUNTY SUPERINTENDENT OF SCHOOLS

Dear Mr. Hill:

We have a vacancy for a mathematics teacher in the inmate education program at San Quentin State Prison for the 1970-71 school year. A California Secondary Credential is required.

Nº 33355

The California Community Colleges

THEODORE PRESTON HILL

The Board of Governors of the California Community Colleges, acting in accordance with the authority vested in it, awards to the person named above a

COMMUNITY COLLEGE INSTRUCTOR CREDENTIAL

This document, earned by meeting the provisions established by law and the requirements established by the Board of Governors of the California Community Colleges, authorizes the holder to perform all services permitted by these provisions and requirements.

When I got to Berkeley, to supplement my meager income from the GI Bill, I explored unusual teaching jobs, including one at San Quentin. I obtained a (now nonexistent) Lifetime California Community College Teaching Certificate and taught school in a nearby Richmond ghetto. [25]

He Wants Bride He Can Fly Away From

By Michael Grieg

A 31-year-old graduate student at the University of California is willing to pay as much as $2000 a year to any airline stewardess who will marry him — in name only.

He doesn't care about looks or age. All that matters is that the airline she works for be an international carrier that offers the customary free travel benefits to employees and their spouses.

This unique way to cut travel costs surfaced in a classified advertisement that appeared this week in The Chronicle:

"Grad student desiring flight privileges will pay to marry stewardess. Preston. P.O. Box 3205. Berkeley 94703."

"I got the idea from friends in Germany who have done the same thing," said the would-be airline groom, who got used to traveling extensively and without charge as a Fulbright scholar and U.S. Army captain.

A stewardess friend, already married, told him that after seven years with an airline she and her husband, her parents, or children have unlimited travel privileges and have to pay only the tax.

A check with Pan American, Trans World, United and American airlines showed that employee travel benefits are, indeed, generous.

In addition to free vacation trips, employees get an increasing number of travel passes, depending on seniority. A small service charge is generally tacked on for going first class. There's often no charge at all, not even the tax, if an employee rides coach.

Aside from applying to a spouse and immediate blood relations, travel privileges on American Airlines even extend to "anyone else supported by and living with an employee," a company spokesman said.

Carrier representives weren't entirely dismayed by the Berkeley student's enterprise.

"This is the first time I ever heard of someone wanting to marry just for free transportation," said one carrier official. "We've had some divorces put off, however, to hold on to the passes."

A Pan American spokesman said the travel privilege has "held more than one marriage aloft." The enterprising student, he said, "should be given an 'A' for being above board."

Preston, the would-be flying spouse who prefers to use his middle name only until he finds a wife, said the stewardess he chooses will probably never even have to see him.

"I'm looking into the possibility that we might even be able to marry by mail or conference phone. After that, I'll be so busy traveling that we may never meet — except by chance, on the same plane."

GRAD STUDENT desiring flight privileges will pay to marry stewardess. Preston, P.O. Box 3205, Berkeley 94703

I realized that the odds of ever finishing my PhD were against me, and missing my days of globetrotting, I hatched a plan to advertise to marry an airline stewardess for free travel. On August 29, 1975, the *San Francisco Chronicle* published this article about my ad. [26]

This photo shows Lester Dubins, my PhD thesis advisor, outside Evans Hall on the Berkeley campus in the late 1970s. Though many found his penetrating intellect intimidating, he also had a fine sense of humor and was a generous host and friend to people from all walks of life. [27]

A friend reading on the stoop of the Blake Street cottage I renovated in exchange for five years of free rent. This was 1976, and I was about to discover, in this same garden, the final key argument for my PhD thesis. [28]

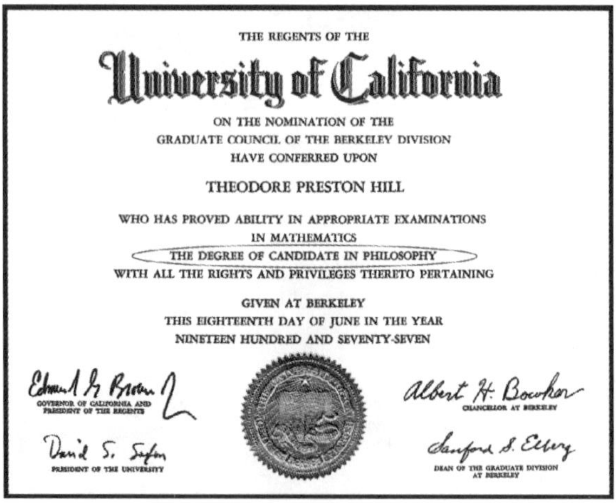

THE REGENTS OF THE

University of California

ON THE NOMINATION OF THE
GRADUATE COUNCIL OF THE BERKELEY DIVISION
HAVE CONFERRED UPON

THEODORE PRESTON HILL

WHO HAS PROVED ABILITY IN APPROPRIATE EXAMINATIONS
IN MATHEMATICS
THE DEGREE OF CANDIDATE IN PHILOSOPHY
WITH ALL THE RIGHTS AND PRIVILEGES THERETO PERTAINING

GIVEN AT BERKELEY
THIS EIGHTEENTH DAY OF JUNE IN THE YEAR
NINETEEN HUNDRED AND SEVENTY-SEVEN

GOVERNOR OF CALIFORNIA AND PRESIDENT OF THE REGENTS

CHANCELLOR AT BERKELEY

PRESIDENT OF THE UNIVERSITY

DEAN OF THE GRADUATE DIVISION AT BERKELEY

In June 1977, I received this unusual Candidate in Philosophy (PhC) degree from Berkeley, which would later cause me trouble with the bureaucracy during my appointment to a tenure-track professorship at Georgia Tech. [29]

Later that summer, I finished my PhD and packed everything I owned into my VW camper to drive from Berkeley to my new job in Atlanta. Here my friend Massoud was helping me load the "borrowed" PhC canoe onto my van. Still visible was the dented roof from the accident that rolled the van near Moscow. [30]

When I returned to Georgia Tech from a year at Leiden University in Holland, I found this Craftsman bungalow on campus that was earmarked for destruction. I saved it, and it became my home for more than twenty years, where I also hosted short- and long-term visitors from more than a dozen countries. Here was where I would make some of my favorite mathematical breakthroughs. [31]

The Math *Ohana* with its ornate woodwork, built-in bookcases and cabinets, beamed ceilings, leaded glass, and three working fireplaces was a unique venue for many academic receptions, celebratory events, and international Thanksgiving dinners. At this one, my sister Margaret (left) was seated next to visitors from Lithuania and China. My PhD student Lisa Bloomer was standing behind graduate students from Venezuela and Peru. [32]

The CBS Evening News team interviewed me in my office, and I verified a successful method to detect winning patterns in a nationwide scratch-card game worth $50 million. The piece appeared on the national Dan Rather news show on December 9, 1985. [33]

In 1989, I graduated my first Georgia Tech PhD student, Martin Jones, who went on to a successful career and full professorship at the College of Charleston. [34]

During my professional years, I continued to alternate periods of intense concentration on mathematics with physical adventures. Here I was hiking on Kauai and on the Fox Glacier in New Zealand, mountain biking the Bluff Trail on California's Central Coast, and teaching rappelling in Arizona. [35]

At Dutch universities, PhD ceremonies are individual, with only one on any given day. They are formal affairs with wine and cheese and many toasts. Here I was speaking at the graduation of my first Dutch PhD student, Frans Boshuizen, in 1991. Also on the committee, seated next to me, was my academic brother, David Gilat from Tel Aviv. [36]

My first request to officiate at a wedding came from my friend Leonid Bunimovich's daughter, Yulia, and her fiancé, Sasha Jeltuhin, in Atlanta in 1995. The toasts at the reception? "What a country . . . even mathematicians can marry people!" Later I would perform several other weddings for close friends, including Yulia's brother, Yuri. [37]

My West Point friend Chan McKearn gave me my first scuba lessons in the Florida Keys before we embarked on our adventures on Grand Bahama Island in 1970.

Over the next four decades, I returned to the island scores of times, honing these diving skills and passing them on to a small core of fellow mathematician adventurers. [38]

My math "dive team" with one day's catch of whelks, conchs, octopi, and lobsters in 2016—no boats, no guides. From left: Vince Ervin (Clemson), Jeff Geronimo (Georgia Tech), and Ryan Hynd (U Penn), born in Australia, Egypt, and Jamaica, respectively. During our evening feasts, we mixed research mathematics with stories of the day's underwater events. [39]

My friend Leonid Bunimovich (standing) hosted an international dinner at his home in Atlanta for visitor Vitaly Bergelson. Seated from left: me, Jean Bellisard, Robin Thomas, Vitaly, and Christian Houdré. This was one of my last social events at Georgia Tech before I took early retirement and moved to California. [40]

At our 40th West Point Reunion in 2006, old Company E-2 plebe comrades Jon Steel, Wes Clark, Chan McKearn, and I enjoyed a formal Cadet Parade Review in our honor. We all agreed that it was better to be watching than marching. [41]

On my first return to Vietnam since the war, my host, mathematician Professor Nguyen Van Thu, greeted me at the University of Hanoi in 2002. I don't know of any other American Vietnam War veteran invited to return to Vietnam to speak about his scientific discoveries. [42]

Vietnamese universities invited me to return again in 2007, and here I was lecturing at the International University in Ho Chi Minh City (formerly Saigon). [43]

My guide Le and I made one last rest stop before summiting Vietnam's well-known Nui Ba Den (Black Virgin Mountain), where I had landed by helicopter during the war. At the top, we were surprised by a clandestine Vietnamese army base camp. [44]

I donated my collection of nearly a thousand Early American mathematics books to the permanent archives at UC Berkeley's Bancroft Library. In 2005 they hosted an exhibition featuring parts of the collection. [45]

Ryan, Lester, and I were exchanging mathematical ideas and enjoying a meal at Saul's—one of Lester's favorite restaurants—a short walk from his Spruce Street home in Berkeley, in 2008. [46]

My strong ties to Central American mathematicians continue. Here I delivered an invited plenary lecture at the 2010 Central American Mathematics Conference in San José, Costa Rica. [47]

Hitchhiking is the only "public transportation" to the dirt track leading to the summit of the Bufa peak near Guanajuato in central Mexico. Here I was taking a break from math research at CIMAT (the Mexican Mathematics Research Center) in 2014 to show Ryan how to get to the peak. [48]

My friend and coauthor Victor Perez-Abreu lived upstairs in my Craftsman bungalow at Georgia Tech. Later, as director general of CIMAT, he invited me to visit and collaborate for three months. Here he and I were relaxing on the CIMAT terraces on a mountain overlooking the eighteenth-century church at Valenciana and the World Heritage Site of Guanajuato. [49]

Here I was heading up to my mathematics *dacha* on the hill behind our home to split wood, start a blaze in the firepit, and think about research ideas. [50]

From inside my math *dacha*, I look out over the open Pacific, Morro Rock, and the Santa Lucia Mountains. A trail right outside my window leads into nearby Montaña de Oro State Park. [51]

12

THE MATH *OHANA*

In my early years at Georgia Tech, when I was not traveling, I lived in the rundown shotgun house on Ninth Street, site of the infamous fall quarter parties. Just before I left for the year in Holland, my landlord decided to sell the house and offered me first option to buy. I thought about it, but I'd never been saddled with home ownership and mortgage debts before, and that had suited my bohemian lifestyle very well. Besides, even if I were tempted to buy that property, I knew I probably would not own it for long. That whole block of Ninth Street was part of Georgia Tech's master campus expansion plan, and they could take it under eminent domain. I turned down the offer.

So I'd left for the year in Leiden knowing I would not have a place to return to. When I got back, I started house hunting once again. I still wanted to be a short walk from my office, even though most property within that distance was either in the tough neighborhood of shabby federal housing projects just south of campus or the run-down, blue-collar neighborhood of Home Park to the north. East and west of campus were mainly derelict warehouses and railroad buildings. None of my colleagues lived within miles of the campus.

I continued my house search in Home Park, asking everyone I met, and one day I heard that the university had recently purchased a house at the southwest corner of Tenth and Atlantic, which put it right *on* campus. The next morning I walked over to take a look and saw that it was in bad shape: peeling paint, rotted-out gutters, dilapidated roof—in fact, just my style. As I stepped back and squinted to mentally wash out the imperfections, what I saw was another architectural gem. This place was a two-story, 1915-era classic Craftsman bungalow, with deeply overhanging eaves, a wraparound porch underneath the exterior of the main roof, exposed rafters, and trapezoidal square columns supporting the veranda, which was raised 4 feet above ground level to catch breezes in Atlanta's notorious summer heat. I walked across the sagging porch floorboards to peer inside and immediately understood why the Craftsman has been described as having Frank Lloyd Wright design motifs and being "Zen-like." Built-in dark wood bookcases and cabinets matched the beamed ceilings and interior square support columns. Two open-hearth brick fireplaces were set diagonally opposite in the front room. A pocket door opened into a den on the street side, and the windows were leaded glass. The two main rooms I could see through the front window had more stone and dark wood trim than actual wall space. The west side of the house had only three small windows, to minimize light from the afternoon sun, but the east side had a small sunroom overlooking Atlantic Avenue. It was still early morning, and I could see kaleidoscopic rays of rainbow beams streaming through the beveled-glass windows onto the hardwood floors. I was starting to fall in love again.

From any reasonable person's standpoint, the house was simply uninhabitable. Plaster was dropping from the ceiling where rain poured in through holes in the roof, the porch floor was rotted through in several places, and many of the main rooms had no electrical outlets at all. Repair-wise, it was a complete nightmare, but not as bad as the Blake Street cottage in Berkeley had been, and I was already imagining myself working on math problems in front of those fireplaces. I made an appointment to talk to Georgia Tech's vice president for planning and real estate.

"My staff has been unable to do anything with that place for over a year," he said. "If we don't find a use for it soon, we'll raze it. It doesn't meet city housing codes, so we can't rent to students or we'll be accused of slumlording."

"Yes, sir," I said. "I can certainly understand the Institute not wanting to rent a building like that to students. But what if a *professor* lives there? I'd waive normal renter's rights, make necessary repairs, paint it, and keep up the yard."

To my amazement, the vice president agreed, and I soon learned why. In his non–Georgia Tech life, he moonlighted—if you could call it that—as a real estate developer. He had just invested heavily in new condominiums diagonally across Tenth Street, whose picture windows looked out over the bungalow. He had a personal financial interest in keeping up the neighborhood, and we worked out the details. The Georgia Tech Physical Plant folks would get the hot and cold water running again and install electrical outlets, not every 6 feet as required by code, but at least one in each room. I would pay minimal rent—$400 a month—for the whole eight-room house and be responsible for some major repairs, including the roof, and all minor maintenance, including painting, electrical, plumbing, and replacement of the rotten boards in the porch floor and banister.

The bungalow's bad odor had intimidated the university facilities inspectors, and that had worked to my advantage in negotiating the rent. They didn't know that this was familiar territory for me. The VP's secretary typed up a lease, I wrote a check for the first month's rent, and we signed. I never dreamed then that that diamond-in-the-rough Craftsman would become my cherished home base, *at that same rent*, for more than twenty years.

The Physical Plant locksmith walked over to the house with me, swapped out the cylinder on the front door lock, and handed me two official brass keys stamped "State of Georgia—Do Not Duplicate."

"The three other external doors are skeleton key jobs," he said. "No cylinders. And as you can see, even this front door lock won't keep people out. Anybody wants in, all they have to do is lean a little against any one of these porch windows." He rattled one to show me.

"Doesn't matter to me," I told him. "I don't own anything valuable anyway. For a burglar, what you see is what you get." I pointed to the empty interior.

"Hey, son," he said. "You know, with that key I just cut for you, and your lease, you are formally the official 24/7 state custodian of this building, just like the guy who is top dog at the library or computer center. That means you get access to the Georgia state surplus warehouse. So if you need a few furnishings, check it out. Down on 200 Piedmont. First go by the campus facilities office and have them issue you the form certifying you as an Authorized User of State Property."

I rolled up my sleeves once again, throwing out garbage, disinfecting, painting inside and out, patching the roof, replacing leaky plumbing and all the rotten floorboards on the porch, and learning basic home repairs as I went, once again mostly by trial and error. When the Craftsman was no longer an eyesore, I emptied my van and drove down to the Georgia state surplus building. I showed them my signed and stamped Authorized User form and my Georgia Tech ID and walked in. I don't know why I was surprised at how huge the warehouse was, since it serves as the repository for every tangible object no longer needed at any state agency in Georgia, from Amicolola State Park to the infamous Milledgeville State Mental Hospital. And here it all was, laid out in unending row after row in this dimly lit building. My eyes widened in disbelief, and I walked to the checkout desk and asked what items I could sign for.

"Anything and everything you want," the clerk said. "Here are some stickers for you to put on the ones you pick."

I couldn't believe my good fortune. After a half hour, I had marked a gray metal government-issue desk, two wooden desks, two sofas, several easy chairs, kitchen and dining room tables and chairs, and several dozen smaller items—a coffee table, two end tables, and an assortment of floor, table, and desk lamps. The desks had coffee cup stains, the lamps were tarnished, and the sofas threadbare, but all were serviceable. Each one was marked with either a barcode sticker or a handwritten state identification number written with a felt-tip marker. I calculated it would take me ten trips in the VW to lug all this loot home, and I walked back to the checkout desk to ask the supervisor what hours the warehouse was open so I could schedule my pickups.

"Oh, that's not necessary," he said. "Since you are the superintendent of a state building, we will deliver. I have the address—328 Tenth Street. Just tell us which days are good for you."

Soon the Craftsman was my new home, right there on campus, and only three minutes on my red Rockhopper mountain bike from both office and library. I was part of campus life like no other professor. The Psi Upsilon fraternity was next door, and at their request, I became their official faculty advisor. Georgia Tech Outdoor Recreation stored its canoes in the triangle two blocks away, so I joined up, earned certification as a whitewater canoe instructor, and began leading trips to the Upper Chattahoochee and Etowah Rivers. The Student Athletic Center was a ten-minute walk from my bungalow, and I spent even more time on the racquetball court than I had before and in the pool as assistant instructor in the university scuba course. The Bobby Dodd football stadium was ten minutes in the other direction, and I added it to my repertoire of illegal midnight tours of university football stadiums.

Friends from the department stopped by on their way home to the distant suburbs and told me that both colleagues and grad students were looking forward to my annual fall term open house party. Was it still on now that I had moved into this bungalow?

"Absolutely," I told them. "This place is even better for parties than the old shotgun house. It's even on campus, with plenty of after-hours campus parking. And it has a special spirit—look at those beam ceilings and beveled-glass windows and fireplaces and try to imagine how many social events have already taken place here since the 1920s! And Tech is going to level it some day, so we should all enjoy it as much as we can before that." I made cassette tape mixes of party music, "Louie, Louie" and most of Michael Jackson's *Thriller* and the like, and replaced the standard light bulbs in the converted gaslight fixtures with bronze and red flickering flame party bulbs. For parties I converted the middle bedroom on the right, with its own fireplace, into a barroom. The first room on the right, the den, held the buffet table. I did not allocate space for the infamous "blue movies" feature of past parties, since the projectionist had left for a legitimate college math teaching job, much to the relief of the more conservative members of the department. I provided chips and pretzels, unlimited beer, wine, and soft drinks, a 20-pound roasted turkey, and a spiral-cut honey-baked ham. I kept another cooked turkey and ham in reserve, and around midnight when the drinking and partying was at its peak and the food running low, I wheeled out the fresh turkey and ham to astonished and very happy faces.

Every year when I was in residence, I advertised to our department and also to friends in the physics and industrial engineering departments, reminding them that everyone was welcome, Tech-affiliated or not. The parties were open to anyone who heard about them, which usually meant a Friday throng of more than 100 people, dancing on the hardwood floors in electric candlelight in the main room or mingling on the huge porch and in the bar and food rooms. For many foreign visitors, it was their first party in America, and the sheer magnitude and informality of the whole event caught them by surprise. Again and again I had to explain why I was not worried about damage to this elegant Craftsman-era home.

One day a Jewish colleague mentioned that it would be nice if some of his Orthodox friends could join in the festivities and asked me if I could possibly shift the annual event to Saturday nights instead. I told him no problem, and that year my updated invitation announced, with a capital *NB*, that the annual party would be on *Saturday*.

The night before the party that year happened to be Halloween, so I decided to set up the flickering lights and dance floor and rock music system ahead of time and arranged to have a private party with my current girlfriend. By 10 o'clock we were completely stoned, with the lights low, music blaring, and flickering electric candles in the wall lights. We were dancing in the main "ballroom" in front of the window-sized mirrors over the fireplace mantels, both in bikini underwear, she with stiletto heels and me wearing a lifelike, full-head, latex Wolfman mask. As we spun around dancing, movement outside the front door caught my eye, but I didn't give it much thought, forgetting that there might be some unexpected trick-or-treaters. I never locked the front door, and now and then street people wandered onto the porch, but none had ever ventured farther. Then the door opened, and I saw two figures enter, a man wearing a conservative sport coat and tie and his companion in a sleek cocktail dress. They hesitated, then walked straight up to us through the empty ballroom. Neither was wearing a Halloween mask, and I immediately recognized Gideon as a friend from the industrial engineering department. I stopped dancing and welcomed him by name. He had a sheepish grin on his face and stuck out his arm with a bottle of wine. I still didn't get it at all and shrugged. Suddenly it hit me.

"Gideon," I said, pulling off my mask. "The party is *tomorrow*!"

"No it isn't," he said, smiling.

He'd been at these parties before, they were always on Friday, and the dancing and dress had always been free-spirited.

"Yes, starting this year it's on Saturday—*tomorrow*. I put it in the invitation." I said, looking at his wife for help.

Suddenly her expression changed to one of partial shock, and she grabbed him by the elbow, pulled him to her side, and whispered something in his ear.

"Look, I figure you probably hired a babysitter for your girls," I told them, and handed him back the wine. "Don't go home, go out to Little Five Points or Buckhead and have some Halloween fun. Then come back tomorrow for the party here."

The next night, Gideon and his wife returned in the same sport coat and dress, with the same bottle of wine, just as though nothing had happened, and reported on their Halloween night on the town.

Mornings after the parties, I made the rounds of the rooms, sorting out the prone figures under blankets and sleeping bags and pointing them to coffee in the kitchen. Most were mathematicians and their friends and companions. Sometimes actual *invited* houseguests were in the mix, as my bungalow had become a stopover for many mathematicians passing through Hartsfield, the world's busiest airport. When my friend Dennis from Kauai visited on one of the party weekends, he smiled.

"What you have here with this bungalow," he said, "is what we Hawaiians call an *ohana*. It means something like extended family and sanctuary, all rolled into one. Nephews and nieces, adopted kids and elders, aunts and uncles, friends' kids—all sharing the same hearth. The beloved home base, the heart and soul of the clan, like an Iroquois longhouse. You even have the open fires! No doubt about it, this place is a Math *Ohana*."

That house became the social center for Georgia Tech's math department. When the Centennial Meeting of the American Mathematical Society was snowed in by a blizzard, that didn't stop the scheduled open party at the corner of Tenth and Atlantic. Conference participants down with cabin fever braved the elements to enjoy the food, drink, and music in the warmth of the Craftsman cottage. Whenever there was some math happening at Georgia Tech, whether it was a conference or a graduate student recruitment weekend, there was sure to be a reception, formal or informal, at 328 Tenth Street.

It fit in perfectly with my traveling lifestyle and growing community of friends and colleagues. Since the house was on campus, I had no difficulty renting it out to visiting professors when I was away. And even when I was in residence, the upstairs unit with its own living room, bedroom, and bathroom made an excellent temporary home for visitors I'd met on my trips abroad. I hosted Ulrich Krengel returning from a backpacking trek to the bottom of the Grand Canyon, Peter Hupfer on his first trip to the US since his trip to West Point on the German Military Academy exchange, and Ester Samuel-Cahn on sabbatical from Jerusalem. Many others had their first "American" experiences of Thanksgiving and Christmas in that beautiful dilapidated old house.

Unlike standard hotels or guest quarters at other universities, the Hill Hotel also came equipped with a company car. For $300 I purchased a gray Buick Skylark from a colleague's mother-in-law and sold it at the same price to math visitors who wanted a car for a semester. Long on years but short on miles, and with an automatic transmission, the Buick was the first car for some of these friends, and the one they learned to drive in. At the end of their stay, I would buy it back for the same amount, ready to sell it to the next visitor. To maintain the steady price, visitors were responsible for any repairs to the car during their temporary ownership. I wondered if the folks at the Motor Vehicle Department downtown did not get curious when they looked at the record of ownership of the Skylark. First Jeffers, then Hill, Boshuizen, Hill, Gilat, Hill, Allaart, Hill, Bunimovich. That Skylark was even mentioned in the thesis of one of my Dutch PhD students, and it ended its days as a Cornell student car for the son of one of my colleagues.

* * *

When I was in residence, 328 Tenth Street became the meeting place of a small group of close friends for what came to be called our Wednesday Boys' Night Out. During my first quarter at Georgia Tech, when my colleagues all left campus for their long commutes home, I stayed on campus to work in my office or the library and to play pinball in the Student Center. The campus film club advertised a series of Alfred Hitchcock movies in the Student Center, a different film each Wednesday at 7 o'clock for just 25 cents. How could anyone pass that up? It was a small theater, not much more than a screening room, and week after week I saw some of the same people, including this one guy in a distinctive Greek fisherman's cap. About a month into the Hitchcock festival, I noticed this same cap on a fellow in our department, and I introduced myself. His name was Jeff Geronimo, and like me, he was also a brand-new visiting assistant math professor bachelor who loved movies. We agreed to link up for a simple dinner before the movie each Wednesday, and when the Hitchcock series ended, Jeff and I decided to continue the simple dinner-and-movie tradition every Wednesday.

Jeff, who is five years younger than I, did his PhD in physics at Rockefeller University. He is solidly built, of medium height, with short jet-black hair so thick that barbers grumble and pull out their special thinning shears. His Jimmy Durante nose, inherited from his Italian-American father, requires a special face mask for skin diving. Jeff is the unlikely combination of partly dyslexic absent-minded professor and natural athlete. We played racquetball and squash and went whitewater canoeing and gold prospecting on the Etowah River. I taught him skin diving and rappelling, taking care to make sure his anchor rope was tied in above the cliff face. Of the score of would-be adventurers I had introduced to the annual Grand Bahama dive trip over the years, Jeff and Vince were, at that time, the only two who came to love it as much as I did and to return year after year for decades.

When friends heard about Jeff's and my midweek outings, several joined us. Every Wednesday night at 6 o'clock, a small group met at the Hill Hotel to exchange new scientific discoveries and good-natured insults and decide on a cheap dinner and a B-grade action movie. The key was always under the doormat, and whoever showed up early knew there would be beer in the fridge. John Oneal sometimes drove over from Tuscaloosa, where he had accepted a tenure-track associate professorship in political science at the University of Alabama, and our little group exchanged teaching philosophies, scientific insights, and tips about refereeing papers, as well as campus gossip. If one of us had a paper accepted for publication that week, our rule was that, to offset this accolade, he had to buy the movie tickets for the whole group. That way he could announce his new success indirectly with a hearty "I'm buying tonight," without sounding like a braggart. Then we'd ask him for details about the paper and quiz him good-naturedly on its logic.

One of the Wednesday night regulars was Ron Fox, regents professor of physics, who had done his PhD apprenticeship under the Dutch physicist George Uhlenbeck, the discoverer of electron spin. A modern Renaissance man in every sense of the word, Ron routinely won Atlanta racquetball tournaments, wrote theoretical physics papers with a thesaurus at hand, entertained visitors with jazz on his electronic piano, and solved the *New York Times* crossword puzzles while carrying on a conversation about the Wednesday movie reviews and new discoveries in physics. *Fe Fox*, as the license plate on his Porsche sports car proclaims, *I-Ron Fox*, often surprised us with his encyclopedic knowledge, ranging from the evolutionary intelligence of octopi to the psychotropic effects and mystical powers of Guatemalan toad secretions.

Universities are filled with bright people by definition, but where Ron has always stood out is his strength of character and his unwavering, Dubins-like integrity. The whole campus recognized these strengths and elected him chairman of the university grievance committee during a scandal at the highest level of the administration. Shortly after refusing to be intimidated by the president of Georgia Tech, Ron submitted a polished sixty-two-page dossier to the Georgia State Board of Regents, who then forced the president to resign. During all those confidential deliberations, our best Wednesday night insults and taunts could not pry loose a single word about the scandal.

Another Wednesday night regular was Leonid Bunimovich, who joined our department during the exodus of top-flight Soviet scientists in the early 1990s. Short, barrel-chested, with red-brown short curly hair and beard, an infectious smile, and dancing hazel eyes, Leonid came to us as a full professor, having already earned international recognition for his work in dynamical systems and physical phenomena that now bear his name: Bunimovich stadium and Bunimovich waves. Even though Kolmogorov himself had served on his PhD committee in the famed Probability School at Moscow State University, Leonid was barred from teaching at a regular university in the Soviet Union because of his Jewish ancestry. His early mathematical discoveries were made on ships where he had served as scientific officer.

I invited Leonid and his family to the Hill Hotel for their first Thanksgiving dinner, shortly after they arrived in the United States with everything they owned packed into a couple of suitcases. I immediately found his humor, energy, and passion for life and mathematics completely irresistible. When he asked if I had ever been to Russia, I told him the story of my attempt to visit Moscow State University in February 1972, when the guards only allowed me to warm up by the radiator before throwing me back out into the snow. They wouldn't let me get within 20 yards of mingling with the Soviet students I could see at the end of the hallway, I told him.

"I was there in 1972!" Leonid cried in a thick Russian accent. "I was graduate student! I had seminars in that corridor and remember exactly where the guards stood. I wish I had known you were there—we had methods to smuggle visitors in. But I never hear anyone make trip like that behind Iron Curtain. I had trouble with KGB myself, without any borders."

On occasion Al Lindseth also joined our Wednesday night group, and hearing his tales of high-stakes law adventures brought us down to earth from our ivory towers. Al described his predawn, commando-like hostile takeover of a multimillion-dollar hotel in Savannah, and his role as the leading attorney for the State of New York in the seven-month trial challenging the adequacy of the New York City public schools' *$12 billion* budget. That quickly put our puny academic research grants and travel awards into perspective.

The Craftsman bungalow would have made a charming base of operations for me wherever it was located, but being on campus and right in the heart of Atlanta, it had unexpected advantages. Just after supper, on a gray November Friday evening, Bob Kertz phoned to tell me that a local TV station needed to talk to an expert in probability about a national Super Bowl lottery contest. One of their reporters wanted to ask a few questions before the story broke on the 11 o'clock news that night. Could he give them my name? I said sure.

Ten minutes later, my phone rang again, and a woman identified herself as Sally Sears, a reporter for WAGA TV, Channel 5 News. She asked if she could come talk to me in person. Had I lived out in Dunwoody or Stone Mountain an hour away, like most of my colleagues, meeting face to face at that eleventh hour would have been impossible. When I said I would be glad to talk to her, she thanked me, doubled-checked my address, and said she was on her way.

Within minutes, her whole film crew arrived at the Hill Hotel. I told them I wouldn't rush my analysis. Her team's deadline was the 11 o'clock news, but mine was not, and I told them if they wanted a clear analysis from me, I couldn't promise to make their deadline, and they might have to wait. They agreed and began setting up the camera lights and microphones.

Ms. Sears, an attractive blonde in her thirties, briefed me on the problem. Beatrice Inc., a Chicago Fortune 500 company, was sponsoring a national contest tied to Monday night NFL games. She explained the rules for the contest, called the *Beatrice Monday Night Winning Line-Up*. The game cards, available for free at convenience stores, listed the eight Monday night games, and below each game, three rows of entries, covered by silver scratch-off paint. The first row contained two silver ovals hiding the two teams' names, and the second and third rows contained eight silver ovals each, concealing the numbers 0 through 7. A contest player could scratch off exactly one oval in each row (otherwise he forfeited that row), and the goal was to uncover, for each week, the winning team, the number of touchdowns, and the number of field goals it scored. A contestant had no idea which team or scores the ovals concealed, so his selections were completely random. Or so everyone thought.

The top prize, if the player uncovered exactly the correct teams and scores in all eight games, was a choice between $20,000 cash or a trip for eight to the Super Bowl in a chartered Learjet. If the player got everything correct except one game, then he won $5,500.

"A young Emory University graduate, Mr. Maggio, claims he found a system to beat the contest," explained Ms. Sears, taking two game cards out of her briefcase and placing them on my desk. "He claims that the cards were *not produced randomly*, but in fact there are only 309 different master cards, and if you scratch off all the ovals for Game One, then you know exactly which of the cards it is, so you also know all the hidden entries for the remaining games. Of course, by scratching off all the entries for the first week, you forfeit that week, but since you then know which card it is, all you have to do is wait and look at the scores in the newspaper to get all the other games correct. In other words, every card you have is now worth $5,500! In doing his rounds as a salesman for Procter & Gamble, Mr. Maggio has accumulated more than four thousand cards. That's over *$20 million*! What I need to know," she said, "is whether he *really* has a system. His proof to me was to give me these two identical cards. But I know that this could have happened by chance alone. What I want you to tell me is whether you think he has a system or not, or whether this could have happened by pure coincidence."

Ms. Sears had done her homework, and her logic was right on the money. If Mr. Maggio was correct, the game producers had cut corners and made only some three hundred master cards, figuring no one would be the wiser. The only way to decide was to figure out the odds of two cards being exactly the same. I did the calculations by slowly punching in numbers on a simple pocket calculator.

"What is your conclusion, Professor Hill?" the reporter asked, motioning me to look at the camera.

"My conclusion," I said, "is that even if Mr. Maggio had *all* the three million cards the company issued, it would have been astronomically unlikely that he would have found a duplicate—*if* the cards had truly been printed randomly. Based on these calculations, however, I am convinced beyond a shadow of doubt that the cards were not produced randomly. Mr. Maggio is definitely on to something."

The film crew quickly collapsed their tripods and packed their gear, while Ms. Sears made small talk.

"You seem to have an interesting lifestyle," she said politely, glancing around the interior of the Craftsman bungalow—queen conch shells from Grand Bahama Island, wallaby skin from Australia, an oil-immersion microscope from Georgia State Surplus, flags from Singapore and Malawi, and Goodwill-reject furniture in front of worn brick fireplaces. "Well," she said, trying not to look in a hurry as her film crew boxed the last camera and microphones, "be sure to watch the 11 o'clock news tonight. You'll be on it."

I thanked her for the tip but told her I didn't own a TV and never had. The rest of the crew, a team of career television professionals, was stunned, but Ms. Sears reacted quickly.

"Tell you what," she said. "Why don't you come be our guest at the studio tonight? Just come to the rear entrance about twenty to eleven. The address is 1551 Briarcliff Road. The guards will be expecting you."

I drove to the WAGA studio a few minutes early. I expected *some* newsroom activity at that eleventh hour, but it was a state of barely controlled chaos. Ms. Sears met me at the guard station and gave me a lightning tour. She was excited.

"I just got the word," she said. "My piece on the Monday Night Football contest made the lead story on tonight's news. That means I'll be sitting with the news team, live on camera, during the 11 o'clock news broadcast."

Ten minutes before going on the air, they were still editing the final version—recording, adding, cutting segments. At the last minute, the turmoil suddenly evaporated, and I joined the technical staff in the studio to watch the broadcast. After it ended, the whole studio crew relaxed. As we passed one office on our way out, a man in a sport coat and tie jumped up from his desk and came to shake my hand. He beamed a big smile and told me his name was Ken Cook.

"Hi," I said. "Ted Hill. Nice to meet you."

A strange blank stare came across his face as he mumbled something and walked quietly back to his desk. My host leaned toward me and whispered, "Weather."

"Of course," I thought, "he must be the Channel 5 weatherman." Everyone else in Atlanta knew that. Another sport coat popped out of another office and introduced himself as Jeff Hullinger. Another vacant look and awkward retreat, and this time the whisper, "Sports." After that they gave up on me.

Different versions of the Beatrice story ran over the weekend, and I happened to be teaching two large calculus classes with nearly two hundred students each, so many of my students had seen me on the Channel 5 news. Most of my students knew that I was a practically computer-illiterate theoretician, and one of them came up to me after the lecture.

"Professor Hill," he asked, "did you see the news Saturday noon?"

I shook my head. I hadn't but knew that different versions of the news are often used for different time slots.

"They said, 'We took this probability question to Professor Theodore Hill in the Mathematics Department at the Georgia Institute of Technology,'" he said, with a widening grin. "And then they showed a close-up of your stubby fingers slowly punching in some numbers on that K-Mart calculator of yours, and said, '*Who put it on the computer . . .*'"

By Monday the Beatrice story made the national news. CBS called and asked to send a Dan Rather team to interview me. Unlike Ms. Sears, the CBS news team didn't want to investigate or learn anything—they just wanted some video footage with their reporter's face and mine, along with a general comment about my professional opinion about whether there really *was* a system to those lottery cards. With no numbers, no explanations, and no examples, the taping took only a few minutes. A few days after that CBS Evening News broadcast, I started receiving a flurry of postcards and letters from long-lost friends and relatives.

When Mr. Maggio filed winning game cards worth $20 million, Beatrice suddenly changed the contest rules and then canceled it completely. Mr. Maggio sued. The case settled out of court, and Maggio retired to Florida as a twenty-six-year-old millionaire. To my way of thinking, he had an excellent idea and deserved every penny. His discovery also pushed back the frontier for design of lottery games and led to several consulting projects for me with companies that produce state and national lotteries.

* * *

Another unexpected payoff from the *ohana's* midtown location came when Atlanta's science museum SciTrek invited me to address a lay scientific audience on "Some Surprises in Probability." My colleagues out in the suburbs were reluctant to return to the inner city for evening events, but I was right there. I prepared for my presentation by rereading the original scientific papers on some of my favorite topics. Among those was the First Digit Phenomenon, or Benford's law, which deals with the unexpected frequencies of the leading digits of numbers in real-life data, such as the numbers appearing in newspapers, the stock market, farmer's almanacs, census data, income tax returns, and tables of physical constants such as the speed of light and the universal gravitational constant. In this data, many more numbers begin with a 1 than with a 2, more begin with a 2 than with a 3, and so on down the line. What is even more striking, however, is that the frequencies of numbers starting with the nine different digits is nearly the same in *each* of these tables and is given by a very concrete logarithmic law. This law, first published in the 1880s by mathematician and astronomer Simon Newcomb in the *American Journal of Mathematics*, says that about 30 percent of the numbers start with a 1, about 17 percent with a 2, and so on down to 9, which is the leading digit less than 5 percent of the time.

I first learned of this curious phenomenon, which surprises even mathematicians, during a formal colloquium lecture that Dubins gave many years ago at Berkeley. In his talk, he cited the abundance of empirical evidence supporting these curious proportions, including the extensive data published by physicist Frank Benford in 1938, and he gave concrete examples to drive home just how counterintuitive the non-uniformity of leading digits is. At the time, there was no proof, or even formulation, in a modern mathematical framework, for a theory predicting the appearance of Benford's law in datasets as varied as tax returns and newspaper articles.

In organizing my thoughts for the SciTrek lecture, the more I read about the failure of modern mathematics to explain Benford's law, the more curious I became. After my lecture, I still could not get this beautiful problem out of my mind, and after several months of playing with it, I hit upon a few key ideas that led to an intuitive explanation and finally a formal proof. Using modern mathematical tools from probability, measure theory, and dynamical systems, I was able to show that Benford's law is the only law for leading digits that remains unchanged under changes of scale, such as converting yards to meters, and the only law invariant under changes of base, say from base 10 to base 100. I published an article in the *Proceedings of the American Mathematical Society* and an expository article in the *American Mathematical Monthly*, finally putting that century-old discovery into a formal mathematical framework. But I still didn't know *why* those Benford numbers appeared.

I continued to think about this question for several years afterward, and although I had finally given the statistical phenomenon of Benford's law a solid mathematical footing, I still was curious why it occurred in real life. Then one evening, I was sitting in the east sunroom of the Craftsman and rereading both Benford's original 1938 paper and the chapter on floating-point calculations in Volume II of *The Art of Computer Programming*. The author, Stanford computer science guru Professor Donald Knuth, wrote that if you don't believe in Benford's law, then just crack open a Farmer's Almanac or tomorrow's *New York Times* and pick numerical data from different pages at random. About 30 percent of the numbers will start with a 1, about 17 percent with a 2, about 12 percent with a 3, and so on—Benford's law. Justifiably skeptical, I pulled down a travel guide on Australia from my living room bookshelf and did an experiment. I selected numbers from various pages at random. One page listed air miles between major cities, another sheep population and rainfall statistics across the country, a third financial data on imports and exports. When they confirmed Knuth's prediction, I knew there *must* be a mathematical theorem that would explain the appearance of those curious percentages in the experiment I just did.

What I was looking for was the analog of Kolmogorov's famous Strong Law of Large Numbers, which explains the layman's observation that in the long run, tosses of a fair coin will result in heads about 50 percent of the time. I went back to basics again and reread the major papers on Benford's law. One day it hit me. *Of course!* The key to solving the Benford problem was breaking one of the cardinal rules drummed into every student from kindergarten to graduate school: "Never mix apples with oranges." You shouldn't combine data from different sources. Then I suddenly realized that if you *break* that rule, then under very general hypotheses the combined data will always follow Benford's law, even when the individual datasets do not.

That explained Knuth's experiment and Benford's original data, which combined numerical data from such disparate sources as areas of rivers, street addresses of famous people, square root tables, baseball statistics, atomic weight tables, and numbers gleaned from *Reader's Digest*. Individually, his data did not fit Benford's law well, but when all the data was combined, it fit to within several decimal points. Similarly, the numbers appearing in newspapers and tax returns and the stock market are often also mixtures of many different sets of numerical data, and thus are likely to follow Benford's law. Roughly 30 percent will begin with a 1, 17 percent with a 2, and so on. The incredible pleasure of making a discovery like that, of being the first person to know a basic scientific fact, was thrilling.

This was my second breakthrough on Benford's law, and I published the mixing-of-data theorem in *Statistical Science*, with an expository article in *The American Scientist*. Since the new theorem explained the appearance of the Benford distribution in real data, the ideas spread like wildfire, especially after accounting professor Mark Nigrini pioneered its use in detecting fraud in financial data. His new idea was simple but powerful. His research had found that true tax data follows Benford's law fairly closely, for which my theorem now gave a mathematical explanation. But when a person or company *fabricates* the data, they usually don't make up data where 30 percent start with a 1, 17 percent with a 2, and so forth. Faked numbers do not fit the distribution predicted by Benford. So all the IRS has to do is check whether numbers in tax returns follow the surprising Benford distribution. If not, there's an invitation to visit their office.

Shortly after the appearance of my 1995 theorem and Mark's paper describing the application of Benford to detection of tax fraud, a *Wall Street Journal* article reported that the district attorney of Brooklyn, in investigating companies doing business with the Borough of Brooklyn, had used Benford's law to catch and convict seven companies of fraud. My Benford's law discoveries soon appeared as the cover story in *New Scientist*, in the French journal *Pour la Science*, and in the Tuesday Science section of the *New York Times*.

The Benford publicity also provided some light moments. A representative of True Believers Ministries contacted me, offering to make me "rich and famous" if I would testify in court on their behalf. Their huge lawsuit, as he explained it, aimed to require public schools to include teaching "intelligent design" in their biology curricula. The judge had rejected the plaintiffs' scripture-based legal argument and instructed them that their argument had to be based on scientific facts, not scripture. The Ministries pored over scientific tables and discovered interesting new empirical evidence, namely that the elements in the sea and in the earth's crust are a very close fit to Benford's First Digit Law. From that, they modified their legal argument: since Benford's law is so counterintuitive and unexpected, such a distribution of the elements could only have been devised by an Intelligent Designer! Alas, when the plaintiff's representative quizzed me on my own personal views on religion, they withdrew their offer and I lost out on my chance to be rich and famous.

Others did manage to make money directly on Benford's law, at least temporarily. Two fellows in Eastern Europe, claiming they were researchers, sent me an email saying they understood how the logarithmic distribution of digits appears in many natural datasets. Then they asked me if it were difficult to generate *artificial* random data that follows the law. They assured me their interest was purely academic. It was certainly a natural mathematical question, so I naively explained that it is very easy to fabricate Benford data—just produce a sequence of random numbers using the standard random number generator on your computer and then raise 10 to those powers. I had completely forgotten the whole exchange when six months later, Dutch colleagues pointed me to a website where those same entrepreneurs explained to readers that to thwart government tax authorities' new fraud-detection software, they would provide foolproof fake data to people who needed it for €25 a pop. Shoot, I missed out again.

In between teaching and research, playing sports, hosting my fall term open house parties and weekly Boys' Nights Out, I still managed to maintain a fairly active social life. I went out dancing and barhopping, either alone or with some of my single friends, and dated a wide variety of women, some short-term and some longer. The social scene in Atlanta was a far cry from the more free-spirited days on the West Coast, and there seemed to be fewer opportunities to meet interesting available women. Many of them found my unusual bachelor lifestyle intriguing and enjoyed visiting the house on Tenth Street in spite of their reservations about its poor condition and the Georgia State Surplus furnishings. But when I started to woo the woman who would turn out to be my life partner, I credit the Math *Ohana* with clinching the deal.

I had first met Erika at a colleague's reception at his home. She was standing alone in the dining room next to a buffet table loaded with Vietnamese delicacies, this gorgeous woman in a black leather miniskirt and the bluest eyes I had ever seen. We struck up a conversation, and I learned she had degrees in modern languages, music, and mathematics. I had never met anyone like her before and was stunned. Unfortunately for me, she was married to a visiting colleague and about to head back to her home in Canada. All I could think was, "Where in the hell did anybody ever find a woman like that?" I sighed silently and tried to concentrate on the other delicacies of the buffet table instead.

When Erika returned to Atlanta alone and unattached a few years later to consult for Philips Medical Systems and work on her PhD in computer science at Georgia Tech, I made sure our paths quickly crossed again. I planned my campaign carefully. I telephoned to welcome her back to Atlanta. I made a *friendly* offer to help her move furniture. When Philips arranged for her to visit their home office in Eindhoven, I gave her *friendly* advice about traveling to Holland. Eventually I even asked her out for a *friendly* date. I learned about her fascination with Art Deco and the architecture of the 1920s, and as my *coup de grâce*, invited her for a *friendly* tour of the Hill Hotel Craftsman bungalow. I'm convinced that she first fell in love with the *ohana* magic and the natural beauty of the house. Turned out that her apartment in an old Little Five Points home looked just like the first floor of the Craftsman. As for me, I was struck by those sky-blue eyes, analytical mind, and outgoing personality, and finally made my move. Thus began what turned out to be the deepest and longest romantic relationship of my life.

Over the years, Erika became an intimate part of the *ohana* life, with all its comings and goings. Sometimes she lived there full-time with me, sometimes part-time as she worked on her dissertation, and sometimes she held down the fort while I was away on one of my fifteen-month absences. Eventually, after landing a tenure-track position at Clark Atlanta University, Erika bought, renovated, and moved into a midtown condominium in

Colony Square, just a few blocks away from Tenth Street. We called our setup the Rat Hole and the Ritz, and I often did my late-night walkabouts through the undeveloped urban blight that lay between our homes to relax in the air-conditioned comfort of her posh condo.

Meanwhile, life on the edge of campus continued as usual. During the day, Tenth Street was often noisy, bustling with student traffic and eighteen-wheelers from the Tenth Street exit on Interstate 75/85. At other times, the sounds were more pleasant. Without leaving the comfort of my study, I could always follow the progress of sports events in the campus stadiums from the fans' reactions—cheers when Garciaparra had blasted another home run in the campus baseball stadium, or loud collective groans when Wake Forest scored a touchdown against the Yellow Jackets in Bobby Dodd Stadium.

But for one short period of thirty-three days in 1996, the Tenth Street neighborhood was as still as a cemetery. Against long odds, on the centennial of the modern Olympic games first held in Athens, the Atlanta city fathers had somehow wrested the Summer Olympics away from Greece. For the first time ever, the Olympic Committee decided that one single campus, Georgia Tech, would serve as the entire Olympic Village, temporary home to more than ten thousand athletes and coaches from July 19 to August 4. The terrorist disaster at the Summer Olympics in Munich in 1972 was still on everyone's mind, and security was a top priority. For starters, the engineers constructed a 10-mile-long, 10-foot cyclone fence around campus as the outer perimeter and then increasingly tighter inner rings inside that.

There was talk of tearing down the Hill Hotel, but after I added a fresh coat of paint, the authorities decided to leave it standing a few feet outside the outer security fence. That fence was guarded around the clock by a combined team of Georgia National Guard soldiers and private Brinks guards. The only traffic on Tenth Street was an occasional official Olympics vehicle, and at night the street was eerily quiet.

"I know what it's like to be on guard duty," I said to the paratroopers. "Must be pretty boring for you. Why not listen to a radio?"

"The captain won't let us," the young paratrooper in his red beret said.

"Well," I said. "This is my house, I'm a Vietnam veteran, and if I want to put a radio on my porch and turn it up, that's my business. What kinda music do you like?"

When they told me, I rolled out an extension cord with a table radio. So there on the outer perimeter, life was good. I even brought out slices of watermelon for them on especially hot days. Unlike me, however, visiting friends as well as the perimeter guards could only hear the festivities inside the Olympic Village and were forbidden to enter.

The university had announced a condensed summer semester and said that no Georgia Tech students, faculty, or staff would be allowed on campus during the Olympics. Exceptions would be granted only for researchers who needed access to their labs, but those personnel needed to undergo an FBI security screening check during the winter quarter. It happened that my office, i.e., my lab, was inside the highest security ring, and I thought it might be interesting to see the goings-on of an Olympic Village. So on a cold, rainy February day, I had boarded the FBI bus to go downtown for the security screening and came back with two different sets of badges and holographic IDs that would allow me to enter the innermost part of the Olympic Village. Apparently none of my previous shenanigans had shown up on the FBI's checklist.

People from all over the world converged on Atlanta, and the International Olympic Committee had brought in numerous consultants and temporary managers. Art Mosley, my West Point and Ranger classmate and Jeep heist comrade, phoned to tell me the Committee had hired him to administer real estate procurement for Olympics events. I hadn't seen him in twenty-five years, when he had slept overnight on a couch in the Lindell mansion while taking a break from a rafting adventure through St. Louis re-creating Mark Twain's *Life on the Mississippi*. Art and I met for dinner, and he filled me in on his recent experiences as city manager of Key West and his current face-to-face hardball Olympics negotiations with Ted Turner, whose widespread Atlanta real estate holdings netted him a huge windfall.

Then I got a call out of the blue from Vince Bruce, the Australian exchange student who had shared my room in the house in Alloway during my senior year in high school.

"I'm here for the Olympics," he said.

"Need any tickets?" I asked.

"No, thanks," he laughed. "I can get all I want. I'm a *judge*."

I remembered his New South Wales track record in the mile and figured he was likely a track-and-field judge. Over dinner he set me straight.

"No, I'm a real courtroom judge, a barrister. This Olympics assignment is a unique legal experience, very fascinating," he told me. "Serious legal issues often arise during the games, such as alleged use of prohibited drugs. So the Olympic Committee always has a set of international judges on hand to decide the issues. We're from all different legal backgrounds—English common law systems like you use here in the US, Napoleonic code systems without juries like they use in Mexico, France, and Japan, and legal systems completely new to me like those in the Middle East. All have different standards of proof and culpability, but we have to work together to come to a single conclusion. Expel the athlete, or let the results stand."

And sure enough, they called him off that very night to help decide a high-profile case involving illegal drug use by several Russian athletes.

But even Olympic officials like Art and Vince couldn't enter the inner sanctum of the Olympic Village, whereas I, a mere mathematician, could waltz right in. I was the only Georgia Tech professor I knew who had taken the trouble to get this special privilege by hopping on the FBI bus and going through the clearance process. Outside events were noisy, full of crowds and vendors and merrymakers of all nationalities. It was a huge citywide street party, and Erika and I attended ticketed judo and track events with friends, as well as the free entertainments that lined the streets. But inside the Village, it was serene and relaxed, with no TV cameras or autograph seekers or throngs of tipsy fans. For the athletes to relax, Olympics contractors had built a temporary dance club, a movie theater, a café, and temporary outdoor swimming pool complete with grass and umbrellas and poolside tables. Inside the fence, everything was free. The café provided not only espressos but also café logo T-shirts and even CDs by the artists and guitarists who were providing the live entertainment.

From my departmental office window in the deserted Skiles Building, I could gaze out at groups of athletes in the moonlight walking back from the dance hall or from the huge tent with state-of-the-art computer games, waving to their teammates and opponents alike, testing English and French and Spanish to find the best common language. In a tent across from my office, the organizers had set up banks of computers with easy-to-use programs for athletes to use email, some for the first time in their lives. Many of them were just teenagers enjoying what they knew would be one of the highlights of their lives, win or lose. What a remarkable gathering of international talent and camaraderie!

But my favorite time to go into the inner ring was late at night, when I could stroll around the transformed campus. Often as not, my path led to one of the 24/7 dining areas, football-field-sized tents filled with fare from all over the world. There were dozens of kinds of bread, exotic fruits and vegetables, meats, fish, and desserts I didn't recognize. And, since the Village was designed to satisfy the athletes' desires, one of the most popular areas of the dining halls was the McDonald's. There were *free* Big Macs and fries and sundaes, as many as they wanted, whenever they wanted. McDonald's had hired several thousand multilingual servers to provide more than a half million meals and even added fresh fruit and yogurt and bagels to their menu for the more particular athletes. I sampled everything except McDonald's and made mental notes of the especially exotic tidbits so I could describe them to my friends outside the fence. For more than a month I had unlimited access to all the food in the world, something I couldn't even have imagined during those weeks of starvation in Beast and Ranger.

When the Summer Olympics ended, life on Tenth Street returned to normal, and I got ready for the new academic term, preparing classes, planning my annual open house party, and scheduling the upcoming year's stream of visitors. Looking back, I felt so fortunate to have enjoyed the past decade of golden years, with its immense freedoms, professional successes, and numerous travel adventures, balanced by the warmth and hospitality of my *ohana*-home and my growing relationship with Erika. But trouble was brewing in our department, and I soon would be called upon to make good on those mental promises I had made about standing up for what's right.

13

THE PENN STATE SYNDROME

My best of times were about to plummet into my worst of times. When I look back at the records of those events even two decades later, my heart sinks. I was a tenured full professor in an institute that *U.S. News & World Report* consistently ranks one of the top ten public universities in America. I had just received the Best Teacher Award among our fifty professors in mathematics, and the head of the department wrote the university president that many considered me one of the best instructors at Georgia Tech. The National Science Foundation had been supporting my research for years, and I'd also won research awards from the Air Force Office of Scientific Research, the Fulbright Program, the US-Israel Binational Science Foundation, and the Dutch National Science Foundation. I had published joint research papers with more Georgia Tech mathematicians than any of my other colleagues. The department elected me president of the Mathematics Faculty Assembly and chose me to deliver the once-a-decade mathematics lecture in the College of Sciences Showcase Lecture Series. The International Statistical Institute elected me to membership, only the second such honor in the history of our department. I designed and wrote a group infrastructure grant proposal for the whole department, and in the summer of 1996, we won one of the six grants from ninety-two competing universities, the largest single award in the history of our department. In short, my life at Georgia Tech up until then was *very* good.

Of course things were not perfect. Every institution has internal politics and favoritism, and I had been warned that Georgia Tech was one of the most autocratic among the many Southern universities with military-like administrative structures. At Georgia Tech, deans appointed directors of departments, and the director of mathematics had almost feudal sovereignty over his unit's fifty professors. He could unilaterally set salaries, raises, teaching loads and assignments, office space, and travel money. He could hire new faculty and staff without consulting any committee or colleague and wielded veto power over all promotions and tenures. And, like the deans and provost and president, the directorship was theoretically a *lifetime* appointment, without review. Most of us just wanted to do our research and teach, not to manage or supervise other professors. We were perfectly happy to let someone else herd the Schrödinger math cats. I had survived US Army regimentation for eight years, and by comparison, the previous two decades in Georgia Tech's extreme autocracy had gone by quite smoothly.

Our newest director had unusual personal charm, encouraged new seminars and joint research, and was very popular. He was often a guest at the Hill Hotel, and my sister and I had dinner with him when she visited Atlanta, just the three of us. But, as I had all too often seen in the Army, from plebe year when the pitiful yearlings Wiley and Boohar hazed Gary Jackson and Wes Clark and me, to the Vietnam War with the smuggling and tennis courts and harassment of POWs, power corrupts even the best. After several quarters, as he began to realize the unusual extent of his power, our new leader Director C. disbanded our elected departmental faculty advisory committee and replaced it with his own handpicked executive committee. He then dispensed with the required annual evaluations, started doling out huge raises to favorites, and travelled almost constantly, not teaching a single course in ten years.

Director C. attended every conference around the globe that interested him and was spending far more state money on his own travel than he allocated to the entire remaining fifty math professors under his care. We senior researchers could often scrape up outside funding, but for young assistant professors who need to attend conferences and visit other researchers to exchange ideas and gain visibility, lack of travel funds is a killer. I heard tales about the creative finances and threats against junior faculty who spoke out, but with my frequent absences from campus, I managed to mostly ignore the politics and to stay in my own happy circle of activity.

However, when the director announced that grant funds specifically earmarked for postdoctoral students would instead be siphoned off into his own pet projects, it was my last straw. Friend or no, I recalled my earlier promise to myself to stand up for young faculty if ever I made full professor. So, at the next annual departmental retreat in Callaway Gardens, I spoke out about allocation of departmental funds. There followed some heated discussion about departmental democracy, and I expected that there would be at least some token improvements as a result. On the contrary, little changed until it came time for the year-end pay raises, which were unilaterally distributed by Director C. in lieu of evaluations. Despite my continued professional accolades, he decided to send me a message by giving me a mediocre pay raise. Two assistant professors known for their independent streaks told me that they too had gotten subpar raises. For me this wasn't about the money, it was his attempt at blatant intimidation.

In research, asking the right question is often the key to solving a problem, and I figured it might also help in this situation. I emailed Director C. and his supervisor, new College of Science Dean S., asking, "Are our raises negotiable?" It was a simple four-word tiny breeze of a question that would soon launch a local hurricane. If they said "No," I figured that would document their dictatorial managerial style, and if they said "Yes," then the queue would commence. At first I heard nothing back, so I emailed again, and this time, I also asked to see a list of faculty salaries and travel allotments by grade, but without names. Since Georgia Tech was a state institution, this information was supposed to be a matter of public record.

Newton's Third Law says that for every action there is an equal and opposite reaction, and I expected as much from the director. But my seemingly simple request precipitated a much greater reaction, and from a completely unexpected direction. Instead of a response from the director of my own department, I was suddenly confronted by an official email from Mr. N., the university's chief legal advisor! Mr. N. informed me that salary information could be obtained through his office via a formal legal request under the Georgia Open Records Act. He had advised the administrators not to correspond with me and perhaps expected that intimidating legalistic communication would quickly put an end to my questions.

I realized then that I must have hit a nerve to warrant such a strong-armed response from the university's top attorney. Instead of caving in, as they expected, I decided to treat the problem just as I did the problem of getting out of confinement at West Point and getting out of the Army. I marched over to the campus library to look up the exact wording of the Georgia Open Records Act. I then made a series of formal open records requests, asking also to see some of the financial records in the department, including those pertaining to one of the director's pet projects, a new Center for Dynamical Systems and Nonlinear Studies that we all knew was burning through hundreds of thousands of dollars of state funds. Now that I started looking into some of these things, I became suspicious of the strong possibility of other financial irregularities as well and asked to see records of departmental travel expenditures. My original intention was to try to ensure fairness in our department and to support and protect junior faculty, not to dredge up financial misdeeds. But that was exactly what turned up.

The Office of Legal Affairs was legally obliged to at least respond to my formal open records requests, and they sent me a huge stack of travel documents. Paging through them, I stumbled upon records of dozens of questionable travel reimbursements to C., including one for a 3,606-mile Jeep trip in the Yukon. Three thousand *hard* miles apparently, since he also received reimbursement for balancing the tires. As for my request to see all financial records for the Center for Dynamical Systems and Nonlinear Studies, the official response came back, in a formal letter signed by the deputy senior attorney in Mr. N.'s office: "No such records exist." When I showed these documents to a few close colleagues, we all agreed something had to be done, if not for us personally, then at least for the taxpayers' sake. But with mortgages and car payments and kids in college, none of them would risk subpar raises for years, let alone possibly losing their jobs. It came down to me, and I now had to face making a commitment to choose the "harder right" of the West Point code. What made it even worse for me was that for the past twenty years, I had repeatedly gone out of my way to avoid academic politics.

I thought it over and decided to try first to address these issues internally rather than go outside to lawyers, the press, or law enforcement agencies. In the past, I'd been successful using logic, a bit of creativity, and by knowing the regulations better than the bureaucratic bosses themselves. I would again work within the system and somehow find a way to use its own rules to my advantage.

The first rule was to go up the chain of command. I made an appointment to see Dean S., a short, humorless man with thin lips and dark circles under his eyes. Dean S. already had a reputation as an iron-fisted administrator. He'd been hired in the mold of Georgia Tech President "It's My Way or the Highway" Crecine, who had unilaterally restructured the university's colleges, not by seeking input and support from professors or students, but by edict. Even after Crecine was ousted, S. continued his top-down management style, once even attempting to solve a problem by sending everyone in the physics department an official memo announcing the installation of surveillance cameras and threatening them with polygraph tests. "OBD," one of our colleagues called him—*Our Beloved Dean.*

Dean S. greeted me with a cold stare and asked what I wanted. He had clearly been forewarned about my visit. I told him I thought there might be problems in the finances and management in the math department.

"There are no problems in the School of Mathematics," he glowered. "You are the problem." Then he proceeded to tell me I was "unprofessional . . . unprofessional . . . unprofessional," and that in his opinion, I was having a "personal crisis."

This unexpected tirade flashed me back to the hazing during plebe year, when a similar Napoleon's complex type forced me to recite, until my voice cracked, "*Intelligence is inversely proportional to the square of height! Intelligence is . . .* ," and the Ranger sergeants had screamed that we were "*lower than whale shit.*" Dean S. was certainly very good at intimidation, but I had seen better.

Still, the encounter left me shaken. When I left his office, I knew that my whole career at Georgia Tech now hung in the balance, and I felt my heart slowly sink. I thought once again about simply leaving, as I had done going to Hawaii. With my professional record even stronger now, I was sure to be able to get a good position elsewhere. But no, this time I decided to stay and fight. I was determined to try to see things set right, not just for my department, but especially for my younger colleagues. I had gone to the next higher authority, as required by institute statutes, and that had failed. I now had to escalate my campaign.

The next internal step was to go through the university's Faculty Grievance Committee, the campus-wide body of full professors elected by the respective colleges to advise the president directly on matters related to the faculty. My strategy was to turn the whole matter over to them, after which I expected my role to be simply to keep them supplied with documents I obtained through open records. I filed a formal grievance asking for return of the cost-sharing funds for postdoctoral students, establishment of a Georgia Tech Ombuds office, and a departmental audit. The head of the grievance committee came to see me in my office.

"This is a very unusual case. We've never heard of a university grievance asking for an *audit*," he said, "in Georgia, or anywhere else. People ask for a pay raise, or larger office, or travel money. Why are you doing this?"

"Things just don't seem right," I told him. "Take a look at these." I handed him a dozen trip expense reports and a copy of the grant cost-sharing promises. "Making corrections will help all of us, so I guess you can look at it like a class-action grievance."

"Listen," he said. "Most people assume our committee is a professor-friendly shoo-in, but I have to tell you this. In the five years I've been on this committee, we have *not one single time* found in favor of the faculty member in any grievance filed by a rank-and-file professor against an administrator. Not once. But we will investigate this."

In retrospect, my optimism was astoundingly naive. Every institution, be it corporation or university, has its small share of lawbreakers, from petty crooks and embezzlers to sexual predators. In big business or in private universities, once the culprits are identified, they can easily be fired or turned over to the police. Nobody bats an eye. But with abuses in public universities, especially ones with powerful and fiercely loyal alumni and fan bases like Penn State or Georgia Tech, things are different. First, the general public *does* care, and second, the red tape required to fire a state employee is formidable. Exposure of internal crimes can wreak havoc with the university's funding, which heavily depends, via the state legislatures, on taxpayers' support. John Q. Public could not care less if a Stanford professor double-bills a trip, since it is not coming out of the public's pocket.

But when an honest, hardworking Georgia taxpaying citizen reads that a highly paid Georgia Tech administrator was reimbursed from state funds for personal expenses, that is a different ball game. If that citizen also happens to be a wealthy Yellow Jackets fan, his annual contribution to the athletic association is likely to reflect his dissatisfaction. Similarly, the exposure of a sexual predator in a private institution is easily handled by firing the perpetrator and turning him or her over to law enforcement authorities. But if the offense occurs in a top-tier public university, especially one whose prime-time basketball and football programs are pulling in millions of dollars in TV advertising funds, the administration's immediate knee-jerk reaction is containment. Keep it out of the press, out of the taxpayers' and legislators' eyes. Put a stop to the abuses, of course, but do it quietly and cover it up as quickly as possible.

Recent events in Penn State and the Catholic Church had brought home to the general public that there are two separate levels of misdeeds, the *crimes* and the *cover-ups*. The crimes usually involve only a few dishonest or immoral culprits at a low or middle level of the organization, but the cover-ups typically involve "cleaners" from various units and at multiple levels. Their goal? Preserve the institution's reputation and keep the state legislature and alumni funds rolling in, at all costs.

So when, much to my amazement, the Georgia Tech Grievance Committee actually found in my favor and recommended an audit, it should have been no surprise that the administration closed ranks. It was still reeling from recent public embarrassment when the Georgia Bureau of Investigation exposed double-billed trips by another Georgia Tech administrator, Norm Johnson. That incident had made local TV news broadcasts and ugly headlines in the *Atlanta Journal Constitution*, and the last thing the Georgia Tech administration needed was another misuse-of-public-funds scandal.

The cover-up began as soon as the grievance committee recommended the audit, when Dean S. made an unexpected visit to our regular math faculty assembly. He announced that he was sending our director on a fully paid year's leave of absence to Singapore, starting in the middle of the fall term, just before the audit was to commence. Get him out of Dodge—a Catholic Church solution. The director departed immediately, and it was business as usual. But by now, I had become adept at making requests through the Open Records Act (ORA), and I just kept on supplying the grievance committee and the auditors with new documents.

I didn't do this just to annoy the higher administration—every new stack of records revealed more evidence of questionable finances. Although I was spending only an hour or so a day on my records requests—less time than my colleagues were sitting in their cars commuting to and from their homes in Cobb County—the sheer volume of my ORA demands kept the administration off balance. Sometimes I requested specific documents or collections of documents that I thought might contain revealing information. At other times I made requests designed to elicit the response "No such documents exist," which also revealed mismanagement and lack of accountability. The Office of Legal Affairs tried all kinds of tactics to discourage me: they suddenly started demanding advance payments for searches, refusing to respond to email requests, and claiming attorney-client privilege. My research showed that all three tactics were in violation of Georgia statutes, and when I confronted them with this fact, the stonewalling stopped. "How on earth could ordinary citizens survive this process?" I wondered. Meanwhile, the Office of Legal Affairs continued to pass along what both the institute auditor and the grievance committee labeled "patently false statements." Even though the internal auditor tried to decipher the web of expenditures and cover-ups, his final report failed to catch dozens of other travel expense payments for the director's international trips. As a result, the incident got bumped up to a higher level of authority, and eventually the Georgia Board of Regents ordered its own independent audit. Even through all this legalistic activity, it still seemed to me like a never-ending, back-and-forth game between the cleaners and me, covering up and uncovering evidence of financial mismanagement.

Then, later that quarter, the exiled director's second-in-command, Acting Director A., summoned me to his office for my annual evaluation, after hours, when the Skiles Classroom Building was dark and nearly empty. He announced he was rating my performance "below expectations" for "activities that were a serious disservice to the school." As it turned out, mine was the only "below expectations" rating in the entire department of fifty professors, in a year when external evaluators later ranked me in the top ten! Up until then I had still innocently believed that all this was simply a paper chase and would blow over with some minor wrist slapping. My face flushed, my voice caught in my throat. I struggled to think. This old friend, who had at one time listed me as the legal guardian of his twin daughters in the event of his and his wife's deaths, was now receiving huge raises from Director C. and had caved in to pressures from the Dean. "Think!" I told myself.

"What disservice are you referring to?" I asked quietly in desperation.

"Your use of the faculty grievance and open records processes," he replied.

Shocked at this blatant admission, I staggered out of his office and down Atlantic Avenue to the Hill Hotel. I knew full well the rating was not his own doing but certainly had been approved if not designed by Dean S. and the exiled Director C. I now realized that this was all going to get very ugly and personal and was not simply about establishing facts and making administrative corrections.

The next day, I mentioned my annual evaluation meeting in a conversation with a member of the grievance committee. No sense filing another grievance, I told him, I just found out exactly where that would lead.

"No," he said. "You *have* to file a grievance on that evaluation! It is extremely important to the university to get this on the record. *Please* file one!"

So, at the grievance committee's *request*, I filed another grievance. During the investigation, Acting Director A. admitted telling me that the reason for the rock-bottom rating was my use of grievances and open records. He could easily have lied or said that he didn't remember, but to his credit, he owned up and didn't lie. He was one of those cleaners in the Penn State syndrome who was inherently honest but still followed orders to cover up as best he could. I also like to think that he knew that telling the truth would help mitigate the damage he'd been ordered to inflict on me and perhaps give me a fighting chance.

The two members of the grievance committee assigned to conduct an "informal inquiry" of the allegations interviewed me, Acting Director A., Dean S., and Chief Legal Advisor N. After the full grievance committee met to discuss the subcommittee's findings, their formal report advised President Clough that certain mathematics administrators, with the support of the Office of Legal Affairs, had made "patently false" statements and had retaliated against me essentially for questioning their authority. They reminded the president that "grievance is the right of all Georgia Tech faculty" and "Open Records Act requests are the right of all citizens of the State of Georgia," and that the Institute should not punish professors for exercising these rights. Their report identified the two main sources of the cover-up and expressed the committee's concern about the involvement of the Office of Legal Affairs in the false statements. They also unanimously recommended that the president give Dean S. a written reprimand for his role in the retaliatory evaluation. All this from a committee that almost never found in favor of professors.

For me, life in the department just got worse. Up until now, the retaliations had come solely from the administration, but now I also began to see it from a small handful of colleagues. Even those who were not getting special privileges had a knee-jerk reaction against questioning authority. Several came to my office and told me my actions could result in unknown consequences for the whole department, and they'd prefer known inequities to unforeseen risks. Others were silent but frowned when they met me in the hallway. There were also a few old friends, guests at my home many times, who were on the director's list of favorites, reaping high raises and low teaching loads, travel bonuses, promotion, and tenure. Instead of giving me the silent treatment or having the guts to talk to me face to face, they sent vicious emails. One colleague emailed me asking why I wanted blood on my hands, and a second, soon to be drafted by Dean S. to be associate dean, wrote asking if I had a drinking problem. A third sent emails to the whole department email list, including graduate students and past and present foreign visitors, accusing me of cowardice and engineering a search of a colleague's office, alluding to "Mein Kempf"[sic]. Eventually he was forced to make a public apology, but for me the interim was hell. I had to walk into my graduate class and try to inspire them with the beautiful mathematics of game theory after they had all been sent an email from a professor in our department accusing me of being a coward. I didn't try to defend myself or even mention the accusation, but I felt miserable.

I discovered that the loneliness of a whistleblower is different from all other experiences. You begin to question your own impressions and motives, and the things the perpetrators do or say to you to cover up are often so outrageous that no one actually believes you when you tell them. Former friends desert and even vilify you. I couldn't sleep and gobbled kava kava tablets like they were candy. Occasionally, faculty and staff from across campus sought me out for advice about using the Open Records Act to address problems in their own departments, and it was some small comfort to know that I wasn't the only one who was being attacked by the system.

On a trip to Berkeley, I met with the campus ombudsperson Ella Wheaton, who also happened to be president of the National Ombudsman Association. When I told her the story of what was going on, she got very quiet.

"Watch where you walk at night," she said. "Look under your car before you drive anywhere. When a university starts sending people out of the country during an audit, it is serious business."

Oh, great. Now I was back in Vietnam, when every time we returned from outside the wires, we used mirrors taped to old telescoping radio antennas to check under our Jeeps for plastic explosives.

I don't know how other whistleblowers cope with the extreme stress, but I resurrected my late-night reveille runs, as I had in Berkeley during periods of intense thesis stress. Scaling the cyclone fences next to the Yellow Jackets athletic track late at night, I ran silently on the spongy red track built for the Summer Olympics, lap after lap after lap, listening to tapes on my Walkman pounding out Spanish verb tenses. Occasionally I would look over my shoulder, then turn back and suck in the fragrance of warm new-mown grass and the fine, cool mist of the spray from the automatic sprinklers.

In the infrastructure grant I had won, a key component was an outreach-lecturing program, and I gladly left Atlanta and traveled throughout the Southeast, giving lectures at more than thirty small colleges that did not have funds to invite visitors. Some of the audiences were as small as three math people—the single math professor in the college and two students—but for me it was a brief respite to be away from the politics and again sharing scientific ideas. Fortunately, my teaching and research continued to flourish, despite the unreal nastiness behind the scenes.

* * *

My closest friends remained loyal and helped me keep my head above the political quicksand. Although Erika had by now moved across the country to take a faculty position in California, we were on the phone every day, sometimes twice a day, as I poured out my story of the latest events, attacks, and abuses. I-Ron Fox, although recently promoted to chairman of physics and thus an official part of the university administration, stayed true to his name as he stood at my side and spoke on my behalf in numerous crucial meetings. And Leonid, my Russian bear of a friend, stuck his neck out by going with me to see Dean S. about the abuse of another junior colleague. He had immigrated with nothing but a few personal belongings, and coming from the former Soviet Union, he too had seen professional intimidation at it best.

"I'm worried about you," Leonid said one day, looking at my long face.

"Then I need to show you Deadman's Reef," I replied, and smiled.

Leonid had heard the stories about what had become an annual dive outing to the Bahamas—catching lobsters and octopi and triggerfish by hand; spearing groupers and flounders; evading moray eels, barracudas, and sharks; and exploring underwater caves and tunnels. Once, he had heard, I even chased a thief at scuba knifepoint, dripping wet from the sea. And on many of the trips, our car had been broken into at remote dive sites. Yes, I told him, it would do us both good, and I organized a weeklong trip for five of us—Vince from Clemson, Bob from Industrial Systems Engineering, and Leonid with his teenage son, Yuri.

On a remote beach at Deadman's Reef, on the southwest shore of Grand Bahama Island, I helped Leonid adjust his fin straps and snorkel and showed him how to spit in the mask to reduce condensation fog. He grinned broadly, pointing to a ½-inch strip of white skin in his curly red beard, just under his nose, where he'd shaved a track for his mask.

"First time I ever shaved part of my beard," he said.

The only novice in the dive group, Leonid took to skin diving immediately, his physical strength and intense curiosity winning out over pain from plugged ears, cramped muscles, and fire coral. I pointed out poisonous stingrays hidden in the sand and told him to avoid the head spikes on the spiny lobster and to just ignore the circling barracudas.

Sharks were more serious, I told him, and I explained the two main types of shark attack. In a hit-and-run attack, a cruising shark takes a bite out of everything he passes and keeps on going—leaving jagged rips and torn flesh but rarely fatal wounds. A bump-and-bite attack, on the other hand, is premeditated murder. The shark identifies a potential victim, circles, and then bumps it firmly, head-on. If satisfied that the target is edible and isn't going to sting or eat *him*, the shark circles again and moves in for the kill.

"We see sharks all the time," I told Leonid. "Nurse sharks, lemon sharks, the more aggressive Caribbean reef sharks. Sometimes we find them sleeping in caves, other times coming up behind to snatch the fish we'd speared—twice they ripped open my net bag and devoured our catch. But they've never attacked us."

Leonid learned quickly, and the third day out, we swam half a mile offshore to the shallow elkhorn coral reef surrounding Peterson's Cay, a 50-foot-long island with three small, hardy cassowary pines. Twenty minutes before reaching the reef, I speared a large brown speckled grouper and put it in the basket trailing on a rope 30 feet behind me in our inner tube float. The belly shot had spilled the grouper's blood and guts into the water, but this had happened often before, and I thought nothing of it.

At a shallow point on the reef, no more than 3 feet deep, I kicked slowly through the sunlit crystal clear Caribbean water, following a school of five squid. Suddenly—*BUMP!*—a broad, leathery black-gray object smashed into my face mask and chest. Instantly, I realized what had happened and raised my head out of the water to shout "Shark attack!" and to try to track the sleek 6-foot shadow as it sliced through the water circling me. I tried to anticipate the direction of the next attack, but it came so fast I could neither scream nor turn. *BUMP!* again. By this time, the other divers had raced to my side, and we formed a tight defensive knot, with our spears and gaffs and dive knives sticking out in all directions, like a giant marine porcupine with metal quills.

"He's over here!" Vince shouted, and a second later, Yuri shouted, "He's here now!" from the other side of our circle. As all of us froze, in shock and anticipated slaughter, the shark suddenly rose out of the water right in front of us and chomped down on our floating catch box with the grouper, shaking it the way a terrier kills a rat. The shark's power and speed and mindless frenzy instantly seared themselves in our memories. We took advantage of its fanatic obsession with the grouper to slowly kick away in tight porcupine formation. When it finished with the grouper, the shark trailed us and backed off only when we reached a shallow sandy bottom.

On the next afternoon dive, I glanced at Yuri and saw his facemask filled with blood and seawater. He had just removed his mouthpiece to say "nosebleed" when I spotted another black shadow and yelled for him not to remove the mask. I saw the shark and pointed Yuri to a small island 100 yards away.

"Kick slowly toward the island," I said, "I'll be right beside you."

The shark followed, repeatedly darting in for closer looks but neither hitting nor bumping. When we returned, we saw that, once again, someone had smashed our window and taken our small stash of money. After these misadventures, I figured no one else would join me on a short night dive on Deadman's Reef. It was risky anyway, and the past four years no one else had volunteered. Each time I had gone on the night dive solo. Leonid, the novice, spoke up.

"I'm going too," he said. Yes, it scared him, but his curiosity overrode everything. "That's exactly why he is such a great scientist too," I thought.

At the end of the week, Leonid slapped me on the back as we boarded the plane in Freeport, taking one last whiff of the tropical salt breeze. "Great trip," he said. "Just like your stories. Lobsters and octopi, night dives, shark attack, getting robbed . . ." I didn't have the heart to tell him they didn't usually all happen on the *same trip*.

On the plane, Leonid recalled one lobster I had struggled to catch, ignoring the fire coral burns and lobster spine lacerations, as I held my breath and fought underwater until finally I broke to the surface, sputtering and gasping for air, but holding the lobster.

"I'm not worried about your mental health any more," he said, with a big smile. "I'm worried about theirs."

"Don't count them out too quickly," I replied. "It's the *land sharks* that will get you."

Back in Atlanta, unexpected official recognition of my efforts to detect and correct problems in Georgia Tech's management of finances began to surface. President Clough met with me twice, one on one, and congratulated me on the recent article in the Tuesday Science section of the *New York Times*. Then he caught me completely by surprise with his remark: "Sometimes universities need a good kick in the ass." In March 1999, he sent me a formal letter thanking me for bringing the funding abuse matters to his attention. And on June 17, after the Board of Regents auditors confirmed the abuses uncovered by the grievance committee, Georgia Attorney General Thurbert Baker wrote Chancellor Portch, Clough's boss, detailing the extent of the misdeeds and confirming the recommended corrective action, including reprimands, reimbursement of thousands of dollars of state funds, and the resignation of Director C.

I thought that at last the end was in sight, and in September I flew to Amsterdam, where the Free University had invited me to deliver a formal lecture at the ceremony honoring the retirement of Professor Piet Holewijn, with whom I had shared three PhD students. At the end of my visit, Wes Clark, still serving as NATO supreme commander, invited me to Belgium to stay overnight with him and Gert at Chateau Gendebien. I hadn't seen them in a year, and since then, much had happened. The Clinton administration's sudden announcement that Wes's tour of duty as NATO commander would be cut short by three months was making world headlines. The rude manner in which it was done, and the Pentagon leak to the *Washington Post*, were seen as intentional snubs of General Clark. The *Atlanta Journal Constitution* reported, "Pentagon officials tried to counter speculation the decision was retaliation for Clark's differences with the administration during the [Kosovo] war." When I read that, I thought, "Retaliation? Differences with the administration? Maybe our plebe room thirty years ago had been infected with some awful anti-authoritarian disease."

I arrived early at the tiny train station in Mons and caught a taxi to the huge iron gate outside the chateau's 23-acre estate. Armed commando guards instantly greeted me by name, opened the gate a shoulder's width, and led me to the command post, where they double-checked my passport and logged me in. Five NATO soldiers sat monitoring a half -dozen security video screens, which were flickering with images from security cameras hidden throughout the compound. The chateau, set on a hill several hundred yards up the circular gravel drive, sparkled in the early afternoon sun. I wanted to walk, but the guards insisted, very firmly, that they would drive me to the front door, where Gert stood waiting with three house servants. Her familiar quick smile, dancing hazel eyes, and delightful freckles took me back three decades.

One of the valets led me to my suite on the second floor, up a sweeping staircase that reminded me of Tara. My last trip to Gendebien had only been an afternoon visit, and I hadn't seen these guest quarters, whose 10-foot arched windows overlooked English gardens on two sides. Between antique cedar chests and dressers was an immense Victorian four-poster bed, and on the marble-topped mahogany writing desk, overlooking a rose garden below, was a telephone and a fresh bouquet of violets and lilies of the valley. A polished silver bowl centered on the writing blotter was filled with flawless strawberries, star fruit, pears, apples, and fragrant Belgian chocolates. Next to them were a heavy sterling silver fork and knife and pure-white linen napkin, on an ivory china plate, embossed with SACEUR—Supreme Allied Commander Europe.

My private bathroom had a walk-in marble shower, 8-foot marble bathtub, marble sinks and floors, and, hidden behind pure-white closet doors, a full-sized refrigerator stocked with soft drinks, premium Belgian beer and chocolates, French Champagne, fresh juices, salted nuts, and an assortment of *hors d'oeuvres*. I paced off the bathroom—20 feet square—and tried on one of the inch-thick, white terry cloth bathrobes in the bathroom *garde robe*, tracing the curves of the gold-embroidered CG (commanding general?) on the pocket with my finger. Matching embroidered towels hung at the foot of the huge bathtub.

Gert waited for me in the small private kitchen below—the industrial-sized stainless-steel kitchen in the basement was used only for state dinners.

She told me Wes would be home in an hour and asked what I'd like to do.

"Take a walk," I said. "Get some fresh air, stroll through the estate. I'll be back in a half hour."

"I'd love a walk too," she said. "I'll show you my greenhouses."

She whispered a few words into the kitchen intercom and led me out through the back patio and onto one of the tree-lined footpaths.

I didn't see the point man until we turned back from the greenhouses and veered off into the forest. Thirty yards out in front, an armed commando, automatic carbine in ready position, anticipated our changing directions. Movement to the side caught my eye, and I spotted the flank security. In the distance were hidden motion detectors and roving patrols of commandos following random azimuths, crisscrossing the grounds. Now and then, helicopters hovered overhead. The White House couldn't have more security. "What a life," I thought. "They can't even go for a simple walk in the woods in their own backyard, it had to be a combat patrol walk."

We returned to the chateau just before Wes arrived, hidden behind the tinted windows of one of the two armored Mercedes in his everyday convoy. I knew that the SACEUR also had his own DC-9 aircraft and two Blackhawk helicopters. Stepping out of his command car, Wes grinned at my Teva sandals and gold earring. Calling them by first names, he introduced me to his bodyguards as his old roommate, The Professor, and immediately made them test my Dutch.

"It's excellent, sir," they told him after exchanging a few sentences with me. "Very few Americans speak Dutch. He says he likes his room here and wants to stay a whole month."

Two of the men were American, clean-cut FBI types, like the one who had come to my cottage in Berkeley to investigate the mysterious Soviet marine canister. The other two were wiry Belgian bodyguards in rumpled clothes. Each of these four men would instantly jump on a grenade or dive in front of a bullet to protect my old friend. "Fluent in French, English, German, and Dutch, the Belgian bodyguards must be Kings of the Pits," I thought, and imagined a hole where 200 bodyguard applicants fought each other tooth and nail until these two alone crawled out alive. That earned them the right to protect one of the world's top generals—"*the* top troop-commanding general in the world," Wes later told me.

"How's your golf?" I asked Wes, reminding him of the past summer's outing, when I had watched his bodyguards frantically charging off into the bushes with loaded Uzis to find the ball he kept slicing or hooking.

"Getting a little better," he said. "Have you taken it up?"

"Not yet," I said. "I'm saving it for my old age. How do you stay awake playing that game—eat caffeine tablets?"

He laughed aloud, as the bodyguards glanced at each other. Never had anyone talked to The General like that before. Wes and Gert and I walked into their private quarters, and the guards stopped outside the door. Wes opened a bottle of French wine and poured three glasses.

"Play any pool?" he asked.

"A little," I said.

"Let's go down to my pool room and shoot a few games of eight ball," he said. "Just you and me, one on one."

I laughed and turned to walk down the wide stairs. Wes pulled my arm and pointed me instead to a tiny Otis elevator. "Let's take the elevator," he said.

The basement billiard room reminded me of the pool table in our Alloway cellar, where Wes and Gert had visited decades earlier. It had the same damp stone walls and musty green felt, the faint whiff of blue-chalk powder and worn wooden cue sticks. I'm not good at pool but made a few lucky shots, winning the first game easily.

"Rack 'em up, *loser*," I teased.

When he scratched on the eight ball and I won again, Wes frowned and hung up his pool cue.

"You should be ashamed of yourself," he said. "A professor shooting pool all the time, instead of doing mathematics."

Still grumbling good-naturedly, Wes led me to the stairs. Halfway up, he suddenly remembered something and stopped in his tracks.

"Going upstairs, Mike," he said, in a loud voice to the wall.

"I'm going upstairs too, Mike," I said. Somewhere in central security the pulsating green blip had left the screen. "That's why the elevator," I thought.

Up in the industrial kitchen, the staff waited, each one a multilingual trained chef, master bartender, and accomplished butler, all rolled into one.

"Probably seventh-degree black belts too," I said to Wes. "Say, General, aren't you going to tell your staff how the pool games went?" I waited for a few long seconds. "What? You mean you didn't win a *single game*? Why, you're just a born loser."

Wes roared with laughter and told them of the Pinball Championship of the Universe I lost to him in his basement in Colorado years ago.

"You keep dredging that up," I said. "Yes, I lost—it was your pinball machine, and you beat me, fair and square. Only thing you ever beat me at, as I recall."

The "kitchen kommandos" blushed, uncertain how to react. "Humor him, General, or kill him?"

"You never were a good loser," Wes said.

"That's right—and I admit it. But I wasn't going to learn that from *you*, now was I?"

Even the bodyguards burst into laughter. Wes had not been number one in the General Order of Merit at West Point, a Rhodes Scholar, and NATO supreme commander because he accepted defeat easily.

Gert, Wes, and I relaxed with a formal dinner at the long table in the East Drawing Room, overlooking a broad patio, green hedges, and vast expanses of rose gardens and lush emerald lawns. Fragrances of fresh bread, roast meat, steamed vegetables, and baked caramel seeped from the kitchen. The house staff, in high starched white collars and pressed black trousers, served a four-course meal, with a main course of razor-thin slices of tender rare lamb, fanned out on the SACEUR china plates beside perfectly aligned asparagus. To me it looked like a Japanese painting. The chef had baked individual French pastries for each of us and had chosen the proper French dessert wine.

I asked Wes how he had made it to the very top. The Army has its share of brilliant officers and energetic workaholics, I said, but to become *the top dog*, there has to be a special reason.

"There is," said Wes. "And it's ironic. I made it because, at each level of promotion, people were jealous and skeptical of my last early promotion. So they gave me the very worst jobs—commands of drug-riddled troops and staff jobs in hopeless armor units. Jobs they considered certain losers. In each one of those jobs, I stayed awake nights, searching for a solution. And I always found one—sometimes building morale by personal example—winning swimming meets myself—other times using pure logic to predict opponents' moves in war games. I turned disaster into triumph and then moved up to the next level of skeptics. If they had given me standard assignments, I would have succeeded too, but so would a lot of officers. I would have been your average general. By giving me the very bottom of the barrel, again and again, intending to destroy me, they ended up giving me opportunity."

After dinner Wes opened up about the retaliation. "Dirty politics," he said, "right from the top."

"Listen," I said, "lighten up. Remember when I saw you in intensive care in Camp Zama? If those AK-47 bullets had been one inch forward, you would have died then and there. As a captain. Now you're the top four star in NATO. Imagine that! You're lucky to just be alive."

Wes agreed, and we clinked our wine glasses for his staff photographer. He then asked about the mess at Georgia Tech, and I told him those problems seemed very petty compared to his. I was sure he didn't want to hear about them.

"Yes, I do," he insisted. "First, Georgia Tech is a fine university, and basic faculty rights and ethics are extremely important—you are responsible for educating the next generation, for setting values. And second . . ." he hesitated. "Second—misery likes company." Wes grinned.

I told him about the retaliations for exposing financial misdeeds, the cover-ups, and the personal attacks from administrators and colleagues.

"Sounds terrible," Wes said. "You know what Kissinger said, after he gave up his full professorship at Harvard to become US Secretary of State, when reporters asked which was worse, real politics or academic politics? 'Academic politics are worse,' Kissinger replied, 'simply because there's so little to fight over.'"

We dropped politics and started talking science. Wes had read my article on Benford's law in *The American Scientist*, and in an instant we were teenage college roommates again, sharing insights about the Second Law of Thermodynamics and making grand plans for new scientific adventures.

Over the next few years, despite the findings of the grievance committees and the kudos from the president, the problems at Georgia Tech continued to fester. The president had acted on some of the Board of Regents' recommendations, forcing the director of our department to step down and pay back thousands of dollars. Even the acting director and the provost had been included in the "cleanup" process. But this only addressed one side of the Penn State syndrome, namely punishing the perpetrators who were directly guilty of financial misdeeds. By leaving the rest of the autocratic structure in place and not reprimanding those involved in the retaliations, false statements, and other cover-ups, it sent a clear message to the rest of the campus.

"I just don't understand it," I told a senior colleague. "The top administrators here at Georgia Tech must be intelligent people, and by now they know we have major problems in leadership. What in the world is going on?"

"They're desperately trying to preserve power," he said, "and to preserve this unique university administrative structure. Have you ever heard of a university where administrators can make unilateral decisions on leadership, hiring, raises, teaching loads, and promotions? These guys want to preserve that system. They know problems will arise from time to time, and they respond in a way that preserves their power and both corrects the problem and discourages faculty activism."

"In the early eighties," the graybeard colleague continued, "the chair of Mechanical Engineering ruthlessly mistreated young faculty. Senior professors objected but were afraid to speak up. Finally, half a dozen untenured assistant professors went to see the dean. The evidence of abuse was clear. What did the administration do? They immediately *fired* all those assistant professors, waited a year, and then fired the chair. That sent a clear message to professors not to question authority and at the same time sent a message to chairs that such behavior was unacceptable. What we're seeing in your case is exactly the same. They're trying to crush you, even though they know you're right. And then, very slowly, they will replace the current regime."

My battle should have been over by now, but it continued, just as my colleague had predicted. My main escape from the hell was my frequent self-paid sabbatical program. By getting away from the unpleasantness in the department as often as I could, I was able to live a parallel life, a life where mathematical discoveries were the main focus of attention. I don't know how whistleblowers who have to report for work every day can possibly survive the intimidation and harassment.

My collaborations in Europe continued to blossom, and the Göttingen Academy of Sciences awarded me a four-month visit as *Gauss Professor.* The Academy also invited me to deliver an evening lecture, *auf Deutsch*, at their formal coat-and-tie meeting, and after the lecture, still charged with adrenaline, I walked through the crunchy snow to my guest office in the same university building where I had been a student three decades earlier. There I found a completely unexpected email message from a Vietnamese mathematician, Professor Nguyen Van Thu.

"I discovered a very interesting point relative to your CV," he wrote. "You were in army in Vietnam and become so great mathematician. Nobody could have such a life. Congratulation! Please come to Vietnam again to visit my institute in Hanoi . . ."

I broke out in goose bumps. I had long dreamed of a return trip to Vietnam but never imagined it would come at the invitation of fellow scientists, because of my mathematical discoveries. "What a privilege it is to be in an academic career," I reminded myself as I happily typed my acceptance.

It turned out that the International Congress of Mathematicians, the main worldwide mathematics conference held once every four years, was to take place in Beijing in 2002. Vietnamese mathematicians had organized a satellite conference in Hanoi and invited me to speak there, so I also submitted a paper to give in Beijing. As I was planning the trip, a Queensland mathematician, Rex Boggs, had read my articles on Benford's law and had discovered evidence of it in the Australian stock market. He sent me spreadsheets of his data and invited me to also visit and lecture at the University of Central Queensland. I sketched out a six-week trip to Queensland, Beijing, and Hanoi, with multiple passes through Cathay Pacific's hub in Hong Kong.

The Australian visa was easy, and the Chinese visa also went surprisingly smoothly, especially compared to my interminable hassles with the East German and Soviet Communist bureaucracies during the Cold War. My guess was that China was trying to improve public relations in anticipation of its bid to host the 2008 Summer Olympics. They were using the International Congress as a dry run.

The red tape for the Vietnam visa application, on the other hand, was a throwback to the Iron Curtain visa authorities thirty years earlier. For a ten-day visit, Vietnamese immigration officials demanded I send them my original passport, official letters of invitation from the University of Hanoi, hand-stamped approval documents from the Vietnamese consulate in Los Angeles, multiple application forms and payment vouchers, and certified copies of air tickets, which, since Cathay Pacific was not permitted to fly into Hanoi, included a Hong Kong–Hanoi stretch on Dragon Air. My last trip to Vietnam, I mused, had been much simpler. As combatants we had arrived in Saigon with virtually no identification except military ID cards and dog tags, in case the return trip to base camp was in a body bag. There were no passports, no customs forms, no immigration papers, not even a driver's license. It was much easier to go off to war than to attend a mathematics conference. Crazy world.

Stepping off the plane in Hanoi, even though I was expecting it, the 90 degree heat and 90 percent humidity hit me like a sauna blast furnace. August averaged ½ inch of rain a day. Instead of the lightweight jungle fatigues I had worn in my last visit to Vietnam thirty-three years earlier, I wore an REI vented nylon trekking shirt, convertible short/long nylon trousers, and Teva sandals that bore an uncanny resemblance to the Viet Cong's classic truck-tire-tread Ho Chi Minh sandals. My host, Professor Thu, met us at the airport in a university van, and we chatted as he drove the 15 miles to the city. I relayed greetings from a common mathematician friend in Tennessee who had been a graduate student with him in Poland in the 1970s.

As the van sped through tiny hamlets, I involuntarily flinched when my eye caught men in dark-green *mu coi* pith helmets and a huge red flag with five-pointed yellow star. For a fraction of a second, I thought I had woken up behind enemy lines in a North Vietnamese Army camp. I slowly relaxed and focused on the more peaceful symbols that were also parts of my old memories: water buffaloes tilling rice paddies and young women in conical straw hats and *áo daì*, the traditional tight-fitting long silk dresses, slit to the waist, over ankle-length, sleek silk pants. Bicycling boys still carried live pigs to the market, and families of four balanced like the Flying Wallendas on sputtering 125cc Yamaha motorbikes.

I asked Thu about the strange architecture of the homes we passed—rectangular boxes one room wide, two or three high, and four or five deep. They looked like gigantic breakfast cereal boxes, balanced upright on their long narrow sides. It reminded me of the shotgun house on Ninth Street, except that it was three stories tall.

"Property taxes in Vietnam base only on width of house," he explained. "This optimal mathematical design."

As we approached the outskirts of Hanoi, traffic slowed and pollution and noise increased. Near the city center, every intersection was jammed with hundreds of motorbikes, coughing and vibrating and spewing smoke. The moving sea of motorcyclists flowed smoothly around both pedicabs and pedestrians and around taxicabs pushing upstream against one-way traffic. It reminded me of the laminar smoke-flow experiments in our West Point wind tunnel labs and swimming through bus-sized schools of silvery jacks off Grand Bahama Island.

Our driver alternated hitting the gas and the horn, rarely using the brakes, and the slow pace gave us a good glimpse of the city, with its tree-lined streets, parks, and 1930s French architecture. Vendors' stalls, temples and storefronts, and open-air markets competed for space with piles of refuse. The streets teemed with shoppers, street children, hawkers, and school groups. The heat and humidity and smells were the same as those I remembered from Saigon over thirty years before—a potpourri of overripe bananas, temple incense, and rotting bamboo leaves, clouds of blue diesel smoke from the trucks, and gray-black fumes from the motorbikes.

On a private excursion to Halong Bay, I struck up a conversation with the driver, who had learned rudimentary English from rock-and-roll lyrics, just like the Polish hitchhiker I had picked up in my Volkswagen van three decades earlier behind the Iron Curtain. He explained that the two primary goals of every young Vietnamese man were, first, to save enough money to buy a motorbike, and if that was successful, to then find a wife and an apartment with at least two rooms to raise a family. He did not even dream of ever owning his own small home.

As we passed through a series of highway toll stations, I asked our driver why we always had to stop twice, once 50 yards in front of the toll booth to buy a ticket from a uniformed official standing on the curb and then once again to give the ticket to the toll booth agent. Why not simply one agent? He blinked at me, bewildered. The two-phase process, he explained, was necessary to prevent corruption. How could you possibly trust the person who was taking the money to also control the tollgate? He frowned in disbelief as I described the outside world's system where one person was trusted to do both jobs.

"Have you been in Vietnam before?" he asked.

"Once," I said. "In 1969. I was a soldier in the Iron Triangle."

"So was my father," he said with a friendly smile. "He was Viet Cong."

The International Conference on Applied Analysis and Applications ICAAA2002 drew only a few mathematicians from North America and Western Europe. Most foreign participants came from former Communist universities in Poland, Russia, and East Germany and were met and attended to by local Vietnamese hosts, who were often former students of theirs, fluent in Polish or Russian or German. Although very basic by Western standards, the conference was clearly extravagant by Vietnamese standards. They arranged for two rooms in the building to be air-conditioned for three hours each day and served hearty but simple three-course conference lunches on long wooden tables covered with oilcloth and decorated with vases of fresh lotus flowers.

The plenary lectures at the conference took place in an auditorium with an ancient public address system, but 90 percent of the audience could not understand much English anyway and just listened politely in silence. The lecture hall looked like a country church, with high ceilings, hard dark wooden benches, a raised podium, and, next to the lectern—instead of a statue of Christ—a larger-than-life white marble bust of Ho Chi Minh. The sculpture struck me as ironic. This courageous tiny country had beaten back the invaders of China in centuries past, and both France and America more recently, only to become mired down in the tyranny and corruption of Communism. But here I was, thirty years after serving in combat against these people, invited to return to Vietnam as a scientist to describe my mathematical discoveries. Instead of treating me like an old enemy, my

Vietnamese colleagues were among the warmest and friendliest people I can remember meeting anywhere. Slowly it sank in. The one hope, the common denominator, was neither one society and system nor the other. What brought us together here was our common curiosity about the secrets of science and mathematics, our shared search for truth and knowledge. On the return flight to Los Angeles, the pilot came on the intercom, identified one of the passengers, a young Army private in desert camouflage uniform, and thanked him for his service to our country. The other passengers loudly applauded their approval. What a difference from my last return from Vietnam in 1970!

But that burst of joy proved to be very short-lived. If I thought the reception in America in 1970 for us combat veterans returning from the war was cold, it was red carpet compared to the reception Dean S. had waiting for me back on campus. Instead of commending me for being perhaps the only Vietnam War veteran ever that Vietnamese universities later invited to return to lecture on his own scientific discoveries, Dean S. had put a stop payment on my state salary. Indefinitely. I went to see the newest director of our department and asked him what my official employment status was. He didn't know, said he'd get right back to me, and two hours later when I ran into him at the copy machine, he shrugged and told me he didn't understand, since his query about my status should have been answered in a few minutes.

"You're new here," I told him. "It's just taking Dean S. and Mr. N. a little time to make something up."

Within the next half hour, the new director came to my office with a sheepish look on his face and told me he had been informed that I was on administrative leave without pay. *Administrative leave without pay?!* That's what they give a cop under investigation for stealing drugs or breaking a student's arm. I shook my head in disbelief and retreated to my office to collect my wits. What now? I had been on voluntary leave without pay many times before and knew that every time a tenured Georgia Tech professor goes on leave of any type, there must be formal approval by the State Board of Regents. There had to be a paper trail. I emailed Legal Affairs to request a copy of the regents' response. They replied the next day that the paperwork had not come back yet. Then I filed an Open Records Act request with the Board of Regents. Several days later, they told me they had never received any leave request for me from Georgia Tech. Dean S. had simply stopped my state salary without notice and without authority. That was the break I needed.

For the past six years, I had been trying to help solve these kinds of abuse problems, and although the president had thanked me repeatedly and even the Board of Regents and state attorney general had weighed in, it was clear that the institution was not going to correct itself. I wanted to move on with my life and research, and I now realized that to wrap this up, I *had* to go outside the state system.

Raised in an anti-union, rural Republican, agribusiness family, I had never even considered asking "the union" for help. After all, I had even worked as a strike breaker in the 1970s Berkeley Teacher's Strike. But now with no salary and my job in jeopardy, I looked up the American Association of University Professors website, which stated its dedication to basic principles of academic freedom, and I contacted their national headquarters. They referred me to Hugh Hudson, executive secretary of the Georgia Branch, who was professor and chair of the history department at nearby Georgia State University.

Upon hearing my story, Dr. Hudson wrote to President Clough, citing the repeated punitive low raises and forced leave without pay. He reminded Clough of the 1940 AAUP Statement of Principles on Academic Freedom and Tenure, *When [professors] speak and write as citizens, they should be free from institutional censorship or discipline*... and wrote, "The Association is thus concerned that the above cited [actions] might be an effort to discipline Professor Hill for exercising his rights, and might therefore constitute a violation of Academic Freedom... which raises serious new questions regarding possible retaliation for the exercise of protected speech." Probably on the advice of the Office of Legal Affairs, Clough never even responded.

But the administration had underestimated this opponent. Dr. Hudson convinced the new chancellor of the University System of Georgia, President Clough's boss, that academic freedom and basic civil rights are crucial to the state's universities. The chancellor ordered President Clough to meet with him and Professor Hudson. All three agreed that I had been a great service to Georgia Tech and corrections were long overdue.

Clough delegated the negotiations to the new provost, Jean-Lou Chameau, who asked me if I would be willing to work out a settlement with Hudson and him alone, without lawyers. After years of fighting for what I knew was right, there now seemed to be a light at the end of the tunnel, and I agreed immediately. During the negotiations, Dr. Hudson was calm, fair, and firm, rescuing the process from stalemate time and again. Chameau maintained a good sense of humor in the proceedings and reminded me that he had inherited the problem and was only trying to find a solution. Then, in a lighter vein, he told me he had been reading Mario Livio's new book *The Golden Ratio*, seen a certain Ted Hill quoted about Benford's law, and checked the credits—yes, it was "his" Ted Hill.

When interviewed by WSB-TV later, Professor Hudson labeled the retaliation against me "severe." He told them that not only is it the *right* of professors to question the status quo, it is their *duty*. "If we did not challenge accepted wisdom," he said, "if we didn't challenge authority, we would still be arguing the world is flat."

In the long run, many things were corrected, and the players in the ordeal also moved on. The negotiations to compensate me for lost salary and several years of punitive raises still came at a price, namely that I would agree to take early retirement. They didn't ask me to leave Atlanta or even to leave campus, but they definitely wanted me out of the hair of Dean S. and Chief Legal Advisor N. and without further access to the grievance process. President Clough and Provost Chameau also both left Georgia Tech, Clough to Washington as Secretary of the Smithsonian Institution and Chameau to California as new president of Cal Tech. Dean S. moved up and down the Georgia Tech administrative ladder, ultimately winding up back down as a chemistry professor.

Chief Legal Advisor Mr. N., on the other hand, continued the tactics the grievance committee had warned President Clough about, but in 2011 that came to a screeching halt. According to the *Atlanta Journal Constitution*, the National Collegiate Athletic Association concluded that N. had "adopted an obstructionist approach" to their investigation into abuses in Tech's nationally prominent athletic program and had "failed to inform the players of the consequences for lying" to investigators. The scandal brought Georgia Tech nasty front-page headlines, a $100,000 fine, four years' probation in intercollegiate football and basketball, and loss of its only Atlantic Coast Conference football championship. Not surprisingly, perhaps, N. was reported to have retired at about the time the NCAA report came out.

Would I speak up again in a similar situation? It's hard to say. If the issues just centered around financial abuses, probably not, although a number of good things came out of the whole struggle at the institutional level: new travel regulations, new annual evaluation processes, and new audit procedures. As far as faculty rights go, I think there was improved understanding of and respect for the Open Records Act, and for the first time in its hundred-year history, Georgia Tech now had an ombudsperson. Conditions did improve slightly for my math colleagues, especially the younger ones, but I didn't see the sweeping changes I'd hoped for. Whistleblowing, as almost everyone knows, is a thankless and absolutely miserable task. It almost always requires a sacrificial lamb, and the collateral damage from the Penn State syndrome is often widespread. Benefits from the battle may not be realized until many years later. All I know was that on the eve of my sixtieth birthday, speaking up had just cost me my job in a damned fine university.

14

PERMANENT SABBATICAL

The AAUP-brokered settlement with Georgia Tech included my early retirement at age sixty, with permanent library and email privileges, shared office space whenever I needed it, and lifetime appointment as professor emeritus of Mathematics. I made plans to head back to California, this time to the Spanish mission town of San Luis Obispo, on the idyllic Central Coast halfway between San Francisco and Los Angeles. Erika was already there, a professor of computer science at Cal Poly, ironically one of the four places on my short list when I had first looked for an academic job all those years ago.

Of course moving west would mean leaving my friends and colleagues in Atlanta, but I was quite sure that many of those friendships would endure, just as they had during my long absences from Tech. The Tenth Street Craftsman bungalow, on the other hand, my home for more than twenty years, would not survive the transition. This unique Math *Ohana* was slated for the bulldozer soon after I left, and although I was greatly relieved that the whistleblower trauma was now behind me, I was also saddened at the imminent loss of this old physical friend.

I wandered through the rooms and reminisced about the huge number of visitors the Hill Hotel had hosted. Some had stayed only a few days or a week, but for many others, the Craftsman had been their Atlanta home for a full semester or more—Ernst from Germany, Victor from Mexico, Vygantas from Lithuania, Christian from Paris, Vince from Australia, Mihael from Moscow, Brett from San Jose, Arno from Austria, Xiao-ling from China, Walter from Belgium, and Marco from Italy. What a privilege it had been for me to share the *ohana* spirit of that charming Craftsman-era bungalow with so many colleagues from around the world.

In my mind, I could see camping gear and dive gear and maps spread out all over the floor. The Craftsman had been the staging ground for many adventures, with Vince to Bonaire and Holland and the Yucatan, with John Oneal to Belize and Luxor and Tikal, and with Massoud to Kauai and Jamaica. A few physical relics still remained, from seashells and flags to a wallaby skin and wall-sized stone print Mayan calendar and a rare six-pointed starfish brought back from one of the annual dive trips to Deadman's Reef.

My thoughts also sped back to the many social events hosted here. The weekly Boys' Night Out gatherings, annual fall quarter parties, math conference receptions, Erika's PhD graduation celebration, an entire wedding ceremony for two of her friends, and Thanksgiving banquets that introduced an international crowd of faculty, friends, and graduate students to this American tradition of food and fellowship. I had especially fond memories of that 1992 Thanksgiving meal where I first came to know Leonid and his family.

Since then we had become exceptionally close over the years, and when his daughter, Yulia, planned to marry, among the fifty-odd wedding guests, I was one of the three non-Russians invited. Leonid had stopped by my campus office the Wednesday before the wedding, looking a bit frazzled.

"We are so delighted you will come to wedding," he said. "We have bilingual friend to share your table. Looks like I'll have to miss Boys' Night Out movie this week, though. Larissa was finally able to book a country club pavilion on the banks of the Chattahoochee River, and we ordered flowers and selected Russian caterer. But we're having trouble getting on the judge's schedule—he doesn't return my calls, and time is getting short."

"Why didn't you ask me?" I said lightheartedly. "I'm an ordained minister—I could have officiated."

He looked at me in disbelief, then shook his head and laughed. "Scuba diver, mathematician, Army Ranger—of course, rabbi too," he said, and ran off to meet his wife.

That night after the movie, my phone rang. I immediately recognized Leonid's strong voice.

"We had family conference," he said. "We want *you* to do the ceremony."

I was stunned. I had been making that offer to friends and relatives for over twenty years. No one had ever taken me up on it before, and by now I considered it a joke.

"Look, Leonid," I said. "I got that license twenty-five years ago from some small church in the Central Valley of California. By mail, from Vietnam. I have no idea if it still exists, or if it does, whether my license is valid here in Georgia."

He was silent for a few long seconds. "Oh," he sighed. "Well, okay, see you tomorrow."

As I lay down to sleep that night, I couldn't get my mind off his sigh. His family really did want me to do the wedding, and the very least I could do was check on the status of my license. The next morning, I phoned information for Modesto, California, and asked for the number for Universal Life Church, "if it still exists," I added. To my surprise, the operator told me there were two numbers listed. I dialed the first, explained my situation to the man who answered, and gave him my certificate number.

"Your ordination is good for life," he said. "You say you're now in Georgia? Let me look it up here on the computer."

I could hear the *clackety-clack-clack* on his keyboard.

"No problem," he said. "Georgia is on the list—you just need two witnesses."

I called Leonid as soon as I hung up, and he was elated. He accepted at once, before I could change my mind, and put his daughter, Yulia, on the phone. She and her fiancé Sasha wanted me to write the service—including the traditional exchange of rings, presentation of family representatives, and vows—but without a single prayer or mention of any deity. I told them I'd do my best.

I rushed off to Barnes & Noble and returned to the Hill Hotel just after midnight with a handful of paperbacks on Western, Eastern, and New Age religious rituals. Using them, I drafted a script built around those aspects of wedding ceremonies that were common across many religions and eras. I simply deleted references and homage to any supreme beings and instead emphasized the historical and logical bases for the rites. Why exchanges of golden rings and not some other object? Gold, because of its beauty and resistance to corrosion, and in the form of a ring since the circle is a universal symbol of eternity, a shape without beginning or end. I wrote it out, read it aloud, polished, and rewrote, again and again. I slept on it, revised once more, and took it to Yulia and Sasha. The wedding was in two days.

They loved the script but requested two changes. First, they wanted the formal ritual to include the official signing of the marriage certificate. In the Soviet Union, they explained, marriage ceremonies often consisted of *the signature alone*, which was done in a special room in the Moscow City Hall. That was no problem. We would set up a small table beside the podium and cover it with a tablecloth of white lace. On top we'd set two tall silver candlesticks with white candles, and between the candles a large silver fountain pen and a pure-white notebook opened on one side to their Georgia marriage certificate, and on the other to my Universal Life Church Ordination Certificate Number 27223, dated February 26, 1969. For their first request, I then simply penciled into the ceremony the phrase "At this point, the final official signature will be affixed to the marriage certificate."

Yulia and Sasha's second request, however, was more challenging. They wanted me to do the vows *in Russian*. Now that was more of a problem, since the few phrases of Russian I remembered from Stanford classes and my trip behind the Iron Curtain were barely intelligible. They had written the words out phonetically, in Roman letters, and tried not to wince as I stumbled through the transliteration. They said it sounded fine, but I knew better.

"Look," I said. "Your job is to try to relax and concentrate on the music and flowers and catering. My job is to learn these lines by Sunday. I have one whole day."

The next morning, I jumped on my mountain bike and sped over to campus, hoping to catch one of our Russian graduate students working on his thesis on Saturday. In the mathematics lounge, I found a student from Bulgaria who was fluent in Russian from his undergraduate years in

Sofia. Unable to suppress a big smile, he coached me through hundreds and hundreds of repetitions of the short vows. First we worked on precise pronunciation of each individual word, one by one. Then we worked on phrases, one after another, and then we put the phrases together and practiced the proper rhythm and intonation. After several hours of drilling, my tutor told me it sounded natural and clear, and for those few phrases, I appeared to be completely fluent in Russian.

Then I rushed home to sort out my wardrobe. In the back of my closet, I found black shoes that were hand-me-downs from Jeff Geronimo and an expensive, sleek, gray Brooks Brothers attorney suit I had diverted from Al Lindseth's latest donation to Goodwill. Its elbows and cuffs were the tiniest bit worn and shiny, so it wasn't good enough for him to appear in court representing millionaire clients, he said. But for my purposes, it was perfect. I added a white banded-collar shirt from Marshall's outlet clothing store, and when I tried on the whole outfit, I looked every inch a bona fide wedding officiant.

During the ceremony the next day, I concentrated on making my English clear, crisp, and strong, since nearly all the guests were Russian émigrés. As the ceremony progressed, I could sense a slight sadness in the audience, a longing for some remnant of the traditions of the old country. When I suddenly broke into effortless Russian for the vows, the shock and delight caused a ripple of spontaneous applause. At the catered Russian feast following the ceremony, the celebrations were frequently punctuated by wedding guests' chants of *Gorka! Gorka! Gorka!*, at which the newlyweds would embrace for long, passionate kisses.

"*Gorka* means bitter, like vodka," explained the man sitting beside me. "Bride and groom have to sweeten it with kiss. Old Russian wedding tradition."

Following the six-course dinner was a series of very formal toasts, delivered by one guest after another, standing at attention, and often reading from several pages of notes. Many of the toasts, an exuberant mixture of Russian and English, alluded to their adventures in this new homeland, with its never-ending surprises and freedoms. More than one of these formal toasts ended in praise for this new land, "*Where even mathematicians can perform marriages!*" That was definitely a high point for me during those difficult last years in Atlanta.

Another high point came from one of Leonid's postdoctoral students. Arno Berger, a thirtyish mathematician from Vienna, had sublet the Hill Hotel shortly before my retirement. I had not gotten to know him or his wife well during my absence, but one late afternoon after I returned to campus, Leonid brought him by my office to have me explain to him the basics of Benford's law.

Lay descriptions of my Benford discoveries had appeared in Mario Livio's *The Golden Ratio* and John Allen Paulos's *A Mathematician Plays the Stock Market*, and these had brought Benford's law to a much wider audience. Applied physicists in Idaho soon discovered empirical evidence of Benford's law in physical experiments with cesium gas and with zinc-bromide liquid solutions and followed that with numerical computer experiments involving classical Lorenz, Henon, and Rösler systems of differential equations. But that was all experimental data, and when we read their paper, Leonid, Arno, and I set out to see whether we could find any example of a common dynamical system that we could mathematically *prove* followed Benford's law.

To our great surprise, we discovered huge general classes of common functions, including essentially all polynomials and exponential functions, which also generate Benford data. For example, if you start with any positive number and keep doubling it, say 3, 6, 12, 24, 48, 96, 192, . . . , the *exact* Benford proportions appear. In all those sequences of numbers, some 30 percent begin with a 1, some 17 percent with a 2, and so on. Same exact percentages if you multiply by 3, or alternate multiplying by 2 and 3. This new revelation about some of the most basic functions in science also came as something of a surprise to the mathematical community and was soon published in the *Transactions of the American Mathematical Society*, the same place I had published my Markov PhD dissertation.

After that first joint collaboration with Arno, he joined me in what would turn out to be the most productive research of my career, lasting more than a decade. Within a week after I had first introduced him to Benford's law, Arno had solved one of the basic problems that had been stumping Leonid and me, and I sensed that Arno was one unusual fellow.

Any question I fired at him was met with deep insights, if not an outright complete answer, and I quickly came to realize that he knew both mathematics and physics at very deep levels. I soon observed that he was always unusually precise in his thinking and speaking, and in that sense, he reminded me of Lester Dubins.

Arno is also remarkably modest and reserved, a true Austrian gentleman scholar and mountain hiker. I knew he had been a product of the elite European *Gymnasium* system, which explained how Latin and literature often worked their way into his conversations. And he had earned his PhD at the Technical University of Vienna. I had known many colleagues with similar backgrounds, but none were quite so precise. One day I looked at Arno's website and saw that his PhD was something specially designated *Sub auspiciis Praesidentis*. I asked him about that.

"My PhD was somewhat rare," he said. "It was personally presented to me in a special ceremony by the president of Austria. My parents made me buy a new suit just for the occasion. Along with the special diploma, I got a gold ring engraved with *Sub auspiciis Praesidentis*, the formal title of the special degree."

"How did you earn that kind of PhD?" I asked, pushing his modesty to the limit.

"A successful candidate essentially has to have straight As in every subject in all nine years of *Gymnasium* and through all university undergraduate and graduate courses and also has to get top grades on his comprehensive exams and defense and thesis. It happens in mathematics maybe once every ten years."

"You mean you also got straight As in ancient Greek and history and English literature, as well as all math and science?" I asked. Yes, he had, and I came to appreciate what a great privilege it was to work with him.

During that last semester on campus before relocating to California, I also met another young man who would soon become an important part of my new life. The room next to my faculty office had been converted into an applied mathematics lab, with desks for several students. As usual I mountain biked from the Hill Hotel to work at my desk, often late at night and on weekends, when the distractions and faculty politics were minimal. One late Friday night, I noticed a light from under the door in the new lab room, and then I saw it again on Saturday night, but this time the door was a few inches ajar. I glanced in and saw a slender young man with close-cropped curly hair who looked to be a little older than other students slumped over his textbooks. These late-night sightings became more frequent, but I never interrupted his studies.

Then, one afternoon when I was ordering a sandwich at the Quiznos café across from campus, I recognized the fellow from the office next door standing behind me in line. Tall, athletic, handsome, now he was alert, with sparkling eyes.

"Say," I said. "Aren't you in the office next to me in Skiles? Are you a math student?"

"Yes, Dr. Hill," he said. "I am. My name is Ryan Hynd."

We shook hands.

"What courses are you taking this term?" I asked, just to be sociable.

"Complex Variables, Abstract Algebra, Undergrad Research Seminar, Statistics," he said, and pursed his brow in thought.

I was just about to tell him it sounded like a pretty heavy load when he continued.

"And Numerical Analysis, Linear Algebra, and Dynamics," he said.

"*Seven math courses this term!*" I exclaimed.

I had never heard of anyone doing more than three university math courses at once, and my first reaction was to thrash the daylights out of his advisor. I figured this nice-appearing young man was practically dead in the water, just because of bad advice. But I restrained myself.

"If you pass all those courses," I said, "then come see me at the end of the semester."

Poor guy, I thought he'd never have a chance, especially being a little older. At semester's end I had forgotten the whole matter when there was a knock on my office door.

"Professor Hill," he said. "You told me to come by if I passed my courses. I got three As, three Bs, and a C."

He handed me his transcript, and I shook my head in amazement as I confirmed it. I reached for my wallet and gave him everything in it, about $100.

"*Congratulations!*" I said. "Too bad you caught me on a light day, this is all I have. Tell you what, next time we're both burning the midnight oil here, I'll take you out to get something to eat. Have a seat."

Ryan told me he was born in Jamaica and had moved with his mother to Florida, where his grand dream had been to play professional basketball. He'd made the playoffs in junior college but could see he'd never make it to the pros, so he transferred to Georgia Tech to study math instead.

"That's why the seven courses," he explained. "I didn't have the math background and had to get up to speed."

That started a wonderful friendship indeed. The rest of my remaining time at Georgia Tech, Ryan and I continued our midnight breaks for late-hour meals of black beans and jerked chicken at Eats on Ponce de Leon. Ryan continued to excel scholastically and won a National Science Foundation scholarship to do his PhD in mathematics wherever he wanted. When he brought me the list of schools that had accepted him, I crossed out Princeton, Cal Tech, and all the others except one. I pointed to the UC Berkeley entry.

"That's where you're going," I said, "*Berkeley*."

"Why there?" he asked.

"First, of course, it has one of the best math departments in the world. And it's on one of the most beautiful campuses you'll ever see, with running streams and redwood glades. Stanford and Princeton and the others have fine campuses too, but the cities they're in are dull. The city of Berkeley has a unique culture and freedom of spirit. You'll see. And as one extra added incentive, I'll soon be moving to the central coast of California and expect to be visiting the Bay Area often. Whenever I do, you get free meals!"

Maybe that pitch helped, but whatever it was, Ryan stopped by Tenth Street to tell me he had chosen Berkeley. I was in the process of closing up the Hill Hotel, and almost everything I owned went to two very appreciative families of immigrant Latin American laborers: Georgia Surplus furniture, lamps, tables, and chairs, followed by kitchen appliances, tools, a lawnmower, ice chests, stereos, and carpets. They filled the open trailer to the brim, trip after trip. I then emptied my Georgia Tech office in the Skiles Math Building, shipped the boxes by UPS, sold my car to a graduate student for $1, and left for California. I was optimistic that the San Luis

Obispo area would be the perfect place to relocate, with its Mediterranean climate and scenic location on Pacific Coast Highway 1, a short Amtrak ride from Santa Barbara and a few hours' drive north on US Highway 101 to San Francisco and Berkeley, or south to Los Angeles.

Although Erika had already bought herself a house in the Laguna Lake section of San Luis Obispo, a typical California three-bedroom, ranch-style home complete with five palm trees, I still secretly hoped to find another condemned house, or at least a fixer-upper. Then we stumbled on a house in the nearby seaside village of Los Osos that elderly friends of hers wanted to sell. The view from the living room was out over Morro Bay, with Hollister Peak and Black Hill in the distance. There were neighbors on the north and south sides, but the west opened out into a grove of live oaks and eucalyptus, and sandy footpaths led right into Montaña de Oro, one of the largest California state parks, right on the Pacific coast.

The house wasn't condemned, but they were selling it "as is," and it definitely needed work. But for me what clinched the decision to buy was the cabin up on the hill behind the main house. An octagonal brown shingle building, it was a little less than 20 feet in diameter, roughly the same size and shape as the tule-thatched huts used by the local Chumash Indians in these same hills for most of the past 10,000 years.

The first thing that hits you when you enter the cabin is the aroma. Natural incense from stacks of Monterey pine, eucalyptus, and sweet California cedar firewood blends with the aromas from decades of wood fires seeping from the porous, unfinished wood walls, just like the inside of a natural cedar chest. The second thing that strikes you is the view through the double-wide picture windows on seven sides. To the west, Pacific waves are crashing on the Sand Spit below. To the north, the volcanic plug of Morro Rock juts up 600 feet out of the blue-green waters at the edge of Morro Bay, and to the east, the horizon several miles away is framed by the Santa Lucia Mountains. In the center of the room, a yard-wide iron firepit under an inverted metal funnel chimney instantly warms the room, even with a small blaze. To the right just inside the door were an electrical outlet and a cold-water sink, everything I needed. I talked to the owner, who also was named Ted.

"I designed that house and cabin," he said. "If you drive up Rodman, you'll notice it's the only house not parallel to the street. I oriented it north-south, for the views and light. I built the cabin for a personal meditation retreat and watched down from there as the main house was being built. It's grandfathered in now, of course, but you can't build anything like that here anymore. When I no longer could walk up to my cabin," he said, "it was time to sell. Not a minute earlier. My knees started giving out when I hit eighty."

As soon as I saw that cabin, I fell in love with the property, and Erika and I joined forces to buy it together, thus ending my long real estate celibacy. I replaced the missing log steps on the spiral trail leading up to the cabin and cleared away the manzanita overgrowth. At barn and garage sales, I found a small hatchet for kindling, a heavier hand axe, two splitting mauls, and a 4-foot one-man tree saw, which I leaned up against the wall just inside the front door. Then I put in a rocking chair, a small oak coffee table, a wooden electric lamp, and a polished pine log futon chair that opens into a narrow sleeping bunk. On the west wall, I installed a wide handmade desk, a shellacked 4x8 sheet of plywood with 135-degree corners cut to fit snugly into the octagon, resting on two old metal file cabinets. I christened the cabin my math *dacha*. In no time it had become my own personal Shangri-La retreat, my Walden.

"You don't have a *real dacha*," said Leonid's son, Yuri, frowning, when I first told him about it. For him and other city-bred Russians, that word conjures up hallowed memories of the rustic summer cabin in the Russian forest that nearly every Muscovite family uses to escape the sweltering summer heat and smog. But when he saw my cabin, his tune changed.

"It even *smells* like a *dacha*!" cried Yuri when he opened the wobbly wooden door and stepped inside. He was immediately hooked and would later return to my little scientific monastery many times, in part to write his Cal Tech PhD thesis in chemistry.

It also called to Ryan, who would hop the Amtrak south from Berkeley to visit us in Los Osos to decompress and hike and to work in my *dacha* on his own Berkeley PhD thesis in mathematics. Lured also by the hiking and tide pooling and wine tasting, a steady stream of visitors started pouring through the new Math *Ohana* West: mathematicians Ulrich Krengel and his wife from Göttingen; Arno and Trudy from Vienna; Frans, José, and Pieter from Amsterdam; Marco from Rome; Massoud from Monterey; and Ron and Leonid from Atlanta. Others included West Point friends of fifty years: Al Lindseth, John Oneal, my Ranger Buddy Jon Steel, my rugby mate Tom Kinane, and my German Military Academy counterpart Peter Hupfer. Our honorary nieces and nephews, the sons and daughters of our friends, all found time to visit and revisit—Jim's son Brett, now a major in the Marines, Jack's sons David and Tom, John Oneal's son and daughter Owen and Adelaide, Wes Clark Jr. and his family. Erika and I added three rooms to the main house to accommodate the constant flow.

Unexpectedly, my own math-related travels still continued year-round. Some were short road trips within California and Nevada, and many others started out of San Luis Obispo's regional airport, with its single gate and baggage carousel. From there I would catch flights to LA or San Francisco or Phoenix, connecting to more distant destinations. Several of the international trips from my Los Osos hub were in service to the greater mathematical community, serving on an external review committee at CIMAT and serving on an accreditation committee for the Ministry of Education of the United Arab Emirates to help establish a new bachelor's program at the University of Sharjah. I also was invited to give talks at the University of Utrecht; the University of Canterbury on New Zealand's South Island; the Tinbergen Institute in Amsterdam; the universities of Naples, Pescara, and Rome; and in Santa Fe as keynote speaker for the first international workshop on Benford's law. One month every year, usually June, I earmarked for my favorite city in the world, Amsterdam, where I continued to mix research and mentoring at the Free University with long bike excursions. With no teaching and no committees and no grant deadlines, I was free as a bird to travel and do mathematics. Permanent sabbatical.

University of Costa Rica mathematician Javier Trejos asked me to speak at the next biannual Central American Mathematics Conference. To help prepare for my upcoming lecture in Spanish, I arrived in San José a week early and arranged an intensive five-day, one-on-one refresher course at the same language institute where I had learned Spanish twelve years earlier. Again my instructor asked about my education, and again the questions about West Point came up. I told her the story about meeting former President Figueres.

Her voice turned soft and sad as she described the recent high-profile corruption scandals that had caused many Costa Ricans to completely distrust their national government. Three former presidents of Costa Rica, she told me, were implicated in fraudulent financial transactions. Two of them, Calderon and Rodriguez, were currently under house arrest after serving short prison sentences. The third had moved to Switzerland shortly after leaving office, following a scandal for receiving a $900,000 payment for consulting services from the French telecommunications firm Alcatel, which at the time was involved in concession contract negotiations with the Costa Rican Electricity Institute. This last culprit was none other than the alleged West Point cheater I had met at the Gran Hotel de Costa Rica, José María Figueres! I guess the "year of reflection" must have worn off by then.

* * *

When I gave a talk at a conference in Banff, Canada, to honor Leonid's sixtieth birthday, the high temperature for the week was on Wednesday afternoon—minus 15 degrees Fahrenheit. After dinner we participants warmed up at a long table in the conference dorm lounge and did what all Russians are genetically engineered to do: we drank vodka and told stories. One of the other mathematicians recalled a fair-division lecture I had given in Germany years before, and then Leonid told the group, mostly expatriate Russian mathematicians, about my Volkswagen camper trip behind the Iron Curtain. None had ever heard of such a trip, and they peppered me with questions. I described the border crossing, the accident, and being barred from world-famous Moscow State University. Many of the mathematicians at the table had graduated from Moscow State and were offended.

"*Certainly* it was possible for Western mathematicians to visit!" one objected, and others immediately agreed, with resounding affirmations of "*Da, da!*"

I stuck to my story, but they insisted that many foreign mathematicians had visited, including Americans. I told them again how guards had expelled me into the snow, and they looked at each other and shook their heads.

"Where exactly were those guards?" one finally asked.

"The front entrance," I answered. They all rolled their eyes.

"Of *course*," one of my new friends cried. "Everybody knew you couldn't use the *front* entrance! That was only for Party bigwigs and KGB officials."

We all laughed, and they shook their heads and clinked their vodka glasses to me.

In March 2007, the new International University of Vietnam in Ho Chi Minh City invited me to speak, and I returned to Saigon for the first time in thirty-eight years. My hosts rolled out the red carpet—a chauffeured government car, invited lectures at two universities, and dinner with the rector (president) of the university, Dr. Phan Quoc Khanh, who told me over stuffed snails about his time as a lieutenant in the North Vietnamese Army during my year in the war.

After my Saigon lectures, I wanted to revisit the two sites I remembered most vividly from the war: Cu Chi, the wartime base of the 25th Infantry's 65th Combat Engineer Battalion, and Nui Ba Den, the 3,000-foot volcanic "Black Virgin" peak in Tay Ninh Province on the Cambodian border. In 1969 I had spent six months with the 65th in Cu Chi and less than an hour on top of the Black Virgin. Four decades later, I found the now-famous tunnels of Cu Chi to be a Disneyland disappointment, surrounded by souvenir stands and Vietnamese fast-food stalls. The original sapper tunnels had been widened and illuminated and ventilated to accommodate Western tourists, and above ground were scores of models of snares, pitfalls, and punji-stake traps used to maim and kill GIs. For me, the tunnel exhibit was tragic and farcical all at the same time.

The trip to Nui Ba Den, on the other hand, was much more powerful and positive. I booked a car and guide, Le, a short, wiry young man from Saigon with a diamond stud in his nose and a suntanned, shaved head. Le spoke very passable English, and we immediately hit it off. Many Vietnamese were also climbing in the 100-degree heat, and they mistook Le for a monk guiding me to the Buddhist cave-temple a third of the way up the mountain. No other Westerners were making the pilgrimage, and after placing offerings of incense and flowers and fruit on the altar, the worshipers all turned back down the mountain.

Le also turned to go down, but I stopped him and pointed farther up to the peak. He'd thought I had meant just going to the temple. He told me neither he nor anyone he knew had ever been to the top, and he didn't know what to expect. I explained that during the Vietnam War, I had been dropped on the summit of Nui Ba Den by helicopter to resupply a tiny radio relay station, where a handful of American troops lived in bunkers surrounded by barbed-wire barricades.

"The view from the top," I told him, "is *well* worth the trouble. Up there you can look down on the fertile plain, flat as a table, far as the eye can see. It's a living mosaic, a multicolored masterpiece with water buffaloes working rice paddies, water shimmering through irrigation canals, and tiny ant people coming and going in their little thatched huts far below. You can even see into Cambodia."

"Okay," he said. "I ready to give it try. We go!"

Le and I began the push upward. The humidity and heat lessened a little as we gained altitude, but still we poured sweat. Halfway up, the path was barely discernible, marked only occasionally by red arrows painted on tree trunks and rock faces. Where it became completely overgrown, we bushwhacked. The trail was now treacherous in places, and we were tiring. "I keep in good physical condition," I reminded myself, "exactly so I can take advantage of unexpected opportunities like this." Now I was keeping up with a climber forty years my junior. At a rest stop, Le revealed that he had brought no water at all—the few bottles in my rucksack would have to do for us both.

Upward we struggled. We used tree roots to pull ourselves up overhangs. With my Swiss army knife, I hacked a bamboo staff to use for probing and for three-point stability on the slippery rainforest slope. Four hours after we started, near the summit, I rested briefly in the cool darkness of a deep lava cave. A small outcropping inside contained a makeshift altar, an earthenware bowl holding incense ashes and bits of tinfoil. I stooped over and picked up a jagged 3-inch piece of rusty shrapnel. When I stepped back out into daylight again, I could see the sky slicing through the base of the trees ahead. We were very near the summit now, and I realized how incredibly lucky I had been during my wartime sortie to the mountain. In 1969 we knew that Viet Cong had infiltrated and occupied the sides of the ancient volcano, but we had no idea just how close the enemy really was. This natural bunker was only a grenade's throw from where our helicopter had landed.

Exhausted and out of water, we finally reached the peak. My heart stopped. There in front of me was another tiny, ramshackle military radio relay and observation post, surrounded by rusty razor wire. Waving from the antenna now, however, in place of the Stars and Stripes, was a flag that had raised terror in our hearts four decades earlier, the Viet Cong's red flag with yellow star. As far as I knew, the mere existence of this outpost could be classified, and I tried to shrink back into the shadows.

But my fears were unwarranted. Two soldiers in shorts and T-shirts came out to greet their unexpected visitors and offered us desperately needed water and sweet, ripe, sun-warmed bananas. Le and I relaxed, and he agreed that the view was all I had promised. After we had rested, we hobbled back down the mountain.

Some friends criticized me for making that hike—failing to take adequate provisions and risking a run-in with Communist soldiers on a remote jungle mountaintop. Others more generally condemned my whole visit to Vietnam. "Why are you supporting a Communist philosophy that wants to destroy us?" But most Vietnam veterans I know have always harbored nagging doubts about their participation in the war, and for me to return, in peace, as a scientist, was a very special privilege. This opportunity to help repair some of the damage inflicted on this remarkable people and culture by a millennium of invaders brought a welcome sense of relief and closure. In my heart, I now knew it was exactly the right thing for me, and those friendly soldiers at the summit had confirmed it.

* * *

My new Los Osos base also offered easy access to Berkeley, my second favorite city, and I made frequent trips there. Dubins had taken what he called "early retirement" at age eighty-four, and over the years he and I had gone from a formal professor-student relationship to one of collegiality and first-name friendship. He had stayed in the Hill Hotel in Atlanta, and I now frequently stayed at the rambling Spruce Street *Ohana* that Lester had bought late into his sixties. He too had a steady stream of international visitors there, and we enjoyed many bicycle rides followed by multicultural buffet dinners around his big dining room table. Immersed in his own PhD thesis challenges at Berkeley, Ryan had also become Lester's fast friend and frequent dining companion. He even began quoting Dubins's sharp insights, often interrupting me with, "Now Lester would question the use of that word."

My relationship with my PhD alma mater continued to deepen, and like many retirees, I started thinking about giving something back, to contribute to the university that had given me a chance to become a mathematician. For starters, and on a lighter note, I decided to give back something that was actually theirs to begin with—the old PhC canoe. Russ had been using it during my foreign travels and had completely restored the classic Old Town under the tutelage of Schuyler Thomson, one of America's few surviving professional wood canoe builders. Russ gave his blessing to my idea immediately.

"Sure," he said, "if Berkeley ever missed it at all. To them it was probably just another inventory item on the shelf."

I called the Berkeley Physical Education Department and asked if anyone on the staff had been in Women's PE thirty years earlier. The receptionist suggested I talk to Professor Emeritus Dr. Roberta Park. When I reached Dr. Park and asked if anyone knew anything about an "old canoe," she interrupted me politely.

"Yes," she said. "We used to have one—it was historical even then and had been part of the department long before my time. It was a blue canoe. A *royal* blue Old Town canoe. It went missing in 1977."

I explained how I had "liberated" it and now wished to return it to Berkeley, if the university was interested. She jumped at the chance and agreed to meet with me and the head of the Women's PE department, Karen Scott, on campus at the Bancroft Library.

Dr. Park was an elegant, silver-haired lady, and Ms. Scott a tall, attractive woman who looked like a former student-athlete. I liked them both and apologized for my "misappropriation" of the Old Town the past three decades, holding out my arms in jest for them to slap on the handcuffs. The Army had considered my misappropriation of their Jeep as a serious offense, but Dr. Park was so thrilled at the prospect of seeing their beloved Old Town again and in mint condition—as I assured them it was—that they almost forgave me on the spot.

I told them that, yes, it had been blue, but I had painted it red the same night I took it, and no one but me knew it had been royal blue.

"But you were mistaken about one thing," I told them. "I borrowed it in 1976, not 1977. You must not have noticed it was gone until 1977."

"That's right," said Ms. Scott. "I was on sabbatical in 1976, and when I returned in 1977 and told my girls to go get the canoe, they said it had *vanished*! I thought I'd never see it again. It had cane seats, beautiful lines."

"I have one more request," said Ms. Scott. "Please write down a brief history of the canoe's odyssey during those decades. People will want to know more about its adventures."

That canoe had made many journeys during its absence. I had taken it atop my Volkswagen van all the way across America, paddling as I went, from Lake Tahoe to the Chattahoochee River and then south into the Okefenokee Swamp and remote swamp trails in the western Everglades. I knew Russ had also taken it on rivers and lakes in Connecticut and Illinois and into the northern lakes of Wisconsin. The Old Town had tasted the tributaries of the Mississippi and even the salt seas of the Atlantic on a short jaunt to a small island off the coast of Rhode Island. Russ and I made good on our promise, flew to Wisconsin, and triple-bubble-wrapped the Old Town like a museum piece for its UPS journey home to Berkeley.

* * *

Besides the canoe, I also wanted to make a *real* contribution to Berkeley, preferably one directly related to mathematics. I thought about the Early American mathematics books I had helped my father accumulate over the past thirty years. The collection, half predating 1850, now totaled nearly 1,000 volumes, including the first American printing of Newton's *Principia*, the only known copy of Fenning's 1789 *Ready Reckoner*, and Lee's 1797 *American Accountant*, which has the first printed appearance of the American dollar sign. Many of the other books in the collection were also very rare, and some were singular works of art. The only book we had parted with during those three decades of collecting was a second edition 1832 copy of Tobias Ostrander's *The Mathematical Expositor: Containing Rules, Theorems, Lemmae, and Explanation of the Mathematical Sciences*. When we learned that it was the only known copy of a book printed by Strong & Grandin Publishers, the first publisher of the Book of Mormon, my father and I donated it to the Church of Jesus Christ of Latter-day Saints. The Ostrander book is now permanently housed in its own display case in the center of the Grandin Building historical museum in Palmyra, New York, the birthplace of the Mormon religion.

Taken individually, the books were of significant historical and pedagogical interest. Taken together, antique book dealers told me, the collection was unique. When I contacted them, the Bancroft librarians at Berkeley told me they'd love to house the collection, and I made the necessary arrangements to transfer it. When I told the rare books librarian at Georgia Tech, she exclaimed, "Oh, why Berkeley is the *perfect* place for those books! You're doing exactly the right thing, making them available to scholars of the history of mathematics."

After the collection arrived in Berkeley, the university library archivist asked me to help select some of the texts for display during Bancroft Library's forthcoming 2005 Exposition on the History of Mathematics at Berkeley. In gratitude he presented me with a detailed draft on the Berkeley Math Department's history, written by Professor Calvin Moore, former chair of Mathematics and dean for Physical Sciences. I always knew that Göttingen had played a central role in the development of American mathematics, but as I read through Moore's manuscript, I realized just how important West Point had also been, not only to American mathematics in general but also especially to Berkeley.

The first full professor of mathematics at Berkeley, appointed in 1869, was William Welcker of the West Point Class of 1851, followed shortly by the first assistant professor, Frank Soule Jr., Class of 1866, exactly one century earlier than Wes and Al and Jon and Gary and I had graduated. Moore wrote that Welcker and Soule "imported the West Point curriculum *en toto*" to Berkeley, including adoption of the standard Academy mathematics textbooks of Davies, Class of 1815, and Church, Class of 1828. I had just donated copies of both those texts to the Bancroft Library! That inspired me to continue searching for additions to the collection, which I would often hand-deliver.

On one of those jaunts up to Berkeley, Jon Steel and Lester and I met for dim sum. Lester had introduced us to the Hong Kong East Ocean restaurant on the Emeryville Peninsula, which juts like a giant curved sea lion tooth out into San Francisco Bay. Jon had never eaten dim sum before and marveled at the fare, from Siamese bird nest and shredded abalone with jellyfish to duck bills and chicken feet. After dining the three of us took a stroll along the Bay, soaking up the sunshine and the fragrant sea salt and cedar air. Jon observed that dim sum was often difficult to share equally, since the dishes arrived in servings of three or four, but we were sometimes a group of five. That led us to reminiscences about dividing chocolate layer cakes via Big Dick at West Point and Lester's famous mathematical paper "How to Cut a Cake Fairly."

Jon asked, "But isn't it always possible to divide things fairly?"

"Well," Lester said, "suppose a man walks up to the three of us and says, 'I have $100 million cash I will give the three of you, but only if you all agree how to divide it amongst yourselves. If you can't agree, nobody gets anything.'"

Eighty-five years old, and with wispy white hair dancing in the wind, his eyes burned with the mischief of an eighteen-year-old mathematician about to let the hammer drop.

"Now," Lester continued, "I immediately pipe up and say that I want $99 million for myself, and you two guys can split the remaining $1 million any way you want. No deals, no discussion. Take it or leave it."

In an instant, the three of us were off in a world of fair-division mathematics and game theory, testing old ideas and trying new ones. Suddenly Jon stopped.

"Wait a minute," he said. "You guys got *paid* to think about stuff like this?"

"Only our whole careers," I said. "Best job in the world, no doubt about it. Paid just to think about things exactly like Lester's $100 million problem. Life simply isn't a fair-division problem."

* * *

One evening I was eating dinner with nonmath friends at home in Los Osos, telling them of my recent travels, when the subject of fair division came up once again. I described Dubins's and Spanier's elegant cake-cutting algorithm.

"That's dessert," teased one friend. "And we're still on the main course. Any math theorems for that?"

"Of course," I replied. "For example, there's the famous Ham Sandwich Theorem of Steinhaus. It says that any *n* objects in *n*-space can be simultaneously bisected by a single hyperplane. In three dimensions, for example, it means that every ham sandwich with three ingredients—say, bread, ham, and cheese—can be cut by a single planar cut of a knife so that each of the three ingredients is simultaneously exactly bisected. Half the bread on each side of the cut, half the ham, and half the cheese. No matter how neatly or how sloppily the sandwich is made."

My companions tried to picture it and frowned.

"Okay," I said. "It's not so easy to visualize. Let's look at the case for two dimensions, which I call the Pizza Pie Theorem. Steinhaus's result says that there is always a way to cut a pepperoni pizza with a straight-line cut so that exactly half the cheese and half the sausage are on each side. Since we're not having Italian food tonight, suppose I sprinkle some salt and some pepper on the table, any amount of each. The theorem says there's always a single straight line that bisects both the salt and the pepper."

I poured some of each on the table and demonstrated. They drew some points on a napkin to try to find a case where there was no such line, but every time I found one.

"Is there any practical application of that?" asked one.

"Maybe," I told them. "I've read that some political scientists are trying to use it to solve gerrymandering problems. You see, the Pizza Pie Theorem also says that in every voting district, there is always a straight line so that exactly half the Democrats are on each side and half the Republicans. No matter how many of each there are."

I demonstrated with Ds and Rs scribbled on a napkin and noticed that I even could always find a bisecting line that always passed through both a Democrat and a Republican. When I couldn't find any examples where it wasn't possible to find such a Democrat and Republican, I figured there might just be another previously undiscovered theorem.

I checked the literature afterward, and when I couldn't find any such theorem, nor find a proof as quickly as I'd expected, I again enlisted my friend and former colleague John Elton, and after a few months, we cracked it. We improved Steinhaus's classical theorem by showing that there is always a bisecting hyperplane that also touches each of the objects. For example, at any given instant in time, *snap!*, there is always one planet, one moon, and one asteroid in our solar system, and a flat plane passing through those three bodies, so that each side of the plane has exactly half the planetary mass, half the lunar mass, and half the asteroidal mass of our entire solar system. John and I published that one in 2011 in the *European Journal of Combinatorics*.

* * *

One afternoon I was sitting in my math *dacha*, watching the fog roll over Morro Rock, talking to Ron Fox on the phone about universal physical constants. We were both interested in the philosophy behind Planck's constant and the speed of light and Newton's universal gravitational constant.

"Is Avogadro's number odd or even?" I teased him.

Avogadro's number, *NA*, is the fundamental physical constant that links the macroscopic physical world of objects that we can see and hold in our hand with the submicroscopic, invisible world of atoms. In theory *NA* specifies the exact number of atoms in a palm-sized chunk of carbon or silicon. More precisely, the official scientific definition says that *NA* is the *exact* number of atoms in 12 grams of carbon-12. The number is an astronomical twenty-four digits long, which means that if you gathered 1 million atoms every single *second* since the Big Bang and multiplied that by ten, you would have close to *NA* atoms. Of those twenty-four digits, only the first eight are known exactly, and laboratories around the world are using different experiments to try to figure out the ninth and tenth digits. No one has any idea what the final twenty-fourth digit is, let alone a clue as to whether it is odd or even.

"Physicists don't ask that kind of question," Ron said with a sniff.

"Well, it has to be an integer, doesn't it?" I said. "Since it's the exact number of atoms in something, any schoolchild could tell you it has to be an integer. So it has to be odd or even."

As soon as I heard Ron's response, I knew we were on to something. Asking an unconventional question is often the key to making progress in science. Ron and I started brainstorming about what kind of number *NA* should be, and it hit me that if you thought of the specimen as a cube of carbon-12, like a sugar cube but made of copper, then *NA* would have to be a perfect numerical cube. And Ron saw immediately that the number of atoms on each side of the cube would only have eight digits, which is well within today's standards of error. When I ran down to the main house for a scientific calculator, I called him back and told him that among the 200 quadrillion values within the internationally accepted range of values for *NA,* only a handful were perfect cubes, and the closest was 84,446,888 cubed.

Suddenly it dawned on us that if you took that number, 84,446,888 cubed, as the *definition* of Avogadro's number, it would be consistent with all current scientific theories and could also solve what was called the Kilogram Problem. The current formal scientific definition of 1 *kilogram* is that a kilogram is exactly the mass of *Le Grand K*, a single unique platinum-iridium artifact housed in a vault outside Paris. All the other six official standard units for physical measurements—length, time, electrical current, temperature, amount of substance, and luminosity—now had purely intrinsic scientific definitions. These definitions could, in principle, be emailed to the other end of the universe to tell alien scientists exactly what units we are using in our experiments. But for mass, we still have to tell our ET correspondents, "Sorry, you have to come to Paris to see what a kilogram is." The related and more pressing earthbound scientific problem is that the official physical object *Le Grand K* changes in size every time it is measured or cleaned, since a few atoms rub off each time. That means that the number of atoms in *Le Grand K* is changing in time, implying that *NA*, and hence the official mass of every single atom of carbon in the universe, is also changing in time. But that contradicts scientific common sense.

Our new proposed exact value for Avogadro's number could also eliminate the necessity of *Le Grand K* once and for all, since using our new definition would mean that 12 grams is simply the mass of 84,446,888 cubed carbon-12 atoms, and thus there would be no need for any manmade artifact ever again. Ron and I were not aware then that the Kilogram Problem was a very hot topic, as scientists had been looking for a way to get rid of the antiquated *Le Grand K* definition for decades. The idea was so clean and simple that I decided to document it by placing it on the open-access physics Internet archives. Within days, David Schoonmaker, editor of *American Scientist*, emailed me that he would like Ron and me to write an article on the idea. It was the first time in over thirty years of publishing scientific research that I had an article accepted within a day of submission and had galleys back within two days.

In trying to choose the best integer for the cube, I contacted the National Institute of Standards and Technology, the keepers of the official values of the fundamental physical constants. I learned that they gather data from different laboratories that use two entirely different methods, one an electronic balance and the other a silicon sphere, to arrive at their recommended values. I asked how they combined the data, and when I learned it was simply adjusted by a human "task force," I figured there must be some better mathematical method for combining the data. When searching the literature did not turn anything up, I talked to statisticians, who told me the problem was ill posed. You can't combine data from two completely different types of experiments. Another challenge.

After six months of trying all sorts of ideas, I finally hit upon a clean and explicit formula that minimized the loss of information in combining the data. Ron suggested the name "conflation," and I spent months checking the complicated proofs and incorporating real-life experimental data from Jack, who was still working at Lawrence Berkeley Labs. Within a week of our posting the results, we received an email from a statistician at Vattenfall, one of Europe's largest generators of electricity, saying our formula was exactly what they needed, and they were already using it. It dawned on me that this idea, too, was based on breaking the old rule of not mixing apples with oranges that had been key in cracking Benford's law.

The Benford ideas also continued to flourish, and in 2015, after a decade of collaboration with Arno, Princeton University Press published our book *An Introduction to Benford's Law*, the first comprehensive mathematical treatment of that phenomenon. Along the way, Arno and I had made many more unexpected discoveries, including the fact that the 300-year-old Newton's method, one of the most widely used algorithms in all applied mathematics, obeys the 125-year-old Benford's law. Nobody ever saw the connection before.

Just as the book was about to appear, two astrophysicists at the European Center for Nuclear Research in Switzerland published a paper with their observation that the current empirical tables of distances to stars and galaxies follow Benford's law quite closely. I posed it as a challenge to Ron for us to come up with a logical argument, based on mathematics and physics, why this might be the case. Ron soon suggested trying to use Hubble's law about the expansion of the universe together with observations about the finite speed of light. After rethinking his ideas, I combined them with two mathematical corollaries of theorems from our new book, and Ron and I completed a math-physics argument for why the distances to stars and galaxies should obey Benford's law. That paper, my first ever in a physics research journal, was soon published in the *Journal of Astrophysics and Astronomy*. I never could have imagined just how much plain fun "retirement" would be!

My Los Osos world turned out to be just a natural extension of my whole life and career, with focus on the two most important parts for me—mathematics and friends. I still have my laboratory in the mind, as well as frequent visitors, both scientific and social. Our annual trips to Deadman's Reef remain welcome adventure breaks, and Vince and I have not missed a single one in the past twenty-five years. Jeff has made most of them, and during the past ten years, Ryan has also become an integral part of the core dive team. We needed new blood and could not have done better than with him, a young mathematician-athlete ready to add ideas and insights to discussions jumping between strategies for catching lobsters and strategies for math finance models. Nearby Cal Poly appointed me Research Scholar in Residence. There I help mentor young faculty and collaborate on research. I'm not at all ready to pack the adventures of science in yet, but the long gray line of mathematicians, including people like Ryan, now professor of mathematics at the University of Pennsylvania, is ready to take the next lap with the mathematics baton.

I'm sure I would have been happy in other professions too, but the only one that seems to even come close is that of inventor. That's not surprising, I guess, since the two professions look like first cousins. Sometimes an inventor's research is motivated by a concrete need, such as an aerosol nozzle for spraying insecticide. At other times, he stumbles on to something quite by accident and only discovers a use for it later, as happened with the nonpermanent glue used in Post-it Notes. I've known several successful inventors personally, and their curiosity and persistence and optimism are infectious. One invented a room-sized machine for packaging frozen fish, and the other modified an unrelated previous contraption of his to invent an automatic piggybank desk calendar.

During our West Point years, Jon Steel and I had visited several Army laboratories, including the Aberdeen Proving Ground. There, in an isolated building reminiscent of the warehouse in the final scene of *Raiders of the Lost Ark*, were stack after stack of crates of obsolete spare parts and military devices. A team of Defense Department inventors had the task of finding uses for these odd objects, be it for fishing weights or children's toys or anything else short of melting them down for scrap metal. That job might have been *almost* as much fun as being a mathematician, but not quite. A mathematician doesn't need tools or scraps or a lab, just paper and pencil, a napkin and a pen, a patch of sand and a stick. For someone like me who loves freedom, both intellectual and physical, mathematics is a glorious life. When friends first visit my math *dacha*, they wonder aloud how in the world I can work in such an idyllic setting.

"Easy," I assure them. "In fact, the beauty of nature is actually one of my keys to deciding what math to work on. When that trail outside looks more enticing than the scribbled math notes on my desk, it's time for me to take a hike. When the hiking and beachcombing get old, I return here to my *dacha*, crank up a roaring blaze in the firepit, settle into the rocking chair, and kick-start the math adventures again. That aroma from wood smoke and eucalyptus buttons you smell brings back memories of a quarter century of math in front of my fireplaces in Berkeley and Atlanta and spurs me happily on to the next theorem quest."

"How do you decide the next direction?" one asked. "How do you keep from getting stuck in one groove and following a dull trail?"

"I let my curiosity lead the way," I said, "just like on a new hike or dive. Then, when I figure I might be on to something, the best initial test for me is to try to phrase the question in very simple terms and run it by my friends. I never work on a problem that I can't explain to them in everyday language."

"Okay, so your mathematical carpet ride has been an adventure, and you say the ride isn't over yet. So what's next?" she challenged me.

But I was already out the door, with rucksack on my back, hiking stick in hand, and a couple of differential equations about rolling stones in my head. I don't know what's next, and don't want to know, either in life or in mathematics. I only hope to continue having the thrills of *eureka!* moments and sharing insights and discoveries with students and friends and colleagues around the world. And, from time to time, coming up with a few more ideas from the laboratory in my own mind to add to the master archive of mathematics.

POSTSCRIPT

Here I am sitting in my math *dacha*, feeding logs into a blazing fire in my beloved redwood octagon, sucking in the sweet scents of pine and cedar. Mathematical ideas are sprawled out on my desk, and I'm longing to get back to them. But after reading a draft of this memoir, friends suggested I end with a few thoughts reflecting on how a mathematical journey is like no other. Are mathematicians different from other creative artists? From other scientists? What are the *eureka!* moments really like, and how does the creative process work in mathematics? Through the *dacha's* picture windows are the distractions of Cerro Alto peak across Morro Bay and the trail outside my window leading into Montaña de Oro State Park. Can I possibly explain the mathematics journey?

In his classic memoir *A Mathematician's Apology*, Cambridge professor G. H. Hardy, one of the leading theoretical mathematicians of the twentieth century, said that he found it a melancholy experience for a professional mathematician to find himself writing about mathematics, since the function of a mathematician is to prove new theorems and add to mathematics, not talk about it. "Exposition," he wrote, "is work for second-rate minds." But I am of a different bent, and not being the melancholy sort, will give it a go as long as the reader accepts in advance that these are my own personal views and are not meant to speak for other mathematicians. These reflections are based on personal experiences with my friends—carpenters and salesmen and nurses, doctors of chemistry and political science and medicine, and artists from sculptors to movie producers. And of course, as with Bob Dylan, some of those friends are mathematicians. It is over fireside chats, Third World trips, and shared physical and intellectual adventures with them that I formed these impressions.

The goal of painters, musicians, poets, and other artists, as I see it, is to create new and beautiful patterns. As Hardy observed, a mathematician, like a painter or a poet, is also a maker of patterns. The difference is solely in the means. Whereas a painter makes patterns with shapes and colors and textures, a musician with sounds and rhythms, and a poet with words, the mathematician makes patterns with *logic*. People often wonder whether getting a PhD in mathematics is harder than getting a PhD in other fields. Among all the people I know who have attempted to get PhDs, the only ones who have struggled more than three decades on a dissertation are mathematicians. But is that because math is "harder"? For me to write a symphony or a PhD thesis in music would be utterly impossible. I don't think mathematics is harder—it's simply different.

In many ways, mathematics is even different from other sciences. When people first meet my physicist and computer scientist and chemist friends, they think they have some idea of what each line of work entails and leave it at that. The physicist measures gravity waves and distances to stars, the computer scientist develops hardware and software, and the chemist mixes multicolored solutions in test tubes and occasionally blows up the lab. But when new acquaintances learn my profession, they invariably declare they have no clue what a mathematician does. They are puzzled, intimidated. Popular films such as *Good Will Hunting* and *A Beautiful Mind* only exacerbate the impression of weirdness, and the reaction is almost never neutral. Either my new acquaintances were always good at math but never pursued it or, more frequently, math was their worst grade in school. It is the only subject I know of which people claim to have a "phobia."

Among fellow scientists, we mathematicians are fond of modestly referring to our field as "the queen of the sciences," and the distinction is largely embodied in the difference between a *theory* and a *theorem*. A theory is educated guesswork about how or why something might be true. Theories come and go. Geocentric theories of the solar system were eventually replaced by heliocentric theories, and one Big Bang theory follows another. A theorem, on the other hand, is a conclusion that can be rigorously *proved* to be true based on accepted premises and pure logic. Theorems do not come and go—they are more or less eternal. As the ancient Greeks discovered and proved, if the lengths of the two sides of a right triangle are *a* and *b*, then the length of the hypotenuse is the square root of $a^2 + b^2$. Not *approximately* the square root of $a^2 + b^2$, or *usually* the square root of $a^2 + b^2$, or the square root of $a^2 + b^2$ until a better formula comes along. It is always *exactly* the square root of $a^2 + b^2$, and always will be. On Earth, on Planet Z, everywhere. Similarly, the Central Limit Theorem and the Fundamental Theorem of Algebra, reverified by successive generations of scholars, are accepted as true by essentially all scientists. And the main "job" of theoretical mathematicians is to find new theorems and prove them.

Where are these theorems to be found? Hungarian Paul Erdös, one of the most prolific and eccentric mathematicians in history, put it this way. An avowed atheist, Erdös maintained that the "Supreme Fascist" in the sky, whom he nicknamed "SF," has a master mathematics Book containing all theorems and their most elegant proofs. The job of mathematicians, Erdös said, is to discover the theorems in the SF's unseen Book.

I met Erdös several times in Atlanta and once played ping-pong singles with him at Oberwolfach. After our match, I asked him about a tiny gem of a conjecture of his in measure theory. Does every planar set of sufficiently large area contain three points that form a triangle of area exactly one? For example, can every county with area at least 250 square kilometers, no matter how irregular its shape, always erect three radio towers so that the triangle they form has area exactly 100 square kilometers? Yes or no? The SF's Book already has the answer, but we do not. Fifty years after Erdös raised the question, we still do not know. And if we want to tackle older problems, the ancient Greeks left us a few easy-to-state challenges about "perfect integers" that no one has solved in two thousand years.

One summer evening, Ryan and I were enjoying a midnight gelato at an outdoor sidewalk café on Haarlemmerstraat in Amsterdam when a new acquaintance expressed surprise at my fluent Dutch. I explained that I had lived in Holland off and on for some three years. Did I speak other languages? Yes, I told her, a fair bit of German and Spanish, and a few words of Japanese, since I had also lived in Germany and Costa Rica and Japan.

"What kind of work are you in, that you can travel so much?" she asked. When I told her I was a mathematician, she got it immediately. "I see," she said, "because mathematics is completely universal."

"Exactly," I replied. "I figure I can parachute into any country on Earth and they will need a mathematician. Maybe it's just basic algebra and trigonometry to estimate crop yields or lay out pyramids, and maybe it's state-of-the-art theory to design security codes or help solve government financial crises."

Many of my colleagues spend their careers looking not for theorems *per se*, but rather for practical solutions to concrete problems like these, problems that originate outside mathematics proper. Others focus on internal mathematical questions so abstract that even the rest of us mathematicians can't begin to understand a word or symbol. I'm very happily in the middle. I often use observations and questions from real life to try to discover basic new mathematical theorems—questions like whether fair borders exist or why numbers on the World Wide Web follow Benford's law. For me, searching for mathematical answers to questions like that is simply irresistible, just as the frontiers of new continents must have been to the early explorers. And because, for me, proving theorems is downright *fun*.

"You've got to be kidding," a friend said recently. "*Fun?* You say that a lot, and I know you told your students you'd be doing mathematics whether or not they paid you, but be honest—that's got to be a line of hooey."

"*Au contraire*," I said. "Look at the evidence—I haven't been paid to prove theorems for ten years now, and I'm still cranking away. And still loving every minute."

I scratched my head to think about how I could begin to explain and remembered that my friend, an outspoken nonscientist, was addicted to Sudoku.

"Think about how you feel when you finally solve a tough Sudoku puzzle," I said. "You get that warm and fuzzy dopamine rush. We get a very similar buzz, only a thousand times more intense. Both types of puzzles, Sudoku and math proofs, are 100 percent logic. The huge difference between them is that a human designed yours, and it has a known solution. But no other mortal has ever solved our theorem puzzles before, and when we do manage to crack one, we're high as a kite. Not only from finally having solved it, but also because when that fat math lady finally sings, a story suddenly appears, a story about cakes or functions or statistical patterns that links it to the whole universe of theorems."

The English physicist Hawking said that making a scientific discovery is like sex, but it lasts longer. As Ron pointed out to me once, there are actually two kinds of math highs: the one where you get the key idea and the one when you actually *prove* it. The first kind, like my thesis insight in the garden at Berkeley, is a delightful burst of optimism and hope. *Eureka! This looks like the key!* When I realized that fixing the Avogadro constant might also solve the Kilogram Problem, I sat bolt upright in bed and smiled until dawn broke. When Ron and I hit upon the idea that Hubble's Law might explain why the distances to stars and galaxies follow Benford's law, we both felt the rush. But those were only hopes for a path to discovery, not discovery itself.

The elation I get when I finally find a *proof* is less instantaneous, because it's never clear that the argument is airtight until every detail in the logic has been checked by me and by independent referees. After the logic has checked out and been verified by experts, *then* the second dopamine rush kicks in. The thrill from verification of a proof is deeper than the thrill from having the key idea and is much longer lasting—*if* the discovery is new.

Sometimes you find out later that someone else has already proved the theorem you found. All that work, and no new result to show for it. You still did enjoy that initial rush when you thought it was new, but then comes a crash. Many colleagues get discouraged and try to forget the whole mess ever happened. I do just the opposite. I keep a yellow notecard on my bulletin board with the *named* theorems I have rediscovered on my own: Levy's Concentration-Variance Inequality, the Dubins-Pitman Martingale, and the Shapley-Folkman Theorem. Glancing at that note now and then reassures me I am working on problems the big guns considered important, and I am *solving* them, so sooner or later I'm bound to hit some they missed. Then I will be the first human to find and prove one of the theorems in the SF's Book, and when that happens, it is a *very* long-lasting rush.

People ask me what the creative process is like in mathematics. For me, it is simply another facet of an inner drive to find things out, to respond to intellectual curiosity attacks that complement more foolhardy physical escapades. I now smile when I think back on how that same curiosity had also caused me problems over the years, whether in railway tunnels facing down speeding locomotives or on rubber plantations surrounded by enemies. The first personal curiosity attack I can remember goes all the way back to when I was about eight years old, playing outdoors with a stick. I saw a dead wasp floating in a rain puddle and wondered, "Can a wasp still sting if it's dead?" I had no idea. So I carefully sliced off the wasp's abdomen with my penknife, inserted a twig into the cavity with the wasp's stinger pointing out like the quill of a pen, and poked it into my left forearm. *Aieee!* I had my answer, with a convincing red welt as proof.

In my world, mathematics is equally as exciting as physical adventures, and it's certainly a lot safer. But it's also far more rewarding in the long run. Luckily I stumbled into a career where curiosity is king. That and persistence, of course, since the answers in mathematics are often years in the making, not like the quick-and-dirty sting from a dead wasp's tail.

I admit it: not everyone finds math questions compelling. Euclid wondered whether there are infinitely many prime numbers. "Who cares?" is a response I often get, even from my closest friends.

"Well, the ancient Greeks cared, and *I* care," I tell them. "And if you do any online banking, then you should care a little bit too, because theories of prime numbers are the bases for almost all state-of-the-art financial security codes. You'll be missing something very beautiful in life if you don't at least get a whiff of how exciting and interesting abstract math can be. Now I know the burden of proof here is on me, so let's see if I can't come up with a math theorem story you'll like."

So I cut cakes in the air, pour salt on the table, tell them how the IRS is using Benford to check their tax returns, and describe the best mathematical strategy for choosing a spouse. In return they ask me questions I had never dreamt of, and the wonderful cycle continues.

PHOTO CREDITS

1. Hill family, courtesy of R. Hill.
2. Fifth-grade class at Seabrook Farms School, courtesy of R. Hill.
3. Football team, and T. Hill with V. Bruce, by Varden Studios Yearbook Division.
4. Cover spine. West Point Company E-2, courtesy of US Army.
5. T. Hill walking area and delinquency report, courtesy of T. Hill.
6. West German High Mountain Pursuit Troops and German Military Academy *Kadetten*, courtesy of A. Lindseth.
7. T. Hill and J. Steel with 1955 Mercury, courtesy of C. McKearn.
8. T. Hill, courtesy of US Army.
9. G. Jackson and T. Hill in the Andes, courtesy of T. Hill.
10. Rugby match, courtesy of J. Steel.
11. Lt. Col. Gibson and T. Hill, courtesy of US Army.
12. General Article 15, courtesy of T. Hill.
13. *Lyons Republican* newspaper article, courtesy of Wayuga Printing and Publishing.
14. Front cover. T. Hill rappelling, photograph by Gene Pospeshil, courtesy of *St. Louis Post-Dispatch*.
15. Rush playing at Forest Park Pavilion, courtesy of The Metro St. Louis Live Music Historical Society, www.stlmusicyesterdays.com.
16. California driver's license, courtesy of T. Hill.
17. T. Hill on motorcycle, courtesy of P. Hupfer.
18. Judo identification, courtesy of T. Hill.
19. T. Hill's 1972 passport photograph, courtesy of US Army.
20. Eastern Bloc passport stamps, courtesy of T. Hill.

21. Checkpoint Charlie, photograph by Roger Wollstadt, courtesy of Wikimedia Commons. This file is licensed under the Creative Commons Attribution-share Alike 2.0 Generic (https://creativecommons.org/licenses/by~sa/2.0/deed.en) license.
22. T. Hill hitchhiking in East Africa, courtesy of R. Hill.
23. T. Hill camping on Zomba Plateau, courtesy of R. Hill.
24. Ugandan passport stamp, courtesy of T. Hill.
25. Letter about San Quentin teaching job and Lifetime California Community College Teaching Certificate, courtesy of T. Hill.
26. *San Francisco Chronicle* article republished with permission of Hearst Corporation, from "He Wants Bride He Can Flay Away From," Michael Grieg, *San Francisco Chronicle*, Friday, August 29, 1975; permission conveyed through Copyright Clearance Center, Inc.
27. L. Dubins, courtesy of G. Bergman.
28. Blake Street cottage, courtesy of N. Lippits.
29. University of California Candidate in Philosophy degree, courtesy of T. Hill.
30. T. Hill with PhC canoe and van, courtesy of N. Lippits.
31. Bungalow on Georgia Tech campus, courtesy of T. Hill.
32. Friends and family dining in the Math *Ohana*, courtesy of E. Rogers.
33. T. Hill interview with CBS, courtesy of CBS News Archives.
34. T. Hill and M. Jones, courtesy of M. Jones.
35. Clockwise from top left: T. Hill on Kauai, courtesy of N. Lippits; T. Hill on Fox Glacier, courtesy of E. Rogers; T. Hill rappelling in Arizona, courtesy of G. Hill; T. Hill on bicycle, courtesy of E. Rogers.
36. T. Hill at Dutch PhD ceremony, courtesy of F. Boshuizen.
37. T. Hill officiating wedding of Y. and S. Jeltuhin, courtesy of Y. Jeltuhin.
38. T. Hill and C. McKearn in scuba gear, courtesy of C. McKearn.
39. V. Ervin, J. Geronimo, and R. Hynd at Bahamas dinner table, courtesy of T. Hill.
40. L. Bunimovich and guests, courtesy of L. Bunimovich.
41. T. Hill, J. Steel, W. Clark, and C. McKearn at West Point reunion, courtesy of E. Rogers.
42. T. Hill and N. Van Thu at University of Hanoi, courtesy of E. Rogers.

43. T. Hill lecturing at International University, Ho Chi Minh City, courtesy of E. Rogers.
44. T. Hill and guide hiking Black Virgin Mountain, courtesy of E. Rogers.
45. T. Hill and display from Early American Mathematics Books collection, courtesy of E. Rogers.
46. T. Hill, R. Hynd, and L. Dubins at Saul's, courtesy of E. Rogers.
47. T. Hill at Central American Mathematics Conference in Costa Rica, courtesy of E. Grigorieva.
48. T. Hill hitchhiking near Guanajuato in central Mexico, courtesy of R. Hynd.
49. T. Hill and V. Perez-Abreu in Guanajuato, courtesy of R. Hynd.
50. T. Hill outside math *dacha*, courtesy of E. Rogers.
51. T. Hill inside math *dacha*, courtesy of E. Rogers.

Front cover: T. Hill, courtesy of E. Rogers.

ABOUT THE AUTHOR

Ted Hill is Professor Emeritus of Mathematics at Georgia Tech, a Distinguished Graduate of West Point's Class of 1966, and a former Army Ranger and Vietnam War veteran who bucked the odds to earn a PhD in mathematics from Berkeley. He has lectured in four languages around the world and is well known for his research in probability, especially Benford's law. He is currently at work on a mathematical theory for the oval shapes of beach stones, as well as several more books, including one on his adventures in hitchhiking. More information may be found at his website, www.tphill.com.